TEACHING ADOLESCENTS
WITH DISABILITIES

This book is dedicated to Judy Petry Tate. For nearly 30 years, Judy was the lead support person in the University of Kansas Center for Research on Learning (KU-CRL) and the Department of Special Education. Judy passed away in September of 2004.

Few have done more to contribute to the strength, stature, and productivity of the KU-CRL and the department than Judy. She was an extraordinarily faithful and loyal friend, colleague, and mentor to all who crossed her path. She gave completely of herself to ensuring the success of others. Spending long nights and weekends tending to countless details was common practice for Judy. She gave so much of herself because she believed so deeply in the missions of the KU-CRL and the Department of Special Education. We all have been the beneficiaries of her creativity, brilliance, tenacity, undying commitment, and work ethic.

Her small stature belied the size of her heart and the strength of her will to accomplish what others often thought to be impossible. The lives of countless thousands have been positively affected by Judy's enormous capacity to do whatever was necessary to accomplish what had to be done. Our center, our department, and our individual lives have been shaped and molded by Judy. We have been so fortunate to have known and worked with this extraordinary human being.

TEACHING ADOLESCENTS
WITH DISABILITIES

ACCESSING
THE GENERAL
EDUCATION
CURRICULUM

Donald D. Deshler | Jean B. Schumaker

CORWIN PRESS
A SAGE Publications Company
Thousand Oaks, California

For information:

Corwin Press
A Sage Publications Company
2455 Teller Road
Thousand Oaks, California 91320
www.corwinpress.com

Sage Publications Ltd.
1 Oliver's Yard
55 City Road
London EC1Y 1SP
United Kingdom

Sage Publications India Pvt. Ltd.
B-42, Panchsheel Enclave
Post Box 4109
New Delhi 110 017 India

Printed in the United States of America

Library of Congress Cataloging-in-Publication Data

Teaching adolescents with disabilities: Accessing the general education curriculum/Donald D. Deshler, Jean B. Schumaker.
    p. cm.
Includes bibliographical references and index.
ISBN 1–4129–1488–4 (cloth) — ISBN 1–4129–1489–2 (pbk.)
  1. Teenagers with disabilities—Education (Secondary)—United States.
I. Deshler, Donald D. II. Schumaker, Jean B.
LC4031.T385 2006
371.9′0473—dc22   2005014774

This book is printed on acid-free paper.

05 06 07 08 09 10 9 8 7 6 5 4 3 2 1

Acquisitions Editor:	Kathleen McLane
Editorial Assistant:	Jordan Barbakow
Production Editor:	Beth A. Bernstein
Copy Editor:	Freelance Editorial Services
Typesetter:	C&M Digitals (P) Ltd.
Proofreader:	Scott Oney
Indexer:	Molly Hall
Cover Designer:	Rose Storey

Contents

Acknowledgments

For more than 25 years, our research center, the University of Kansas Center for Research on Learning, has had as its mission the design and validation of interventions that dramatically impact the performance of struggling adolescent learners, including those with disabilities. When we've learned lessons and made progress, it's been because practitioners, researchers, and support staff have come together in pursuit of a common goal. Educational research that makes a difference in the lives of students and their families is very difficult to do—it can't be accomplished without a strong team that is committed to coming up with solutions that improve the quality of life for at-risk adolescents.

Much of our center's research has been supported by the U.S. Department of Education, Office of Special Education Programs (OSEP). For years, this agency has been extraordinarily resourceful in supporting research agendas that lead to socially significant outcomes on behalf of individuals with disabilities. We are indebted to the professionalism of the many project officers from OSEP who have helped to guide our research over the years. We are especially grateful to Louis Danielson and Bonnie Jones, who were instrumental in supporting the research that led to this book.

Without a doubt, one of the greatest strengths of our research center is the extraordinary support team with whom we have been privileged to work. This book and the many activities that we have undertaken in our quest to find answers to an endless array of research questions related to adolescents with disabilities has been made possible through the tireless efforts of Barb Babcock, Mary Brieck, Jamin Dreasher, David Gnojek, Jeannie Heil, Jean-Ellen Kegler, Cameron Knight, Pete Mynstead, Darrell Mooney, John Radar, Janet Roth, Belinda Schuman, Julie Tollefson, and Shanna Williams. For the extra hours and the extraordinary care and dedication spent in preparing the multiple drafts of this book, we owe special thanks to Jeannie Heil, Mary Brieck, and Jamin Dreasher.

Although they were not directly involved in this particular project, we wish to acknowledge the work of our colleagues Mike Hock, Jim Knight, and Barbara Ehren—they influence our thinking on a daily basis and continually challenge our ideas. As a result, our thinking gets sharpened. They always help us to come up with better solutions. Additionally, we wish to acknowledge Eleanor Womack and Peggy Showalter, who served as the primary support staff in our research center during its first 20 years. We will be forever indebted to them for all they did to teach us what teamwork is all about, as well as to establish a strong collegial atmosphere within our center.

We are deeply indebted to Kathleen McLane, consulting acquisitions editor at Corwin Press, for her encouragement and leadership through the entire publication process. Her knowledge of and commitment to students with disabilities and the teachers who work with them is unparalleled. In light of those great attributes, her role in helping us to shape and refine this manuscript has been very important.

We owe the most to our families, who have supported our work for years and have unhesitatingly supported and encouraged us to pursue our professional goals. Don is deeply indebted to Carol and his four children, Reed, Jill, Todd, Chad, and their spouses. Jean is likewise profoundly grateful for the support of her family, especially Jesse and Scott.

—Donald D. Deshler and Jean B. Schumaker

About the Editors

 **Donald D. Deshler** is Director of the University of Kansas Center for Research on Learning (KU-CRL) and a Professor in the Department of Special Education. The work of the KU-CRL focuses on the validation of academic strategies for adolescents who struggle with becoming good readers, writers, and learners. Don's work also focuses on designing instructional routines that can be used by secondary teachers to help them more effectively teach subject-matter content to academically diverse classes in secondary schools. Don and his colleagues have completed in excess of $80 million of contracted research and development that has resulted in the validation of the Strategic Instruction Model (SIM), a comprehensive instructional model for improving outcomes for at-risk adolescents.

Through the KU-CRL's International Professional Development Network, more than 400,000 educators have been trained to use different components of the SIM. Don's most recent text, *Teaching Content to All: Evidence-Based Inclusive Practices in Middle and Secondary Schools*, details several of the instructional practices validated through KU-CRL research. Additionally, KU-CRL researchers have produced in excess of 50 teacher-use curriculum materials for teaching struggling adolescent learners.

Don is the recipient of numerous awards, including the J. E. Wallace Wallin Award from the Council for Exceptional Children and the Learning Disabilities Association Award from the Learning Disabilities Association of America for outstanding research and service for at-risk populations.

 **Jean B. Schumaker**, PhD, is Associate Director of the University of Kansas Center for Research on Learning and a Professor in the Departments of Special Education and Applied Behavioral Science. She is also President of Edge Enterprises, Inc., a research and publishing company focusing on the area of special education. She has spent the last 32 years studying the problems of adolescents and developing educational interventions for them.

In addition to her research on the Strategic Instruction Model (SIM), Jean has conducted programmatic research related to social-skill performance and instruction. Her research studies in this area have described the related to social skills of several populations of at-risk youths and have reported the development and validation of instructional procedures for social skills. Her current work in this area focuses on the instructional procedures for social skills in inclusive classrooms in which students with disabilities are enrolled.

Jean has been the principal investigator for more than $30 million of funded research and development projects. She is an author of the *Learning Strategies Curriculum*, a curriculum that comprises 15 teacher's manuals for teaching students learning strategies; *Social Skills for Daily Living*, *ASSET*, and the *Cooperative Strategies Series*, three social skills curricula; eight manuals in the *Content Enhancement Series*, a series developed to improve the delivery of content in mainstream classrooms; and numerous articles and chapters.

Jean was president of the Division for Learning Disabilities within the Council for Exceptional Children during 1999–2000. In 1996, she received the division's Award for Outstanding Contributions to the field of learning disabilities. In June of 2004, she received the Distinguished Achievement Award from her undergraduate alma mater, Lawrence University in Wisconsin.

Introduction

When the Education for All Handicapped Children Act (P.L. 94-142) was passed in 1975, provisions were established to guarantee that students with disabilities would be educated with, not apart from, their peers—that is, they were to have access to and be educated in the same *place* as their normal-achieving peers. In the 1990s, the access component of this legislation was expanded beyond place to include access to the *general education curriculum.* In other words, the Individuals with Disabilities Education Acts (IDEA) of the 1990s and beyond have provided that students with disabilities should have full access to the same learning experiences, materials, and curriculum elements as their normal-achieving peers. Hence, they are not merely to be in the same physical location as their peers; they are to experience the same curriculum as their peers. Although this expansion of the legislation was heralded as a philosophical and moral victory for individuals with disabilities, it presented some very significant instructional challenges to teachers and administrators— especially to those working with adolescents in high school settings.

One of the major challenges faced by school personnel relates to the skill deficits of these students. For most adolescents with disabilities, there is a large gap between their current level of performance and the demands of the curriculum they are expected to meet. Unless students have mastered the necessary skills and strategies to respond to the heavy curriculum demands of rigorous subject-matter classes, they will encounter failure and great frustration. Figure I.1 on the next page illustrates the challenge faced by teachers and students in today's high schools. The upper, straight line represents the path of "normal" acquisition of knowledge or skills by typical students. That is, at the conclusion of one year of instruction, on average, students should have acquired "one year's worth" of knowledge and skills, represented by Point A on that line. At the end of the second year, they should be performing at the level of Point B, and so on. Students who acquire skills and knowledge at this pace are, in turn, able to successfully deal with the curriculum demands that are presented to them. In other words, they can successfully "access the curriculum."

The performance of students with disabilities, on the other hand, does not usually follow this line of progress. On average, they perform at the level of Point A at the end of one year of schooling and travel a path similar to the one depicted by the dotted curved line. The area between the solid line (representing normal achievement) and the dotted line (representing underachievement) depicts the "performance gap," the gap between what students with disabilities are expected to do and what they actually can do. Over time, this gap grows larger and larger, and it is especially exacerbated in the later grades, when the academic growth of students with disabilities plateaus. As a result of this performance gap, these students are unable to access the general education curriculum and meet the demands of required courses for graduation from high school. Their resulting failure leads to discouragement and disengagement from school, and, for too many, this disengagement manifests itself in dropping out of school altogether.

Significantly, the dotted line in the figure (and the achievement of students with disabilities) tends to plateau by the time these students reach the seventh grade in school. Hence, the magnitude of the gap grows exponentially because the demands of the curriculum that students encounter during their middle and high school years increase dramatically because of the volume of content covered, its complexity, and, in many instances, its abstract nature. Assignments and tests associated with this content become more complex as well.

Although this figure helps to profile the challenges faced by adolescents with disabilities, its greatest value is in providing a focus for interventions that should be employed to close the performance gap to a point where students are able to truly access and benefit from the general education curriculum. Given the shortage of instructional time available to secondary

Figure I.1 The Performance Gap

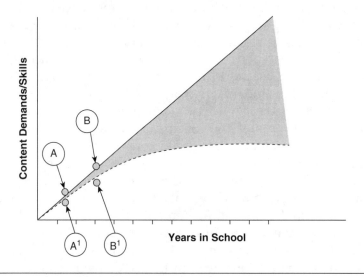

teachers, they need well-designed instructional interventions and materials that have been validated through research studies demonstrating that when they are used with fidelity and sufficient intensity, significant gains will result that effectively close the gap.

The purpose of this book is to provide classroom teachers and administrators with a comprehensive review of research-validated practices that have been shown to be effective with adolescents with disabilities. The chapters in this book emerged as part of a research grant funded by the Office of Special Education Programs (PR#324S990001) to study ways to improve access to the general education curriculum for adolescents with disabilities in high schools. The students who were the target of the project were those who had the capacity, given high-quality instruction associated with well-designed interventions, to successfully complete high school and receive a standard high school diploma.

The first chapter describes the extraordinarily complex context within which teaching adolescents with disabilities must occur. Each of the remaining chapters describes specific research-validated practices that are available to classroom teachers. Each chapter deals with a critical component of the instructional process that must be considered in constructing comprehensive and well-designed instructional programs for adolescents with disabilities. Additionally, each chapter points out what instructional practices have some grounding in research, as well as areas where there is a shortage or complete absence of supporting research. However, in spite of the many questions that remain to be answered, there is much that is known and that can be effectively leveraged to dramatically improve outcomes for adolescents with disabilities and to put them on the road to successfully completing their high school education.

Specifically, Chapters 2 through 7 address the following topics, all of which can play an important role in facilitating access to and success in learning the general education curriculum for adolescents with disabilities. Specifically, Chapter 2 provides an in-depth analysis of the various dimensions of teacher planning. How general education classroom teachers make instructional plans in light of the academic diversity of students in their classes, as well as the large amounts of complex content, is a critical first step in enabling the type of instruction that can be understood by students with disabilities. Chapter 3 describes a broad array of instructional practices that can be used, primarily by the subject-matter teacher, to facilitate the mastery of critical content within the context of the general education classroom. Chapter 4 focuses on specific learning strategies that can be taught to adolescents for the purpose of changing how they think about and approach problems that they need to solve and how they work on assignments they are given. In short, this chapter reviews what is known about teaching adolescents with disabilities how to learn. Chapter 5 addresses one of the biggest barriers to academic success for students with disabilities—namely, instructional materials that are "inconsiderate" and not sensitive to the information-processing difficulties of many students with disabilities. Specifically, this chapter discusses how to optimally design instructional materials and teaching sequences to maximize student outcomes. Chapter 6 describes how technology, as an instructional tool, can help teachers provide needed supports for struggling learners, including how it can facilitate guided practice, instructional reinforcement, and assisting teachers to effectively leverage their personal attention to targeted learners at strategic times during the lesson. The final chapter addresses an array of instructional practices that are central to enhancing nonacademic growth and outcomes. Among the critical topics covered in this chapter are self-determination, transition planning, and social-skill instruction.

In short, this book will provide the reader with a thorough understanding of

- the context in which adolescents with disabilities are educated,
- the principles leading to instructional plans that help teachers effectively differentiate their instruction for all learners in their class,
- instructional practices that teachers can use to promote commensurate instructional gains for *all* subgroups within subject-matter classes (including students with disabilities),
- methods for changing the way that students learn and perform tasks by teaching them specific learning strategies that enable them to be more independent in performing their schoolwork,
- ways to choose and design instructional tools that will optimize student outcomes,
- the principles for effectively leveraging the rapidly growing benefits of technology to enhance the instructional environment, and
- strategies for enhancing nonacademic outcomes for students with disabilities.

High Schools and Adolescents With Disabilities: Challenges at Every Turn

Donald D. Deshler, Jean B. Schumaker
Yvonne Bui, and Sue Vernon

June 6, 2005, was a very special day for Jason Warner. It was also a real highlight for his parents. At 7:30 that evening, Jason joined 289 of his classmates to receive his high school diploma from Woodland High School. Receiving a standard high school diploma was not something that happened by accident or by luck—it was an event that took place largely because of some very deliberate decisions and commitments that had been made by key administrators and teachers in Jason's district several years earlier.

While going through the North Central Accreditation process in 1995, school leaders in Jason's district were alarmed to learn how low the graduation rate was for high school students with disabilities. A few years later, when statewide assessments were implemented and requirements added for schools to meet adequate yearly progress (AYP) standards for all students as a result of the No Child Left

Behind (NCLB) Act, school leaders knew that significant steps would have to be taken to alter outcomes for students with disabilities. In an attempt to significantly improve assessment performance and, ultimately, the graduation rate, these school leaders committed to putting four components at the heart of their district's plan for all adolescents with disabilities: (1) use research-based interventions as the foundation of all instruction; (2) actively involve all teachers in programming and teaching decisions on behalf of students with disabilities, not just the special educators; (3) make parental and community involvement a central feature of each student's program; and (4) ensure that each student's program was carefully coordinated across settings and personnel—given the complex nature of secondary schools, orchestration of plans and resources on behalf of students was deemed a very high priority. This chapter describes the broader context in which thousands of adolescents with disabilities, like Jason, must try to succeed.

Educating high school students with disabilities has always been difficult (e.g., Lenz & Deshler, 2004). This challenge has recently been exacerbated by the AYP accountability requirement called for in the NCLB Act, whereby each state must establish a set of high standards to improve the quality of education for all students.

The difficulty of meeting this challenge is underscored by the findings of both the initial National Longitudinal Transition Study (NLTS1; Wagner, Blackorby, & Hebbeler, 1993) and the second National Longitudinal Transition Study (NLTS2; Newman, 2004). For example, NLTS1 found that a disproportionate number of students with disabilities (38%) drop out of school compared with the general population (25%). Indeed, in some locations, as many as 85% of the students with disabilities drop out of school (Ehren & Lenz, 1986). Before dropping out of school, these students show a broader array of performance and adjustment problems than students in the general population, including (1) higher rates of absenteeism, (2) lower grade point averages, (3) higher course failure rates (Wagner et al., 1993), (4) more feelings of poor self-esteem, and (5) higher rates of inappropriate social behaviors (Schumaker, 1992). Predictably, only a small minority of these individuals (approximately 25%) pursue postsecondary education (Wagner et al., 1993).

In NLTS2, general education teachers were found to set reasonably high expectations for students with disabilities, but many of them failed to meet those expectations. Additionally, these students were found to be less likely to respond orally to questions, work independently, or work effectively with a peer or group (Newman, 2004). In short, success for students with disabilities in high schools has fallen short of the hopes of educators, parents of adolescents with disabilities, and the students themselves. Most important, although these students have struggled to cope with the demands of high school curricula, they have not been prepared to face the even higher expectations of the globalization of commerce and industry, the dramatic growth of technology, the dramatic transformation of the workplace, and the very nature of work itself (Martin, 1999; Oliver, 1999; Rifkin, 1995).

Subsequently, the passage of the NCLB Act in 2001 established a new set of expectations for students with disabilities. Namely, the accountability provisions of that legislation require schools to report achievement outcomes for all students by disaggregating their data into key subgroups, and students with disabilities constitute one of the these subgroups. Hence, educators now must be as concerned with the academic success of students with disabilities as they are with typically and high-achieving students in their schools.

THE NEED FOR A NEW APPROACH

A dramatically new approach to educating students with disabilities in high schools is necessary to meet these outcome goals. Historically, educators have tried to understand and serve adolescents with disabilities from a limited perspective that focuses on individual characteristics. That is, the prevailing assumption has been that if an adolescent is not performing well in a criterion environment (for instance, the general education classroom), the problem must reside within the student. Hence, detailed explanations for a student's poor performance are sought by administering one battery of tests after another. After a thick file describing the "student's problem" is assembled, an intervention program is designed to "fix" or "change" the student.

But in reality, the difficulties that students with disabilities face cannot be accurately described by merely analyzing the students' behavior alone. A more valid and helpful perspective carefully considers not merely learner attributes, but also environmental factors. High school students with disabilities are, first and foremost, *adolescents* who are trying to understand, cope with, and respond to the pressures associated with comprehensive high school settings. Additionally, as these students gain independence, the way they are perceived and the roles they play in their families and communities change dramatically. All of these pressures and changes, which are different and independent from their personal characteristics as learners, can have dramatic effects on their academic performance. Hence, the performance of adolescents with disabilities is best understood by viewing their behavior as the result of interactions between an individual's characteristics and the environmental conditions within which he or she must live and cope: $B = E \times I$. Efforts to understand and intervene with these students, therefore, should be made in light of a complex array of factors that are present within the individual (I), the environmental settings or contextual factors (E), and the product of an interaction between the two (B).

Numerous studies and reviews have investigated the individual factors associated with adolescents with disabilities, but few reviews have focused on the environmental or contextual factors that they face and how those factors interact with their individual characteristics. The purpose of this chapter is to discuss a host of contextual factors that might interact with the characteristics of adolescents with disabilities to have a potentially significant impact on their academic performance. Interventions must be designed in light of contextual realities such as the unique structures of secondary schools and a myriad of trends that characterize secondary education in America today.

We will briefly discuss eight contextual factors or trends that relate to the education of students with disabilities within today's high schools. Although they will be presented in isolation, these factors clearly do *not* operate in isolation. Rather, the different ways that they can be combined and the varying degrees to which they are present (or absent) create the extreme cultural complexities within which adolescents with disabilities are expected to succeed. The eight factors are not meant to represent an exhaustive list, but to serve as examples of some of the major contextual forces that currently operate in most high schools.

The eight factors are (1) legislative mandates, (2) the standards-based reform movement, (3) curricular and structural demands, (4) the absence of comprehensive service delivery systems, (5) confusion with regard to the role of special educators, (6) cultural and linguistic diversity, (7) the prevalence of violence and fear, and (8) family and community dynamics.

LEGISLATIVE MANDATES

The national context is the largest context within which high school students with disabilities are educated. During the past several decades, a series of federal legislative initiatives have been directed at improving the quality of services for adolescents and young adults. Although the full intent of these mandates has not yet been realized, nonetheless, they create a set of conditions for governing educational decision making and for evaluating current practices at the high school level. While the Individuals with Disabilities Education Act (IDEA) and NCLB are the most prominent pieces of federal legislation, several other legislative actions are also germane to the way adolescents and young adults with disabilities are educated and supported. These actions, along with IDEA and NCLB, are briefly described in the paragraphs that follow.

First, in 1989, at the historic governors' meeting in Charlottesville, Virginia, the 50 state governors mandated that by 2000, eight National Education Goals for the education of all students in the United States would be addressed. Although all of these goals apply to students with disabilities as well as to other students, five of them have particular implications for students with disabilities in relation to preparing them for life during and after high school. These five goals are as follows: (1) the high school graduation rate will increase to at least 90%; (2) all students will leave Grades 4, 8, and 12 having demonstrated competency over challenging subject matter, including English, mathematics, science, foreign languages, civics and government, economics, the arts, and history and geography; (3) every school in America will ensure that all students learn to use their minds well so they may be prepared for responsible citizenship, further learning, and productive employment in our nation's modern economy; (4) all adult Americans will be literate and will possess the knowledge and skills necessary to compete in a global economy and to exercise their rights and responsibilities of citizenship; and (5) every school will promote partnerships that will increase parental involvement and participation in promoting the social, emotional, and academic growth of children.

Second, as activities related to these National Education Goals were being implemented by the governors and their states, the Americans with Disabilities Act of 1990 (P.L. 101-336) added further protection by prohibiting discrimination against persons with disabilities and by affording protections under the law in the workplace. Additionally, the 1990 amendments to the Individuals with Disabilities Education Act introduced transition service requirements that call for a statement of needed transition services to be written in the individualized education program (IEP) for each student with a disability, beginning no later than age 16 or younger, if appropriate. These legislative changes represent a move toward preparing students with disabilities for their future, for work, and for life after high school.

Third, in 1994, to further underscore the importance of schools ensuring that their students meet the National Educational Goals, Congress passed several pieces of legislation (the Goals 2000: Educate America Act, the School-to-Work Opportunities Act, and the Improving America's Schools Act) to promote success by raising academic and occupational standards, encouraging students to work harder to meet them, improving teaching strategies, and strengthening student and parent involvement for all students, including students with disabilities.

Fourth, in 2004, the Individuals with Disabilities Education Improvement Act (P.L. 108-466) was reauthorized. The primary purpose of this legislation was to ensure a free and appropriate public education for all individuals with disabilities that emphasizes special education and related services designed to meet their unique needs and prepare them for employment and independent living. The authors of IDEA 1997 recognized that if children and youth with disabilities are to be successful, it is necessary to focus on instruction and experiences that prepare them for later educational experiences and postschool opportunities, including independent living, formal and informal postsecondary education, and, if appropriate, employment. Thus, Part B of this act sets forth specific requirements in the areas of transition planning and services that must be implemented at age 16. It is important to note that IDEA 1997 (P.L. 105-17) had expanded earlier transition requirements by lowering the age by which a transition plan must be implemented to no later than age 14. States still have the option to require transition plans to be made by age 14, but the federal law no longer mandates these plans at the younger age level. A major change in the 2004 legislation is to bring its statutes into alignment with the NCLB Act relative to accountability systems and performance goals and indicators.

Fifth, the Carl D. Perkins Vocational and Technical Act of 1998 (P.L. 105-332) and the Workforce Investment Act (P.L. 105-220) were designed to work in concert with and support IDEA 1997 by focusing federal investments on high-quality vocational and technical education programs, as well as creating an integrated one-stop system of workforce investment and educational activities for youth and adults.

Sixth, the goal of the Government Performance and Results Act is to improve results for individuals with disabilities by assisting state and local education agencies in providing children with disabilities with access to a high-quality education that will help them meet challenging standards and prepare them for employment and independent living. This goal is to be accomplished by (1) ensuring that all students have IEPs that include a statement of transition service needs focusing on their course of study and that coordinates a set of activities designed to promote movement from school to postschool activities; (2) increasing the percentage of students exiting school who graduate with a diploma; (3) decreasing the drop-out rate; (4) increasing the percentage of students who go on to postsecondary education or employment; and (5) reducing the gap between the average hourly wage of individuals with disabilities and that of peers without disabilities.

Finally, the NCLB Act of 2001 is the most comprehensive piece of educational legislation to be signed into law during the past 50 years. Its implications for all students, including those with disabilities, are significant and far-reaching. In essence, NCLB was designed to change the culture of America's schools by closing the achievement gap, offering more flexibility, giving parents more options, and teaching students based on instructional practices grounded in scientific research. Under the act's accountability provisions, states must describe how they will close the achievement gap and make sure that all students, including those who are disadvantaged, achieve academic proficiency. Further, they must produce annual state and school district report cards that inform parents and communities about state and school progress. Schools that do not make progress must provide supplemental services, such as free tutoring or afterschool assistance; take corrective actions; and, if they are still not making adequate yearly progress after five years, make dramatic changes to the way the schools are run.

In summary, numerous recent pieces of legislation and other initiatives have been directed at the education of students with disabilities, and many of them are directly related to the high school education of these students. Accordingly, high schools are being required to educate students with disabilities in the least restrictive environment, to give them *real* access to the general education curriculum, to ensure that they meet outcome goals, and to help them plan successful transitions into their adult lives. These initiatives may be used to create a positive climate for students with disabilities in high schools. However, some of the trends and factors also present challenges that must be met to create that positive climate.

THE STANDARDS-BASED REFORM MOVEMENT

One movement that may create a barrier to the education of students with disabilities is the national school improvement effort commonly known as *standards-based reform*. As defined by Nolet and McLaughlin, "standards-based reform is a policy response to the dissatisfaction with the performance of American schools—major elements of standards-based reform are (a) higher content standards, (b) the use of assessments aimed at measuring how schools are helping students meet the standards, and (c) an emphasis on holding educators and students accountable for student achievement" (2000, p. 2). Although the movement toward standards-based reform began in the mid-1980s, standards-based reform was formally introduced as a full-blown policy framework in 1994 through the Goals 2000: Educate America Act, which provided incentives to states to adopt an accountability system based on standards and aligned assessments.

The same year, the reauthorization of the Elementary Secondary Education Act (ESEA) as the Improving America's Schools Act required that states develop an accountability framework based on standards and assessments and that Title I schools demonstrate annual yearly progress toward student proficiency on state assessments. In spite of these legislative initiatives, states moved toward the adoption of standards at an uneven pace and varied widely in their approaches to standards-based reform. In 1994, only 11 states were in compliance with the reauthorized ESEA. As a result, the 2002 reauthorization of the ESEA as the NCLB Act mandated that states develop an accountability system based on standards and assessments, extended the AYP requirement to all schools, and imposed a system of sanctions on schools, districts, and states that fail to comply. Paige (2004) reported that on June 10, 2003, all 50 states plus the District of Columbia had approved accountability plans based on standards and assessments.

The NCLB legislation requires that state assessments of reading and mathematics, and, by 2005–06, science, be administered to all students in Grades 3 through 8 and at least once during the high school years. To achieve AYP, schools must demonstrate that at least 95% of students participated in the assessments and made progress toward achieving state-determined targets for proficiency. Moreover, schools must report on participation rates and assessment scores for specified subgroups of students, including students with limited English proficiency and students with disabilities. State accountability systems vary as to the stakes of assessments. At present, NCLB mandates that schools must demonstrate their students are progressing toward the goal of universal proficiency by 2013–14. Some states, however, place the burden of achieving proficiency on individual students. At present, 24 states have exit exams that students must pass to graduate from high school with a standard diploma. President Bush's acceptance speech to the Republican National Convention on September 2, 2004, suggested the administration's intent to require exit exams as part of NCLB (Cavanagh, 2004). In addition to these exit exams, many states require that students pass state exams before they matriculate to the next grade.

Naturally, teachers are being required to teach students the information and skills contained on state tests required by NCLB. For example, in the state of Louisiana, teachers must help students pass the LEAP 21 tests at the fourth- and eighth-grade levels in the areas of English, mathematics, science, and social studies if they are to pass into the fifth and ninth grades. They also must help students pass tests in the tenth and eleventh grades in the areas of written composition, English language arts, mathematics, science, and social studies if they are to graduate from high school (Louisiana Department of Education, 2000).

The impact of this standards-based reform movement on all students and teachers in American schools has been significant (Howell & Nolet, 2000). The ramifications for students with disabilities are especially problematic (e.g., McDonnell, McLaughlin, & Morrison, 1997). Before the passage of the NCLB, a survey by the National Center of Educational Outcomes reported that educators in approximately half of the 43 states that had adopted standards reported they were using the same standards (or some variation of the standards) for students with disabilities that they used for general education students. Educators in eight states reported they were developing different standards for students with disabilities, and educators in 14 states reported they were uncertain as to which standards they would use (Sack, 2000). In addition, only 23 states could provide data on how many students with disabilities were participating in state assessments and the types of accommodations that were provided (Sack, 2000).

However, the NCLB Act now mandates that all students must meet the same state standards. Although provisions have been made for students with the most severe disabilities to participate in alternate assessments, no more than 1% of students' alternate assessment scores can be counted toward AYP (any scores in excess of 1% must be calculated as nonproficient), and alternate assessments must be based on alternate achievement standards and aligned with state standards that apply to all students (U.S. Department of Education, Title I, 2003).

Before the passage of the NCLB, there were some indications that many students with disabilities were being left out of state assessments altogether. According to testing experts, students with disabilities were not being included because their scores could negatively skew overall scores (e.g., Kleinhammer-Trammill & Gallagher, in press). A study by the National Assessment of Educational Progress confirmed that most students with disabilities were not taking state assessments (Sack, 2000). Another study by the National Center on Education Statistics estimated that nearly half of all students with special needs (including students with limited English proficiency) were excluded from state assessments between 1992 and 1994 (Council of Chief State School Officers, 1998). In spite of the NCLB mandates, several states have failed to make AYP because of widespread non-participation of students with disabilities (U.S. Department of Education, Title I, 2003)

Clearly, there are serious problems associated with excluding students with disabilities from state assessments. Exclusion denies students with disabilities and their families their legal rights under the IDEA. Indeed, the 1997 amendments to the IDEA represent a major advancement in ensuring not only that students with disabilities receive the basic civil rights protections of a free and appropriate education, but also that they receive additional benefits designed to improve the quality of their education. To ensure the quality of education for these students, the 1997 reauthorization specified that students with disabilities should have access to challenging curricula and that their educational programs should be based on high expectations. Hence, this new legislation shifts the focus of educational programming from *physical* access to general education classes to *real* access to the general education curriculum and improved educational performance. In essence, the purpose of IDEA 1997 was to increase the degree of alignment of special education services (programs and policies) with the standards-based reform movement. In addition, both IDEA 1997 and the NCLB ensure that students with disabilities are part of the overall accountability system and make schools responsible for their progress.

Standards-based assessments, then, play a crucial part in determining whether students with disabilities are getting an appropriate education. If these students are not participating in state assessments, no one can determine what they are learning in comparison to what other students are learning and how their educational programs can be changed to help them learn better. According to some experts, excluding students with disabilities from state assessments ignores their academic needs and maintains low teacher expectations for their achievement (McLaughlin & Warren, 1992). Their exclusion also translates into no accountability for their teachers and administrators.

Clearly, the exclusion of students with disabilities from state assessments is problematic. On the other hand, the inclusion of students with disabilities in standards-based assessments to determine promotion and graduation has its own problems. Currently, 24 states require that all students pass a graduation exam with the same passing score (regardless of whether they have a disability) to receive a standard diploma. Unfortunately, many students with disabilities do not have the skills and knowledge required to pass these exams. Because of these students' lack of skills, some states are being challenged legally. For example, in Indiana, there is a current lawsuit challenging the exit exam required for high school graduation for 1,000 students with disabilities. The lawsuit alleges that the state violated the students' due process rights by changing graduation requirements too quickly and by not allowing enough time for the students to learn the skills and knowledge required on the tests. In addition, the lawsuit alleges that the state violated IDEA by failing to provide adequate testing accommodations (Olson, 2000a).

Because of these problems, the interaction of the standards-based reform movement and special education has been the focus of a great deal of study and debate. A recent report released by the Center for Policy Research on the Impact of General and Special Education Reform, titled *Reforming High School Learning: The Effect of the Standards Movement on Secondary Students With Disabilities* (Dailey, Zantal-Wiener, & Roach, 2000), speaks directly to the impact of this movement on adolescents with disabilities. Among the major findings of this report are the following:

- There is a lack of interaction between special education programs and policies and district- and school-based reform efforts. While most state-level reforms do specify that all students will be part of reform efforts, few states provide guidelines about aligning standards with student IEPs.

- Several factors associated with high schools greatly inhibit the capacity and collaboration among special and general educators needed to include students with disabilities in a standards-based curriculum and related assessments. Such factors as departmental structure, subject-matter focus, lack of professional development opportunities, lack of common planning time, credit and graduation requirements, and course scheduling place limitations on the extent to which students with disabilities can access and benefit from a standards-based curriculum.

- There are few service delivery models in high schools that truly facilitate the inclusion of students with disabilities and promote the application of and engagement in a standards-based curriculum.

- Instructional materials that focus on the content subjects and standards often are not designed for students with disabilities. Teacher guides that accompany high school texts often do not provide suggestions or accommodations for diverse learners. Moreover, special education teachers often report using discarded materials from general education.

- District and school leaders often articulate support for including students with disabilities in a standards-based curriculum; however, they often do not provide the resources, incentives, and organizational structures to implement promising practices that engage and apply standards to students with disabilities.

- Both general and special education teachers often lack the necessary knowledge of how to link pedagogy, standards, and content.

- Both general and special education teachers lack the knowledge and skills to coteach in a classroom. In some teaming situations, special educators perceive themselves as assuming the role of an instructional aide. Issues regarding content, delivery of instruction, and grading policies are often unresolved and result in fewer coteaching or teaming situations.

- All teachers reported that time was among the major resources needed to reflect on and plan for the implications of state standards for students with disabilities and to develop appropriate strategies and services to include these students in standards-based instruction.

CURRICULAR AND STRUCTURAL DEMANDS

Simultaneous with the standards-based reform movement has been a major trend in high schools toward enrolling a large percentage of students with disabilities in general education classes for a majority of the school day (e.g., Fisher, Schumaker, & Deshler, 1995; King-Sears & Carpenter, 1996; Lenz & Deshler, 2004; Newman, 2004). In large measure, this trend is the result of efforts to promote access to the general education curriculum among students with disabilities. Thus, the vast majority of students with disabilities are receiving their education in the same environment as their peers and being afforded the same opportunities to learn and the same quality education as their peers. Unfortunately, because of the standards-based reform movement, which has taken place simultaneously with the full-inclusion movement, the demands associated with general education courses have increased dramatically. That is, in required high school general education courses, students are expected to do more academic work and learn more than ever before. They are being challenged to read, write, think, and compute at very complex levels (Brand & Partee, 2000).

One demand within required high school courses that is getting more and more difficult to meet is the reading demand (Kamil, 2003). With the emphasis on excellence in education and the explosion of information, high school textbooks have not only become thicker (many are two and a half inches thick) and larger, by they also contain very complex information. Whereas biology students once needed to learn the definition of

DNA, for example, they now need to know the chemical components of DNA, how they are organized and replicated, and their varying roles in genetic processes. Thus, in today's high schools, students are not only required to read more pages of more complex information, they are also required to read them at high readability levels (Mastropieri, 2003).

Other demands associated with required high school courses are equally complex and challenging. For example, students are required to research and write long, typed papers (Schumaker & Deshler, 1984). They are required to listen and take notes from lectures, which make up 70% of the instruction they receive (Suritsky & Hughes, 1996). They are required to master 60 to 80 facts per test, answer in excess of 40 questions per test, and provide extended written response to approximately 40% of the test questions (Putnam, Deshler, & Schumaker, 1992). They are required to complete projects over relatively long periods of time, and they are required to complete daily homework, sometimes involving two to three hours of independent study each evening (Rademacher, Schumaker, & Deshler, 1996).

Additionally, the instruction in these classes takes place at a rapid pace. Teachers focus on covering the specified material. If students do not learn it, they do not return to old information to ensure mastery; they simply move on to new material (Lenz, Alley, & Schumaker, 1987). In fact, general education teachers report that they tend to focus on their high-achieving students in diverse classes of learners. Thus, when these students are ready to move on, the whole class moves on. Similarly, when these students reject an activity or teaching method, that activity or teaching method is discarded (Lenz et al., 1987).

Another critical factor affecting instruction is the length of classes. Because block scheduling is often used in today's high schools (Queen, 2000), students find themselves in the same general education class for as long as two and a half to three hours at a time. This means they need to be able to sit in their seats and concentrate on the same subject, and sometimes the same activity, for that length of time.

Indeed, the very structure of high school classes and schedules creates demands on students. Because students are enrolled in several courses at the same time, they need to be able to divide their attention among these courses, as well as keep track of all of the assignments in all of the courses at the same time. Because their general education teachers work with approximately 150 students a day and have little time to really know and attend to individual students, students have to be independent learners who are able to recruit the help they need. Further, because whole-group instruction is the norm for high school classes, students need to be able to learn and perform within that context.

A final high school demand that impacts students with disabilities is new course requirements for high school graduation and entrance into postsecondary educational settings. For example, in most states, students are now required to pass an algebra course to graduate, whereas in previous years they only had to pass a general math course (Elmore, 1998). For another example, many postsecondary educational settings are requiring students to be fluent computer users. They can either pass a high school computer course that focuses on the competencies required, or they can pass a test of the competencies (Kansas Board of Regents, 2000).

This constellation of demands associated with high school general education courses influences the success of students with disabilities who are enrolled in them. First, these students often have several skill deficits that hamper their attempts at meeting the demands. For example, students with learning disabilities enter high school reading, on average, at the fourth-grade level. Although a large proportion have mastered basic mathematical facts for the addition and subtraction of whole numbers, they often have not mastered the facts for multiplication and division, nor have they learned how to work with fractions and decimals (Warner, Schumaker, Alley, & Deshler, 1980). They typically cannot write a variety of complete sentences, and they do not know how to organize and write paragraphs and themes (Schmidt, Deshler, Schumaker, & Alley, 1989). They hand in an average of 40% of their assignments (Hughes, Ruhl, Deshler, & Schumaker 1995). They do not know how to study for tests, and they often do not pass tests, earning an average of 57% of the points (Bulgren, Schumaker, & Deshler, 1988).

Because of these skill deficits, many students with disabilities enter required general education courses without the prerequisite skills for success. Thus, students who read at the fourth-grade level cannot gain information from textbooks written at the tenth-grade level and above. Students who cannot multiply, divide, and work with fractions cannot do algebra. Students who cannot write a complete sentence cannot write a 10-page paper. And students who cannot pass tests can rarely pass a course.

Second, students with disabilities, especially those with attention deficit disorder, attention deficit hyperactivity disorder, and behavioral and emotional disorders, often have difficulty staying in their seats and concentrating for long periods of time. They need opportunities to move around, as well as frequent changes in activities to stay focused (Carpenter & McKee-Higgins, 1996). Not surprisingly, these students report that they lose interest in a class after about 15 to 20 minutes and rarely do much work after that (Schumaker, personal communication, 2000). Additionally, they have difficulty learning within large-group frameworks (Mercer, Lane, Jordan, Allsop, & Eisele, 1996) and need individual and elaborated feedback to learn efficiently (Kline, Schumaker, & Deshler, 1991).

Clearly, these disparities between the demands of required courses and the skills of students with disabilities impact whether they have true access to the general education curriculum. Although they might be enrolled in general education courses, these students might not truly have the same opportunities as other students to learn within those courses.

ABSENCE OF A COMPREHENSIVE
SERVICE DELIVERY SYSTEM

The full-inclusion movement and the standards-based reform movement have produced changes not only within general education, but also within special education. In fact, the special education services now offered to students with disabilities in high schools are in a state of flux. As described previously, students who used to receive a large proportion of their education in self-contained and resource room environments are now enrolled in general education classes for a majority of the school day (Lipsky & Gartner, 1997). As a result, the services and instruction that special education teachers deliver have changed. Whereas these teachers once may have focused on teaching students how to read, write, and do math, they now have to focus on helping students meet the difficult demands of the general education courses in which they are enrolled.

This means that students who are scheduled to be present in the resource room for an hour a day may receive some assistance in completing their assignments. At best, assistance takes the form of traditional tutoring (Carlson, 1985), which may involve a teacher actually doing an assignment for the student (Hock, 1998). Such tutorial assistance promotes dependence and does not prepare the student to do similar assignments independently (Hock, Deshler, & Schumaker, 1999a). At worst, students use the resource room as a study hall where they can recruit assistance with assignments if they wish. Because the scheduling of resource room hours typically results in a diversity of students being present in the room at the same time, there is no opportunity for group instruction on skills needed by students, and opportunities for individual assistance and instruction are infrequent and short in duration.

Worse yet, in some high schools, students with disabilities no longer receive any services in a resource room; instead, their special education teachers are assigned to teach required courses. In some cases, they coteach with a general education teacher. This can result in a misuse of special education funds: Research has shown that team teaching is often characterized by the special education teacher spending considerable time in a support role in the classroom as an observer who occasionally acts as an aide for the general educator (that is, passing out papers and completing other noninstructional tasks) (Boudah, Schumaker, & Deshler, 1997). Additionally, because the number of courses in which students with disabilities may be enrolled in a full-service high school is large, and because the number of courses in which special education teachers can team teach is limited, this type of service does not reach all of the students with disabilities who need it in all of their courses. Alternatively, special education teachers might teach watered-down versions of required courses to students with disabilities and other at-risk students (Hock, Deshler, &

Schumaker, 1999b). This tactic can be problematic as well because these teachers often are not certified to teach the subject matter in the courses to which they are assigned. Moreover, students with disabilities do not receive the same instruction and the same quality of education as their peers, and as a result may not pass state assessments. Finally, data supporting coteaching instructional arrangements for adolescents with disabilities are extremely limited; of those studies that have been done, the outcomes are equivocal at best (Murawski & Swanson, 2001).

In still other schools, the special education teachers are supposed to act as consultants to the general education teachers. They are to meet with the general education teachers and suggest accommodations and modifications for each activity and assignment that will enable the students with disabilities to succeed in targeted courses. Unfortunately, general education teachers report that this is not a practical way of helping students. Because they are given just a few minutes to plan each day, they want to spend that time planning their upcoming lessons, grading assignments, and taking care of the day's business. They do not want to spend that time planning to accommodate just a few students among the 150 students they see each day, nor are they willing to devote time within their classes to accommodate a small number of students (Lenz, Schumaker, & Deshler, 1991).

Finally, in some schools, and for some students with disabilities, special education services have been substantially altered so that students receive all instruction in their general education classes. Thus, they receive very little assistance outside of what is typically available to students at large, usually supplied through their general education teachers. Unfortunately, these teachers' lives are stressed and stretched thin as they attempt to educate 150 students each day. Not surprisingly, the amount of attention and assistance given to students with disabilities is minimal.

These types of service delivery systems for high school students with disabilities usually supply too little help in situations that require comprehensive support if these students have any hope of meeting the demands of challenging courses. Although comprehensive service delivery programs have been designed for students with disabilities to promote their success in required high school courses (Hock et al., 1999a; Schumaker & Deshler, 1984), the use of these programs is more the exception than the rule. These students need a combination of (1) intensive instruction in the prerequisite skills needed for success in required courses (Hock et al., 1999a), (2) homework assistance that helps them to become independent learners and aids their completion of assignments, and (3) specially designed learner-friendly instruction in their required courses (Hock et al., 1999a). Unfortunately, most high schools are not supplying this combination of services.

CONFUSION WITH REGARD TO
THE ROLE OF SPECIAL EDUCATORS

Closely aligned with the lack of comprehensive service delivery systems for high school students with disabilities is a general confusion about the role of special educators in the education of students with disabilities. Although policy by the Council for Exceptional Children (2000) has underscored that specialists should be certified in each exceptionality, many agencies and organizations are pushing noncategorical certification for special education teachers. This is of great concern because many current and future special education teachers are not receiving in-depth training related to particular exceptionalities. Additionally, some agencies are providing alternative routes to licensure, which, again, do not involve in-depth training of specialists. To maximize meager resources, many school districts are emphasizing consulting or coteaching roles for special education teachers; as a result, many of these teachers have been relegated either to being "paper pushers" or to sitting at the rear of classrooms serving as glorified aides. They are disheartened, their morale is low, and the turnover rate in special education positions is high (Mainzer, Deshler, Coleman, Kozleski, & Rodriguez-Walling, 2003). Not surprisingly, districts are having more and more difficulty finding qualified applicants for special education positions.

Regardless of the confusion and the emphasis on noncategorical services, specialists are needed within special education. Take, for example, the field of learning disabilities, which serves the largest subpopulation of students with disabilities. Specialists are needed in this field for a variety of reasons. First, recent research shows that a large majority of students with learning disabilities can be taught the basic skills associated with reading, writing, solving math problems, listening, and speaking if certain instructional methods are used (Vaughn, Gersten, & Chard, 2000). Proper use of these methods requires in-depth training that involves practice as well as feedback from someone who knows how to use them. Nevertheless, many individuals graduating from professional development programs lack the competencies for teaching students with learning disabilities these basic skills (Otis-Wilborn & Winn, 2000).

Second, research has also shown that students with learning disabilities who have learned the basic skills associated with reading, writing, math, and speaking can learn the more complex skills and strategies needed for success in high school and postsecondary school. They also can succeed at a level that is comparable to typically achieving peers in these educational settings (Schumaker & Deshler, 1992). Again, however, the individuals who are to teach these skills and strategies to students with learning disabilities need extensive training.

Third, research is showing that the kind of instruction that enables students with learning disabilities to be successful must be intensive and explicit. Specifically, students with learning disabilities must have many opportunities to practice and receive feedback on a daily basis, and teachers must focus on the mastery of the skills and strategies for individual students (Deshler et al., in press).

Unfortunately, the conditions for this type of instruction are rarely present in today's schools. For example, in general education classrooms, which contain heterogeneous groupings of students (including those who learn quickly), instruction moves forward regardless of what each student has mastered. Also, because of the number of students enrolled in these classes, the provision of meaningful individual feedback is difficult to arrange. Additionally, general education classes often focus on learning subject-matter information rather than learning skills such as reading, especially in grades where most students have already acquired those skills.

Sometimes these conditions are not present in noncategorical special education programs either. Teachers often state that because of the mix of students within each class hour, there is no time to provide the intensive instruction that students with learning disabilities need. They find themselves dealing with the latest crisis, often related to a student with emotional problems, and unable to devote the time and effort necessary for intensive instruction.

Fourth, research is showing that there is no quick fix for students with learning disabilities. These students need special types of instruction until they learn all of the skills necessary for success at the secondary and post-secondary levels. If specialized instruction proceeds intensively across the grades for at least an hour a day, many students with learning disabilities can learn these skills by the 10th or 11th grade (Schumaker & Deshler, 1992). Thereafter, their performance must be carefully monitored and assistance provided as needed. This means that learning disabilities specialists must be available across the grades to teach these students the skills and strategies they need to be successful lifelong learners in today's competitive world.

Clearly, individuals with learning disabilities need learning disabilities specialists, just as students with other exceptionalities need specialists who know how to meet their unique needs. Unfortunately, today's high school teachers and administrators often find themselves working in conditions that make providing their students with the "appropriate instruction and support" very difficult—in some cases, impossible. Some indications of the adverse conditions that educators face were recently reported by the Council for Exceptional Children in its report *Bright Futures for Exceptional Learners: An Agenda to Achieve Quality Conditions for Teaching and Learning* (Kozleski, Mainzer, & Deshler, 2000). This report was the product of a presidential commission that studied the conditions that today's teachers face in trying to provide quality instruction to our country's most challenged learners. Although the report focuses primarily on the challenges that special education teachers face in meeting the needs of students with disabilities, its conclusions reflect the mounting pressures that all teachers face in meeting the needs of increasingly diverse student populations.

The concerns discussed in the report were identified as accounting for the fact that special educators are leaving the teaching profession at almost twice the rate of general educators. To fill the void, school districts often recruit inexperienced or unqualified teachers to teach some of the most difficult-to-teach students. In light of this reality, the presidential commission concluded that "the special education field is facing a crisis of capacity: more students and a growing demand for special educators. To stem the loss of our most accomplished special educators, the field must understand the underlying reasons for the attrition rates (these issues) are placing an oppressive burden on educators and create the need for action" (Kozleski et al., 2000, p. 22). Among the most pressing concerns raised in the report are the following:

• *Ambiguous and competing responsibilities:* Special educators face ambiguous, conflicting, and fragmented expectations from other educators, families, administrators, and the public. The shift in the way special educators spend their time is a reflection of the significant changes that have occurred in the roles of these teachers. Many came into the field expecting to work intensively with a small group of students with exceptional needs. Intensive instruction has been the hallmark of special education. However, 68% of special educators report that they spend less than two hours per week in individual or small-group instruction with their students. Increasingly, special educators are expected to engage in collaboration, coteaching, coaching, and mentoring.

• *Overwhelming paperwork:* One of the most frequently reported barriers to quality teaching is the oppressive amount of paperwork necessitated by federal and state regulations. While special educators applaud the important role of IEPs, they struggle with the amount of clerical work that the process requires. The average length of the typical IEP is 8 to 16 pages, with an estimated four hours of premeeting planning time going into each IEP conference. The majority of special educators report spending one day or more per week on paperwork, and 83% report spending one half to one and a half days per week on IEP-related meetings. IEPs, however, are just the beginning of paperwork responsibilities for educators. Many teachers reported that they are expected to do considerably more record keeping today to "keep the school system out of a lawsuit."

• *Inadequate district and administrative support:* Many administrators lack the knowledge, skills, and time to support services for students with exceptionalities. Some of this may be tied to the fact that licensing for administrators rarely addresses the knowledge and skills that administrators need to provide effective leadership for establishing and running effective programs on behalf of exceptional learners. Additionally, special educators report that they often do not have the necessary materials they need to provide quality instruction. In many schools, the special education program is still the last on the list for books, instructional materials, classroom space, and equipment. To make up for some of these shortages, teachers regularly spend as much as $500 each of their own money on classroom supplies and materials.

- *Significant teacher isolation:* Special educators report being isolated from both their special education and general education colleagues. With few opportunities to collaborate, this sense of separation is often combined with a feeling of powerlessness to participate in, let alone influence, major decisions and policies that guide their work and things done on behalf of students with disabilities.

- *Insufficient focus on improved student outcomes.* To help each student achieve high-quality learning results, teachers must select instructional approaches and strategies that match the learning needs of individual students. Unfortunately, too many widely adopted approaches to teaching in specific content areas lack evidence of successful student outcomes. Furthermore, many learning approaches, materials, and interventions are ineffective for students with disabilities. In spite of available research identifying teaching methods and strategies that produce learning results, valuable instructional time is spent using weak teaching strategies (Kozleski et al., 2000, pp. 4–5).

In summary, students with disabilities need people with the knowledge and skills to teach them what they need to know to be successful learners; they need people who can focus their attention on them and provide them with the intensive instruction and feedback they need; they need people who can set up instructional conditions that are conducive to their learning; and they need sustained contact with a series of such teachers across the grades. Unfortunately, because of the current confusion over special education teachers' roles and the emphasis on generalization rather than specialization in teacher preparation programs, many students with disabilities do not have access to teachers who are specially trained to teach them. In addition, because special education teachers often labor under conditions that are not conducive to optimal learning, and because they often do not receive support from their administrators, even teachers who are trained to provide research-based instruction often cannot implement it.

CULTURAL AND LINGUISTIC DIVERSITY

Another major trend that impacts high school students with disabilities and their special and general education teachers relates to the dramatic increase in diversity among the U.S. student population. Because of the increase in cultural and linguistic differences among students, the prevailing context of many high schools is dramatically different from previous decades. In 1998, almost 40% of all public school students were students of color, and nearly 25% of those students were living in households where languages other than English are spoken (Mazzeo, Carlson, Voekl, & Lutkus, 2000).

Additionally, the composition of the population of students with disabilities is changing. In fact, 1996 National Assessment of Education Progress assessment data indicated that one out of every five (20%) limited English proficiency students was also classified as having a disability (Mazzeo et al., 2000). Furthermore, an analysis of special education prevalence data shows that, in some states, as many as 27% of students with limited English proficiency receive special education services. These rates are significantly higher than the national disability prevalence rate of 12% (Robertson, Kushner, Starks, & Drescher, 1994).

Clearly, these increased numbers of English-language learners pose complex challenges in terms of referral, assessment, and instruction. For example, studies of the referral, assessment, and placement of culturally and linguistically diverse learners with disabilities indicate that many teachers and support personnel are unable to distinguish linguistic differences and characteristics of second-language acquisition from language or learning disorders (Ortiz, Garcia, Wheeler, & Maldonado-Colon, 1986; Wilkinson & Ortiz, 1986). As a result, many such learners are inaccurately labeled as having disabilities.

Regardless of the difficulties inherent in educating these students, the prevailing notion is that they are to receive the same education and assessments as other students. The Improving America's Schools Act, for example, encouraged educators to serve students with limited English proficiency in general education classrooms whenever possible to ensure their access to the general education curriculum. Additionally, increased expectations for culturally diverse learners are clearly manifested in curriculum standards (that is, goals that indicate what students should have learned upon completion of their public school education) that guide the work of general education teachers. These standards have been developed and promoted by a range of professional organizations for *all* children. For example, the authors of the Standards for the National Council of Teachers of Mathematics stated, "We believe that *all* students can benefit from an opportunity to study the core curriculum specified in the *Standards*" (1989, p. 259). The staff of the National Center for History in the Schools stated, "A reformed social studies curriculum should be required of *all* students in common, regardless of their 'track' or further vocational and educational plans" (Pyne, Sesso, Ankeney, & Vigilante, 1992, p. 9). Members of the National Committee on Science Education Standards and Assessment stated, "The commitment to science for all implies inclusion not only of those who traditionally have received encouragement and opportunity to pursue science, but of all racial and ethnic groups, students with disabilities, and those with limited proficiency in English" (1993, p. 1). Finally, members of the National Council of Teachers of English (1996) stated that their goal is to promote equality of educational opportunity and higher academic achievement for *all* students. These pronouncements clearly indicate that general education teachers are expected to adjust the nature of their instruction to meet the needs of all students, including those with disabilities and those who are bilingual.

Additionally, these students are expected to take part in the same types of assessments as other students. Both the *21st Annual Report to Congress* (U.S. Department of Education, 1999) and the National Association for Bilingual Education (1999) emphasized the need to include limited English proficiency and bilingual students in state and national assessments. They also emphasized the need to provide these students with accommodations or alternative assessments similar to those given to students with disabilities.

The change in the composition of the student population in recent decades has had several implications for high school students with disabilities. First, the composition of general education classes is more diverse. Not only are classes filled with a variety of learners (high achievers, typical achievers, low achievers, and students with disabilities); they are also filled with students who speak a variety of languages and have a variety of background experiences. In some schools in California, more than 100 languages are spoken by students (Williams, personal communication, 1999). This puts tremendous pressure on general education teachers as they try to deliver instruction in their courses. The likelihood that these teachers will be able to give attention to individuals with disabilities who already speak English is diminished if they also have to focus on students who cannot speak English.

Second, the composition of any special education class will be more diverse. Again, special education teachers who once may have had time to teach students learning strategies may now have to devote a great deal of time to teaching these students how to read, speak, and write English. Thus, the presence of students who cannot speak English well may have a deleterious effect on the amount of time and attention that can be devoted to students with disabilities.

THE CLIMATE OF VIOLENCE WITHIN TODAY'S SCHOOLS

Another major trend in high schools, which may or may not be associated with the diversification of the student population and tensions among student subgroups, has been an overall change in the way students treat each other. Aggressive, antisocial, and violent behavior is a reality in today's high schools. The National Association of School Psychologists estimates that, every day, 160,000 students stay home from school because of a fear of bullies (Vail, 1999). In a 1993 survey of 6,504 6th- through 12th-grade students in the United States, 71% reported that bullying, physical attacks, or robbery had happened at their school (Nolin & Davies, 1993). Similarly, in another study, 77% of the respondents indicated that they had been victims of bullies at school (Vail, 1999). Although a recent report for the U.S. Department of Justice suggested that violent crime among juveniles is decreasing, it also noted that 47% of all teens believed their schools were becoming more violent (Brooks, Schiraldi, & Ziedenberg, 1999). The authors of the report suggested that a gap exists between statistics related to youth and school violence, what students think of their schools, and what Americans think is or could be happening in their children's schools. They stated, "Sadly, many of the policy changes being enacted across the country are based on policymakers' sense of adult perceptions, and not the actual incidence of crime, or the experiences of children in school" (Brooks et al., 1999, p. 8).

Indeed, the statistics on violent crime rates may not tell the whole story. Researchers who monitor school climate suggest that it is more hazardous than in previous years and that bullying is rampant (Limber & Nation, 1998; Portner, 2000). Among males in some high schools, as many as 21% reported having seen a person sexually assaulted; 82% reported having witnessed a beating or mugging in school; 46% reported having seen a person attacked or stabbed with a knife; and 62% said that they had witnessed a shooting (Singer, Anglin, Song, & Lunghofer, 1995). Similarly, in a survey of junior high and high school students, Limber and Nation (1998) reported that 88% had witnessed bullying and 77% had been victimized by bullies. These authors further noted that bullying occurs more frequently on school grounds than on the way to or from school. In contrast, the results of a National Household Education Survey taken in 1993 revealed that 20% of high school students were worried about becoming victims at school, 8% reported they had been personally victimized, and 6% reported having been bullied at school. Thus, bullying seems to be more frequently reported in recent surveys. Unfortunately, student surveys suggest that teachers seldom discuss bullying in class and seldom intervene effectively when problems occur (Banks, 2000). When adults do become involved, their interventions often make the situation worse (Vail, 1999). Indeed, bullying is often underreported, minimized, or unacknowledged by school staff members (Vail, 1999).

This is cause for concern. High schools have become fearful and unhappy places for many students. Victims' grades deteriorate, and their fear often leads to absenteeism, truancy, or dropping out of school (Vail, 1999). Some authors have suggested that victims run an increased risk of isolation at school (Banks, 2000) and mental health problems, as well as an increased likelihood that they, too, will commit acts of violence (America's Children, 2000; Davis, Nelson, & Gauger, 2000). Victims of bullies report higher levels of loneliness, distress, and negativity toward school than nonvictims (Kochenderfer & Ladd, 1996), and, as adults, victims of bullying are at an increased risk for depression, poor self-esteem, and additional mental health problems (Limber & Nation, 1998). More alarming are reports that children who are bullied are more likely to commit suicide (Portner, 2000). According to Portner, childhood suicide has tripled during the past 30 years and is the third-leading killer of 10- to 19-year-olds in the United States. However, only 1 in 10 schools has a plan to prevent it.

This overall change in high school climate can have an especially devastating effect on students with disabilities, who often are isolated, alienated, and experience difficulty becoming an integral part of the high school community. In fact, students with disabilities have been consistently found to be rejected by their peers (Gresham & Reschly, 1986), bullied more than their peers (Sabornie, 1994), and ignored and treated in negative ways within cooperative groups (Vernon, Schumaker, & Deshler, 1994). They also have fewer social skills than their peers (Hazel, Sherman, Schumaker, & Sheldon, 1986). Some investigators have reported that students with disabilities in inclusionary settings experience heightened feelings of "disconnectedness" (King-Sears & Cummings, 1996). Given the current climate within high schools, one could predict that students with disabilities might fall prey to loneliness (Margalit & Levin-Alyagon, 1994), victimization (Sabornie, 1994), and alienation (Bryan, 1986) even more than ever before.

FAMILY AND COMMUNITY DYNAMICS

Besides the contextual factors present in today's schools, how well high school students perform academically and how well they deal with the uncertainties and pressures of adolescence are influenced, in a significant way, by the nature of their family situation and the quantity and quality of interactions with adults in their lives. Two factors in particular have contributed to increased instability in the homes of U.S. teenagers during the past quarter of a century: poverty and the absence of parents.

With regard to poverty, numerous research studies have indicated that economic hardship or poverty at the family and neighborhood level affect adolescent mental health and school achievement. In 1997, the U.S. Census Bureau revealed that when poverty was defined as an annual income of $16,036 or below for a family of four, 35.6 million Americans were found to be living below the poverty line. Poverty rates were three to four times higher for black youth, five times higher for female-headed families, and consistently higher in nonmetropolitan areas (Dalaker & Naifeh, 1998).

Other variables seem to interact with poverty to impact children. For example, the duration of poverty, family conflict rates, and the presence of maternal depression and family violence are all variables that can significantly influence the magnitude and type of impact that poverty has on children and adolescents (Garrett, Ng'andu, & Ferron, 1994).

Indeed, the duration of economic deprivation is often neglected as an important variable influencing the effects of poverty. For adolescents, the number of years that the family lives in poverty is a highly significant predictor of school attainment and early career outcomes (Corcoran, Gordon, Laren, & Solon, 1992). In terms of onset, the combination of family poverty and welfare use during adolescence has been shown to be a significant predictor of increased high school drop-out rates (Haveman, Wolfe, & Spaulding, 1991).

Predictably, studies have shown that economic stress adversely influences the quality of family relationships (Elder, Conger, Foster, & Ardelt, 1992; Voydanoff, 1990). Poverty is directly linked to depression and loneliness in adolescents because youth are significantly affected by the disruptions in parent–child relations caused by parental preoccupation with the economic needs of the family (Flanagan, 1990; Lempers, Clark-Lempers, & Simons, 1989). For example, in one study of 378 white families, economic stress was associated with the number and severity of parent–adolescent conflicts and marital discord (Conger, Ge, Elder, Lorenz, & Simons, 1994). These conflicts often were manifested as parent hostility toward the adolescent, which was associated with increased risk that the adolescent would develop behavioral problems (Conger et al., 1994). Additionally, families with youth with special needs are more likely to demonstrate conflict or aggression in their interactions than other families (Robinson & Jacobson, 1987).

Economic hardships are particularly difficult for single mothers. The effects of poverty and sustained unemployment are often manifested in increased levels of depression experienced by mothers, as well as levels of punishment given to adolescents in their homes. In turn, the adolescents of single mothers have been found to evidence higher levels of stress and depressive symptoms than other adolescents living in poverty (McLoyd, Jayaratne, Ceballo, & Borquez, 1994).

Finally, according to the *Nineteenth Annual Report to Congress* (U.S. Department of Education, 1997), family poverty is closely linked to the increased likelihood of disabilities and participation in special education (LaPlante & Carlson, 1996; McLoyd, 1998). In an analysis of the National Health Interview Survey of 25,000 households from 1983 to 1996, researchers concluded that the odds of having a child with a disability were 88% higher in a single-parent household than in a two-parent household and that poverty was the most significant predictor of disability status (Fujiura & Yamaki, 2000).

Closely related to the adverse effects of family poverty are the effects of the neighborhood in which a youth resides and associates (Mayer & Jencks, 1989). Unfortunately, as a result of structural changes in postindustrial society, there has been an increase in the number of poor and jobless families in inner-city neighborhoods. Neighborhoods with poverty rates of 40% or more are often termed "ghetto" neighborhoods (Wilson, 1991). The number of poor neighbors becomes more important for children as they enter school, and especially as they reach adolescence (Duncan, Brooks-Gunn, & Klebanov, 1994). A poor neighborhood is more likely to have a substantial number of youth who are using drugs, having early unprotected sexual intercourse, and dropping out of school (Crane, 1991). All of these factors tend to negatively influence adolescent behavior (Steinberg, 1998). Neighborhood poverty has been found also to have significant implications for students with disabilities. Namely, these students experience more stress, victimization, and violence because of the deleterious effects of violence and poverty in their neighborhoods (Groves, Zuckerman, Marans, & Cohen, 1993; Osofsky, 1994).

With regard to their home lives, many adolescents experience uncertainty and disruption and have parents who are largely absent from their lives (Stepp, 2000). Whether they are victims of the dramatic increase in the divorce rate in American families (Holtz, 1995) or circumstances that allow them limited access to their parents, adolescents are increasingly experiencing a significant void in adult role models in their lives. Economic pressures are keeping parents in the workplace for longer hours (Oliver, 1999) and requiring both parents to be engaged outside the home for a significant portion of the day. For example, only one in five teenagers report spending time with their fathers daily (Steinberg, 1998). In a classic study on adolescent activities, Csikszentmihalyi and Larson (1987) found that adolescents spent only 4.8% of their time with parents and 2% of their time with adults who were not their parents. In short, as youth move into their teenage years, there is a marked separation from significant adults in their lives.

Hersch (1998) describes the effects of this separation as follows:

> America's adolescents have become strangers. They are a tribe apart; somewhere around age 14 the nation's kids slip into the netherworld of adolescence and estrangement. Today's teens have grown up in the midst of enormous social change that has shaped, reshaped, distorted, and sometimes decimated the basic parameters for healthy development. They live in families that have difficulty fitting in child rearing—[child rearing] needs to compete with the energies put into earning a living. At a time when teens need role models to emulate, the adults around them seem to be moving targets. (p. 147)

Hersch (1998) further argues that because of the altered dynamics within many homes and extended families, teenagers often experience a significant sense of disconnection from adults who, in previous generations, played a central role in the lives of adolescents.

The teens of the 1990s were more isolated and more unsupervised than other generations. Today, mom is at work. Neighbors are often strangers.

Relatives live in distant places. This changes everything. It changes access to bed, the liquor cabinet, and cars. These days, kids can more easily be good or bad without others knowing about it. Exchanges do not take place between generations. Conversations do not get held; the guidance and the role modeling are not taking place. The wisdom and traditions are no longer filtering down. How can teens imitate and learn from adults if they seldom talk to them? What kids need from adults is not just rides, pizza, and chaperones. They need the telling of stories and close, ongoing contact so that they can learn and be accepted. Without a link across generations, kids only learn from their peers. In the absence of a community within the family and the neighborhood, students have separated themselves and set up their own community as "a tribe apart!" (Hersch, 1998, p. 153).

In short, one of the major struggles that teenagers face is a lack of connection to significant traditions and older mentors. Related to this void is the noted decrease in teenage involvement in extracurricular school activities (Stepp, 2000). Increasingly, many teenagers find meaningful relationships and interests in the mall or in groups (in some cases, gangs) that are set apart from the formal fabric of the high school scene (Brand & Partee, 2000). Indeed, today's adolescents often learn to depend on each other for the sense of community they long for and often do not find within their families. Regrettably, some of the role models that they find among their counterparts are not always positive. In many cases, youth find few individuals or groups with whom to associate and experience a significant sense of isolation and aloneness (Hersch, 1998).

To summarize, the effects of poverty and disrupted home lives on adolescents can be devastating in terms of their feelings of stability and connectedness. If adolescents who are poor live in poor neighborhoods, have little contact with their parents, have home lives marked by conflict, have no other positive role models with which to connect, and also have disabilities, their chances of success in the complex environment of today's high schools are diminished. Take, for example, the academic demand that they complete two to three hours of homework per day. If their home lives are chaotic, stressful, and conflictual, they will not be able to concentrate well enough to do homework. If their study time is not structured and supervised, and if assistance is not available to them when they encounter difficulty, they are not likely to complete their assignments. Thus, adolescents with disabilities, many of whom come from poor families, seem to be at a particular disadvantage because they are the very students who need the most adult support and stability.

CONCLUSION

Although federal mandates are in place requiring that students with disabilities have real access to the general education curriculum and receive the assistance they need to succeed within that curriculum, many other contextual factors present in today's high school serve as barriers to these students' success. First, for the most part, state standards are driving the high school curriculum. The demands associated with required high school courses are complex and difficult enough that most students with disabilities, given their skill deficits, cannot meet them. Second, there is an absence of comprehensive service delivery systems and confusion about the role of special education teachers. Instead of focusing their time and energy on using validated instructional methods to provide students with disabilities the intensive instruction and assistance they need to become independent learners, these teachers are often acting as aides in general education classrooms, dealing with paperwork, teaching watered-down courses, or tutoring students. Third, the diversity of today's student population adds a new set of challenges for teachers who are already stressed by the new levels of accountability to which they are answerable. Fourth, the social climate of today's high schools often is not conducive to helping students feel part of the school community and motivated to learn. The frequency of bullying is growing, and many students live with fear as a daily part of their lives. Further, the culture of negativity prevents many students from even trying to do schoolwork. Finally, poverty, chaotic home lives, problematic neighborhoods, and the absence of adults in many teenagers' lives create a context within which many students have difficulty concentrating and performing academically.

These serious contextual conditions must be met with serious interventions if the nine outcome goals in IDEA 1997 are to be met. We offer the following recommendations for creating a better context in which to ensure that adolescents with disabilities succeed in high school. These recommendations are based on the assumption that high expectations will be maintained for students with disabilities. Further, they must be accompanied by equal access for these students to a standards-based curriculum. Finally, the recommendations that have emerged from this research synthesis build on and support those highlighted by the recently published document from the Center for Policy Research on the Impact of General and Special Education Reform (Dailey et al., 2000).

- The IEP should be the tool for negotiating, reconciling, and determining supports needed for students with disabilities to participate within a standards-based curriculum.
- Preservice and inservice professional development experiences should prepare general education teachers to deal with the demanding realities of implementing a standards-based curriculum in a manner that allows diverse groups of students to be successful.
- Preservice and inservice professional development experiences should prepare special education teachers to provide the types of

specialized instruction that subgroups of students with disabilities need to be successful in a standards-based curriculum.

- Districts should experiment with models for organizing high schools as interdepartmental and interdisciplinary structures that bring general and special educators together in planning and instructional configurations that optimize student performance.
- Comprehensive service delivery models based on research-validated methods must be made available so that students with disabilities receive learner-friendly instruction in their required courses, as well as intensive instruction in the skills and strategies they need to be successful in those courses. They also need appropriate homework assistance so that they can become independent learners who are capable of motivating themselves to learn and complete their work, regardless of the conditions around them. Additionally, these models must provide students with disabilities with instruction in how to deal with the negative social culture prevalent in many schools so that they can respond in productive ways to bullying and negativism and build positive relationships with other students and mentoring relationships with adults.

Insofar as a central goal of IDEA 2004 is to improve the academic outcomes of students with disabilities, and given that this improvement must take place within the larger context of standards-based reform efforts, educators must use instructional practices that have the greatest probability of preparing students to successfully respond to these demanding standards and compete with typically achieving peers. Indeed, *real* access to rigorous general education curricula must make available the instruction, supports, and accommodations necessary to ensure these students' academic success, as well as their feelings of connection to their school community.

REFERENCES

America's Children. (2000). *The state of America's children yearbook.* Washington, DC: Children's Defense Fund.

Banks, R. (2000). Bullying in schools. *ERIC Review: School Safety: A Collaborative Effort, 7*(1), 1–3.

Boudah, D. J., Schumaker, J. B., & Deshler, D. D. (1997). Collaborative instruction: Is it an effective option for inclusion in secondary classrooms? *Learning Disability Quarterly, 20*(2), 293–316.

Brand, B., & Partee, G. (2000). *High schools of the millennium.* Washington, DC: American Youth Policy Forum.

Brooks, K., Schiraldi, V., & Ziedenberg, J. (1999). *School house hype: Two years later.* Washington, DC: Justice Policy Institute, Center on Juvenile and Criminal Justice.

Bryan, T. (1986). Self-concept and attribution of the learning disabled. *Learning Disability Focus, 1*(2), 82–89.

Bulgren, J. A., Schumaker, J. B., & Deshler, D. D. (1988). Effectiveness of a concept teaching routine in enhancing the performance of LD students in secondary-level mainstream classes. *Learning Disability Quarterly, 11*(1), 3–17.

Carlson, S. A. (1985). The ethical appropriateness of subject-matter tutoring for learning disabled adolescents. *Learning Disability Quarterly, 8*(2), 310–314.

Carpenter, S. L., & McKee-Higgins, E. (1996). Behavior management in inclusive classrooms. *Remedial and Special Education, 17*(4), 195–203.

Cavanagh, S. (2004, September 3). Bush touts ed. law's successes, promises high school reforms. *Education Week.* Retrieved September 6, 2004, from www .edweek.org/ew/ew_prinstory.efm.slug+02bush_web.h24

Conger, R. D., Ge, X., Elder, G. H., Jr., Lorenz, F. O., & Simons, R. L. (1994). Economic stress, coercive family process, and developmental problems of adolescents. *Child Development, 65,* 541–561.

Corcoran, M., Gordon, R., Laren, D., & Solon, G. (1992). The association between men's economic status and their family and community origins. *Journal of Human Resources, 27,* 73–106.

Council for Exceptional Children (CEC). (2000). *What every special educator must know: The standards for the preparation and licensure of special educators* (4th ed.). Arlington, VA: Author.

Council of Chief State School Officers. (1998). *State education accountability reports and indicators: Status of reports across states.* Washington, DC: Author.

Crane, J. (1991). The epidemic theory of ghettos and neighborhood effects on dropping out and teenage childbearing. *American Journal of Sociology, 96,* 1126–1159.

Csikszentmihalyi, M., & Larson, S. (1987). The ecology of adolescent activity and experience. *Journal of Youth and Adolescence, 32*(3), 281–294.

Dailey, D., Zantal-Wiener, K., & Roach, V. (2000). *Reforming high school learning: The effect of the standards movement on secondary students with disabilities.* Alexandria, VA: Center for Policy Research on the Impact of General and Special Education Reform.

Dalaker, J., & Naifeh, M. (1998). *Poverty in the United States: 1997* (Current population reports, Series P60-201). Washington, DC: Government Printing Office.

Davis, J. L., Nelson, C. S., & Gauger, E. S. (2000). *The Boys Town model: Safe and effective secondary schools.* Boys Town, NE: Boys Town Press.

Deshler, D. D., Schumaker, J. B., Lenz, B. K., Bulgren, J., Hock, M. F., Knight, J., & Ehren, B. J. (in press). Ensuring content-area learning by secondary students with learning disabilities. *Learning Disabilities Research and Practice.*

Duncan, G. J., Brooks-Gunn, J., & Klebanov, P. K. (1994). Economic deprivation and early childhood development. *Child Development, 65,* 296–318.

Ehren, B. J., & Lenz, B. K. (1986). *Final report: A proposed dropout identification system.* Submitted to the Florida Legislature and the Florida Department of Education, Student Support Services.

Elder, G. H., Jr., Conger, R. D., Foster, E. M., & Ardelt, M. (1992). Families under economic pressure. *Journal of Family Issues, 13,* 5–37.

Elmore, R. (1998). Progress toward implementing standards-based reform. In *Annual report on implementation of Goals 2000 Education Act.* Washington, DC: U.S. Department of Education, Office of Educational Research and Improvement.

Fisher, J. B., Schumaker, J. B., & Deshler, D. D. (1995). Searching for validated inclusive practices: A review of the literature. *Focus on Exceptional Children, 28*(4), 1–20.

Flanagan, C. A. (1990). Change in family work status: Effects on parent-adolescent decision making. *Child Development, 61,* 163–177.

Fujiura, G. T., & Yamaki, K. (2000). Trends in demography of childhood poverty and disability. *Exceptional Children, 66,* 187–199.

Garrett, P., Ng'andu, N., & Ferron, J. (1994). Poverty experiences of young children and the quality of their home environments. *Child Development, 65,* 331–345.

Gresham, F. M., & Reschly, D. J. (1986). Social skill deficits and low peer acceptance of mainstreamed learning disabled children. *Learning Disability Quarterly, 9,* 23–32.

Groves, B., Zuckerman, B., Marans, S., & Cohen, D. (1993). Silent victims: Children who witness violence. *Journal of the American Medical Association, 269,* 262–264.

Haveman, R., Wolfe, B., & Spaulding, J. (1991). Childhood events and circumstances influencing high school completion. *Demography, 28,* 133–157.

Hazel, J. S., Sherman, J. A., Schumaker, J. B., & Sheldon, J. (1986). Group social skills training with adolescents: A critical review. In D. Upper & S. M. Ross (Eds.), *Behavioral group therapy: An annual review* (pp. 203–246). New York: Plenum Press.

Hersch, P. (1998). *A tribe apart: A journey into the heart of American adolescence.* New York: Fawcett Columbine.

Hock, M. F. (1998). *The validation of a strategic-tutoring intervention.* Unpublished doctoral dissertation, University of Kansas.

Hock, M. F., Deshler, D. D., & Schumaker, J. B. (1999a). Closing the gap to success in secondary schools: A model for cognitive apprenticeship. In D. D. Deshler, J. B. Schumaker, K. R. Harris, & S. Graham (Eds.), *Teaching every adolescent every day* (pp. 73–97). Cambridge, MA: Brookline Books.

Hock, M. F., Deshler, D. D., & Schumaker, J. B. (1999b). Tutoring programs for academically underprepared college students: A review of the literature. *Journal of College Reading and Learning, 29*(2), 101–121.

Holtz, G. T. (1995). *Welcome to the jungle.* New York: St. Martin's Griffin.

Howell, K., & Nolet, V. W. (2000). *Curriculum-based evaluation.* Atlanta, GA: Wadsworth.

Hughes, C., Ruhl, K., Deshler, D. D., & Schumaker, J. B. (1995). *The Assignment Completion Strategy.* Lawrence, KS: Edge Enterprises.

Individuals with Disabilities Education Act, 20 U.S.C. § 1474(b) (1997).

Kamil, M. (2003). *Adolescents and literacy: Reading for the 21st century.* Washington, DC: Alliance for Excellent Education.

Kansas Board of Regents. (2000). *Regents curricula: The right combination—A student guide to curricular requirements for regents universities.* Topeka: Kansas Board of Regents.

King-Sears, M. E., & Carpenter, S. L. (1996). Introduction to the topical issue: Inclusion, Part 2. *Remedial and Special Education, 17*(4), 194–195.

King-Sears, M. E., & Cummings, C. (1996). General educators' inclusive practices. *Remedial and Special Education, 17*(4), 14–23.

Kleinhammer-Trammill, J., & Gallagher, K. (in press). Goals 2000 as inclusive education policy. In W. Sailor (Ed.), *Inclusive education and school/community partnerships.* Baltimore: Paul H. Brookes.

Kline, F. M., Schumaker, J. B., & Deshler, D. D. (1991). Development and validation of feedback routines for instructing students with learning disabilities. *Learning Disability Quarterly, 14*(3), 191–207.

Kochenderfer, B. J., & Ladd, G. W. (1996). Peer victimization: Cause or consequence of school maladjustment? *Child Development, 67,* 1305–1317.

Kozleski, E., Mainzer, R., & Deshler, D. D. (2000). *Bright futures for exceptional learners: An agenda to achieve quality conditions for teaching and learning.* Reston, VA: Council for Exceptional Children.

LaPlante, M. P., & Carlson, D. (1996). *Disability in the United States: Prevalence and causes, 1992* (Disability Statistics Report No. 7). Washington, DC: U.S. Department of Education, National Institute on Disability and Rehabilitation Research.

Lempers, J., Clark-Lempers, D., & Simons, R. (1989). Economic hardship, parenting, and distress in adolescence. *Child Development, 60,* 25–49.

Lenz, B. K., Alley, G. R., & Schumaker, J. B. (1987). Activating the inactive learner: Advance organizers in secondary content classrooms. *Learning Disability Quarterly, 10*(1), 53–67.

Lenz, B. K., & Deshler, D. D. (2004). Adolescents with learning disabilities: Revisiting the educator's enigma. In B. Y. Wong (Ed.), *Advances in learning disabilities* (pp. 301–337). New York: Guilford.

Lenz, B. K., Schumaker, J. B., & Deshler, D. D. (1991). *Planning in the face of academic diversity: Whose questions should we be answering?* Chicago: American Educational Research Association Conference.

Limber, S. P., & Nation, M. M. (1998). Bullying among children and youth. *Juvenile Justice Bulletin, 27*(3), 121–137.

Lipsky, D. K., & Gartner, A. (1997). *Inclusion and school reform: Transforming America's classrooms.* Baltimore: Paul H. Brookes.

Louisiana Department of Education. (2000). *Increasing student performance.* Baton Rouge, LA: Office of Student and School Performance, Division of School Standards, Accountability, and Assistance.

Mainzer, R. W., Deshler, D. D., Coleman, M. R., Kozleski, E. & Rodriguez-Walling, M. (2003). To ensure the learning of every child with a disability. *Focus on Exceptional Children, 35*(5), 1–12.

Margalit, M., & Levin-Alyagon, M. (1994). Learning disability subtyping, loneliness, and classroom adjustment. *Learning Disability Quarterly, 17,* 279–310.

Martin, C. (1999). *Net future.* New York: McGraw-Hill.

Mastropieri, M. A. (2003, December). *Feasibility and consequences of response to intervention (RtI): Examination of the issues and scientific evidence as a model for the identification of individuals with learning disabilities.* Paper presented at the National Research Center on Learning Disabilities Responsiveness-to-Intervention Symposium, Kansas City, MO.

Mayer, S. E., & Jencks, C. C. (1989). Growing up in poor neighborhoods: How much does it matter? *Science, 243,* 1441–1446.

Mazzeo, J., Carlson, J. E., Voekl, K. E., & Lutkus, A. D. (2000, March). *Increasing the participation rate of special needs students in NAEP: A report on 1996 NAEP research activities.* Washington, DC: U.S. Department of Education, Office of Educational Research and Improvement.

McDonnell, L. M., McLaughlin, M. J., & Morrison, P. (1997). *Educating one and all: Students with disabilities and standards-based reform.* Washington, DC: National Academy Press.

McLaughlin, M. J., & Warren, S. H. (1992). Outcome assessments for students with disabilities: Will it be accountability or continued failure? *Preventing School Failure, 36*(4), 29–33.

McLoyd, V. C. (1998). Socioeconomic disadvantage and child development. *American Psychologist, 53*, 185–204.

McLoyd, V. C., Jayaratne, T. E., Ceballo, R., & Borquez, J. (1994). Unemployment and work interruption among African American single mothers: Effects on parenting and adolescent socioemotional functioning. *Child Development, 65*, 562–589.

Mercer, C. D., Lane, H. B., Jordan, L., Allsop, D. H., & Eisele, M. R. (1996). Empowering teachers and students with instructional choices in inclusive settings. *Remedial and Special Education, 17*(4), 226–236.

Murawski, W. W., & Swanson, H. L. (2001). A meta-analysis of co-teaching research. *Remedial and Special Education, 15*(3), 73–85.

National Association for Bilingual Education (NABE). (1999). *About NABE: Education, language and culture.* Washington, DC: Author.

National Committee on Science Education Standards and Assessment. (1993). *National science education standards.* Washington, DC: National Science Teachers Association.

National Council of Teachers of English. (1996). *Standards for the English language arts.* Urbana, IL: Author.

National Council of Teachers of Mathematics. (1989). *Principles and standards for school mathematics: An overview.* Reston, VA: Author.

Newman, L. A. (2004). *Findings from the national longitudinal transition study–2 (NLTS2): Improving academic performance and access to the general education curriculum for secondary youth with disabilities.* Washington, DC: U.S. Department of Education, Office of Special Education and Rehabilitative Services.

Nolet, V. W., & McLaughlin, M. J. (2000). *Assessing the general curriculum: Including students with disabilities in standards-based reform.* Thousand Oaks, CA: Corwin.

Nolin, M. J., & Davies, E. (1993). *Student victimization at school.* Washington, DC: U.S. Department of Education, National Center for Education Statistics, National Household Education Survey.

Oliver, R. W. (1999). *The shape of things to come.* New York: McGraw-Hill.

Olson, L. (2000a). Indiana case focused on special education: Suit challenges high stakes testing. *Education Week, 38*, 1–15.

Olson, L. (2000b). Worries of a standards "backlash" grow. *Education Week, 30*, 1–13.

Ortiz, A., Garcia, S., Wheeler, T., & Maldonado-Colon, E. (1986). *Characteristics of limited English proficient Hispanic students served in programs for the speech and language handicapped: Implications for policy, practice and research. Part III* (Report of the Office of Vocational and Adult Education). Washington, DC: Division of National Vocational Programs.

Osofsky, J. (1994). Introduction. In J. Osofsky & E. Fenichel (Eds.), *Caring for infants and toddlers in violent environments: Hurt, healing and hope* (pp. 3–6). Arlington, VA: Zero to Three/National Center for Clinical Infant Programs.

Otis-Wilborn, A., & Winn, J. (2000). The process and impact of standards-based teacher education programs. *Teacher Education and Special Education, 23*(2), 78–92.

Paige, R. (2004, February 24). Letter to Senator Edward M. Kennedy and members of the Senate Education, Labor, and Pensions Committee and the House

Education and the Workforce Committee detailing the progress made since No Child Left Behind was enacted. Retrieved September 6, 2004, from www .ed.gov/news/pressreleases/2004/02/02242004.html

Portner, J. (2000). Suicide: Many schools fall short on prevention. *Education Week, 19*(32), 4–5.

Putnam, M. L., Deshler, D. D., & Schumaker, J. B. (1992). The investigation of setting demands: A missing link in learning strategies instruction. In L. J. Meltzer (Ed.), *Strategy assessment and instruction for students with learning disabilities: From theory to practice* (pp. 325–351). Austin, TX: Pro-Ed.

Pyne, J., Sesso, G., Ankeney, K., & Vigilante, D. (1992). *National standards for history.* Washington, DC: National Center for History in the Schools.

Queen, J. A. (2000). Block scheduling revisited. *Phi Delta Kappan, 33*(4), 214–222.

Rademacher, J. A., Schumaker, J. B., & Deshler, D. D. (1996). Development and validation of a classroom assignment routine for inclusive settings. *Learning Disability Quarterly, 19*(3), 163–178.

Rifkin, J. (1995). *The end of work: The decline of the global labor force and the dawn of the post-market era.* New York: Putnam.

Robertson, P., Kushner, M. I., Starks, J., & Drescher, C. (1994). An update of participation rates of culturally and linguistically diverse students in special education: The need for a research and policy agenda. *Bilingual Special Education Perspective, 14*(1), 75–90.

Robinson, E. A., & Jacobson, N. S. (1987). Social learning theory and family psychopathology: Make room for daddy. *Psychological Bulletin, 111,* 387–412.

Sabornie, E. J. (1994). Social-affective characteristics in early adolescents identified as learning disabled and nondisabled. *Learning Disability Quarterly, 17,* 268–279.

Sack, J. L. (2000). States report trouble with special ed. testing. *Education Week, 27,* 24.

Schmidt, J. L., Deshler, D. D., Schumaker, J. B., & Alley, G. R. (1989). Effects of generalization instruction on the written language performance of adolescents with learning disabilities in the mainstream classroom. *Reading, Writing, and Learning Disabilities, 4*(4), 291–309.

Schumaker, J. B. (1992). Social performance of individuals with learning disabilities. *School Psychology Review, 21*(3), 387–399.

Schumaker, J. B., & Deshler, D. D. (1984). Setting demand variables: A major factor in program planning for the LD adolescent. *Topics in Language Disorders, 4*(2), 22–40.

Schumaker, J. B., & Deshler, D. D. (1992). Validation of learning strategy interventions for students with learning disabilities: Results of a programmatic research effort. In B. Y. L. Wong (Ed.), *Contemporary intervention research in learning disabilities: An international perspective* (pp. 22–46). New York: Springer-Verlag.

Singer, M. I., Anglin, T. M., Song, L. Y., & Lunghofer, L. (1995). Adolescents' exposure to violence and associated symptoms of psychological trauma. *Journal of the American Medical Association, 273*(6), 477–482.

Steinberg, L. (1998). Autonomy, conflict, and harmony in the family relationship. In J. Feldman & L. Elliott (Eds.), *At the threshold* (pp. 215–233). New York: Baxter.

Stepp, L. S. (2000). *Our last best shot: Guiding our children through early adolescence.* New York: Riverhead Books.

Suritsky, S. K., & Hughes, C. A. (1996). Notetaking strategy instruction. In D. D. Deshler, E. S. Ellis, & B. K. Lenz (Eds.), *Teaching adolescents with learning disabilities* (2nd ed., pp. 267–312). Denver, CO: Love Publishing.

U.S. Department of Education. (1997). *Nineteenth annual report to Congress on the implementation of the Individuals with Disabilities Education Act.* Washington, DC: Author.

U.S. Department of Education. (1998). *Twentieth annual report to Congress on the implementation of the Individuals with Disabilities Education Act.* Washington, DC: Author.

U.S. Department of Education. (1999). *Twenty-first annual report to Congress on the implementation of the Individuals with Disabilities Education Act.* Washington, DC: Author.

U.S. Department of Education, Title I—Improving the Academic Achievement of the Disadvantaged: Final Rule. 68 Fed. Reg. 68,698 (Dec. 9, 2003).

Vail, K. (1999). Words that wound. *American School Board Journal, 37*(4), 33–40.

Vaughn, S., Gersten, R., & Chard, D. J. (2000). The underlying message in LD intervention research: Findings from research syntheses. *Exceptional Children, 67*(1), 99–114.

Vernon, D. S., Schumaker, J. B., & Deshler, D. D. (1994). *Cooperative strategies in the classroom.* (SBIR Phase I Final Report, 1R43MH47211-01A1). Bethesda, MD: National Institute of Mental Health.

Voydanoff, P. (1990). Economic distress and family relations: A review of the eighties. *Journal of Marriage and the Family, 52,* 1099–1115.

Wagner, M., Blackorby, J., & Hebbeler, K. (1993). *Beyond the report card: The multiple dimensions of secondary school performance of students with disabilities; A report from the National Longitudinal Study of Special Education Students.* Menlo Park, CA: SRI International.

Warner, M. M., Schumaker, J. B., Alley, G. R., & Deshler, D. D. (1980). Learning disabled adolescents in public schools: Are they different from other low achievers? *Exceptional Education Quarterly, 1*(2), 27–35.

Wilkinson, C. Y., & Ortiz, A. A. (1986). *Characteristics of limited English proficient and English proficient learning disabled Hispanic students at initial assessment and at reevaluation.* Austin: University of Texas, Department of Special Education, Handicapped Minority Research Institute on Language Proficiency. (ERIC Document Reproduction Service No. ED283314)

Wilson, W. J. (1991). Public policy research and "The truly disadvantaged." In C. Jencks & P. E. Peterson (Eds.), *The urban underclass* (pp. 460–481). Washington, DC: Brookings Institution.

Planning Practices That Optimize Curriculum Access

Keith Lenz and Gary Adams

From the very beginning, Jason struggled in school. Early in the third grade, he was diagnosed with a severe learning disability. He was significantly behind in both reading and written expression and had great difficulty organizing and remembering information. After qualifying for special education services, he received intensive instruction during his elementary years. This instruction allowed him to benefit from most of the education provided in the general education classroom. Jason was more successful in some general education classes than others. As teachers tried to determine why, they discovered that the classes in which Jason was most successful were ones in which his teachers engaged in thoughtful planning for the academically diverse classes they were teaching. Teachers who used planning tools such as the Lesson Organizer, Unit Organizer, and Course Organizer were most successful in meeting Jason's unique needs as a learner. At the same time, students who were normal and high achievers in his class also benefited from the instruction.

P lanning tools, such as the ones described in the scenario above, help teachers to plan what they will teach and how they will teach it. If they are teaching students with disabilities, they will need to choose ways to teach the targeted content that will enable these students to succeed. Unfortunately, research on teacher planning is relatively new and typically has not focused on meeting the needs of students with disabilities. Most references to planning in the literature are connected to the model proposed by Ralph Tyler (1949), which is based on an "objectives first" approach referred to as the *rational model for planning*. A significant amount of attention was given during the late 1970s and 1980s to research on how teachers plan (e.g., Brown, 1988; Clark & Elmore, 1979; Clark & Peterson, 1986; Clark & Yinger, 1979; Kerr, 1981; McCutcheon, 1980; Shavelson, 1983; Yinger, 1980; Yinger & Clark, 1985). Much of this research challenged Tyler's rational model, suggesting that teachers generally start planning by first targeting content and then developing instructional activities. Thus, contrary to what Tyler proposed, research has indicated that objectives play a smaller role in the planning process of teachers compared with the role of content and activities.

During this period, most research on teacher planning for general education instruction focused on describing how teachers plan, not on changing planning processes to reach more learners, such as students with disabilities. Attempts to change how teachers plan have focused primarily on planning for effective instruction and have taken place in preservice teacher education programs (e.g., Cooper, 1999; Dick & Reiser, 1989; Floden & Clark, 1988; Reiser, 1994). The research most closely associated with changing teacher planning has focused on professional development and the growth of teachers related to integrating and sustaining new classroom practices (Allen, Rogers, Hensley, Glanton, & Livingston, 1999; Gersten, Chard, & Baker, 2000; Glickman, 2002; Vaughn, Klinger, & Hughes, 2000). However, this body of research primarily focuses on macro-level factors that support teacher change, ultimately relying on teachers to orchestrate specific plans that will be implemented in the classroom.

In 1990, the U.S. Department of Education's Office of Special Education and Rehabilitative Services (OSERS) extended a request for proposals to examine how general education teachers could plan to better meet the needs of students with disabilities. Research teams at the Education Development Center, Inc., the University of Miami, the University of Kansas, and Vanderbilt University were subsequently funded. As a result, the literature on general education teachers' planning increased (e.g., Fuchs, Fuchs, Hamlett, Phillips, & Bentz, 1994; Lenz, Schumaker, & Deshler, 1991; Riley, Morocco, Gordon, & Howard, 1993; Schumm, Vaughn, & Leavell, 1994). Specifically, researchers conducted studies that focused on identifying barriers to planning for students with disabilities and on planning methods that teachers can use to better meet these students' needs.

Recently, attention to planning has reemerged as a result of new technologies and an emphasis on instructional systems design (e.g., Baylor, Kitsantas, & Chung, 2001; Driscoll, Klein, & Sherman, 1994; Reiser, 1994, 2001a, 2001b). Although special education planning approaches have also taken advantage of technology and systems design (e.g., Rose & Dolan, 2000), recent initiatives have not yet led to new research on how secondary teachers can make their planning more sensitive to the needs of students with disabilities.

Finally, core curriculum planning for students with disabilities has received some attention through efforts in the broader education community to reach students who are enrolled in academically diverse classes using "differentiated instruction" (Tomlinson, 1995, 1999, 2000, 2003; Tomlinson & Allan, 2000). Tomlinson (2000) described differentiated instruction as a way of thinking, a philosophy, and a set of beliefs about teaching and learning, not a recipe or instructional strategy. Nevertheless, the literature on differentiated instruction contains references to many practices—for instance, creating a learning environment with flexible spaces and learning options; presenting information through auditory, visual, and kinesthetic modes; encouraging student exploration; and allowing students to work alone or with peers. (See Tomlinson, 1999, for more strategies that support differentiated instruction.) These efforts appear to be consistent with the goals of inclusive practice; however, to date no data have been published on how differentiated instruction changes the way teachers plan for students with disabilities or how this approach ultimately influences the learning of students with disabilities enrolled in secondary core curriculum classrooms.

PLANNING REALITIES: FINDINGS FROM THE JOINT COMMITTEE ON TEACHER PLANNING

The most comprehensive set of research findings on improving planning for students with disabilities resulted from the efforts of four research teams funded in 1990 by OSERS. Writing as the Joint Committee on Teacher Planning for Students with Disabilities (1995), researchers at the University of Miami (Vaughn & Schumm), the University of Kansas (Lenz, Schumaker, & Deshler), the Education Development Center, Inc. (Morocco, Gordon, & Riley), and Vanderbilt University (Fuchs & Fuchs) summarized conditions in the K–12 educational system that should be taken into consideration when designing interventions to influence the types of planning that could improve educational outcomes for youth with disabilities. Their findings from the four years of federally funded studies were organized into two groups: "Ways the School Culture Affects Teacher Planning" and "How Teachers Plan." The findings provide a framework for understanding the context in which planning must occur in secondary schools. They are summarized here.

Ways the School Culture Affects Teacher Planning

This summary describes how the overall conditions and structure of the school environment, which are shaped primarily by tradition and school structure, affect teacher planning.

• General education teachers are expected to work alone, with few opportunities for collaboration with colleagues, including special education teachers. Teachers question the support they get from administrators. They frequently do not view professional development activities as support provided by administrators, nor do they see a connection between these activities and day-to-day classroom demands. Although inclusive education is expected, teachers feel that efforts to be inclusive are not truly valued by their administrators or by other general education teachers.

• Teachers struggle with expectations to "cover the curriculum" within a specific time frame. However, they point out that "covering" and "teaching" the curriculum are not the same. Although teachers express little enthusiasm for the coverage approach, they do not feel they have much choice, given the demands placed on them by the school culture and the standards-based reform movement. Thus, teachers feel that they must move from lesson to lesson and from unit to unit at a steady pace, even though some students may not have learned the material at all, including students with learning difficulties.

• Time available for teacher planning affects planning. Teachers agree that most of the planning time made available is not quality planning time. Out of necessity, the time formally scheduled to plan instruction during the school day is primarily used for administrative tasks that are not directly related to instructional planning. However, because there is insufficient time in the daily school schedule for planning, many teachers recognize that deeper, more substantial planning at another time is necessary. Such planning usually takes place over time, at home or in places where teachers can reflect on what they need to do to teach well. According to the teachers, when this kind of planning does not occur, student learning suffers. When planning decisions are made, teachers report that the impromptu planning required for daily instruction is rarely recorded in their planning books.

• Teachers acknowledge that tests are important for grading, but they do not figure prominently in their planning. Objective tests are the standard for evaluation in secondary schools. Memorization of lists of facts and details and demonstrating control of this knowledge on objective tests is the rule for secondary teachers. Although teachers recognize the limitations of this approach, most of them believe that barriers associated with time, class size, and accountability will not be addressed in the near future to warrant a change in approach. This approach to assessment seems to send a message to students (and those who help students) about what is important to learn in a class. Even though testing determined grades, test results are not used to help teachers plan future instruction. When teachers received information from tests that indicated students were not learning, they did not feel that they had time to either redirect their teaching or reteach.

How Teachers Plan

This summary describes how teachers approach and engage in the overall planning process.

• When teachers plan, they focus on group learning; more individual-ized planning may occur, but it occurs much less frequently than whole-class planning. As a result, individual accommodations frequently conflict with the goals set up for the group. Planning decisions are often made with a "meta-student" in mind. Such a student is characterized as a typical B-grade-earning student. Such planning involves general plans to accomplish broad goals, with little reflection on questions such as "What if they don't learn this?" If prompted to address this question for students with disabilities, teachers are not sure how to plan and tend to focus on what students cannot do rather than on what they can do. Even when teachers create alternative plans, they screen these plans and may abandon them if they believe the classroom activities may not be attractive to other students. This can occur even when their alternative plans may result in higher rates of learning for students with disabilities.

• Course planning appears to define the mind-set for all teaching. It lays a framework for how units and lessons will be experienced by students rather than what they will learn. If the course framework does not take into consideration instructional concepts related to academic diversity, inclusive teaching, or accommodation, the teacher is unlikely to make or maintain changes after a course is launched. Once course and unit decisions are made, lesson planning is frequently improvised at the last minute. It is frequently guided by decisions that have already been made in course and unit planning. More time is spent on unit planning than on any other planning level. In secondary schools, once a unit is planned, very little day-to-day lesson planning is conducted, and any requests to alter individual lesson activities on behalf of students with disabilities are not likely to be fulfilled. This has serious implications for special educators working to adapt course content.

- Although general education teachers value students' "learning how to learn," teaching students how to learn is not planned and is rarely part of instruction. Nevertheless, students report wanting to learn strategies that will help them learn. Further, teaching students strategies and making instructional accommodations are almost never part of high school teachers' plans and are not viewed as feasible while promoting instruction for the rest of the class within the current realities of classrooms (class size, range of student diversity, amount of planning time, etc.). In fact, the high school structure and culture are barriers to individualization and infusing a learning-how-to-learn perspective.

CHANGING HOW TEACHERS PLAN TO INCREASE LEARNING FOR ADOLESCENTS WITH DISABILITIES

In addition to contextual information about planning for the inclusion of students in the secondary curriculum, information about what type of planning is required to meet the needs of students with disabilities in the core curriculum is also important. Generally, most inclusion advocates argue that interventions designed to alter the way teachers plan to improve the performance of youths with disabilities should be based on students' instructional needs. However, whether teachers understand the needs of youths with disabilities is not clear. Many teachers are aware that youths with disabilities have difficulty mastering basic skills such as reading, writing, and mathematics, but they may not understand that these students' underlying problems may require alternate forms of instruction. For example, Lenz and Schumaker (1999) suggested that there were at least 12 major design issues related to the curriculum, whether transmitted by the teacher or through text, that should influence teacher plans related to students with disabilities. These design issues include abstractness, organization of content, relevance, interest, skills needed, strategies needed, background assumed, complexity, quantity of content, structure and sequence of activities, outcome expectations, and response requirements.

To address some of these issues, Kameenui and Carnine (1998) proposed a set of six principles that should be used in developing curricula to maximally address the needs of students with disabilities while accelerating the performance of the classroom group. Focusing on the design rather than the delivery of instruction, these design principles include (1) focusing instruction on *big ideas*; (2) using *conspicuous strategies* to show the steps involved in solving problems; (3) preteaching *background knowledge*; (4) providing personalized guidance, assistance, and support through *mediated scaffolding*; (5) regularly reviewing previously learned critical information through *judicious review*; and (6) ensuring that new knowledge is linked to old knowledge through *strategic integration*.

Indeed, previous research on students with learning disabilities has indicated that these students benefit most from explicit instruction (e.g., Carnine, Jones, & Dixon, 1995; Gersten, 1998; Hollingsworth & Woodward, 1993) and support these design principles. Gersten (1998) proposed that explicit instruction should be based on using (1) examples to demonstrate a concept or process; (2) models of proficient performance and step-by-step strategies; (3) advance organizers and guiding questions to focus attention and prompt critical thinking; (4) opportunities for students to share decision-making processes; (5) authentic, interactive, and adequate practice; and (6) frequent feedback and support for performance.

In a meta-analysis of instructional components that predict positive outcomes for students with learning disabilities, Swanson (1999) identified 10 components that increased learning: (1) sequencing (for instance, breaking down the task); (2) drill-repetition-practice-feedback; (3) segmentation of information; (4) technology (that is, visual and structured presentation media); (5) control of task difficulty (for instance, scaffolding); (6) models for problem-solving steps or tasks; (7) presentation of cues to prompt strategy use; (8) supplementation of teacher instruction with homework or tutoring; (9) small, interactive groups; and (10) directed response and questioning of students.

Swanson (2001) also conducted a subanalysis focusing on interventions with adolescents. The purpose of this synthesis was to identify instructional models for adolescents that could predict success related to improving problem-solving skills or higher-order processing. The components found to predict treatment outcomes included (1) sequencing (for instance, breaking down the task); (2) step-by-step prompts; (3) drill-repetition-practice-feedback; (4) directed questioning and responses; (5) individualization combined with small-group instruction; (6) segmentation (for instance, breaking down a targeted skill into smaller units and then synthesizing the parts into a whole); (7) technology; and (8) small interactive group instruction. Thus, in both syntheses, Swanson found that interventions that included a direct or strategy instruction derivative were more effective for students with learning disabilities than other interventions.

Teachers are aware of the need to select and plan for different types of activities that might address the needs of students with disabilities. For example, Vaughn and Schumm (1995a) reported that teachers rated the use of a wide variety of adaptations to increase learning for youths with disabilities as very desirable. However, in the same study, many of the adaptations that teachers rated as desirable were rated as not feasible, given the conditions of the school setting. This indicates that although simple interventions (for example, if the youth cannot read, have him listen to an audiotape or have someone read aloud to him) may be perceived as effective and desirable, the context within which teachers must make planning decisions often seems to make such interventions impossible to implement. Similarly, Lenz, Schumaker, Deshler, and Kissam (1991) found that although secondary teachers did not believe that students with learning disabilities had a negative impact on their classes and that they preferred heterogeneously grouped classes over homogeneously grouped classes, they did not feel particularly confident or effective in their ability to work with these students.

In sum, although the type of instruction or adaptations that need to be planned and implemented for students with disabilities may be clear, specific feasibility and sustainability barriers exist. To better understand this issue, Lenz, Schumaker, Deshler, and Kissam (1991) conducted a series of focus group interviews with secondary core curriculum teachers to determine what conditions are important for sustained acceptance of alternatives in their classrooms. The researchers analyzed responses from 14 focus group meetings attended by junior and senior high school science and social studies general education teachers. A total of 51 teachers participated in groups of four to eight teachers across the 14 focus group meetings. Based on the data gathered in these meetings, the researchers concluded that alternatives were more likely to be adopted by teachers if they

- resulted in observable changes in students (that is, the teachers could see their efforts pay off);
- had the potential for improving the performance of the majority of students in the class;
- did not single out individual students as "different" from others in the class;
- resulted in activities that were acceptable and motivating to students, especially high-achieving students;
- could be incorporated in a manner that did not require major preparation or implementation time;
- could be prepared mentally through reflection without significant paperwork;
- enabled teachers to gather information about students for evaluation and feedback;
- did not negatively influence the performance of any student in the class (that is, they especially did not reduce the opportunity to learn for the more able);
- promoted the acquisition of important content (that is, did not involve watering down the curriculum); and
- resulted in products or outcomes that were personally satisfying to the teacher and built the teacher's resources and skills for use in future teaching situations.

Sadly, because many of the interventions that are effective for youth with disabilities require teachers to provide more explicit and intensive instruction, they will remain desirable but not feasible.

Components of Teacher Planning Requiring Intervention

In addition to understanding the conditions that might make planning interventions acceptable to teachers, the dilemmas facing teachers as they plan for instruction also must be understood and taken into consideration. Overall, teachers face three planning dilemmas when trying to provide appropriate educational experiences for students with disabilities in the core curriculum.

First, educators must sort through information and determine which outcomes are most critical so that students can meet rigorous standards, graduate from high school, and be prepared for postsecondary educational opportunities. Such sorting is particularly critical for students with disabilities who may not have the same background information as their peers or who have trouble distinguishing important from less important information in teacher presentations (Lenz, 1984; Lenz, Alley, & Schumaker, 1987). In addition, the task of processing various dimensions of information in problem-solving activities is difficult for many students with disabilities (e.g., Brownell, Mellard, & Deshler, 1993; Hutchinson, 1993).

Curriculum specialists have argued that, too often, the goal of teachers has been content coverage rather than learning. Wiggins and McTighe (1998) described this approach as "teaching by mentioning it," or covering topics and ideas by drawing attention to them without developing them. The challenge is to help teachers think differently about the curriculum and what students should know and be able to do as a result of curriculum experiences. To that end, Wiggins and McTighe argued for a curriculum planning approach called *backward design*. Here, teachers sort information into three levels: "enduring understanding," "important to know and do," and "worth being familiar with" (Wiggins & McTighe, 1998, pp. 9–10). Other educators over the last three decades have made similar suggestions (e.g., Beane, 1995; Blythe & Associates, 1998; Bruner, 1960, 1973; Caine & Caine, 1997; Lenz & Deshler, 2004; Perkins, 1992), and their suggestions are slowly beginning to shape how high schools deliver the core curriculum (Erikson, 1998; Lenz & Deshler, 2004).

The second planning dilemma that teachers face is translating the curriculum into instructional experiences to ensure students' mastery of critical information or skills. As described in a previous section, research on youths with learning disabilities has indicated that these students benefit most from explicit instruction. However, few studies have examined how explicit instruction can be translated into methods that meet the demands associated with the large-group instruction that is frequently encountered in high school general education settings. To benefit students with disabilities, instructional planning should create plans that lead to instruction that results in higher rates of learning in critical content areas.

The third planning dilemma that teachers face is finding the time and support to identify content, plan activities that result in explicit instruction, and then incorporate those activities into the available instructional time. Because most of the available planning time during the school day is not quality planning time (Joint Committee on Teacher Planning for Students with Disabilities, 1995), planning interventions must also meet the test of palatability and sustainability.

The remaining sections of this chapter will extend the discussion of the research on planning for students with disabilities and how secondary core curriculum teachers have addressed this challenge in their classrooms. Specifically, four topics will be addressed. First, different kinds of planning interventions will be defined. Second, the general approach taken in this synthesis will be explained, based on the status of research on teacher planning. Third, studies on teacher planning will be described and critically analyzed. Finally, results of the synthesis will be summarized and recommendations will be provided for future research.

HOW ARE TEACHER PLANNING INTERVENTIONS DEFINED?

Using the context for intervention design presented by the Joint Committee on Teacher Planning for Students with Disabilities (1995), a variety of activities may be defined as teacher planning. For example, taking the broadest approach possible, teacher planning could include everything that a teacher decides to do before, during, and after classroom interactions. Researchers in teacher planning (e.g., Lampert & Clark, 1990) have argued that teacher planning must take into consideration the minute-by-minute decisions that teachers make in the classroom as they interact with students. Although this may be true, it complicates the task of defining what research is required for improving access to the general high school curriculum for students with disabilities.

For the purposes of this review, the conceptual framework proposed by Lenz, Schumaker, and Deshler (1991) will be used to think about interventions related to teacher planning. Specifically, Lenz, Schumaker, and Deshler (1991) proposed three types of interventions that might be developed to alter teacher planning. As shown in Figure 2.1, interventions may be (1) planning *heuristics* based on preparing for a course, unit, or lesson (for example, I am using a lesson-planning strategy to plan); (2) specific guidelines used or provided for planning instruction to achieve an *outcome* focused on learning content, acquiring a skill or a strategy, influencing motivation, influencing attitudes, or changing interactions or a behavior (for example, I will follow the procedures in this guidebook to teach the concept of "commensalism" to students); or (3) an *experience* that leads to teacher participation in a collaborative, cooperative, exploratory, investigative, or reflective activity designed to increase student learning outcomes (for example, I attended the student's IEP meeting and have been collaborating with the special education teacher to increase the student's learning in my course).

Each of these intervention approaches may involve decisions related to a large group of students making up a class or a whole course, a smaller group or subset of a class, or individual students. At another level, planning

Figure 2.1   Types of Interactions

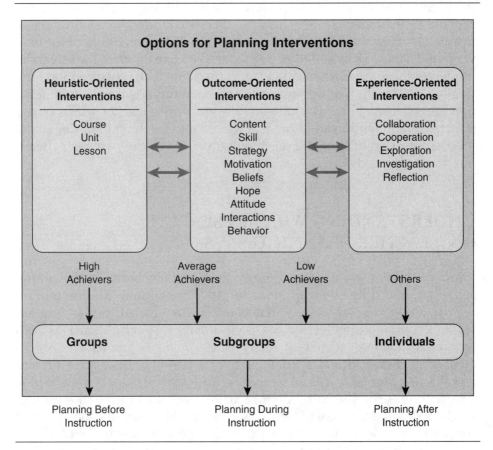

may be targeted at students in traditional achievement groups, such as students who are high achieving, average achieving, or low achieving. Planning may also be targeted for other students who do not fit nicely into an achievement category and may move between achievement categories because of the subject, the teacher, or circumstances. Finally, planning decisions may be made and activities conducted before, during, or after instruction. Nested within these interventions may be decisions related to (1) selection or development of adaptations or accommodations, (2) teacher-led versus student-led instruction, (3) promoting in-class versus out-of-class learning, and (4) consideration of stages for learning (such as acquisition, guided practice, independent practice, fluency, and generalization).

The conceptual framework shown in Figure 2.1 provides a comprehensive way to think about teacher planning in relation to curriculum, instruction, and assessment. However, the comprehensive nature of this framework goes far beyond the scope of this chapter. The research synthesis in this chapter will focus on research that has been conducted on heuristics that relate to planning the delivery of a course, unit, or lesson.

Papers and studies in which teacher planning was only a phase in a broad intervention effort will not be reviewed here. Although such studies could contribute to understanding how teachers make decisions and prepare instruction, they rarely focus on the decision-making dimensions of the intervention. That is, the intervention is prepared by a researcher, the researcher implements or the teacher is taught to implement the intervention, and, finally, data on student performance and sometimes teacher implementation are collected. However, data on how and why a teacher selects or constructs an intervention and how it is woven into teaching practices so that it becomes a part of a regular teaching sequence typically are not collected or are not reported.

UNDERSTANDING WHAT RESEARCH ON TEACHER PLANNING SAYS

Three methods were used to identify the works included in the synthesis. First, the ERIC, Exceptional Child Educational Resources, and PsychINFO databases were searched for entries related to planning and students with disabilities for the period 1985 through August of 2004. Second, a manual search of *Exceptional Children, Journal of Learning Disabilities, Remedial and Special Education, Learning Disabilities Research and Practice, Journal of Special Education,* and *Teacher Education and Special Education* was conducted to identify articles related to general education teacher planning for students with disabilities. Third, unpublished research reports on secondary-level teacher planning generated from OSEP (Office of Special Education Programs) funding were also reviewed. These three search methods yielded 392 citations. From this list, only works that included course-, unit-, or lesson-planning efforts at the secondary level (middle and high school) for students with high-incidence disabilities likely to be enrolled in and expected to master core curriculum courses (that is, students with learning and behavioral disabilities) taught by general education teachers were selected. Using these filtering criteria, 31 citations were identified.

These citations were reviewed to determine how many focused on some type of quantitative or qualitative evaluation. Thus, the definition of research was quite broad. Because few studies have been conducted on general education teacher planning to meet the needs of students with disabilities in high school settings, studies conducted at the middle school level that shed light on secondary content-area planning were also included. In addition to experimental studies published in peer-reviewed journals, other sources that presented quasi-experimental and qualitative studies reporting changes in teacher planning were included. This filtering process yielded several planning studies that are reviewed in the following sections.

STUDIES PROMOTING
SECONDARY INCLUSIVE PLANNING

The studies on secondary inclusive planning have been organized into three areas: lesson planning, unit planning, and course planning. The studies on lesson planning relate to how teachers plan instruction about topics included in a unit. A lesson is defined as instruction that takes place on one or more days; two or more lessons make up a unit. The studies on unit planning focus on the major divisions of a course and involve linking multiple lessons together with a bigger idea and end in some type of summative evaluation, usually a test or performance assessment. Therefore, a unit may include information from one or more chapters of a textbook. Finally, the studies on course planning relate to how a teacher plans how to orchestrate standards and district curricula over a year or semester, depending on how the course is structured. Each course comprises several units and decisions about methods and ideas that must be maintained as all the units are taught.

Lesson-Planning Research

Several studies have focused on inclusive planning at the lesson level. Using case study methodology, Schumm et al. (1995) described the planning of content-area instruction of four elementary, four middle school, and four high school teachers over the school year. The 12 general education teachers studied were identified by administrators as effective in working with students with learning disabilities. Schumm et al. concluded that teachers who are judged to be effective with students with learning disabilities, especially secondary teachers, do not plan ahead to meet the needs of these students. Consistent with other research findings, the planning of the four secondary teachers involved in the study was centered on whole-group instruction, rarely taking into consideration the needs of individuals and subgroups of students. Across all grades, but especially at the secondary level, teachers stated that the expectations and evaluation criteria for students with learning disabilities should be the same as for students without disabilities. The researchers reported that there was little evidence of adjustment in methods, materials, or student assessment at the secondary level. Once a plan was created, teachers made accommodations primarily by circulating through the room and checking on progress.

The finding that general education teachers do little to support students with learning disabilities enrolled in core curriculum classes is consistent with other findings indicating that, although teachers accept these students, they treat them like other students in the class and provide few adaptations (Vaughn & Schumm, 1994). Similarly, Schumm and Vaughn (1991) reported that although teachers found many of the adaptations that students needed to be desirable, they did not find implementing them to be feasible given the instructional conditions of the general education setting.

However, Schumm et al. (1995) did report that teachers were willing to structure classrooms to ensure that students with disabilities would be accepted by peers. At the secondary level, this meant making sure everyone was treated equally. It also meant structuring activities to ensure youth involvement through peer-assisted and cooperative-group work. Once students started to work, teachers were willing to check to see whether students were following directions and staying on task. Indeed, checking in more frequently with certain students was the primary adaptation used by secondary teachers. As they circulated through the room, their checks were usually related to low-level tasks, such as completing an assignment or staying on task. Although teachers would attempt to correct a misunderstanding when it was discovered, often there were not enough interaction opportunities with a student for teachers to discover misunderstandings. They reported that students with learning disabilities infrequently asked for help or for assistance, did not volunteer to answer questions, participated in teacher-directed activities at a lower rate, and interacted with the teacher and peers at a lower rate than nondisabled students. The finding that students with disabilities have a very low level of classroom participation and interaction is similar to the results reported by Vaughn and Schumm (1994).

Schumm et al. (1995) found that if secondary-level students needed help beyond what was provided during in-class question-and-answer opportunities, it was their own responsibility to seek it. Because most opportunities offered by teachers were during lunch and before and after the school day, few students took advantage of the help offered. Although students were in contact with special education teachers, the special education teachers were viewed by the general education teachers as simply a resource. Thus, little collaboration took place. Secondary teachers referred to IEPs rarely and only contacted special education teachers when there was a severe problem, which was usually behavioral in nature. Overall, Schumm et al. concluded that secondary teachers believed that providing differential support for students with disabilities was wrong.

To alter teacher planning in an effort to provide more effective instruction to students with disabilities as part of whole-group planning, Schumm et al. (1994) developed a framework called the *Planning Pyramid*, which is a mental template to guide reflection and self-questioning about plans (see Figure 2.2). One set of key questions prompted by the Planning Pyramid template is, what do I want all students to learn? What do I want most students to know? And what do I want some students to know?

Once these three questions are answered and the information is sorted into the three categories, other questions are prompted. They may be related to the teacher's experience with each level of content, the nature of the content, possible contexts for learning the content, issues related to individual students, and possible instructional practices. Schumm et al. (1994) field-tested the Planning Pyramid process with general education

Figure 2.2   Planning Pyramid

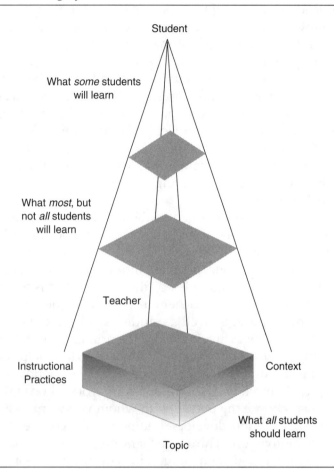

teachers at the elementary, middle, and high school levels, but they reported specifically on a fifth-grade teacher's use of the tool. Data on 13 teachers who used the Planning Pyramid over one semester showed that its use helped teachers move to an increased level of detail and clarity in their planning. However, no data on student learning were reported.

In another descriptive study on lesson planning, Bulgren and Lenz (1998) investigated teacher planning of lessons that were intended to be learner-sensitive. Sixteen teachers were selected during the end of a school year. Four taught middle school science, four taught high school science, four taught middle school social studies, and four taught high school social studies. Questionnaires and group interviews were used to collect information about the teachers. Teachers met with researchers and each other eight times over the summer in large- and small-group meetings to plan a detailed lesson for teaching a targeted concept. In groups of four, teachers were challenged to select an important but difficult concept that they would be willing to teach in one of their courses in the coming year.

They were also asked to work together to develop a lesson on that concept that would lead to mastery of that concept by everyone in the class, including students with learning disabilities. Additionally, they were asked to develop a test to measure student mastery of the concept. The processes that the teachers used to plan their lessons were evaluated through direct observation by the researchers (audiotapes and researcher notes) and by evaluating the teachers' planning logs. Finally, the teachers were observed during the school year as they implemented the lessons developed during their summer planning. Data were collected from (1) observations of teachers as they taught the lessons, (2) interviews about changes they made in lessons before they were implemented, and (3) planning logs to determine how the summer planning information was infused into their general teaching plans.

Certain characteristics emerged as the teachers developed their inclusive lessons. First, teachers selected concepts that were not simply the focus of a single lesson, but were important to the overall understanding of course content. These concepts were introduced in the targeted lesson, and, after the lesson was completed, the teachers revisited the concept throughout the year. Second, teachers responded to the needs of students with learning disabilities, as well as students judged as being at risk for academic failure or low-achieving students, primarily by setting up cooperative learning groups or by pairing students needing help with students who were more task oriented. They also gave students options (for instance, choose a topic, choose a way to present your work, choose the resources you want to use, choose the person with whom you want to work, choose a place to work, etc.) and developed entertaining activities to encourage attention and motivation. Third, teachers often used visual devices or graphics to organize and focus attention. Fourth, hands-on activities or activities that led to student involvement were commonly included. Fifth, linking content to real-world events or problems was discussed frequently by each teacher and emerged in each plan.

Several planning components were not emphasized in the plans. First, teachers did not develop many new assignments. They valued the assignments other teachers had already developed and suggested and often transferred them to their own lessons with no changes. Second, the lesson-planning process did not appear to prompt teachers to develop new assessments, even when the content and activities had changed. The main focus of their planning in this regard was the percentage of points required to pass objective tests. Even when teachers mentioned that students should "think about how they are thinking," they did not specify how this would be assessed. Overall, student success was defined by a broad range of results related to student outcomes. These included student knowledge of content, completion of assignments, practice at home, correct answers, use of the problem-solving process, work in groups, on-task behavior, good feelings in the classroom, and perceptions of student motivation.

An analysis of teacher time spent in planning meetings and entries in the planning logs indicated an emphasis on content. According to a survey of time spent on types of planning activities, 37% of planning was devoted to determining what content in a lesson was critical for all students to know and then planning how to organize the critical content for instruction. Another 28% of planning time was devoted to developing ways or activities to help students understand, remember, or organize new information to promote learning. The remaining 35% of the planning time was spent primarily on examining, discussing, debating, and exploring materials and resources that would match the targeted content to the targeted instructional activities.

Bulgren and Lenz (1998) also evaluated how lessons were actually implemented in their classrooms. Although all teachers implemented the lesson plan, all teachers exceeded the time that they had predicted the lesson would require. Indeed, 14 of the 16 participants took twice as long to teach the content as they had projected. Further, there was great diversity among implementations, even when teachers had planned the lesson together and had been instructed by researchers to present the same lesson. This was true for both the quantity of examples presented and the quality of the presentations. Most of the changes occurred when a teacher implemented a lesson in several classes over the day. That is, the first class in which the lesson was introduced was the "testing ground." Teachers found out what was right and wrong with their plan and then changed it accordingly. Teachers reported that they constantly refined their implementation of a lesson throughout the first day's presentation, but had few plans to make any changes beyond that. Therefore, most of the changes were not planned, but were made as teachers interacted with students on the day the lesson was implemented. Finally, using measures that the teachers had developed to evaluate mastery, only about 65% of the students with learning disabilities met the teachers' criteria for mastery. Nonetheless, teachers reported that the lessons were highly effective for all students and effective for students with learning disabilities.

Thus, Bulgren and Lenz (1998) found that although a lesson might be sensitive to the needs of students as a result of careful advanced planning, teachers had difficulty reaching the level of explicitness required to ensure student mastery in a targeted area. Even when experienced teachers planned what they considered to be "best shot" lessons specifically designed to meet the needs of students with disabilities, they still had to adjust the lessons as they were implemented to make them more effective. Nevertheless, in the final analysis, a large proportion of students with disabilities did not learn the targeted content.

The same dilemma was illustrated in a study by Lenz, Boudah, Schumaker, and Deshler (1993). These authors attempted to alter teacher planning to benefit students with learning disabilities by asking teachers to plan lessons in which a learning strategy was introduced to the class as part of an ongoing routine. Six teachers (three sixth-grade teachers and three seventh-grade teachers) volunteered to provide strategy instruction to their students. Seven teachers volunteered to serve as comparison teachers. The six strategy teachers participated in a one-hour professional development session to provide instruction to their students in a paraphrasing strategy called "TAPE." The strategy was designed to enable students to Tune in to the lesson material being presented, Ask themselves questions about the information, Put the information into their own words (either through rephrasing the information or summarizing it), and Elaborate on the information. The teachers also learned a planning process for designing lessons that would help students with disabilities learn how to rephrase, summarize, and elaborate on content.

Throughout the year, the researchers attended 10 lesson-planning sessions at about three-week intervals with each teacher. During these sessions, the researchers evaluated the teachers' planning related to implementing the strategy in their classes and their overall lesson plans. A checklist was used to evaluate their planning processes. After each planning session, the class in which the lesson was targeted was observed. In each class, in addition to the teacher's presentation, two high-achieving students, two average-achieving students, two low-achieving students, and all students with learning disabilities were observed to determine class participation, response to the instruction, and on-task behavior.

Students' performance of the strategy was measured using a researcher-designed written test before the teachers participated in the professional development session and after instruction had been implemented for two months. On the test, students were asked to read and rephrase single sentences, read and summarize single paragraphs, and elaborate on the paragraphs. The students with learning disabilities received an oral form of the test in addition to the written form.

Two experimental designs were used. A multiple-baseline across-teachers design was used to determine whether teacher behavior had changed as a function of the training session. A pretest–posttest comparison-group design involving intact classes was used to determine whether students' skills had changed as a function of the strategy instruction.

Lenz, Boudah, et al., (1993) found that the teachers who had learned about the strategy instruction changed the way they taught students, and they integrated the strategy instruction into their content instruction in a variety of ways. The teachers who did not learn about strategy instruction did no paraphrasing strategy instruction during the study. Some of the teachers who received training in the strategy instruction increased the number of paraphrasing prompts they used during their lessons (sixth-grade teachers); others did not (seventh-grade teachers). On the whole, the teachers who increased the number of paraphrasing prompts during lessons did not increase that number substantially. For example, one teacher who prompted summarizing once during three baseline sessions prompted summarizing an average of 3.3 times across 10 observed intervention sessions.

The teacher planning data showed that most of the teachers' lesson plans had been shaped by decisions made at the course and unit levels by the teacher or by the department. The instructional materials used by the teachers often defined most of their plans, but clearly the teachers had made decisions about lesson content as they had planned the unit in which the lesson fit. With the exception of planning when they would prompt the use of the paraphrasing strategy by students, the teachers demonstrated very little lesson-specific decision making during the lesson-planning sessions.

The students with learning disabilities received infrequent opportunities to practice using the strategy in class. The largest number of total prompts given to these students across all 10 of the observed classroom periods during the school year by a teacher was four. Not surprisingly, students with learning disabilities made no gains with regard to paraphrasing information in either written or oral form. By comparison, students without disabilities in the sixth-grade classes, who received the same two months of strategy instruction as the students with disabilities, made significant gains with regard to rephrasing but made no gains with regard to summarizing and elaborating. Students in the seventh-grade classes made no gains in any area.

Although Lenz, Boudah, et al. (1993) demonstrated that general education teacher planning could be changed to incorporate plans about instruction in a strategy, like Bulgren and Lenz (1998), they found that the instruction was not explicit or intensive enough to influence the performance of students with learning disabilities. From a lesson-planning perspective, Lenz et al. found that the teachers had difficulty shaping lesson plans because previously adopted unit and course plans had already limited the degree to which their lessons could be changed. This is a significant point for educators who are responsible for guiding classroom-based practices. If educators try to intervene or support students with disabilities in core curriculum classes only through day-to-day lesson-level interactions with teachers, they are likely to find that lesson plans have already been limited by earlier unit and course planning.

In a continuation of this study, Boudah, Deshler, Schumaker, Lenz, and Cook (1997) followed three of the six teachers who had implemented instruction in the paraphrasing strategy into a second year. The purpose of this study was twofold: (1) to better understand why the lesson-planning process was so resistant to incorporating explicit and intensive types of instruction that would benefit students with disabilities, and (2) to continue to try to shape teacher lesson planning. A case study approach was used. The researchers interacted with the teachers in a number of ways in a collaborative attempt to learn about planning and instruction of students with disabilities in the general education classroom. Specifically, researchers interacted with the teachers in monthly study meetings, during debriefings after classroom observations, and through the written logs the teachers kept over the course of the second year. Each of the teachers was also observed during instruction approximately once a month and received individual or group feedback that same day regarding his or her integration of the instruction of the paraphrasing strategy (TAPE) into the lesson and the inclusion and performance of targeted students in the lesson activities.

Among the sixth-, seventh-, and eighth-grade teachers, those who had completed secondary-content teacher education training were more content oriented. That is, they demonstrated less evidence of thinking about, planning, and instructing differentially for different subgroups or individual students; they paid more attention to content coverage than to student learning; they incorporated instruction in paraphrasing less; they were more structured; they placed greater importance on students' prior knowledge; and they predominantly used whole-group activities and assessments.

By comparison, the two sixth-grade teachers who had an elementary education teacher-training background were more student oriented. That is, they demonstrated more evidence of thinking about, planning, and instructing differentially for different subgroups or individual students and less attention to content issues; they incorporated instruction in paraphrasing more and in a holistic way; they were less structured; they placed less importance on prior student knowledge; and they used individual as well as whole-group activities and assessments. However, the one secondary-trained teacher who had participated in both years of the study became more student oriented, paid more attention to subgroups and individuals, provided more instructional modeling, and increased her use of individual activities and assessments.

The work of Boudah et al. (1997) indicates that, although explicit and intensive instruction may be difficult to infuse into planning and teaching activities, ongoing coaching and support may pay off. This finding supports the professional development literature, which indicates that a change in teacher practices must be supported over time if it is to be sustained (Allen et al., 1999; Gersten et al., 2000; Vaughn et al., 2000). At the same time, it points to how lesson-planning interventions might be conceptualized. That is, any changes in instruction must be conceptualized as involving the integration of practices into already fixed teaching routines. Such integration will require time and modification of course and unit plans to allow day-to-day lessons to evolve to include better practices. Thus, lesson-planning interventions need to be incorporated within long-term, intensive, collaborative professional development efforts research with secondary content teachers to produce meaningful and lasting change in academically diverse classrooms.

Some researchers have adopted a collaborative development approach with core curriculum teachers to increase the chances of implementing interventions for students with disabilities in general education settings (e.g., Boudah, Logan, & Greenwood, 2001; Morrocco, Riley, Gordon, Howard, & Longo, 1994). For example, Scanlon, Schumaker, and Deshler (1994) and Scanlon, Deshler, and Schumaker (1996) reported on the collaborative development and instruction of a content-organizer strategy with sixth- and seventh-grade social studies teachers. Rather than introducing a ready-made strategy to teachers, as did Lenz, Boudah, and colleagues (1993), the researchers engaged in a collaborative effort with teachers to develop the strategy to be tested.

Scanlon et al. (1996) employed two research designs to evaluate the collaboratively developed instructional program. First, a multiple-probe design (Horner & Baer, 1978) was used to determine the effects of the collaboration and professional development activities on the teachers' implementation of the instruction. Second, a pretest–posttest comparison-group design was employed to determine the effects of the strategic instruction on the students' creation of graphic organizers. The study was conducted over a three-month period. The researchers expected the collaborative process to lead to improved outcomes over other studies in which strategy instruction had been embedded within general education classes. However, they reported that the teachers perceived a mismatch between strategy instruction and their regular teaching routines. The quality of implementation varied among the teachers, and the amount of strategic teaching, as measured through classroom observations, actually decreased during the instructional condition. Correspondingly, the students did not make significant progress in learning the strategy when compared with the types of gains achieved when a strategy is taught in a separate classroom by special education teachers.

This study again illustrates the difficulty that general educators have incorporating the types of instruction that have proved effective in teaching students with disabilities. Even when teachers endorsed a philosophy of promoting the development and instruction of learning strategies and worked collaboratively with researchers, they did not necessarily achieve the level of explicitness required to produce socially significant differences in the learning of students with disabilities and other students.

However, one notable difference is revealed when the study described by Boudah et al. (1997) is compared with the study reported by Scanlon et al. (1996)—the length of the intervention. That is, Boudah et al. did not witness the content-centered teacher moving to a student-centered approach (a possible prerequisite for providing explicit instruction) until the second year of working intensively with researchers. The study described by Scanlon et al. was conducted over a three-month period. Thus, time and level of support may be important factors related to achieving and sustaining effective inclusive practices.

Another important line of research related to planning classroom activities focuses on developing student assignments. A variety of authors have identified practices that might be used to increase the completion of assignments and homework by students with disabilities. These practices include increasing home–school communication (Callahan, Rademacher, & Hildreth, 1998; Karustis, Habboushe, Leff, Eiraldi, & Power, 1999; Martin & McLaughlin, 1981); training parents to provide homework help; increasing homework variety (Rademacher, Schumaker, & Deshler, 1996); using free time as reward (Martin & McLaughlin, 1981; Strandy, 1979); increasing choice in assignments (Rademacher et al., 1996); using peer mediation (O'Melia & Rosenberg, 1994); student goal setting and charting (Olympia, Sheridan, Jenson, & Andrews, 1994; Tollefson et al., 1986); teaching organizational skills (Anday-Porter, Henne, & Horan, 2000; Bever, 1994); providing instruction in assignment-planning skills (Anday-Porter et al., 2000; Rademacher et al., 1996); and meeting with students to coconstruct assignments (Maher, 1987). Only two of these studies provided specific information related to the lesson-planning process of general education teachers at the high school level.

The first relevant study was conducted by Maher (1987). He studied the effects of coconstructing assignments with 49 students classified as having behavioral disorders. Researchers instructed four general education teachers (two language arts and two math teachers) to meet with students individually on a weekly basis. They taught the teachers how to work one-on-one with high school students with disabilities to construct assignments, set goals, scale goal attainability, identify instructional strategies to help students learn, and monitor progress toward meeting goals. Each teacher engaged in a collaborative planning process and met weekly throughout the year with each of four to six students. A comparison teacher group participated in a general professional development session about the nature and needs of high school students with disabilities and used a traditional planning process that did not involve individual meetings with students.

Results indicated that the collaborative process was successful at increasing student learning. In addition, both students and teachers rated the intervention as feasible in terms of time. Teachers reported that they liked the explicitness of the steps involved in the coplanning sessions. They also reported that they enjoyed the structured yet informal way of establishing rapport with students and that they were pleased with the apparent ease of scheduling students into teacher preparation time during the school day.

Although the authors did not follow up on the school, teachers, or students involved in the study to determine whether the routine of meeting individually with students was maintained, the results indicate that one-on-one interactions with students may be a direct way of changing teachers' plans. However, this may be true only when teachers have four to six students with disabilities enrolled across their classes. In addition, and consistent with other findings (Boudah et al., 2001), this procedure's success may be attributed to the yearlong duration of the intervention and the implementation of a routine that was initiated before the school year began and sustained through regular meetings with students.

The second study relevant to assignment planning was conducted by Rademacher et al. (1996), who examined the degree to which they could influence the types of assignments teachers gave. The researchers used a multiple-probe, single-subject design (Horner & Baer, 1978) to evaluate teacher change and a pretest–posttest comparison-group design to evaluate student change. The intervention phase was preceded by a development phase in which teachers and students identified the characteristics of high-quality assignments. Twelve middle school general education teachers participated in the intervention portion of the study, which included 14 students with disabilities and 13 students without disabilities.

In the phase of the study that targeted identifying assignment characteristics, 11 assignment characteristics were generally deemed to be important by both students and teachers: clear directions, understood purpose, product evaluation criteria, optimal challenge, personal relevance, assignment completion feedback, format variety, available resource lists, creative expression opportunities, interpersonal and social interactions, and completion-time considerations. There were some disagreements between teachers and students, however, about how they perceived the relative importance of each characteristic. One characteristic, student choices, was rated highly by students but was rated lowest by the teachers. Both students and teachers rated nine factors as highly important components of explanations that teachers provide to students: giving clear directions, stating purpose and completion benefits, providing models and examples, considering time factors, stating quality-work criteria, providing social interaction direction, providing student choices, encouraging creative expression, and naming available resources.

Results of the intervention phase of the study showed that the teachers had learned the routine. They (1) designed assignments according to a set of validated high-quality assignment dimensions, (2) presented assignments using a set of validated explanation factors, and (3) evaluated assignments and provided feedback to students in a way that was consistent with recommendations from the literature. Teachers were generally satisfied with the goals, procedures, and outcomes of the routine. They perceived that their assignments had improved. They were explaining assignments in more effective ways, and they were providing better feedback on the quality of students' work. They were also providing students with more choices and chances for participation in the assignment process. However, teachers were dissatisfied with the amount of time required to implement the various steps of the routine. Students were somewhat pleased with the goals, procedures, and outcomes of the routine. They perceived that the types of assignments they were given had improved, that teachers were explaining assignments in more effective ways, that teachers were placing more emphasis on quality work, and that they were given more opportunities to make choices in the assignment process. However, the students were somewhat dissatisfied with the amount of time required to record the assignment information.

Because secondary teachers place so much emphasis on assignments, and because at-risk students often do poorly on assignment completion, assignment planning is an important area of study and potential intervention. These results indicated that the quality of assignments given can be markedly improved in academically diverse classes. However, issues related to the palatability of the routine for the classroom teacher were still a concern. The finding that teachers and students differed on the attribute of "student choice" appears to be consistent with Boudah et al.'s (1997) findings in terms of the difficulty that content-centered teachers have in moving toward a student-centered approach. Inasmuch as freedom to choose is a highly valued attribute for most adolescents and the need to maintain control of circumstances is highly valued by secondary teachers, factors underlying this basic difference need to be explored to determine whether this is a variable that should shape planning.

A number of other intervention-development studies have focused on inclusive practices. These studies, though they do not describe or focus specifically on lesson planning, nevertheless have implications for lesson planning. They identify practices that have been found to produce positive changes under empirical conditions for students with disabilities enrolled in secondary core curriculum classes. These interventions may be grouped as either classroom instructional practices or as technology, media, or materials that teachers may select and use to deliver content. Research-based interventions that focus on instructional classroom practices are reviewed by Bulgren and Schumaker in Chapter 3, whereas interventions that focus on technology, media, and materials are reviewed by Davis, Caros, and Carnine in Chapter 6. Several important factors emerged from these reviews that should be considered in shaping planning interventions.

In their review of validated secondary classroom instructional practices, Bulgren and Schumaker report that most evidence-based interventions involve teacher and student construction of a specific teaching device used as part of a "teaching routine" or as part of a lesson. Each routine and the associated teaching device serves to compensate for students' lack of skills or strategies. To use such a routine, the teacher has to plan a very targeted, teacher-directed activity that uses the graphic organizer device and involves leading a whole class of students through an important learning process. Bulgren and Schumaker report that several achievement groups of students in the classrooms benefited from the teaching-routine interventions. The extent of the interventions' positive effects for students *other* than those with disabilities seemed to be an important criterion for teacher adoption and continued use, because the interventions require more time to plan and implement than typical instruction. A more detailed discussion of the research on teaching routines is provided in Chapter 3.

One important point that Bulgren and Schumaker make is that each of the studies reviewed focused on teacher planning and the use of a single intervention. Studies have not yet been conducted in which a teacher incorporates a variety of interventions that facilitate a variety of learning processes for youth. What happens when students' needs dictate that a teacher plan and use multiple devices for organizing, understanding, and recalling information is not known. How teachers might approach preparing and sustaining this type of instruction over time is not known.

The success of implementing and sustaining inclusive practices may rest in the degree to which technology, media, and materials can be designed to provide more explicit and intensive support of classroom instruction. Studies on the use of technology, media, and materials in the secondary core curriculum are reviewed by Davis et al. They conclude that the processes related to the types of planning required to effectively select and integrate technology and media to support lesson planning on behalf of students with disabilities have not yet been addressed. Furthermore, whether the selection and orchestration of technology and media makes planning easier or more complicated is not clear. A significant factor is the effectiveness of the design of the technology, media, and materials. That is, if the design can accommodate for disabilities and facilitate the learning of strategies and skills, the idea of adopting such interventions is likely to be more compelling.

Grossen, Davis, Caros, and Billups (2001) addressed this issue in their review by citing research supporting six design principles that accommodate the learning needs of students with disabilities in heterogeneous classes. Although research supports the use of the design principles cited in the development of technology, media, and materials, none of the reviewed studies addressed how teachers might use these principles to guide planning and decision making; select appropriate technology, media, or materials; or adapt or design their own materials. These principles may be useful in materials design; however, how they may shape teacher planning is unclear. A more detailed discussion of the design principles that should be used to guide decision making in selecting technology, media, and materials is provided in Chapter 5.

Unit-Planning Research

Vaughn and Schumm (1995b) proposed a separate version of the Planning Pyramid, described earlier, as a template for unit planning. Use of the Unit Planning Pyramid to structure reflection and self-questioning enabled 13 teachers studied by Vaughn and Schumm over a semester to become more explicit about unit planning. Although data on the impact of the Unit Planning Pyramid have been reported primarily through case study reports and data on student learning have not been reported, the framework provided by the model may offer a useful way to approach some of the content-coverage challenges faced by general education teachers.

In another example of unit planning aimed at promoting inclusion, Jorgensen (1997) described how unit planning was nested in the process of moving an entire high school toward inclusion. In case study fashion, Jorgensen described how Souhegan High School in Amherst, New Hampshire, developed an inclusion model over a three-year period. Working within the principles of the Coalition for Essential Schools, the faculty followed a curriculum-design model for planning units that comprised four stages. Stage 1 consisted of identifying themes, essential questions, and outcomes and planning exhibits of student work. Stage 2 consisted of planning unit-learning activities that involved exploration, materials selection, student grouping, student support, and opportunities for practice. Stage 3 consisted of designing evaluation activities around a portfolio that included classwork, homework, tests, and exhibits. Finally, Stage 4 consisted of determining how grades would be determined through self, peer, teacher, and community evaluations.

The unit-planning process described by Jorgensen was not focused on a single discipline, but on interdisciplinary planning. It involved a unit topic, title, or theme that would guide instruction across disciplines. Essential, overarching questions were then constructed to guide student study of the unit. The goal was to craft questions that any student could use to gain knowledge. Students learned through hands-on and exploratory learning activities and demonstrated the knowledge they gained through performances. Although Jorgensen does not provide data on learning outcomes for students with disabilities, the process used to change the way teachers plan instruction at the high school level may be an important component in changing how units are planned.

Lenz, Schumaker, et al., (1993) reported the results of a study designed to alter the unit plans of core curriculum secondary teachers and the impact on students. Using a single-subject, multiple-baseline research design to evaluate teacher implementation of a unit-planning routine and student learning, the study moved systematically from focus groups on teacher planning, to teacher involvement in the coconstruction of a unit-planning routine, to classroom implementation of the routine over the course of one school year.

Initially, the researchers conducted focus groups with 50 secondary-level social studies and science teachers and then individually interviewed the six teachers participating in the study to identify how they had planned the first four units of the school year. Teachers were asked to identify (1) the steps they typically followed in planning units, (2) the organization of major topics in units, (3) how they took into consideration the needs of different kinds of learners in their planning, (4) adjustments they made to plans as they went through the unit, and (5) the amount of planning time they spent prior to beginning the unit versus the amount of planning time spent throughout the unit.

After the focus group and interview data were collected, data were shared with the six teachers involved in the intervention study. These teachers then collaborated with the researchers to create a generic process for planning and implementing units that they judged would be sensitive to the needs of students with disabilities enrolled in their courses while simultaneously meeting the needs of all students. Planning was divided into three activities: introducing the unit, maintaining unit ideas as the unit was being taught, and processing unit information to study and prepare for the test. These three activities made up the planning routine used in the study.

The unit-planning intervention consisted of preparing a two-page graphic organizer (see Figures 2.3 and 2.4) in which the teacher had to identify (1) how the unit fit in with other units and the course, (2) how the information was conceptually structured overall as the unit would unfold, (3) content relationships that were intended learning outcomes (such as cause and effect), (4) a set of self-test questions for guiding and testing learning, and (5) assignments and due dates that would be used to promote and evaluate learning throughout the unit. Teachers prepared the plan and used it as a guide to introduce the unit, maintain and check mastery of unit ideas, and guide unit review. The first page of the graphic organizer (Figure 2.3) was used to plan how the unit would be launched on the first day of the unit, and the second page of the graphic organizer was used to plan how the content of the unit would be added as the unit progressed (Figure 2.4). Alternatively or in addition, the content could be planned using a graphic organizer that focused on a section of the unit or a lesson of the unit showing how the lesson fit within the context of the overall structure of the unit. This alternative approach is shown in Figure 2.5 as a lesson organizer. Each student had the graphic organizer available to refer to under teacher leadership and to use as an organizing guide to monitor progress throughout the unit.

Six teachers (science and social studies teachers, three middle school and three high school teachers) participated in a two-legged, multiple-baseline design with two teachers in each design to evaluate their use of the organizer in class. To evaluate student learning, each teacher was asked to select eight students of varying ability and achievement levels: two high-achieving students, two average-achieving students, two low-achieving students, and two students with learning disabilities. Student performance was evaluated through structured interviews about content learning, unit tests, and student satisfaction. Teacher implementation of the planning routine was evaluated through an analysis of teacher plans and materials and interviews.

The teachers' use of the unit-planning organizer appeared to enhance the ability to organize, discuss, and recall information for students with learning disabilities, for low-achieving students, and for about half of the averaging-achieving students. The performance of high-achieving students did not improve. Students indicated that they were satisfied with the teachers' use of the organizer. The researchers indicated that, although the use of the graphic organizer in the classroom resulted in varying

62

Figure 2.3 First Page of Unit-Planning Graphic Organizer

The Unit Organizer

④ BIGGER PICTURE

DATE 4/1

| ② LAST UNIT/Experience Invertebrates | ① The Animal Kingdom | ③ CURRENT UNIT Vertebrates | Interrelationships | NEXT UNIT/Experience Ecology |

⑤ UNIT MAP

is about …

the most advanced and intelligent animals on the earth pp. 427–482

such as the — fishes

such as the — amphibians

such as the — reptiles

such as the — birds

such as the — mammals

⑥ UNIT RELATIONSHIPS

explanation

compare/contrast

⑧ UNIT SCHEDULE

4/1	Introduce vertebrates
4/4	Fish/Amphibian of choice report due
4/5	Fish/Amphibian quiz
4/10	Reptile quiz
4/12	Trip to natural history museum
4/15	Trip report due
4/16	Bird/Mammal quiz
4/17	Lab report due
4/18	Review
4/19	Test

⑦ UNIT SELF-TEST QUESTIONS

What are the basic differences among the major groups of vertebrates?

In what ways is life on land more difficult than life in water?

What is meant by cold-blooded and warm-blooded?

Which of the major groups of vertebrates is the most successful group? Why?

Figure 2.4   Second Page of Unit-Planning Graphic Organizer

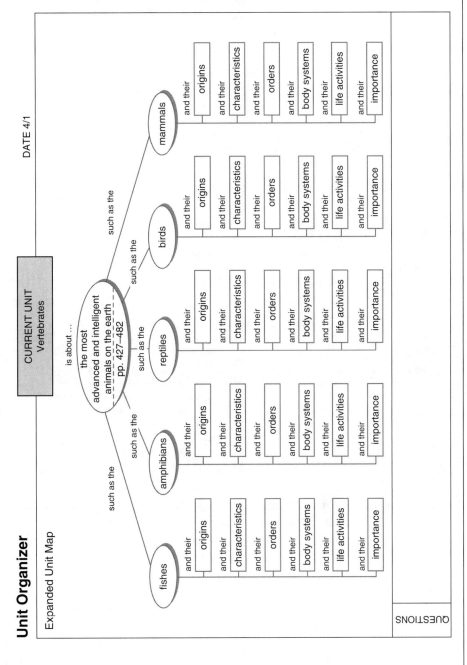

Figure 2.5   Lesson Organizer

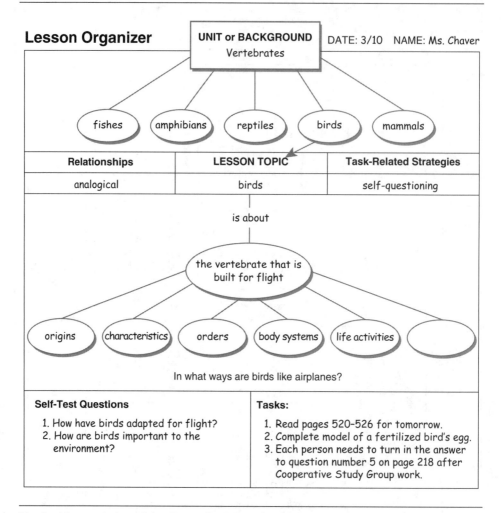

degrees of success for different learners, teachers reported that it significantly improved their approach to planning and the degree to which they could reach students with disabilities. In addition, they reported that the Unit Organizer appeared to help other students in the class even more. Teachers cited the translation of instructional plans into the graphic organizer form as particularly useful. They remarked that it helped them think about the content and become more explicit about the importance of information and the relationships between items of information. The researchers contacted participating teachers the following year and found that eight of the nine teachers continued to use the planning organizer independently in their courses. Further, although one teacher was not using the planning organizer with students as a classroom teaching guide, that teacher was using it as a unit-planning tool to prepare instruction.

One interesting finding reported by Lenz, Schumaker, et al. (1993) related to their testing methods. Most teachers participating in the study did not alter their methods of testing or evaluating student performance. Even though they referred to the planning organizer and focused on "the bigger picture" in class, most teachers tended to stress recall of detail when testing. The researchers noted that the teachers' approach to testing influenced the information students chose to learn, as well as the information students were able to recall during the structured interviews. Thus, the researchers concluded that the teachers' approach to testing sent a strong message to students regarding not only *what* was important to learn, but *how* one should learn (that is, one should memorize random facts).

The researchers also reported on the qualitative data collected over the year. Several themes emerged during the interviews conducted prior to developing and implementing the planning organizer. During this pre-implementation phase, teacher comments and concerns were character-ized by frustration with the degree of organization and clarity of the information and content, including key ideas, concepts, vocabulary, and how to help students differentiate important from unimportant informa-tion. After the planning organizer was created and introduced, themes emerged that focused on the classroom changes teachers were seeing. For example, teachers indicated that creating and sharing their planning orga-nizer with students made (or "forced") them to become more organized. They spent more time (especially up front) planning units and began to think more about the selection of content and materials, even question-ing or abandoning the structure of the text they were using. Finally, the teachers reported that, although the visual depiction of unit information was particularly helpful for students with learning disabilities and for low-achieving students, it was helpful for any student, regardless of achievement level, who did not already have efficient strategies for orga-nizing and understanding chunks of information.

Confirming some of the findings of the studies on lesson planning, Lenz, Schumaker, et al. (1993) noted that lesson planning began to change as the teachers revised unit plans. That is, the bigger unit decisions affected how explicit lessons could become. In addition, as teachers shared their unit plans with special education teachers, the latter reported that they were better able to support students' daily work by knowing what the teacher was emphasizing at the unit level. Finally, by the end of the study, the teachers reported that they had begun to think so differently about their teaching and the organization of their content that they were rethink-ing how they organized their courses.

Course-Planning Research

Although yearlong case studies of planning and implementation of units and lessons provide insights into many dimensions of the planning process, they have not provided insights into how a teacher thinks, plans, launches, maintains, and gains closure on a whole course. In general, the professional literature does not address the challenge of course planning that individual teachers face in translating various mandates and expectations into the total course experience. In addition, research indicates that teachers' mind-set or philosophy about how inclusive their courses should be is closely aligned with the course-planning process (Joint Committee on Teacher Planning for Students with Disabilities, 1995).

Research on course planning is not a clear area of study in the teacher-planning literature. Course planning falls somewhere between efforts to promote school restructuring and efforts to link units, assignments, and grading policies within a course syllabus for students and parents. Efforts to guide unit development around certain criteria, as described in the summary of the unit-planning process reported by Jorgensen (1997), may be seen as a broad way of defining course planning. Broader yet are the various examples of how schools have embarked on schoolwide efforts to promote inclusion (e.g., Sage, 1997). Specifically, district or departmental efforts to identify when and how national and state standards should be addressed in the curriculum could define another type of course planning. However, teachers are still responsible for following district guidelines and choosing and sequencing materials that will translate standards into meaningful classroom activities. Evidence suggests that teachers struggle with this charge (e.g., Maccini & Gagnon, 2002).

In the only study on course planning for students with disabilities, Lenz, Deshler, et al. (1993) reported on an effort that involved shaping how teachers planned their courses to increase the success of students with learning disabilities in secondary core curriculum courses. The research was conducted over a two-year period. During the first year, approximately 35 teachers provided suggestions about ways to structure and introduce courses that included students with disabilities through four focus group meetings and written questionnaires. These suggestions were converted to a questionnaire that was given to the same 35 teachers plus an additional 35 teachers, asking them to rank course-planning dimensions in terms of their importance.

During the summer following the end of the first year of research, eight teachers from the same school district were recruited to participate in a course-planning study. Four teachers (one middle school science, one middle school social studies, one high school science, and one high school social studies teacher) were assigned to an experimental group that would test a course-planning intervention. The other four teachers (one middle school science, one middle school social studies, one high school science, and one high school social studies) were assigned to a comparison group that would not use the course-planning intervention. A total of 224 students participated in the study: 116 students in the experimental classes and 108 in the comparison classrooms. Seventeen students with learning disabilities were enrolled in the experimental classrooms, and 13 students with learning disabilities were enrolled in the comparison classrooms. Teachers were asked to target two students who were high achieving, two who were average achieving, two who were low achieving, and two who had been identified as having a learning disability. The researchers reported on the effects of the course-planning process on these students' performance.

Over the summer and during the school year, qualitative data were collected through observations, planning interviews, teacher journals, group discussion with the teacher teams, and interviews with selected students in the classes of the four comparison teachers and the four intervention teachers. In addition, quantitative data were collected through teacher observations, student satisfaction questionnaires, student tests that were based on 10 course questions designed by each experimental and comparison teacher, and student expectation surveys.

The course-planning intervention required teachers to use a graphic organizer to name the course, paraphrase what the course was about, create 10 critical or "big idea" questions that all students would be able to answer by the end of the year, and identify how performance would be evaluated and progress communicated to students. They had to create a map of the units, identify a set of critical course concepts, identify a set of classroom or community principles that would guide how they would work together, identify ongoing learning rituals that would be routinely used throughout the course (that is, teaching routines, learning strategies, social-skill strategies, and communication systems that would be introduced and used to promote learning), and create performance options that would define the accommodations and adaptations that would be available to address individual learning needs. Figures 2.6 and 2.7 show the first and second page of the course-planning organizer used in the study. Teachers shared this organizer with their students at the beginning of the course using a specific teaching routine and then used it to review course ideas at the end of every unit and at the end of the year. Teachers met with researchers monthly to discuss course planning as well as the progress of targeted students.

After the teachers in the experimental group learned to use the initial version of the course-planning routine and understood instructional methods that could be used with diverse classes of students, they spent more time introducing major course ideas, concepts, themes, and routines to students than teachers in the comparison group. In addition, teachers in the experimental group introduced an average of eight innovative instructional practices related to responding to classroom academic diversity over the school year. Moreover, of these eight, they maintained seven practices through the end of the year. The comparison teachers introduced an average of four innovative instructional practices across the year, but only maintained, on average, one of these innovative practices through the end of the year.

Figure 2.6 First Page of Course-Planning Organizer

The
Course Organizer

Teacher(s): Mr. Sanders	Student: Nancy Nolder
Time: 8:05–8:57	Course Dates: 9/98–5/99

À THIS COURSE:

Biology

(is about) → How living things exist in the world around us.

Á COURSE QUESTIONS:

1. How do the forms of matter relate to each other?

2. How are organic macro molecules the basis for life?

3. How does the cell theory relate to life?

4. How are groups of organisms organized?

5. How do molecular characteristics of organisms determine heredity?

6. What is the connection between biological evolution and the classification of organisms?

7. How does the interdependence of organisms affect the world?

8. How do matter, energy, and organisms interact?

9. What defines and/or influences the behavior of animals?

10. Why are natural resources important or not important to living things?

11. How does natural selection provide an explanation for evolution?

Á COURSE STANDARDS:

What?	How?	Value?
CONTENT:		
1. *Critical unit concepts*	Unit tests	20 pts.
2. Examples of concepts	Unit tests	10 pts.
3. Relationships	Demonstrations	20 pts.
4. Facts	Daily work	10 pts.
		60 pts.
PROCESS:		
4. Paraphrasing	Class demo.	20 pts.
5. Teamwork	Class demo.	10 pts.
6. Being prepared	Class demo.	5 pts.
7. Journaling	Journal	5 pts.
		40 pts.

COURSE PROGRESS GRAPH

Total Score for Grade
Content Score
Process Score

UNITS 1 2 3 4 5 6

A = 100–90
B = 89–80
C = 79–70
D = 69–60
Less than 60 Redo

Used with permission of the Center for Research on Learning, University of Kansas.

Figure 2.7   Second Page of Course-Planning Organizer

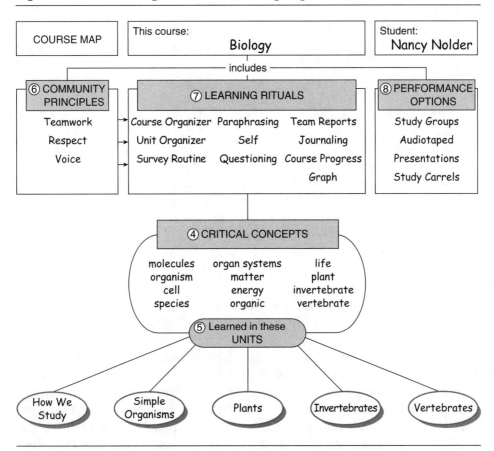

In terms of student performance, none of the students with learning disabilities could answer the 10 critical big idea questions correctly at the beginning of the year on written tests or in interviews. At the end of the course, students with learning disabilities enrolled in classes taught by teachers in the experimental classrooms answered an average of eight big idea course questions correctly, whereas students with learning disabilities in the comparison classes answered an average of three course questions correctly at the end of the course.

At the end of the school year, teachers in the experimental group reported that working to create a connected community of learners was very important to them. Observations and interviews showed that they had repeatedly used the "learning community" ideal to judge their progress and success. They indicated that they had used the Course Organizer to achieve this. They indicated that creating and revising the 10 course questions, creating course maps, and selecting target students to guide their reflection were the course-planning components that were most useful in helping them become more learner-sensitive. Descriptive results indicated that the experimental teachers had developed a mind-set about teaching academically diverse classes that was different from the mind-set of teachers in the comparison group. Specifically, they noted that responding differently to individuals with special needs in the context of the group when planning and teaching lessons and units was more important than the teachers in the comparison group indicated.

Lenz, Deshler, et al. (1993) also found that before using the planning and teaching routines, teachers often lost sight of the big ideas of their courses. They frequently became bogged down in trying to cover masses of information. As a result, their students had difficulty understanding the relationships among clusters of information within the course. They also reported that using the routine helped them focus their instruction and assessment activities and helped students understand important relationships. Having the freedom to modify the planning routine to suit their own needs helped them use the routine successfully. However, the researchers also found that teachers struggled to articulate what was important about their content. For example, they reported that all four of the experimental teachers asked if they could revise their course questions halfway through the school year.

Although this initial study on course-planning yielded positive results, several factors remain unclear. First, teachers in the experimental group collaborated with researchers on developing and implementing the routine, and therefore they were motivated to use it. In other words, teachers who *wanted* to invest time and energy in being more effective with diverse groups of students were successful in using the routine. Second, there were only eight teachers in the study, and all of these teachers represented the content areas of either social studies or science. As a result, the effects of the course-planning approach on teacher planning in other subject areas are not known. Third, although different types of students were involved, the sample of students was probably not representative of all the different types of learners for which teachers are responsible.

SUMMARY OF LESSONS LEARNED

Reforming the educational experience that high school students receive is a major challenge for those who advocate that no child be left behind and that all students be included in the educational process. The literature that describes how high school teachers approach the inclusion of students with disabilities is not optimistic. Many secondary teachers believe that students with disabilities who are enrolled in core curriculum classes should adapt and that teachers should not have to plan for their success. As Schumm and Vaughn (1992) indicated, although teachers are willing to have students with disabilities in their classes and are willing to make adaptations when students experience problems, they are not willing to plan ahead to prevent academic failure.

After reviewing the planning of secondary teachers, Schumm et al. (1995) recommended that future research should focus on developing interventions that enable secondary teachers to address the needs of the whole class to meet the content-coverage dilemma, while simultaneously providing the kinds of instruction needed by students with disabilities. Similarly, in a descriptive study of the classroom practices of secondary teachers, Nolet and Tindal (1993) concluded that teachers' knowledge of the subject matter and how they assessed students' acquisition of that subject matter were the two most important influences on whether students with disabilities gained access to the core curriculum. They argued that content-area teachers must clearly identify what content is critical for students to learn and how they can use this information to solve problems, and then focus communication with special education teachers on this content. They suggested that once the content is identified, teachers can collaborate on how to provide more explicit instruction for students with disabilities.

This review of planning research aimed at helping high school teachers increase student access to the core curriculum supports the conclusions of Schumm et al. (1995) and Nolet and Tindal (1993). It also offers some additional observations.

First, planning interventions that focus on making whole-group instruction more sensitive to the needs of students with disabilities are more likely to be adopted and maintained than planning interventions that focus on individual students. Because content mastery is the primary focus of the high school experience—and this emphasis has been reinforced through national endorsement of standards-based testing—efforts to alter teacher planning on behalf of students with disabilities must build on this directive. Interventions that help teachers make decisions about the importance and organization of content information (Lenz, "with" an's not needed 1994; Vaughn & Schumm, 1994) seem to help teachers meet a general planning demand and are more likely to be adopted. In addition, the process of graphically depicting plans and sharing these plans with students also seems to promote change in teacher planning and teaching behavior. This finding may indicate that creating a graphic device that can guide planning and be used as a teaching tool (in the form of teaching routines; see Chapter 3) may increase palatability and sustainability.

Second, the studies that involved in-depth and sustained work with teachers to support planning changes appeared to be more effective than shorter studies. This finding is consistent with other research on professional change. However, the type of collaborative process that best facilitates change is not known. Although close and sustained collaboration between researchers and teachers seemed to contribute to change, how this approach could be translated into the natural process of supporting teachers across many high schools is not known.

Third, studies that involved asking teachers to target individual students to determine the effects of their planning tended to positively influence teacher change. This may suggest that teachers are more willing to adopt an intervention change when it involves direct communication with youth or enables them to see growth in particular youths. As reported in previous planning literature, getting to know individual students can lead to changes in whole-group planning and instruction.

Although some intervention efforts indicate that planning can be influenced, the research in this area is sparse. The types of studies reported here demonstrate that research designs must take into consideration that there are few students with disabilities enrolled in high school core curriculum classes. For example, almost all of the studies included here used case studies or quasi-experimental designs to examine changes. In most of the classes studied, teachers had only one or two students with disabilities enrolled. This situation creates problems in selecting research designs that can produce generalizable results related to teacher and student outcomes. Research must be conducted on why students with disabilities are rarely included in these classes and how to employ adequate and cost-effective research designs that can be used when students are included in core curriculum classes.

Another dilemma is the uncertainty about what general education teachers can be expected to do. Currently, there are no clear criteria for successful inclusion in high schools. When inclusion *and* success in the core curriculum are considered, there is even more confusion. As a result, the success of interventions that prompt teachers to change their planning on behalf of students with disabilities is likely to vary.

Overall, the challenge of helping teachers move to the level of explicitness and support that is necessary to ensure the access of students with disabilities to the core curriculum has not yet been met. Teachers struggle to move to the level that researchers request. The in-class *and* out-of-class time required to ensure student success seemed excessive to the teachers in many of the studies described here. Although the studies reviewed here indicate that some tactics are more effective than others (for instance, graphic organizers used as planning devices seems to help teachers become more explicit and focused and form a firm foundation for effective teaching routines) and provide some overall direction for how educators might think about supporting change in teacher planning, several major dilemmas remain unsolved.

Future research should focus on further validation of some of the basic planning interventions described here. Does creating graphic organizers and sharing plans with students lead to more explicit instruction than when teachers do not use these tools? What types of information about students will influence planning, and how do teachers acquire and use this information to shape plans? Such studies should investigate planning in terms of the content, implementation, and contextual challenges teachers face while simultaneously helping teachers provide supports that are maximally feasible and socially acceptable. In addition, the degree to which these supports are adequate or inadequate for successful access to the curriculum needs to be examined, and the additional supports that are necessary need to be identified.

Educational Applications and Implications

Personnel in schools and school districts are utilizing some of the planning routines described in this chapter to plan their secondary general education courses. For example, in one midwestern school district, all of the algebra teachers across all of the schools have met to review the state standards and benchmarks related to algebra. In addition, they have worked together to create Course Organizers, Unit Organizers, and, in some cases, Lesson Organizers to be used by all algebra teachers. These organizers are closely aligned with and incorporate the benchmark knowledge and skills required by the state standards. To provide support for the highly transitory population of students who often transfer from one school to another within the district, the teachers have adopted a standardized timeline for presenting the units of the algebra course so that students who transfer will not miss important content and skills.

For another example, science teachers in a northeastern high school have worked together to plan their shared physical science course. Like the algebra teachers just mentioned, they have aligned their Course Organizer and Unit Organizers with state standards. They have created new unit tests to align with the content being taught and with the required state standards. They also have created a schedule for when the units will be taught.

Other schools have adopted the use of the planning methods described in this chapter schoolwide. Personnel in each department in these schools have been responsible for working together to address state standards and create planning organizers. Teachers have worked together not only to coordinate shared courses, but also to ensure that the information is sequenced across courses that build on one another (for instance, U.S. History II builds on U.S. History I; English II builds on English I). Teachers of electives such as technology, industrial arts, and music courses have participated in these efforts alongside teachers of required subject-area courses.

For efforts such as these to succeed, the necessary supports must be in place. First, teachers need to participate in professional development experiences related to new planning practices. Second, they need to be given access to state standards and other pertinent documents, as well as time to work together so that the necessary planning can take place. Third, during this planning, they often need the help and expertise of a trained coach who can answer their questions and help them polish the planning organizers they have created.

Administrators need to orchestrate the availability of the needed professional development, planning time, and coaches as teachers begin this new endeavor. In addition, they need to provide their own measure of enthusiasm to the project by observing teachers in their classes and by providing assistance and resources as necessary.

For more information on how to obtain assistance with professional development experiences for some of the planning interventions reviewed in this chapter, visit the University of Kansas Center for Research on Learning Web site at www.kucrl.org or contact the center's director of professional development at 785-864-4780.

REFERENCES

Allen, L., Rogers, D., Hensley, F., Glanton, M., & Livingston, M. (1999). *A guide to renewing your school: Lessons from the league of professional schools.* San Francisco: Jossey-Bass.

Anday-Porter, S., Henne, K., & Horan, S. (2000). *Improving student organizational skills through the use of organizational skills in the curriculum* (Research Report). Chicago: Saint Xavier University and Skylight Professional Development.

Baylor, A., Kitsantas, A., & Chung, H. (2001). The instructional planning self-reflective tool: A method of promoting effective lesson planning. *Educational Technology, 41*(2), 56–59.

Beane, J. (Ed.). (1995). *Toward a coherent curriculum: The 1995 ASCD yearbook.* Alexandria, VA: Association for Supervision and Curriculum Development.

Bever, V. (1994). *Increasing productivity in non-productive at-risk elementary resource students* (Research Report). Chicago: Saint Xavier University.

Blythe, T., & Associates. (1998). *The teaching for understanding guide.* San Francisco: Jossey-Bass.

Boudah, D., Deshler, D., Schumaker, J., Lenz, K., & Cook, B. (1997). Student-centered or content-centered? A case study of a middle school teacher's lesson planning and instruction in inclusive classes. *Teacher Education and Special Education, 20*(3), 189–203.

Boudah, D., Logan, K., & Greenwood, C. (2001). The research to practice projects: Lessons learned about changing teacher practice. *Teacher Education and Special Education, 24*(4), 290–303.

Brown, D. (1988). Twelve middle-school teachers' planning. *Elementary School Journal, 89,* 69–87.

Brownell, M., Mellard, D., & Deshler, D. (1993). Differences in the learning and transfer performance between students with learning disabilities and other low-achieving students on problem-solving. *Learning Disability Quarterly, 16,* 138–156.

Bruner, J. (1960). *The process of education.* Cambridge, MA: Harvard University Press.

Bruner, J. (1973). *The relevance of education.* Cambridge, MA: Harvard University Press.

Bulgren, J. A., & Lenz, B. K. (1998). *The role of social studies and science concepts and content in planning lessons for academically diverse classes at the secondary school level* (Research Report). Lawrence: University of Kansas Center for Research on Learning.

Bulgren, J., & Schumaker, J. (2001). *Instructional practices designed to promote success for students with disabilities in inclusive secondary content classrooms: A review of the literature* (Research Report). Lawrence: University of Kansas Center for Research on Learning.

Caine, R. N., & Caine, G. (1997). *Education on the edge of possibility.* Alexandria, VA: Association for Supervision and Curriculum Development.

Callahan, K., Rademacher, J., & Hildreth, B. (1998). The effect of parent participation in strategies to improve homework performance of students who are at risk. *Remedial and Special Education, 19*(3), 131–141.

Carnine, D., Jones, E., & Dixon, R. (1995). Mathematics: Educational tools for diverse learners. *School Psychology Review, 23*(3), 406–427.

Clark, C., & Elmore, J. (1979). *Teacher planning in the first weeks of school* (Research Report No. 56). East Lansing: Michigan State University, Institute for Research on Teaching.

Clark, C., & Peterson, P. (1986). Teachers' thought processes. In M. Wittrock (Ed.), *Handbook of research on teaching* (3rd ed., pp. 255–296). New York: Macmillan.

Clark, C., & Yinger, R. (1979). Teachers' thinking. In P. L. Peterson & H. J. Walberg (Eds.), *Research on teaching*. Berkeley, CA: McCutchan.

Coalition for Essential Schools. (2002). *The common principles: Elementary and secondary school inclusive.* Retrieved from www.essentialschools.org/pub/ces_docs/

Cooper, J. (Ed.). (1999). *Classroom teaching skills.* Boston: Houghton Mifflin.

Dick, W., & Reiser, R. (1989). *Planning effective instruction.* Englewood Cliffs, NJ: Prentice Hall.

Driscoll, M., Klein, J., & Sherman, G. (1994). Perspectives on instructional planning: How do teachers and instructional designers conceive of ISD planning practices. *Educational Technology, 34*(3), 34–42.

Erickson, L. (1998). *Concept-based curriculum and instruction: Teaching beyond the facts.* Thousand Oaks, CA: Corwin.

Floden, R., & Clark, C. (1988). Preparing teacher for uncertainty. *Teachers College Record, 89*(4), 506–524.

Fuchs, L., Fuchs, D., Hamlett, C., Phillips, N., & Bentz, J. (1994). Classwide curriculum-based measurement: Helping general educators meet the challenge of student diversity. *Exceptional Children, 60,* 518–537.

Gersten, R. (1998). Recent advances in instructional research for students with learning disabilities: An overview. *Learning Disabilities Research and Practice, 13,* 162–170.

Gersten, R., Chard, D., & Baker, S. (2000). Factors that enhance sustained use of research-based instructional practices: A historical perspective on relevant research. *Journal of Learning Disabilities, 33,* 444–457.

Glickman, C. (2002). *Leadership for learning: How to help teachers succeed.* Alexandria, VA: Association for Supervision and Curriculum Development.

Grossen, B., Davis, B., Caros, J., & Billups, L. (2001). *Promoting success in the general education curriculum for high school students with disabilities: Instructional technology, media, and materials* (Research Report). Lawrence: University of Kansas Institute for Academic Access.

Hollingsworth, M., & Woodward, J. (1993). Integrated learning: Explicit strategies and their role in problem-solving instruction for students with learning disabilities. *Exceptional Children, 59,* 444–455.

Horner, R., & Baer, D. (1978). Multiple-probe technique: A variation of the multiple baseline. *Journal of Applied Behavioral Analysis, 11,* 189–196.

Hutchinson, N. (1993). Effects of cognitive strategy instruction on algebra problem solving of adolescents with learning disabilities. *Learning Disability Quarterly, 16,* 6–18.

Joint Committee on Teacher Planning for Students with Disabilities. (1995). *Planning for academic diversity in America's classrooms: Windows on reality, research, change, and practice.* Lawrence: University of Kansas Center for Research on Learning.

Jorgensen, C. (1997). Including all students in high school: The story of Souhegan High School, Amherst, New Hampshire. In D. Sage (Ed.), *Inclusion in secondary schools: Bold initiatives challenging change* (pp. 11–43). Port Chester, NY: National Professional Resources.

Kameenui, E., & Carnine, D. (1998). *Effective teaching strategies that accommodate diverse learners.* Columbus, OH: Merrill.

Karustis, J., Habboushe, D., Leff, S., Eiraldi, R., & Power, T. (1999, April). *From clinic to school: Adapting a homework intervention program for ADHD in school settings.* Paper presented at the annual convention and exposition of the National Association of School Psychologists, Las Vegas, NV.

Kerr, S. (1981). How teachers design their materials: Implications for instructional design. *Instructional Science, 10,* 363–378.

Lampert, M., & Clark, C. (1990). Expert knowledge and expert thinking in teachers: A response to Floden and Klinzing. *Educational Researcher, 19,* 21–23.

Lenz, B. K. (1984). *The effect of advance organizers on the learning and retention of learning disabled adolescents with the context of a cooperative planning model.* Final research report submitted to the U.S. Department of Education, Office of Special Education and Rehabilitative Services. Lawrence: University of Kansas Center for Research on Learning.

Lenz, B. K., Alley, G., & Schumaker, J. (1987). Activating the inactive learner: Advance organizers in the secondary content classroom. *Learning Disability Quarterly, 10*(1), 53–67.

Lenz, B. K., Boudah, D. J., Schumaker, J. B., Deshler, D. D. (1993). *The lesson planning routine: A guide for inclusive lesson planning* (Research Report). Lawrence: University of Kansas Center for Research on Learning.

Lenz, B. K., with Bulgren, J. A., Schumaker, J. B., & Deshler, D. D., & Boudah, D. J. (1994). *The Unit Organizer routine.* Lawrence, KS: Edge Enterprises.

Lenz, B. K., & Deshler, D. D. (2004). *Teaching content to all.* Boston: Allyn & Bacon.

Lenz, B. K., & Schumaker, J. B. (Eds.). (1999). *Adapting materials for middle-school students with disabilities.* Reston, VA: Council for Exceptional Children.

Lenz, B. K., Schumaker, J. B., & Deshler, D. D. (1991, March). *Planning in the face of academic diversity: Whose questions should we be answering?* Paper presented at the conference of the American Educational Research Association, Chicago, IL.

Lenz, B. K., Schumaker, J. B., Deshler, D. D., Boudah, D., Vance, M., Kissam, B., Bulgren, J., & Roth, J. (1993). *The Unit Planning Routine: A guide for inclusive unit planning* (Research Report). Lawrence: University of Kansas Center for Research on Learning.

Lenz, B. K., Schumaker, J. B., Deshler, D. D., & Kissam, B. J. (1991). *Planning in the face of academic diversity: Whose questions should we be answering?* (Executive Summary, Research Report). Lawrence: University of Kansas Center for Research on Learning.

Maccini, P., & Gagnon, J. (2002). Perceptions and application of NCTM standards by special and general education teachers. *Exceptional Children, 68*(3), 325–344.

Maher, C. A. (1987). Involving behaviorally disordered adolescents in instructional planning: Effectiveness of the GOAL procedure. *Journal of Child and Adolescent Psychotherapy, 4*(3), 204–210.

Martin, R., & McLaughlin, T. (1981). Comparison between the effect of free time and daily report cards on the academic behavior of junior high students. *Journal of Special Education, 5*(4), 303–313.

McCutcheon, G. (1980). How do elementary school teachers plan? The nature of planning and influences on it. *Elementary School Journal, 81,* 4–23.

Morrocco, C., Riley, M., Gordon, S., Howard, C., & Longo, A. M. (1994). *Changing teacher mindset through collaborative planning* (Technical Report). Newton, MA: Education Development Center.

Nolet, V., & Tindal, G. (1993). Special education in content area classes: Development of a model and practical procedures. *Remedial and Special Education, 14*(1), 36–48.

Olympia, D., Sheridan, S. M., Jenson, W. R., & Andrews, D. (1994). Using student managed interventions to increase homework completion and accuracy. *Journal of Applied Behavioral Analysis, 27*(1), 85–99.

O'Melia, M., & Rosenberg, M. (1994). Effects of cooperative homework teams on the acquisition of mathematics skills by secondary students with mild disabilities. *Exceptional Children, 60*(6), 538–548.

Perkins, D. (1992). *Smart schools: From training memories to educating minds.* New York: Free Press.

Rademacher, J. A., Schumaker, J. B., & Deshler, D. D. (1996). Development and validation of a classroom assignment routine for inclusive settings. *Learning Disability Quarterly, 19*(3), 163–178.

Reiser, R. (1994). Examining the planning practices of teachers: Reflections on three years of research. *Educational Technology, 34*(3), 11–16.

Reiser, R. (2001a). A history of instructional design and technology: Part I. A history of instructional media. *Educational Technology Research and Development, 49*(1), 53–64.

Reiser, R. (2001b). A history of instructional design and technology: Part II. A history of instructional design. *Educational Technology Research and Development, 49*(2), 57–67.

Riley, M., Morocco, C., Gordon, S., & Howard, C. (1993). Walking the talk: Putting constructivist thinking into practice in classrooms. *Educational Horizons, 71*(4), 187–196.

Rose, D., & Dolan, R. P. (2000). Universal design for learning. *Journal of Special Education Technology, 15*(4), 67–70.

Sage, D. (1997). *Inclusion in secondary schools.* Port Chester, NY: National Professional Resources.

Scanlon, D., Deshler, D., & Schumaker, B. (1996). Can a strategy be taught and learned in secondary inclusive classrooms? *Learning Disabilities Research & Practice, 11*(1), 41–57.

Scanlon, D., Schumaker, J., & Deshler, D. (1994). Collaborative dialogues between teachers and researchers to create educational interventions: A case study. *Journal of Educational and Psychological Consultation, 5*(1), 69–76.

Schumm, J. S., & Vaughn, S. (1991). Making adaptations for mainstreamed students. *Remedial and Special Education, 12,* 18–27.

Schumm, J. S., & Vaughn, S. (1992). Planning for mainstreamed special education students: Perceptions of general education teachers. *Exceptionality, 3,* 81–98.

Schumm, J., Vaughn, S., Haager, D., McDowell, J., Rothlein, L., & Samuell, L. (1995). *Exceptional Children, 61*(4), 335–352.

Schumm, J., Vaughn, S., & Leavell, A. (1994). Planning pyramid: A framework for planning for diverse student needs during content area instruction. *The Reading Teacher, 47*(8), 608–615.

Shavelson, R. (1983). Review of research on teachers' pedagogical judgments, plans, and decisions. *Elementary School Journal, 83,* 392–413.

Strandy, C., McLaughlin, T. F., & Hunsaker, D. (1979). Free time as a reinforcer for assignment completion with high school special education students. *Education and Treatment of Children, 2*(4), 271–277.

Swanson, H. L. (1999). Instructional components that predict treatment outcomes for students with learning disabilities: Support for a combined strategy and direct instruction model. *Learning Disabilities Research and Practice, 14*(3), 129–140.

Swanson, H. L. (2001). Research on interventions for adolescents with learning disabilities: A meta-analysis of outcomes related to higher-order processing. *Elementary School Journal, 101*(3), 331–348.

Tollefson, N., et al. (1986). Teaching learning disabled students goal implementation skills. *Psychology in the Schools, 23*(2), 194–204.

Tomlinson, C. (1995). *How to differentiate instruction in mixed ability classrooms.* Alexandra, VA: Association for Supervision and Curriculum Development.

Tomlinson, C. (1999). *The differentiated classroom: Responding to the needs of all learners.* Alexandria, VA: Association for Supervision and Curriculum Development.

Tomlinson, C. (2000). Reconcilable differences: Standards-based teaching and differentiation. *Educational Leadership, 58*(1), 6–11.

Tomlinson, C. (2003). Deciding to teach them all. *Educational Leadership, 61*(2), 6–11.

Tomlinson, C., & Allan, S. (2000). *Leadership for differentiating schools and classrooms.* Alexandria, VA: Association for Supervision and Curriculum Development.

Tyler, R. (1949). *Basic principles of curriculum and instruction.* Chicago: University of Chicago Press.

Vaughn, S., Klinger, J., & Hughes, M. (2000). Sustainability of research-based practices. *Exceptional Children, 66*(2), 163–171.

Vaughn, S., & Schumm, J. (1994). Middle school teacher's planning for students with learning disabilities. *Remedial and Special Education, 15*(3), 152–161.

Vaughn, S., & Schumm, J. (1995a). The lesson planning pyramid. In Joint Committee on Teacher Planning for Students with Disabilities, *Planning for academic diversity in America's classrooms: Windows on reality, research, change, and practice* (pp. 11–120). Lawrence: University of Kansas, Center for Research on Learning.

Vaughn, S., & Schumm, J. (1995b). The unit planning pyramid. In Joint Committee on Teacher Planning for Students with Disabilities, *Planning for academic diversity in America's classrooms: Windows on reality, research, change, and practice* (pp. 8–10). Lawrence: University of Kansas, Center for Research on Learning.

Wiggins, G., & McTighe, J. (1998). *Understanding by design.* Alexandria, VA: Association for Supervision and Curriculum Development.

Yinger, R. J. (1980). A study of teacher planning. *Elementary School Journal, 80*(3), 107–127.

Yinger, R. J., & Clark, C. M. (1985). *Using personal documents to study teacher thinking* (Occasional Paper No. 84). East Lansing: Michigan State University, Institute for Research on Teaching.

3

Teaching Practices That Optimize Curriculum Access

Janis A. Bulgren and Jean B. Schumaker

During the last semester of the eighth grade, careful plans were made to ensure that Jason would make a smooth transition to high school. Extra care was taken to ensure that the classes to which he was assigned in the general education curriculum would be led by teachers who had demonstrated an ability to make the necessary curricular adaptations and accommodations to enable all students in their classes to master the content and respond to the high-stakes assessments that Jason would need to take to graduate. Many of the general education staff at Woodland High School had been trained to use a host of Content Enhancement Routines. These routines were used by many of Jason's teachers on a regular basis to assist not only students with disabilities but also the broad array of other students who experienced problems in understanding and mastering the content.

Teachers like Jason's are constantly called on to respond to numerous instructional challenges in inclusive secondary classes that include both students with disabilities and other students of diverse abilities.

Teachers are expected to be experts in their content areas, in learning, and in instructional techniques that are appropriate for students with a variety of needs. The challenges facing today's teachers have been highlighted by recent legislation in the No Child Left Behind Act of 2001 (2002), which mandates the disaggregation of data by student groups, including those with disabilities.

Such legislation early in the 21st century sets the expectations for our schools that instructional practices should be designed to promote success for all students. Indeed, these expectations directly relate to the "core of educational practice," which Elmore describes as "how teachers understand the nature of knowledge and the student's role in learning, and how these ideas about knowledge and learning are manifested in teaching and classwork" (1996, p. 2). Implicit in these expectations is the notion that teachers are expert instructional mediators for all students. They must select, organize, and transform critical content information so that all students can become active and proficient learners (Bulgren & Lenz, 1996).

The teacher's role as a mediator has been described by several authors. For example, Jones, Palincsar, Ogle, and Carr (1987) built on the work of Feuerstein (1980) to explain that teacher mediation means that teachers intercede between learners and their learning environments to help students organize and interpret information. Because teachers must meet the multifaceted challenge of teaching students of diverse abilities, they must translate their knowledge into practice in three distinct areas: content, student learning, and instruction. In each case, they must be experts in the relevant theories and foundational knowledge; then, they must relate that general knowledge to the strengths and needs of each of their students. In essence, they must be strategic teachers who are constantly thinking and making decisions, using a rich knowledge base of both content and teaching and learning strategies and functioning as both models and mediators in their classrooms (Jones et al., 1987).

To shed light on the instructional practices that teachers can use to ensure that students with diverse abilities learn in their classrooms, teachers' roles with regard to choosing what content students will learn, recognizing the cognitive learning skills of their students, and teaching those skills will be described in detail. Then, experimental research that relates to these roles and to enhancing the performance of students with diverse abilities in secondary general education classes will be reviewed.

MEDIATING THE INSTRUCTIONAL PROCESS

As teachers work to fulfill these roles, they must think about how they can mediate learning in terms of important content information, characteristics of diverse students and how they learn, and ways to use that information as the foundation for instructional techniques.

Mediation of Content: What Must All Students Learn?

With regard to content, teachers are expected to be experts in extensive bodies of knowledge related to their subject areas (such as math, science, history, literature). One need only look at the rapidly expanding size of textbooks to appreciate the enormousness of this challenge. Keeping up with the explosion of information and the variety of resources available is a difficult task. Perhaps because of this difficulty, teachers often equate the textbook with the curriculum (Thornton, 1991), and many teachers accept texts as the major source of content (Borko & Niles, 1987). However, often all of the information contained in a textbook cannot be covered in a course, and most texts do not cover all of the information that might appropriately be addressed in a course.

Therefore, teachers must decide what information is most important to teach if they want students to become content-literate citizens. This may mean selecting the most important information in a text in an effort to prepare students to move on to the next level of courses, instead of simply proceeding through a text at a pace that students can manage and stopping instruction at whatever point has been reached when the semester or year ends. The latter approach results in students mastering some less critical information but lacking other critical information that is a prerequisite for their progress to the next level in the subject area.

Additionally, teachers may have to use other sources, including their own expertise, to teach all that is required. Often, teachers who are expert mediators in their content areas consider the main course textbook as only one source of information rather than the sole determiner of course content. Such a vision is necessary because of the learning demands associated with today's secondary content courses. These demands require students to not only comprehend information from texts but also recall and manipulate content from multiple sources and generalize that information as they complete inquiry, application, and performance tasks.

These latter types of tasks are becoming more and more prevalent in content-area classes as a result of standards-based reform movements, such as the one in science education (National Research Council [NRC], 2000), in which scientific inquiry and scientific argumentation are being emphasized. For example, students are often expected to question the relationships between evidence and explanation, construct and analyze explanations, and communicate scientific arguments (Driver, Newton, & Osborne, 2000; NRC, 1996, 2000). The same types of tasks are being developed in other subject areas (National Center for History in the Schools, 1996). Therefore, teachers must think carefully about how to teach important information and how to help students develop the ability to gather information, think critically about it, and use it.

Another area in which teachers must function as content experts involves standards and assessments. Many states have set content standards and designed assessments that correspond to those standards. In addition, professional groups have proposed national standards and benchmarks (NRC, 1996). When serving a recognizably mobile student population, teachers who are content experts must understand the standards and assessments for different regional areas. They also must plan and teach in ways that support responses to assessments based on these standards so that students will be able to meet the standards no matter where they are when they take the tests.

When attempting to mediate content, teachers may choose the most critical information for their courses by using planning techniques such as the "Curriculum Pie" (Lenz, Bulgren, Kissam, & Taymans, 2004). This planning technique was developed to help teachers select a relatively small critical mass of information that *all* students must know, a somewhat larger amount of information that *most* students should learn, and an extremely large amount of content information that only *some* students, because of high interest or career goals, might learn. The importance of thinking about the most critical information that all students must learn has been supported by Wiggins and McTighe (1998), who argued that teachers must rethink their approach to teaching and decide what to teach by sorting information into (1) that information that should be enduring, (2) information that is important to know and do, and (3) information with which students should have some familiarity. Erickson (1998), too, indicated that instruction should revolve around essential understandings.

To summarize, subject-area teachers need to be experts in both content knowledge and how that knowledge must be applied and demonstrated by students. As a result, they are responsible for determining how to compensate for the inadequate, overloaded, or confusing presentation of content information in some textbooks. To accomplish this, even the most expert teacher in a content area must also be an expert in another arena. That is, teachers must understand learning theories and be able to identify matches or mismatches between an individual learner's characteristics and content-learning demands.

Mediation of Learning: Who Learns in Special Ways?

The second area in which teachers must function as mediators is in the area of learning theory and how it relates to an individual learner's characteristics. This means that teachers must know the types of cognitive learning skills that students are expected to exhibit to be successful in secondary content classes.

According to Mayer (1987), the demands that students must meet relative to understanding content-area information minimally include (1) learning concepts; (2) applying or generalizing learned concepts to novel situations; (3) comparing and contrasting concepts; (4) learning rules and propositions (which specify the relationships between concepts); (5) learning and integrating main ideas and details; (6) learning procedures, processes, or sequences of actions; (7) learning cause-and-effect relation-ships; and (8) exploring problems, making judgments, and arriving at solutions. Once teachers have knowledge of these demands, their role then includes determining which of these learning demands are present in a course. Additionally, the teacher's role includes understanding how students of diverse abilities learn and how they can be supported in their learning, as well as recognizing and understanding the diversity of partic-ular groups of students in terms of their strengths and weaknesses. Only then can teachers organize and manipulate the course content in ways that will help all students to understand and become active, literate, and lifetime learners.

To understand students' weaknesses as learners, teachers must be aware of problems that many students have processing information. Swanson and Ransby (1994) suggested that students with learning disabil-ities (LD), for example, have problems with several information-processing components, including sensory memory, short-term memory, working memory, long-term memory, and executive processing, in addition to prob-lems integrating these information-processing components. Although they cite the need for research that will lead to an understanding of the cognitive abilities of students with LD, these authors suggested that research on the academic performance of students with LD be conceptualized as an inter-action between these students' deficient cognitive processes and a variety of external variables, such as instruction and context.

Thus, content-area teachers not only must be the expert mediators of learning for all students, they also must pay attention to students with dis-abilities or other students who are at risk for failure, for whom they must be particularly mindful mediators of learning. Teachers must determine whether students in their classes have limited background experiences, difficulty understanding key conceptual information, memory problems, executive-processing problems, unfamiliarity with processes or methods of inquiry, difficulties with written formats, or an inability to generalize a specific skill from one area to another. Once they determine what deficits students have, they can choose appropriate adaptations, enhancements, and accommodations to use in their instruction.

Performing all of these tasks is particularly important because of emerging data that point to the increasing diversity among students in our nation's classrooms (Hodgkinson, 1991). Such diversity is partly the result of the inclusion of more students with disabilities in general education courses, where they are expected to receive the same instruction and take part in the same courses and statewide assessments as other students.

Fortunately, research indicates that students who are enrolled in general education classes are amenable to the adaptations that teachers make. Indeed, Vaughn, Schumm, and McIntosh (1991) reported that students liked teachers who adapted instructional procedures, provided special assis-tance, and arranged class groupings. Students were particularly receptive to adaptations that promoted learning, and they saw teachers who provided these adaptations as better able to meet the needs of students.

Mediation of Instruction: How Can Students Be Taught to Learn?

Having a thorough knowledge of content, learning theory, and student needs is an important foundation, but it works only if this knowledge can be translated into instruction that focuses on both critical content knowledge and the management of an environment that facilitates learning for all students. A particularly important framework for this kind of instruction involves students in a *learning partnership* with the teacher (Bulgren & Lenz, 1996). This can occur in a variety of ways, depending on the students' backgrounds and repertoires of learning strategies. The teacher recognizes that students who use learning strategies have found ways to approach learning tasks that guide their personal thinking and actions, help them reflect on outcomes, and adjust their actions as needed. The teacher as expert also recognizes that when students do not use or have knowledge of learning strategies, they are not learning independently in efficient or effective ways.

Therefore, the teacher is not merely a presenter of content information to those who are best able to assimilate that information. The teacher also is a mediator who is mindful of how a variety of students learn and the supports and instruction that some students may need to become learning partners. As a mediator, the teacher explains teaching techniques to students, clarifies expectations related to students acting as partners in the learning process, and holds students accountable for their role in the learning process. In short, such teaching unites the teacher and students in a learning partnership by providing informed, explicit, and interactive instruction. Such teaching also prompts students to activate their own background knowledge and bring it to bear as part of the group learning process by encouraging them to contribute their insights and knowledge. This type of instruction is particularly important for students with learning disabilities, who often do not recognize the usefulness or even the existence of innovative teaching practices when the teacher uses them (Lenz, Alley, & Schumaker, 1987).

Unfortunately, for the most part, teachers do not provide explicit instruction; that is, they do not lead students through the rationales, procedures, and expected outcomes associated with learning (Bulgren & Lenz, 1996). Nevertheless, a central instructional principle to which teachers must adhere is that they must inform students about the elements of instruction and learning partnerships, and they also must guide students in how to benefit from that instruction so that they move to the level of independent learners. This principle is based on research findings that cut across the areas of curriculum, instruction, educational psychology, and special education. It can guide teacher thinking, planning, and teaching in content areas and define the teacher's role as a professional, a content expert, a mediator of student understanding, and a partner in the learning process. This principle has been a major theme running through the experimental literature in the area of secondary content-area instruction.

WHAT THE RESEARCH LITERATURE TELLS US

Several instructional techniques that are based on the principles discussed previously have been developed and investigated for teacher use in general education courses to create learning partnerships with students. The instructional techniques that qualified for inclusion in this review are those that teachers can use to help students of varying backgrounds, skills, and abilities meet complex content-area course demands. Specifically, the techniques that were selected for this review are those that (1) focus on student acquisition of content knowledge, (2) have been used at the secondary level, (3) have been used in content-area classes in which students with disabilities were enrolled or could be used in those classes, and (4) are based on teacher mediation of learning. Experimental studies were included if they (1) employed an experimental design that controlled for the effects of extraneous variables, (2) presented student performance data associated with the use of the technique, and (3) reported positive effects related to the use of the technique.

This research synthesis focuses on studies that were conducted in inclusive secondary content classes or in classes that replicated such classes as closely as possible. However, a few exceptions were made by including studies that were part of lines of research that may have been conducted in resource rooms or laboratory settings and that focused on instructional techniques that may eventually be used in inclusive secondary content instruction.

The scope of this review was defined in such a way that planning interventions and instruction associated with technology-assisted instruction were not included because they are covered in other chapters of this book. (See Chapter 2 for a review of planning for inclusive classes and Chapter 6 for a review of technology-assisted instruction.) In addition, this review was specifically limited to interventions described by Deshler et al. (2001) as Level 1 interventions. These interventions are designed for use by subject-area teachers with diverse classes to compensate for limited levels of literacy presented by some students and to promote all students' understanding and mastery of content information.

Two types of Level 1 instructional techniques were found: (1) methods designed to help students organize and comprehend information from the course textbook, and (2) methods based on mediation of content information by teachers and students using a variety of sources in addition to the main text. In other words, instructional procedures varied depending on the information source and the extent of teacher mediation.

In some cases, the source of the content information was the course text, and the teacher used an innovative instructional technique to help students organize and comprehend that information. This type of instructional technique is often used before students read a passage; that is, it serves as an advance organizer for a reading assignment. An advance organizer is information delivered in advance of the learning task to help students understand what they need to do or learn as they complete the learning task. Varying degrees of teacher guidance and interaction with students may be combined with advance organizers. Still other instructional techniques may be used as the student is reading a text or after the student has completed reading a text. All of the instructional interventions that focus on the text as the major information source will be referred to as *text-based interventions*.

In other interventions included in this review, the teacher and students constructed an understanding of the information using both the prior knowledge of individuals in the class and information derived from primary sources and materials in addition to the main text. Interactions between students and the teacher are usually an important component of these interventions. They will be referred to as *multiple-source-based interventions*.

This distinction between text-based and multiple-source-based interventions reflects classifications associated with the demands of today's secondary courses. In some cases, students are asked to answer *textually explicit* questions (the answer is stated directly in a text) or *textually implicit* questions (the answer is found in several places in a text or requires reader knowledge that is not present in the text). In other cases, students are asked to answer *scripturally implicit* questions (the answer must come from the mind of the reader but is directly related to the interpretation of a text) or *textually-scripturally implicit* questions (the reader must search for sources in the text and use prior knowledge to construct an answer) (Kansas State Board of Education, 1995). Thus, instructional techniques are based on these and even more complex demands involving the active construction of knowledge on the part of students.

Many of the text-based and multiple-source-based interventions reviewed here include a teaching device, that is, a visual or auditory stimulus that is designed to achieve a singular goal in promoting learning. In general, devices may be designed to help students organize, understand, and/or recall content information. Visual devices include study guides, sketches, pictures, maps, demonstrations, and a range of diagrams such as semantic maps or webs, grids, matrices, tables, and other graphic organizers. Auditory devices include stories, analogies, verbal organizers, role-play activities, and even critical questions. Often, these devices are presented by the teacher to students or created by teachers and students working together using an instructional "routine." Routines, in this context, are sequenced sets of instructional procedures. They are used by teachers to present or develop a specific teaching device that promotes broad learning goals associated with acquiring and demonstrating content knowledge.

One set of routines that focuses on constructing learning devices and has been designed to help all students, including students with disabilities learn in general education classes is called the *Content Enhancement Routines* (Lenz & Bulgren, 1995; Schumaker, Deshler, & McKnight, 2001). These routines are used to *enhance content learning* by all students enrolled in a course, and they entail the following on the part of the teacher: thinking deeply about critical content that students need to learn; organizing and manipulating that content to make it learner friendly; delivering that content in a way that keeps students active in the learning process; and reviewing the information in a way that enhances students' retention of it.

Each routine is a combination of teaching behaviors targeted to a particular instructional goal. All of the routines are founded on several research-based learning principles: (1) students learn more when they are actively engaged in learning activities; (2) students learn abstract content more easily if it is presented in a concrete form; (3) students learn more information when the structure or organization of that information is presented to them first and when relationships among pieces of information are explicitly discussed; (4) students are more likely to learn new information if it is tied to information they already know; and (5) students learn more important information if that information is distinguished from unimportant information.

Studies have been conducted on three kinds of Content Enhancement Routines that are relevant to this review: *Organizing Routines, Understanding Routines*, and *Recall Routines*. Specifically, teachers use Organizing Routines to show students how course information is organized and related; they use Understanding Routines to teach students about major concepts in a course, such as the concept of "democracy"; and they use Recall Routines to help students understand and remember important details related to a course.

In addition to the studies focusing on Content Enhancement Routines, studies have been conducted by other researchers in the areas of organization, understanding, and remembering of content information using other types of devices and routines. All of these studies will be reviewed together within the three categories of routines, as well as within the categories of text-based and multiple-source-based interventions.

INSTRUCTIONAL PRACTICES RELATED TO ORGANIZING INFORMATION

Organizing devices and routines often serve as advance organizers to prepare students to learn content information. Teachers can use advance organizers to strengthen a student's cognitive structures, which Ausubel (1963) defined as the student's knowledge of a subject matter at a given time with regard to its organization, clarity, and stability. Because students with disabilities often lack relevant background knowledge, are unable to organize information so that it can be easily retrieved, are frequently not motivated to learn, and are typically inactive during learning activities, advance organizers are especially useful for them. Advance organizers can serve as vehicles for presenting the background knowledge required to understand a lesson, for highlighting organizational patterns about which students should be aware, for motivating students to learn, and for communicating to students expectations about what they should be doing during instructional activities.

In planning for instruction that optimizes access to the curriculum for all students, teachers often use planning routines and associated devices. These are developed prior to instruction and help teachers identify what content information is most important to teach so that all students learn the most critical information (see Chapter 2). In addition, these planning routines and associated devices can be used in classroom instruction to convey the structure of the information and to emphasize the most important information. Therefore, planning routines also may be used in instructional practice as both text-based and multiple-source-based interventions.

Text-Based Interventions

Advance organizers have been used to prepare students to learn from texts or other written material. For example, Lenz (1984) conducted a study to determine the effects of an advance organizer on students' learning and retention of written information. The advance organizer provided background and organizational information about a reading assignment before the students had read the assignment. Students with learning disabilities and peers without disabilities participated in the study and were randomly assigned to an experimental or a control group. The study was conducted outside school hours (that is, not in general education classes). Students read three passages and, after reading each passage, took a test (with 36–40 items) on the information. The tests contained an equal number of questions about important and unimportant information in the passages. Considerable effort was devoted to making the passages and tests parallel and equivalent. Students in the experimental group received an advance organizer before they read each passage; those in the control group did not.

A posttest-only control-group design revealed significant differences between the recall performance of students with LD in the experimental group ($M = 19$ questions answered correctly) and students with LD in the control group ($M = 13$ questions answered correctly). (No differences were found for the students without disabilities.) Additionally, students with LD in the control group correctly answered significantly more questions about unimportant information than about important information. Those in the experimental group answered significantly more questions about important information than about unimportant information.

Lenz's results indicated that the teacher's use of organizers helped students with LD to discriminate important information from unimportant information. In addition, the organizers helped them store that important information so that it could be recalled later for a test on the information. The result of this more efficient storage was that the performance of students with LD on a test covering important information was not substantially different from the performance of learners without disabilities when they did not receive an advance organizer (19 questions answered correctly vs. 21 questions answered correctly). These findings suggest that an advance organizer that precedes a reading assignment can be a beneficial tool for enhancing the test performance of low-performing students. However, the effects of the use of advance organizers before reading assignments have not been formally determined in general education subject-area classes in relation to typical reading assignments in those classes. Thus, their utility for such purposes is unknown.

Multiple-Source-Based Interventions

In a companion study, Lenz et al. (1987) tested the use of advance organizers in relation to multiple-source-based information, particularly in relation to lectures and other activities that took place in a variety of secondary subject-area classes. They developed a Lesson Organizer Routine consisting of several components and trained general education teachers to use it in their secondary courses (history, English, and physical science). Designed to be used at the beginning of each lesson, the components of the routine required the teacher to tell students about

- the purpose of the advance organizer for the lesson,
- the actions to be taken by the teacher and the students during the lesson,
- the topic and subtopics to be covered in the lesson,
- background knowledge related to the lesson,
- concepts to be learned,
- reasons for learning the information,
- new vocabulary,
- organizational frameworks for the information in the lesson, and
- desired lesson outcomes.

The effects of the routine were evaluated through a multiple-probe across-students design (see Figure 3.1 for an example of this design). Students with learning disabilities were interviewed after each class to see what they had learned from the lesson. These students had been enrolled in the general education classes as part of an inclusion effort. Lenz et al. (1987) found that teachers who used only a few of the Lesson Organizer components at the start of the study could be trained in less than an hour

Figure 3.1   Example of a Multiple-Probe Across-Students Design

Probe Test Sessions

	Before Interventions			After Interventions			
Student 1	X	X	X	X	X	X	X
Student 2	X	X	X	X	X	X	X

to implement the routine above the 80% mastery level in the classroom. They also found that, when students with disabilities were specifically taught to attend to the teacher's use of the Lesson Organizer Routine, the number of relevant statements they made after the lesson about the lesson content increased substantially, compared with the number of statements they made after lessons when they had not been informed about how to attend to the Lesson Organizer. For example, one group made an average of 13.7 statements before any training, 18.5 after teacher training, and 29 after student training. Another group made an average of 22 statements before any training, 26.8 after teacher training, and 29 after student training.

For the unit level of instruction, Lenz, Bulgren, Schumaker, Deshler, and Boudah (1994) created the *Unit Organizer Routine*, which is designed for use when introducing a unit of instruction in subject-area courses and for keeping students apprised of progress through the unit. They defined a unit as "any chunk of content that a teacher selects to organize information into lessons and that ends in some type of test or closure activity" (p. 2). To introduce such a unit of content using the routine, teachers explained to students the relationship between the new unit and the course as a whole and other units in the course. They also created a visual map of the unit's content and explained the relationships between parts of the unit (see Figures 2.3 and 2.4 in Chapter 2 for an example). Additionally, they shared with students a schedule of activities and assignments to be completed during the unit, major questions that would be answered during the unit, and cognitive strategies to be used during the unit to process information.

Six secondary teachers of general education science and social studies courses (three at the middle school level and three at the high school level) used the Unit Organizer Routine. The researchers studied the teachers' use of the routine and the routine's effects during an eight-month period in heterogeneous classes in which students with disabilities were enrolled. They found that teachers could learn to use the routine above the 80% mastery level in their classes after about three hours of workshop instruction. Further, when teachers used the routine, on average, understanding and retention of information by low-achieving students, students with LD, and average-achieving students improved substantially over baseline.

This was reflected in unit test scores and in scores on unit content maps and explanations of those maps. Students of teachers who had referred to the Unit Organizer regularly and consistently scored an average of 15 percentage points higher on unit tests than students of teachers who had referred to it only once or twice during the units (Joint Committee on Teacher Planning for Students with Disabilities, 1995).

For the course level of instruction, Lenz and colleagues created the *Course Organizer Routine* (Lenz, Schumaker, Deshler, & Bulgren, 1998). Like the Unit Organizer Routine, this routine is designed for use when introducing a body of content; however, it is designed for use when introducing a whole course and for keeping students apprised of progress throughout the course. After the Course Organizer is introduced at the beginning of the year, the routine is used after each unit has been completed to help students integrate what was learned in the unit with the "big picture" of the course as a whole and to explain how the upcoming unit fits into the course and relates to other units. When using the Course Organizer Routine, teachers share with students approximately 10 course questions that will drive their progress through the course; a visual map of the course units (see Figures 2.6 and 2.7 in Chapter 2); guidelines and criteria for grading student performance during the course; principles, routines, cognitive strategies, communication systems, and options to guide their interactions and learning; and major concepts to be learned in the course.

The researchers worked with 12 secondary subject-area teachers who taught heterogeneous general education classes in which students with disabilities were enrolled. The teachers learned to use the Course Organizer Routine at mastery levels after about three hours of instruction. The teachers who used the routine spent more time at the beginning of the course introducing major course ideas, concepts, themes, and routines to students than did the comparison teachers. They integrated an average of eight innovative instructional practices into their courses, whereas comparison teachers integrated an average of one innovative practice into their courses. Furthermore, students with LD enrolled in their classes correctly answered an average of three course questions at the beginning of their courses and eight course questions (out of 10 essay questions) at the end of the courses, whereas comparison students with LD (enrolled in other similar courses) correctly answered an average of three course questions at the beginning of the courses and four at the end of the courses (Joint Committee on Teacher Planning for Students with Disabilities, 1995).

INSTRUCTIONAL PRACTICES FOR IMPROVING UNDERSTANDING OF INFORMATION

In addition to helping students organize information, instructional devices and routines can be used to promote students' understanding of information.

Such understanding may involve the acquisition of vocabulary; the comprehension of content information; the analysis and manipulation of facts, concepts, relationships, and evidence; or the generalization of learning. As with instructional practices associated with the organization of information, some research studies in this area have focused on text-based interventions, whereas others have targeted multiple-source-based interventions.

Text-Based Interventions

One intervention that has been used to promote student understanding of written information is the study guide. To prepare a study guide, the teacher identifies important sections of a text, analyzes them, identifies important content within them, and then develops questions or incomplete sentences (that is, sentences in which important words have been blanked out) about that information to include on the study guide. The teacher may also write the page number on which the answer can be found next to each item on the guide. The compiled study guide is copied and distributed to students, who subsequently read the passage, answer the questions or fill in the missing words in the sentences, and check their answers against an answer key (Lovitt & Horton, 1988).

Lovitt, Rudsit, Jenkins, Pious, and Benedetti (1985) researched the use of such a study guide to help secondary students learn science information. The specific study guide was created based on a chapter in the students' seventh-grade physical science text. It consisted of incomplete sentences that the students had to complete as they listened to the teacher's lecture on the chapter, vocabulary exercises with words for students to define, definitions for which students were asked to provide the correct word, and lists of words and definitions that the students were asked to match.

Three randomly selected groups of students enrolled in seventh-grade science courses participated: (1) students who were taken out of the regular classroom in a small group for 10 minutes per day and were given the answers by the science teacher to fill in on their study guides (the study-guide group); (2) students who were taken out of the classroom in a small group for 10 minutes per day, were supervised by the researcher, and quizzed each other in pairs on the information using structured practice sheets (the precision-teaching group); and (3) a control group who took part in traditional instructional activities (such as lectures, labs, and reading assignments) in the classroom. The routine that the science teacher used in conjunction with the study guide involved lecturing, placing transparencies of the study guide pages on the overhead projector, modeling how to fill in the answers on the study guide, asking questions about the information, and arranging games related to filling in the study guide.

The researchers found a significant difference between the gain scores of the combined group of experimental students and the gain scores of the control students on a multiple-choice test in favor of the combined group of experimental students. However, the actual mean scores that the groups earned on the posttest did not differ much. Specifically, students in the experimental and control groups earned mean pretest scores of 47% and 55% and mean posttest scores of 67% and 65%, respectively. There were no differences between the two experimental groups (that is, the group that received the study guide and the group that received precision teaching). The gain scores for medium- and low-achieving students in the experimental groups were significantly different from the gain scores for those types of students in the control group. However, the scores earned by students with LD were not separated from the scores of the other low-achieving students (there was only one student with LD in each low-achieving group), so determining how those students performed is not possible.

An important consideration related to this study is that the teacher worked with the students on the study guide in the study-guide group and did not work with the students in the other groups. This difference in teacher attention may have confounded the study's results. Additionally, the routine was not applied during whole-class activities, and the data for students with disabilities were not separated from the other data. Thus, the effects of study guides in large classes and on students with disabilities cannot be determined from this investigation.

In two later studies on study guides reported by Horton and Lovitt (1989), the data gathered from students with LD were segregated from the data gathered from remedial students and regular students, and general education teachers implemented the interventions in their social studies and science classes. In both studies, the study guides comprised 15 short-answer questions based on passages in the students' textbooks. In the first study, a counterbalanced design was used to compare the effects of a teacher-directed study-guide condition (similar to the one described previously) with the effects of a self-study condition. In the teacher-directed condition, the students read and reread a passage and completed a study guide while the teacher directed the activity by modeling how to fill it out using an overhead projector, and then the students studied the guide on their own. In the self-study condition, students read and reread a passage, took notes, and studied as they normally would. Significantly higher scores on multiple-choice tests were earned by students with LD ($M = 68\%$), remedial students ($M = 85\%$), and general education students ($M = 86\%$) when the teacher helped them complete their study guides than when they studied the passages on their own ($M = 49\%$, 68%, and 73%, respectively).

In the second study conducted by Horton and Lovitt, a similar design was used to compare a student-directed study-guide condition with a self-study condition. In the student-directed condition, students used study guides that contained page number references to help them locate answers to the questions in the assigned passage. Again, the study-guide condition resulted in significantly higher test scores among students with LD ($M = 77\%$), remedial students ($M = 81\%$), and regular students ($M = 87\%$) than the self-study condition ($M = 43\%$, 53%, and 55%, respectively). This study supported earlier findings reported by Bergerud, Lovitt, and Horton (1988) that showed favorable effects when high school students with LD used student-directed study guides with science materials in a resource room.

Instead of study guides, graphic organizers in the form of semantic webs, matrices, or other branching diagrams have been used to help students understand information in a text. Horton, Lovitt, and Bergerud (1990) conducted a series of three studies on the use of graphic organizers in inclusive science and social studies classes at the 7th- and 10th-grade levels to help students understand their texts. The graphic organizers were prepared for passages selected from textbooks using a hierarchical format arranged by major and minor categories, similar to an outline. Most of the participating classes included students with learning disabilities and general education students. One class contained remedial students only.

Each of the three studies evaluated the effects of one of three conditions of graphic organizer use: teacher-directed graphic organizers, student-directed graphic organizers with text references, or student-directed graphic organizers with clues. In the teacher-directed condition, students read the passage, and then the teacher put a transparency of the graphic organizer on the overhead projector, asked the students questions, and gradually uncovered different parts of the organizer for the students to copy. In the student-directed with-text-references condition, the students read the passage and filled in their own graphic organizers by answering written questions about the passage and using page and paragraph numbers corresponding to the reading passage. Finally, in the student-directed clues condition, the students read the passage and filled in their own graphic organizers by answering written questions with an answer chosen from a list of randomly ordered items. Students in all of the conditions were given five minutes to study their organizers. A counterbalanced design was used in each of the three studies to compare the effects of the graphic organizer interventions to self-study of the reading passage.

Horton et al. found that all three graphic organizer conditions produced significantly higher student performance on a graphic organizer test than when students studied the information on their own. To complete the graphic organizer test, students were asked to fill in the boxes of a graphic organizer similar to the one they had studied. Students with LD earned a mean score of 73% in the teacher-directed condition, a mean score of 71% in the student-directed with-text-references condition, and a mean score of 67% in the student-directed with-clues condition compared with the self-study mean scores of 30%, 19%, and 10%, respectively. The scores of the remedial students and general education students showed the same general pattern, with significant differences in all cases.

This series of studies on graphic organizers indicated that use of graphic organizers can improve student learning in general education classes. However, because the test that was used simply required students to fill in components of an empty graphic organizer that was exactly like the one they had previously constructed, there is no way of knowing how much understanding of the information the students gained. Additionally, because the students in the self-study condition were seeing the graphic organizer for the first time when they took the test, they probably had no idea how to construct the information in it.

A third type of device that has been studied in conjunction with understanding text-based information is called the *relationship chart*. The routine that is used in conjunction with this device is called semantic feature analysis (Bos & Anders, 1990). To prepare a relationship chart, the teacher examines a text passage before class and identifies important vocabulary words and features associated with each important word. These words and features are entered into the relationship chart. The words are listed on one axis of the relationship chart and the features on the other. During class, the teacher puts a transparency of the chart on the overhead projector and conducts a discussion with the students to introduce the words and the features. When necessary, definitions are created for words with which the students are not familiar by using a dictionary. Then the students predict the relationships between the words and the features on the chart and enter symbols into boxes on the chart to depict those predicted relationships. Next, the students independently read the targeted passage from their textbooks to confirm or disconfirm their predictions and to clarify unknown relationships. Finally, the students discuss their findings and change the chart as needed.

Anders, Bos, and Filip (1984) conducted an initial study, and Bos, Anders, Filip, and Jaffe (1989) conducted a follow-up study on the use of a relationship chart and semantic feature analysis related to a textbook passage covering the Fourth Amendment to the U.S. Constitution. Participants were high school students with LD who were enrolled in English and social studies classes taught in a resource room by a special education teacher. These intact classes were randomly assigned to either (1) a condition in which the students participated in a semantic feature analysis (SFA) exercise, as described previously, or (2) a condition in which they looked up and wrote definitions of the targeted vocabulary words (the vocabulary look-up condition). The textbook was written at the sixth-grade level. The students in the SFA condition earned significantly higher scores than students in the vocabulary look-up condition on a multiple-choice test of vocabulary knowledge and conceptual understanding immediately after instruction and six months after instruction. Specifically, students in the SFA condition earned a mean score of 8 points on both the conceptual understanding items and the vocabulary items, whereas those in the vocabulary look-up condition earned a mean score of 6 on the conceptual items and 5 on the vocabulary items (out of 10 points in each case).

Because this research was conducted in self-contained content classes with students with LD only, and because the researchers implemented the instruction, questions remain with regard to the effects of this routine on the same population in general education classes, teachers' reaction to it, and its effectiveness in promoting learning by a variety of types of students.

Multiple-Source-Based Interventions

In addition to the studies that have been conducted on text-based interventions to promote student understanding, research has also been conducted on instructing students so that they can understand the critical information needed to succeed throughout a course. Such understanding often requires teacher mediation of more than one source. In these cases, the teacher must identify the critical concepts or conceptual relationships that are prerequisites for success in a course and use a variety of sources, including his or her own expertise, to mediate understanding for all students.

Several studies have focused on using Understanding Routines and devices for this type of mediation. In these cases, the aim of the mediation process is to ensure that students acquire new information by integrating that information with prior knowledge and by becoming actively engaged in analyzing and manipulating the new information. Much research has provided a foundation for developing methods to help students understand critical information (Ausubel, Novak, & Hanesian, 1968; Bruner, Goodnow, & Austin, 1956; Gagné, 1965; Klausmeier & Associates, 1979; Klausmeier & Ripple, 1971; Merrill & Tennyson, 1977). Several components have been used within Understanding Routines to enhance students' content understanding: (1) attributes, properties, or characteristics according to which items are placed in a specific category; (2) rules by which these attributes are joined in a concept class; (3) hierarchical patterns of superordinate, coordinate, and subordinate concepts into which a concept fits; and (4) instances or examples of a concept.

All of the studies on Understanding Routines that integrate these components have been based on the content enhancement approach described previously. The purpose of these routines is to teach information about complex, abstract concepts (for instance, "democracy," "thesis," or "equation") in a way that enhances students' understanding and memory of the information. Bulgren, Schumaker, and Deshler (1988) conducted a study in this area on the *Concept Mastery Routine* (Bulgren, Deshler, & Schumaker, 1993). This routine uses a Concept Diagram, a graphic device that organizes concept information into categories that (1) name and define the concept; (2) relate to characteristics that are always, sometimes, or never present in the concept; and (3) relate to examples and nonexamples of the concept (see Figure 3.2 for an example). The teacher prepares a rough draft of the Concept Diagram before class. During class, the teacher leads a discussion about the concept, and then the teacher and each student fill in blank Concept Diagrams about the concept. The final diagram is a product that is coconstructed by the teacher and students and uses information from a variety of sources, in addition to the main course text.

Figure 3.2 Concept Diagram

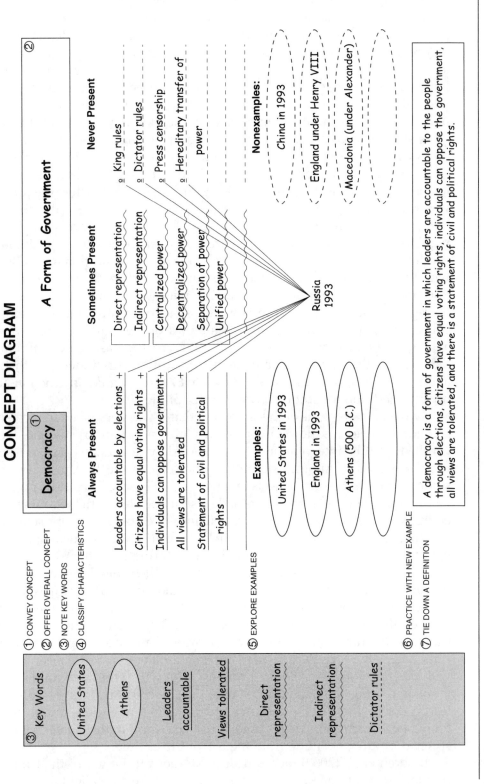

Used with permission of the Center for Research on Learning, University of Kansas.

Through the use of multiple-baseline designs, Bulgren et al.'s (1988) study evaluated whether secondary teachers could learn to use the Concept Mastery Routine and determined the effects of its use on students' performance in general education courses. The results showed that the teachers learned to use the routine at mastery levels in less than three hours. Furthermore, student performance was enhanced in a variety of ways when the teachers used the routine to introduce one concept during each unit. With regard to notetaking, for example, both students with LD and other students wrote three times more concept-related information in their notes when the teachers used the routine than in the baseline condition.

With regard to specially designed concept tests, mean test scores increased above baseline levels for all groups of students when the routine was used. Concept test scores improved even further when the concept information was reviewed before the test along with other material in the regularly scheduled review session, from an average of 40% in the baseline condition to 62% during the instruction and review condition for students with LD, and from 49% in the baseline condition to 83% during the instruction and review condition for students without disabilities. Test scores on regularly scheduled unit tests were also significantly higher when the concept information was reviewed as a part of the regular review. Here, average student scores increased from 60% in the baseline condition to 71% during the instruction and review condition for students with LD, and from 72% in the baseline condition to 87% during the instruction and review condition for students without disabilities.

Two major strengths of this study are that it was conducted in inclusive secondary general education classes in which a variety of students were enrolled, and the intervention was conducted by teachers who were teaching those classes. Another strength is that one of the measures was the students' unit test scores on tests that were actually scheduled to be given in the classes. These were publisher-made tests associated with the course textbooks. As such, they represent a real-life measure of student performance.

Bulgren, Deshler, Schumaker, and Lenz (2000) conducted another study on the instruction of conceptual information after designing a second Understanding Routine, the *Concept Anchoring Routine* (Bulgren, Schumaker, & Deshler, 1994). This routine may be used to help students connect new knowledge about a concept to prior knowledge by using a device called the *Anchoring Table* (see Figure 3.3 for an example). Like the Concept Diagram, the teacher creates a draft of an Anchoring Table before class. This table is used to display information about a new concept along with paired information about a concept with which the students are very familiar. During class, the teacher uses the Concept Anchoring Routine to lead a discussion. As the discussion proceeds, the teacher and students fill in blank Anchoring Tables. Again, the final draft of the table is a coconstructed product resulting from the use of the routine.

Bulgren et al. (2000) reported three studies on the use of the Concept Anchoring Routine. In the first, two concepts were taught in general

Figure 3.3   Anchoring Table

(**Anchoring Table**)

Unit: _____   Name: _____   Date: _____

③

Known Information → furnace	② **Known Concept** Temperature control systems in modern buildings		① **New Concept** Temperature control systems in warm-blooded animals
	④ **Characteristics of Known Concept**	⑥ **Characteristics Shared**	⑤ **Characteristics of New Concept**
air conditioner 72 degrees	Building temperature is set to stay the same (72 degrees). →	Inside temperature is supposed to stay the same.	Body temperature stays the same (98.6 degrees). ←
thermostat notices change	Thermostats notice temperature changes. →	Something notices temperature changes.	Nervous & endocrine systems notice temperature changes. ←
set temp. anywhere	When temperature changes, thermostat sends electronic signals. →	When temperature changes, a sensor sends signals.	When temperature changes, nervous & endocrine systems send signals. ←
electronic signals	Signals start action in furnace or air conditioner. →	Signals start other systems.	Signals start action in circulatory system or muscles. ←
	Furnace or air conditioner corrects building temperature to 72 degrees. →	System corrects temperature.	Circulatory system & muscles correct body temperature. ←

----

⑦ **Understanding of the New Concept**

Temperature control systems in warm-blooded animals are like those in modern buildings because the temperature is supposed to stay the same, but when the temperature changes, something notices. A sensor sends signals to start other systems that correct the temperature.

ANCHORS Linking Steps:	1. Announce the New Concept	2. Name Known Concept	3. Collect Known Information	4. Highlight Characteristics of Known Concept	5. Observe Characteristics of New Concept	6. Reveal Characteristics Shared	7. State Understanding of New Concept

Used with permission of the Center for Research on Learning, University of Kansas.

education science classes by one of the researchers. A counterbalanced design was used with two experimental conditions: (1) the use of the routine and Anchoring Table, and (2) the use of traditional lecture methods (see Figure 3.4 for a depiction of the design). A 32-item multiple-choice test served as the outcome measure. Results showed that when students with LD participated in the Concept Anchoring Routine along with other students assigned to their general education classes, they earned an average test score of 69% on one concept and 55% on another. In comparison, students with LD who participated in traditional instruction about the same concepts earned an average test score of 40% on one concept and 36% on the other, respectively. Comparable differences were found for other low-achieving students and for normally achieving students.

In the second study, Bulgren et al. (2000) trained 10 teachers to use the routine in their secondary general education classes. Using a multiple-probe across-teachers design, they found that the teachers learned to use the routine in three hours so that they could perform it in their classrooms at mastery levels.

In the third study, one of the teachers who had participated in the first study taught four concepts to the students in her seventh-grade life science classes. She taught two of the concepts using the Concept Anchoring Routine and the Anchoring Table and the other two concepts using traditional lecture methods. When the students took a test on the four concepts, they earned average test scores of 87% and 70% on the concepts taught through the use of the routine and average test scores of 27% and 42% on the concepts taught through traditional means. The differences between the student scores were significant for each pair of concepts taught.

More recently, Bulgren, Schumaker, Deshler, Lenz, and Marquis (2002) conducted a study on a third Understanding Routine, the *Concept*

Figure 3.4   Experimental Design for the Concept Anchoring Routine Study

| | Condition 1 | | | | Condition 2 | | | |
	HA	NA	LA	LD	HA	NA	LA	LD
Concept 1	CAR	CAR	CAR	CAR	T	T	T	T
Concept 2	T	T	T	T	CAR	CAR	CAR	CAR

Note: HA = high-achieving students; NA = normal-achieving students; LA = low-achieving students; LD = students with learning disabilities; CAR = Concept Anchoring Routine; T = traditional lecture-discussion methods.

Comparison Routine (Bulgren, Lenz, Deshler, & Schumaker, 1995). This routine was designed for helping students compare and contrast two or more concepts. Before class, the teacher drafts a graphic display of how two or more concepts are alike and different. This graphic display or device, called a *Comparison Table,* shows the similar and dissimilar characteristics of each concept. During class, the teacher uses the Concept Comparison Routine to lead an interactive discussion with the students and help them create a Comparison Table. Again, the final product of the activity is a graphic device that is constructed by the teacher and the students working together (see Figure 3.5).

Results of the study, which was conducted with stratified randomly assigned groups in a counterbalanced design with researchers delivering the instruction (see Figure 3.6 for a depiction of the design), showed that, when the Concept Comparison Routine was used, students with LD recalled significantly more information than when traditional instruction was implemented, with a mean difference of more than 14 percentage points in favor of the experimental condition. On average, other groups of students, including low-achieving, average-achieving, and high-achieving students, also performed better in the experimental condition.

Bulgren et al. (2002) also conducted a study with 10 secondary general education teachers. Through the use of a multiple-probe across-teachers design, they showed that teachers could learn to use the Concept Comparison Routine in their classrooms at mastery levels given three hours of training. They did not collect data on student performance in actual general education classes after the students had participated in the routine.

Another routine that can be used with information taken from multiple sources is the *ORDER Routine.* After students have taken notes during a lecture or after they have read an assignment, teachers can use this routine to help students decide what information is important to know, choose a format for visually depicting that information, draw a graphic organizer fitting that format (see Figure 3.7 for an example), explain the graphic organizer to someone else, and then use the graphic organizer to study for a test or to guide written work.

Scanlon, Deshler, and Schumaker (1996) studied the use of this routine by 12 middle school teachers and their students in general education classrooms. Six classes were randomly assigned to the experimental condition, and six were randomly assigned to the comparison condition. During the pretest and posttest, students were given a reading passage and asked to identify the structure of the information and create a graphic organizer for the information in the passage. Results showed that the students in the experimental classes earned significantly higher scores on the posttest than their counterparts in the comparison classes after controlling for their pretest scores. On both the pretest and posttest, students without LD earned higher average scores than the students with LD. Nevertheless, experimental students with LD made greater pretest-to-posttest gains than did the experimental students without LD.

Figure 3.5   Comparison Table

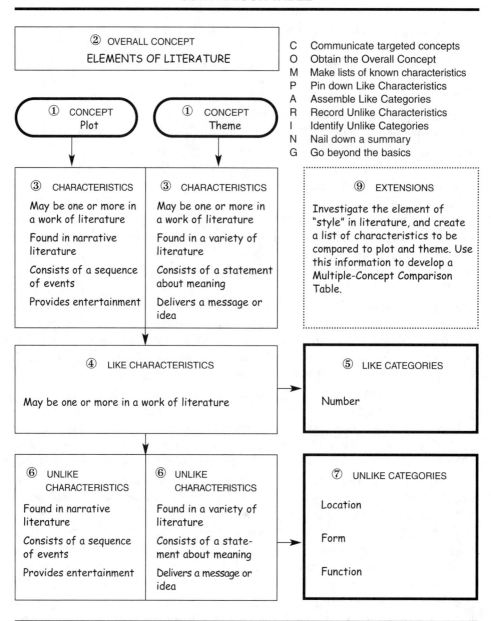

COMPARISON TABLE

② OVERALL CONCEPT
ELEMENTS OF LITERATURE

C   Communicate targeted concepts
O   Obtain the Overall Concept
M   Make lists of known characteristics
P   Pin down Like Characteristics
A   Assemble Like Categories
R   Record Unlike Characteristics
I   Identify Unlike Categories
N   Nail down a summary
G   Go beyond the basics

① CONCEPT
Plot

① CONCEPT
Theme

③ CHARACTERISTICS

May be one or more in a work of literature

Found in narrative literature

Consists of a sequence of events

Provides entertainment

③ CHARACTERISTICS

May be one or more in a work of literature

Found in a variety of literature

Consists of a statement about meaning

Delivers a message or idea

⑨ EXTENSIONS

Investigate the element of "style" in literature, and create a list of characteristics to be compared to plot and theme. Use this information to develop a Multiple-Concept Comparison Table.

④ LIKE CHARACTERISTICS

May be one or more in a work of literature

⑤ LIKE CATEGORIES

Number

⑥ UNLIKE CHARACTERISTICS

Found in narrative literature

Consists of a sequence of events

Provides entertainment

⑥ UNLIKE CHARACTERISTICS

Found in a variety of literature

Consists of a state-ment about meaning

Delivers a message or idea

⑦ UNLIKE CATEGORIES

Location

Form

Function

⑧ SUMMARY

Two elements of literature are plot and theme. They are alike in terms of the number used in any piece of literature (there may be more than one plot or theme in a piece of literature). They are different in their location in literature, the form they take, and the function they serve.

Used with permission of the Center for Research on Learning, University of Kansas.

Figure 3.6   Experimental Design for the Concept Comparison Routine Study

	Control				Experimental			
	HA	NA	LA	LD	HA	NA	LA	LD
Class 1	A	A	A	A	B	B	B	B
Class 2	B	B	B	B	A	A	A	A
Class 3	A	A	A	A	B	B	B	B
Class 4	B	B	B	B	A	A	A	A
Class 5	A	A	A	A	B	B	B	B
Class 6	B	B	B	B	A	A	A	A

Note: A = first randomly assigned half of the class; B = second randomly assigned half of the class; HA = high-achieving students; NA = normal-achieving students; LA = low-achieving students; LD = students with learning disabilities.

Preliminary results from other studies involve the use of a *Question Exploration Routine* that was designed to help students explore and answer difficult questions. Teachers use this routine and a visual device to display a critical question that is related to the content being studied and to help students explore key terms related to the question, answer supporting questions, create an answer to the critical question, and apply learned information to new topics (see Figures 3.8 and 3.9).

Results of one study conducted in an experimentally controlled setting indicated that students who learned content information through the use of this routine scored significantly better on tests designed to assess knowledge, application, and generalization of information than did students who were taught the same information in a traditional lecture-discussion format (Bulgren, Lenz, Deshler, Schumaker, & Marquis, 2004b). Results of another study conducted in randomly assigned intact classrooms indicated that when teachers used the routine to teach a regularly scheduled English literature unit, students performed better on classroom tests when the routine was used than when the traditional lecture-discussion format was used (Bulgren, Lenz, Deshler, Schumaker, & Marquis, 2004a).

A final type of multiple-source-based intervention tested to promote student content understanding is *peer instruction*. This type of instruction includes peer tutoring, student learning teams, and cooperative learning groups. In this type of intervention, students are expected to help each other learn in some way; however, the teacher, as the instructional mediator, must arrange, direct, and monitor activities associated with peer

Figure 3.7 Example of Graphic Organizer

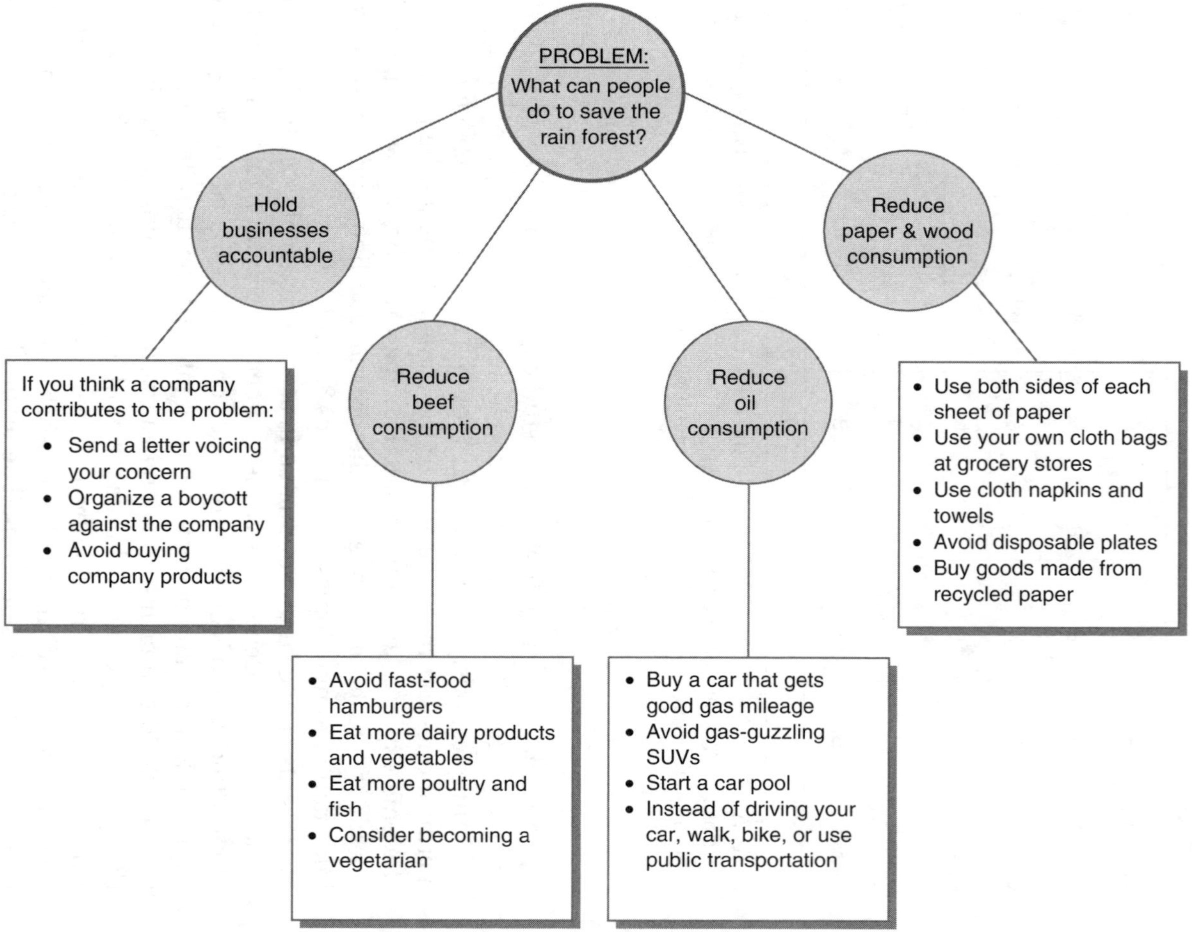

PROBLEM:
What can people do to save the rain forest?

Reduce paper & wood consumption
- Use both sides of each sheet of paper
- Use your own cloth bags at grocery stores
- Use cloth napkins and towels
- Avoid disposable plates
- Buy goods made from recycled paper

Reduce oil consumption
- Buy a car that gets good gas mileage
- Avoid gas-guzzling SUVs
- Start a car pool
- Instead of driving your car, walk, bike, or use public transportation

Reduce beef consumption
- Avoid fast-food hamburgers
- Eat more dairy products and vegetables
- Eat more poultry and fish
- Consider becoming a vegetarian

Hold businesses accountable

If you think a company contributes to the problem:
- Send a letter voicing your concern
- Organize a boycott against the company
- Avoid buying company products

Figure 3.8   Example Question Exploration Guide for the Critical Question
"How do the larval and amphibians differ?"

Question Exploration Guide

Title/standard: _Changing percentages to decimals_

Student name: _____   Date: _March 15, 2002_

Course Question #: _____   Unit Question #: _____   Lesson Question #: ___4___

① What is the Critical Question?

   How do the larval and adult stages of amphibians differ?

② What are the Key Terms and explanations?

Amphibians?	Vertebrates that are usually aquatic as larvae & terrestrial as adults.
Larval stage of amphibians?	Fishlike feeding stage that develops from an egg through metamorphosis.
Metamorphosis?	Marked transformation in form & mode of life during development.

③ What are the Supporting Questions and answers?

A. What are the characteristics of the larval stage?

B. What are the characteristics of the adult stage?

C. What are the categories of differences?

A. Characteristics of larval stage	C. Differences	B. Characteristics of adult stage
1. Breathe with gills	1. Respiratory system	1. Breathe with lungs/skin
2. Single-loop circulation	2. Vessels of circulatory system	2. Double-loop circulation
3. 2-chambered heart	3. Heart in circulatory system	3. 3-chambered heart

④ What is the Main Idea Answer?

The respiratory and circulatory systems of the adult stage of most amphibians are more complex than those of the larval stage.

⑤ How can we use the Main Idea?

   What advantage does an amphibian have as an adult that it does not have as a larva?

⑥ Is there an Overall Idea? Is there a real-world use?

   • Find and discuss an environmental problem that inhibits the development of an amphibian from the larval stage to the adult stage.

Figure 3.9   Example Question Exploration Guide for the Critical Question "Why is knowing how to change a percentage to a decimal important when you are shopping at a store?"

Question Exploration Guide

Title/standard: _Changing percentages to decimals_

Student name: _____   Date: _March 15, 2002_

Course Question #: _____   Unit Question #: _____   Lesson Question #: ___4___

① What is the Critial Question?

Why is knowing how to change a percentage to a decimal important when you are at a store sale? ("Pay only 80% of original price for this $100 coat.")

② What are the Key Terms and explanations?

Percentage	Examples of percentages:	75%	100%	50%
Decimal	Examples of decimals:	.75	1.00	.50

③ What are the Supporting Questions and answers?

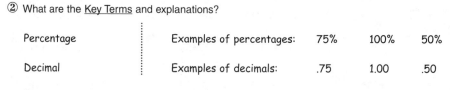

How can you write 80% as a decimal? → .80

Why is the decimal useful in the calculation? → It allows us to multiply to get the price.

How is the calculation set up? →

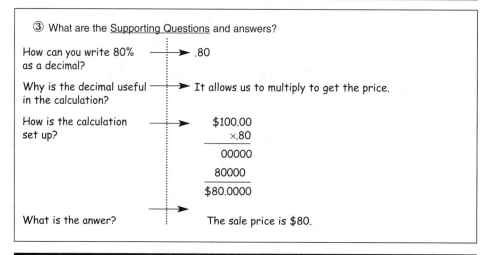

$100.00
×.80
_____
00000
80000
_____
$80.0000

What is the anwer? → The sale price is $80.

④ What is the Main Idea Answer?

Knowing how to change a percentage to a decimal allows us to accurately calculate the sale price.

⑤ How can we use the Main Idea?

What other steps would be necessary if the sign said, "20% off the original price?"

⑥ Is there an Overall Idea? Is there a real-world use?

• You are helping someone prepare a tax return. The directions tell you to calculate 6% of $12,500. How would you compute that problem? Explain your work so that the person can do it himself next year.

interaction. The goal associated with these interventions is to transfer teaching responsibilities from the teacher to a student's peer or peer group. Each student also assumes mediational responsibilities to participate in the group activity in a specified capacity. However, to optimize learning, the teacher, as the instructional mediator, arranges the groups, materials, tasks, evaluation procedures, feedback, reinforcement structures, and orientation to the process.

A number of researchers have described procedures that are designed to promote conditions that facilitate students' mediational responsibilities (e.g., Aronson, 1978; Delquadri, Greenwood, Whorton, Carta, & Hall, 1986; Jenkins & Jenkins, 1985; Johnson & Johnson, 1975; Slavin, 1983; Slavin, Madden, & Leavey, 1984). Within these interventions, the teacher becomes a special learning mediator by making students aware that they are members of a team and that each member has a role and must identify and respond to others' actions and performance. Students also must be aware of the goals of cooperation and interdependence and how attaining these goals can affect all team members' performance.

Much of the research on peer tutoring and small-group cooperative structures has been conducted at the elementary level, focusing on the acquisition of basic skills. However, Meheady, Sacca, and Harper (1987) investigated one study on a form of peer instruction, called *Classwide Student Tutoring Teams*, in general education 9th- and 10th-grade math classes that included students with and without disabilities. The classes had smaller enrollments than typical classes (15–20 students), and three to six students with disabilities were included in each class. Weekly 30-item math practice sheets were created by the general and special education teachers based on the instructional objectives set forth for the week. Each item contained a math problem and a solution to the problem.

To evaluate intervention effects, the researchers used a multiple-baseline across-settings design combined with a reversal design. During baseline, teachers implemented traditional math instruction (lecture-discussions, demonstrations, board work, math assignments), and gave students a weekly practice sheet to help them study for the upcoming weekly math quiz. During the intervention, the teacher lectured and gave demonstrations for the first two days of the week. For the next two days, the students worked together in heterogeneous groups of three students to complete problems on the practice sheet. One student acted as the tutor and read a selected problem from the sheet. The other two students then calculated an answer to the problem. If one of the students solved the problem incorrectly, the tutor explained how to solve it and required the student to solve it correctly three times. The weekly quiz was given on the last day of the week.

Results showed that weekly math quiz scores were higher in the intervention condition than in the baseline condition for students at both grade levels. For example, for ninth graders, the mean baseline quiz score was 62% compared with a mean intervention score of 83%, representing a 21-percentage-point gain. Although mean scores were not reported for students with disabilities, the authors reported that their mean score improved by 19 percentage points.

The results of this study are promising because they indicate that peer instruction can improve student performance in a class that includes students with disabilities. However, because the study was conducted in smaller classes, the feasibility and efficacy of this approach in regular-sized general education classes are unknown. Additionally, the applicability of this approach to other content areas besides math has yet to be tested.

Mastropieri, Scruggs, Spencer, and Fontana (2003) also conducted a study to evaluate the effects of peer tutoring. They compared the effects of their peer-tutoring intervention to the effects of teacher-directed guided notes on the learning of world history information by secondary students with mild disabilities. Special education teachers led the instruction. However, the number of students (16 with mild disabilities, including 15 students with LD), the length of time involved in the instruction (a nine-week quarter), and the focus on world history suggest this intervention may be useful in inclusive secondary content classes. Assignment to conditions was nonsystematic, but student achievement was similar in both conditions. Tests included pre- and posttests of reading fluency, comprehension strategies, and content tests, including end-of-chapter tests, cumulative delayed-recall tests, and a delayed-recall final exam covering the entire year, as well as interviews with teachers and students regarding their instructional preferences.

Findings indicated that students who had participated in peer tutoring significantly outperformed those who had participated in the guided-notes condition on content-area tests. Results of the student interviews suggested that students responded positively overall to tutoring and guided notes, and they provided specific relevant insights on each procedure.

INSTRUCTIONAL PRACTICES FOR IMPROVING RECALL OF INFORMATION

Another set of instructional practices that has been suggested to help students succeed in content classes, particularly in helping them recall information for tests, involves the use of mnemonic or memory devices. Mnemonic devices include keywords, pegwords, acronyms, symbolic pictures, literal pictures, phonic mnemonic devices, spelling mnemonic devices, and number-sound mnemonic devices.

Based on numerous mnemonic instruction studies conducted with their colleagues, Scruggs and Mastropieri (1990, 1992) have made a case for including mnemonic instructional practices in classrooms. They have traced the evolution of their research from theory-driven laboratory research to classroom application (Scruggs & Mastropieri, 1990). Much of their research has been conducted in special education classrooms or experimentally controlled settings using materials adaptations. They have reported promising studies suggesting that using mnemonic instruction in self-contained junior high school classes helps students to understand content in areas such as American history (Scruggs & Mastropieri, 1989b), state history (Mastropieri & Scruggs, 1989), and science (Scruggs & Mastropieri, 1989a). They have contended that their studies demonstrate that "mnemonic instructional methods and materials, both teacher- and researcher-developed, can provide dramatic gains in classroom learning for special education students" (Scruggs & Mastropieri, 1990, p. 29). However, they point to the importance of determining the applicability of mnemonic devices within the context of general classroom settings, especially because they reported that teaching students to develop their own mnemonic devices can be time-consuming (Mastropieri & Fulk, 1990).

Two studies have been conducted on a recall routine called the *Recall Enhancement Routine* (Schumaker, Bulgren, Deshler, & Lenz, 1998) that builds on this research on mnemonic devices. This routine involves the coconstruction of mnemonic devices (memory tools) by the teacher and students to help the students remember information. For example, if students are required to remember that the capital of Jamaica is Kingston, they might design a visual mnemonic device consisting of an image of a king (derived from "Kingston") eating from a jar of jam (derived from "Jamaica") to help them remember this fact. For another example, if students are required to remember that Joseph Swan invented an early form of the light bulb, they might visualize a swan holding a lightbulb in his beak (see Figure 3.10 for an example of this visual device). To use the routine, the teacher cues students that certain information is important to remember and explains why, helps students construct a mnemonic device for remembering the information, and finally, supervises student review of the information.

In the first study conducted on this routine, Bulgren et al. (1994) randomly assigned students with LD and students without disabilities in the seventh and eighth grades to experimental and control groups. All of the students received the same lecture, in which 40 facts were embedded, and participated in a review of the information. The review for students in the experimental group included presentation of mnemonic devices that students could use to remember half of the important facts in the lecture. The review for the control group included re-presentation of the same important information. All of the students took a 40-item multiple-choice test (half of the items were related to reviewed facts and half were related to nonreviewed facts).

Results showed that students with LD answered more test items related to reviewed facts correctly when the routine was used (their mean score was 71%) than when facts were simply repeated (their mean score was 42%). A similar difference was found for students without disabilities.

Another experimental study on the same routine (Bulgren, Deshler, & Schumaker, 1997) showed that nine teachers could learn to use the Recall

Figure 3.10   Example of a Memory Device

Enhancement Routine at mastery levels in their classrooms within a three-hour workshop. It also showed that students whose teachers used the routine chose the most appropriate type of mnemonic device for particular items to be learned for 18% more of the items to be learned than students whose teachers did not use the routine.

Another instructional review method that has been used to enhance students' recall of information for a test is a form of peer instruction called *Classwide Peer Tutoring*. Meheady, Sacca, and Harper (1988) conducted a study on this review method with 10th-grade students using social studies content. Classes were smaller than a typical social studies class (15–20 students), and the regular content-area teachers received the consultative services of special educators. Three to six students with disabilities were included in each class. A multiple-baseline across-settings design was used. Treatment was withdrawn during some lessons, resulting in a reversal (ABAB) design combined with the multiple-baseline design. Data were collected for both students with mild disabilities and students without disabilities. Weekly study guides were created that contained questions and answers related to weekly instructional objectives.

In the baseline condition, students received weekly study guides and were prompted to study them before taking the weekly 20-item written quiz. During the intervention condition, after each class was divided into two teams, pairs of tutors and tutees were identified within each team. The teams were given the study guides, and the tutor and tutee worked together to ask each question, answer each question, award points, and then switch roles. The two teams competed with regard to scores on the weekly 20-item written quizzes on material studied during the tutoring sessions.

Results revealed higher student quiz performance in the intervention conditions compared with the baseline conditions, as well as high levels of satisfaction on the part of both students and teachers. The mean baseline quiz score was 66% (with about 33% of the students earning failing grades), and the mean intervention score was 88%. Although the results for students with disabilities were not reported separately from results of the class as a whole, the authors reported that the mean quiz score of students with disabilities in the baseline conditions "did not differ much" (Meheady et al., 1988, p. 55) from the class mean. They also reported that the mean gain for the students with disabilities was 23 points, and the mean gain for the total class was 22 points.

In summary, both mnemonic and peer-assisted review methods appear to be helpful for enhancing the recall of information on a test by students with disabilities. Nevertheless, because the effect of neither method was evaluated with regard to student performance on regularly scheduled tests on actual content presented in rigorous secondary general education classes, these effects remain unknown.

SUMMARY

This chapter has revealed important findings across the combined group of studies. First, students with disabilities did not score well on pretest and baseline performance measures of learning course content. Specifically, across all studies that used traditional instructional methods in baseline or comparison conditions, students with disabilities earned failing mean scores. Although most of the studies used researcher-constructed tests as a measure, the one study that used regularly scheduled unit tests (Bulgren et al., 1988) as an outcome variable supported the claim that students with disabilities, on average, are not performing at passing levels on tests related to general education content. In that study, the mean baseline unit test score for students with disabilities was 55%, and 57% of these students were failing the tests. This is an important finding because it provides support for the notion that simply enrolling students with disabilities in general education classes will not result in success for a large proportion of them, especially given the fact that a large percentage of a student's quarterly grade in a secondary general education course is based on test scores.

A second major common finding across the studies is that implementation of carefully planned and structured instructional routines, most of them based on a teaching device, can result in improved learning by students with disabilities. The studies showed that as a group, on average, students with disabilities made performance gains when instructional practices related to organizing, understanding, and recalling content information were used. In addition, other students enrolled in the same classes made comparable gains. Thus, based on this body of work, the notion that general education teachers can enhance the organization, understanding, and recall of information by students with disabilities and other low-achieving students enrolled in their classes seems to be a viable one.

In all of the studies except one (Lenz, 1984), the mean test scores of the students with disabilities during intervention conditions were above the passing level, and many of them were at the C or B levels. Depending on the intervention, the differences between conditions or gains achieved by students with disabilities ranged from 11 to 43 percentage points. Most of these gains represent substantial and socially significant improvements in terms of a student's life. That is, if an intervention can take a student well into the passing range in terms of course grades, the student will be more likely to stay in school and graduate from high school.

Another major finding that cuts across many of the studies is that, when innovative instructional routines and procedures are used, the performance of students without disabilities improves along with the performance of the students with disabilities. This is an important side benefit of the instructional methods because teachers are unlikely to use methods that enhance the learning of just a small proportion of students in their classes, especially if such methods require additional planning or effort.

One important commonality among the studies is that positive findings were achieved with *single* interventions. That is, in all of the studies, one intervention was compared with traditional instruction or some other type of instruction. To date, none of these effective interventions has been combined with others into a package to evaluate the effects of the package as a whole. Whether additional improvements in student performance could be achieved by using several interventions in combination is unknown.

Thus, future research needs to focus on packages of the various interventions discussed here, in addition to refining current interventions for use in today's schools. For example, in one course, Organizer Routines could be used to introduce a course, units, and lessons. Concept routines could be used to develop information related to a major concept in each unit. Study guides and graphic organizers could be used to help students understand reading assignments. Finally, Classwide Peer Tutoring and mnemonic devices could be used to help students practice and review information for a test. Conceivably, such an integrated sequence may have an even greater effect on student performance and success in content courses than the routines in isolation. In addition, a broad array of interventions, such as those described by Deshler et al. (2001) and Lenz and Ehren (1999), which can be conceptualized as a content-literacy continuum, need further research. This would provide more information on how effective and feasible instructional packages are in promoting success for everyone in inclusive content classrooms.

Because most of the studies reviewed here were restricted to examining the effects of interventions on students with LD, students with other exceptionalities need to be included in future studies focusing on single interventions and combined packages of interventions. Additionally, some of the routines need further study to determine under what conditions they are most effective and practical. Practicality is an especially important consideration as the use of devices such as semantic feature analysis or other charts, study guides or other study aids, and variations of graphic organizers and their associated routines are integrated into inclusive secondary content classes. Clearly, if teachers find that preparing or using several interventions is unwieldy, they will choose not to use them.

Further, because several researchers reported that some students with disabilities in their samples were still failing even after a new instructional method had been used, research is needed to identify factors associated with no change in particular students, as well as to study the effects of multiple interventions on these students' learning.

Research should also be conducted on innovative instructional routines that address the new and challenging content demands that are being set forth in state and national standards and assessments. Specifically, instructional practices are needed to help students respond to increasingly challenging content-area standards and assessment practices in all content areas. Students are being called on to engage in higher-order thinking and inquiry into challenging questions and problems in secondary-level inclusive content classrooms. For example, students are being asked to engage in scientific argumentation (Driver et al., 2000), that is, to look at data, evaluate claims made by others, and make decisions based on those claims. Furthermore, students are being asked to pose questions themselves rather than rely on a question provided by the teacher or formulate their own explanations from evidence (NRC, 1996, 2000). Similarly, in history classes, students are being asked to identify historical problems and analyze proposals for dealing with the problems (National Center for History in the Schools, 1996). Responding to assessments is often even more challenging when students are asked for written responses, reports of projects, or participation in cooperative efforts. Thus, future research needs to focus on these challenging areas so that students with disabilities can be taught to meet the demands associated with succeeding in high school in the 21st century.

For this future research to be most useful, the types of methodologies used must be carefully considered. A variety of methodologies were used in the studies reviewed here. In some, experimental designs were used with randomly selected students or with randomly selected intact groups within sets of circumstances that are different from typical class environments. For example, researchers provided the instruction, instruction took place in classes other than general education classes, and materials were different from course textbooks. In other studies, interventions took place in actual general education classes and were implemented by the teachers regularly assigned to the classes, but the intervention was not integrated into ongoing instruction. In still others, interventions took place in general education classes, teachers provided the instruction, and intervention was integrated into class activities for extended periods of time.

Clearly, as researchers move further along the continuum toward integrating an intervention into the natural secondary class milieu, fewer experimental controls are possible. Intact classes must be included in the studies. The different content of the classes must be taught, and different outcome instruments need to be used across classes. Nevertheless, this type of research must be conducted to determine the feasibility of using an intervention or a package of interventions week in and week out under natural school conditions.

Ideally, a series of research studies would be conducted on each intervention. First, focus group studies could be conducted to involve teachers in developing a new intervention. This would help to prevent the development of interventions that are neither practical nor needed. Next, an initial, tightly controlled study with students randomly assigned to groups might be conducted to determine the effects of an intervention under controlled conditions with students with disabilities. Then, once an intervention has been validated under controlled conditions, studies with intact classes might be conducted in a variety of subject areas. Here, teachers would need to implement the intervention using actual course materials and focusing on actual course content, and scores on actual tests, quarterly grades, and scores on state assessments would serve as some of the dependent variables. Further, maintenance of knowledge must be measured across time. Researchers need to listen carefully to teachers participating in these studies to gather information about the time required for planning and their concerns related to a given intervention so that it can be adjusted to the realities of today's schools. Finally, the intervention needs to be taken to scale; that is, it must be integrated in many different subject-area classes in several different kinds of schools (rural, urban, and suburban) to determine its cumulative, long-term, and life-quality effects on students.

To date, this proposed sequence of research has not been conducted for any of the interventions reviewed here; however, some of the researchers are approximating the sequence. Bulgren and colleagues, for example, have involved focus groups, and they have conducted tightly controlled studies and studies in actual general education classes in which students with disabilities were enrolled. Although this is clearly a step in the right direction, more research is needed to fill in gaps of the described research sequence.

As performance challenges grow more difficult for all students, they are becoming even more difficult for students with disabilities enrolled in inclusive secondary content classes. Simultaneously, instructional challenges for their teachers are also increasing. Research must keep pace with these challenges and supply research-based instructional practices to help teachers act as mediators so that all students learn.

To conclude, the field of education must turn to research-based practices as it strives to respond to the challenge of helping all students succeed in school. The research presented here suggests practices that have sufficient research support to recommend their use in inclusive secondary classrooms. Common elements found in many of these practices involve the use of a variety of presentation formats, including graphic and visual devices that help organize and explore information, as well as verbal presentations; active student engagement achieved in whole-class or peer-group formats; explicit instruction on how students are to participate in active learning; scaffolded and coconstructed knowledge; and a recognition and valuing of differences among students.

Educational Applications and Implications

Personnel in schools and school districts are using many of the interventions described in this chapter in secondary general education courses. For example, in one California high school, all of the social studies teachers met to review the state standards and benchmarks related to their courses. In addition, they have worked together to create graphic devices for their courses that correspond to the routines that they want to use to present the content of their courses. For example, they carefully planned the key concepts to be taught in each course so that later courses could build on concepts taught in earlier courses. Then they chose the most appropriate graphic device (e.g., a Concept Diagram, Anchoring Table, or Comparison Table) and routine for teaching each concept.

Other schools have adopted the use of interventions described in this chapter and the planning tools described in Chapter 2 schoolwide. Personnel in each department in these schools have been responsible for working together to address state standards, create devices, and implement the routines across the school year. Efforts are being made to ensure that each unit in required courses is taught using a variety of routines. For example, the course is introduced using the Course Organizer Routine; a unit is introduced using the Unit Organizer Routine; critical questions in the unit are addressed using the Question Exploration Routine; a key concept is analyzed using the Concept Mastery Routine; other key concepts are compared using the Concept Comparison Routine; key information is reviewed using the Recall Enhancement Routine; and major assignments are introduced using the Quality Assignment Routine.

Again, specific supports must be in place for such efforts to succeed. Teachers need to participate in a professional development experience for about three hours to learn how to use each routine. They also need time to work together so that the coordination can take place across shared courses and across a sequence of courses. Such coordination requires the alternation of work periods with sharing and feedback sessions. Again, the expertise of a trained coach can be very helpful during this process.

Finally, sometimes teachers need someone to observe and videotape them in class, provide demonstrations in class, and give them helpful feedback on their performance of the routines. Analyzing videotapes of performance can be very helpful.

The administrator's role in this process involves organizing and attending professional development sessions, setting up time for teachers to work together, making such collaboration a part of expected school activity, and arranging for coaches to help the teachers. Once the teachers begin using the routines, the administrator can learn how to observe teachers and then regularly visit classrooms to provide feedback to teachers.

For more information on how to obtain assistance with professional development experiences for some of the interventions reviewed in this chapter, visit the University of Kansas Center for Research on Learning Web site at www.kucrl.org or contact the Center's director of professional development at 785-864-4780.

REFERENCES

Anders, P. L., Bos, C. S., & Filip, D. (1984). The effect of semantic feature analysis on the reading comprehension of learning-disabled students. In J. A. Niles & H. Newton (Eds.), *Changing perspectives on research in reading/language processing and instruction* (Thirty-Third Yearbook for the National Reading Conference, pp. 162–166). Rochester, NY: National Reading Conference.

Aronson, E. (1978). *The jigsaw classroom.* Beverly Hills, CA: Sage.

Ausubel, D. P. (1963). *The psychology of meaningful verbal learning.* New York: Grune & Stratton.

Ausubel, D. P., Novak, J. D., & Hanesian, H. (1968). *Educational psychology: A cognitive view* (2nd ed.). New York: Holt, Rinehart & Winston.

Bergerud, D., Lovitt, T. C., & Horton, S. (1988). The effectiveness of textbook adaptations in life science for high school students with learning disabilities. *Journal of Learning Disabilities, 21*(2), 70–76.

Borko, H., & Niles, J. A. (1987). Description of teacher planning: Ideas for teachers and researchers. In V. Richardson-Koehler (Ed.), *Educators handbook: A research perspective* (pp. 167–187). New York: Longman.

Bos, C. S., & Anders, P. L. (1990). Toward an interactive model: Teaching text-based concepts to learning disabled students. In H. L. Swanson & B. Keogh (Eds.), *Learning disabilities: Theoretical and research issues* (pp. 247–262). Hillsdale, NJ: Lawrence Erlbaum.

Bos, C. S., Anders, P. L., Filip, D., & Jaffe, L. E. (1989). The effects of an interactive instructional strategy for enhancing learning disabled students' reading comprehension and content area learning. *Journal of Learning Disabilities, 22*(6), 384–390.

Bruner, J. S., Goodnow, J. J., & Austin, G. A. (1956). *The study of thinking.* New York: Wiley.

Bulgren, J. A., Deshler, D. D., & Schumaker, J. B. (1993). *The Content Enhancement Series: The Concept Mastery Routine.* Lawrence, KS: Edge Enterprises.

Bulgren, J. A., Deshler, D. D., & Schumaker, J. B. (1997). Use of Recall Enhancement Routine and strategies in inclusive secondary classes. *Learning Disabilities Research and Practice, 12*(4), 198–208.

Bulgren, J. A., Deshler, D. D., Schumaker, J. B., & Lenz, B. K. (2000). The use and effectiveness of analogical instruction in diverse secondary content class-rooms. *Journal of Educational Psychology, 92*(3), 426–441.

Bulgren, J. A., & Lenz, B. K. (1996). Strategic instruction in the content areas. In D. D. Deshler, E. S. Ellis, & B. K. Lenz (Eds.), *Teaching adolescents with learning disabilities: Strategies and methods* (2nd ed., pp. 409–473). Denver, CO: Love Publishing.

Bulgren, J. A., Lenz, B. K., Deshler, D. D., & Schumaker, J. B. (1995). *The Concept Comparison Routine.* Lawrence, KS: Edge Enterprises.

Bulgren, J. A., Lenz, B. K., Deshler, D. D., Schumaker, J. B., & Marquis, J. G. (2004a). *The effects of a Question Exploration Routine in inclusive secondary English class-rooms.* Unpublished manuscript, University of Kansas–Lawrence.

Bulgren, J. A., Lenz, B. K., Schumaker, J. B., Deshler, D. D., & Marquis, J. G. (2004b). *The use and effectiveness of a Question Exploration Routine in inclusive secondary content classrooms.* Unpublished manuscript, University of Kansas–Lawrence.

Bulgren, J. A., Schumaker, J. B., & Deshler, D. D. (1988). Effectiveness of a Concept Teaching Routine in enhancing the performance of LD students in secondary-level mainstream classes. *Learning Disability Quarterly, 11*(1), 3–17.

Bulgren, J. A., Schumaker, J. B., & Deshler, D. D. (1994). The effects of a Recall Enhancement Routine on the test performance of secondary students with and without learning disabilities. *Learning Disabilities Research and Practice, 9*(1), 2–11.

Bulgren, J. A., Schumaker, J. B., Deshler, D. D., Lenz, B. K., & Marquis, J. G. (2002). The use and effectiveness of a comparison routine in diverse secondary content classrooms. *Journal of Educational Psychology, 94*(2), 356–371.

Delquadri, J., Greenwood, C. R., Whorton, D., Carta, J. J., & Hall, R. V. (1986). Classwide Peer Tutoring. *Exceptional Children, 6*(52), 535–542.

Deshler, D. D., Schumaker, J. B., Lenz, B. K., Bulgren, J. A., Hock, M. F., Knight, M. J., & Ehren, B. J. (2001). Ensuring content-area learning by secondary students with learning disabilities. *Learning Disabilities Research and Practice, 16*(2), 96–108.

Driver, R., Newton, P., & Osborne, D. (2000). Establishing the norms of scientific argumentation in classrooms. *Science Education, 84*(3), 583–590.

Elmore, R. F. (1996). Getting to scale with good educational practice. *Harvard Educational Review, 66*(1), 1–26.

Erickson, L. (1998). *Concept-based curriculum and instruction: Teaching beyond the facts.* Thousand Oaks, CA: Corwin.

Feuerstein, R. (1980). *Instrumental enrichment.* Baltimore: University Park Press.

Gagné, R. M. (1965). *The conditions of learning.* New York: Holt, Rinehart & Winston.

Hodgkinson, H. (1991). Reform versus reality. *Phi Delta Kappan, 73*(1), 8–16.

Horton, S. V., & Lovitt, T. C. (1989). Using study guides with three classifications of secondary students. *Journal of Special Education, 22*(4), 447–462.

Horton, S. V., Lovitt, T. C., & Bergerud, D. (1990). The effectiveness of graphic organizers for three classifications of secondary students in content area classes. *Journal of Learning Disabilities, 23*(1), 12–22.

Jenkins, J. R., & Jenkins, L. M. (1985). Peer tutoring in elementary and secondary programs. *Focus on Exceptional Children, 17*(6), 1–12.

Johnson, D. W., & Johnson, R. T. (1975). *Learning together and alone.* Englewood Cliffs, NJ: Prentice Hall.

Joint Committee on Teacher Planning for Students with Disabilities. (1995). *Planning for academic diversity in America's classrooms: Windows on reality, research, change, and practice.* Lawrence: University of Kansas Center for Research on Learning.

Jones, B. F., Palincsar, A. S., Ogle, D. S., & Carr, E. G. (1987). *Strategic teaching and learning: Cognitive instruction in the content areas.* Alexandria, VA: Association for Supervision and Curriculum Development in cooperation with North Central Regional Educational Laboratory.

Kansas State Board of Education. (1995). *Kansas Assessment Program: Results of 1995 mathematics, reading, and social studies assessments.* Topeka: Author.

Klausmeir, H. J., & Associates (1979). *Cognitive learning and development: Information-processing and Piagetian perspectives.* Cambridge, MA: Ballinger.

Klausmeir, H. J., & Ripple, R. E. (1971). *Learning and human abilities: Educational psychology.* New York: Harper & Row.

Lenz, B. K. (1984). *The effect of advance organizers on the learning and retention of learning disabled adolescents within the context of a cooperative planning model* (Final research report submitted to the U.S. Department of Education, Office of Special Education and Rehabilitative Services). Lawrence: University of Kansas Center for Research on Learning.

Lenz, B. K., Alley, G. R., & Schumaker, J. B. (1987). Activating the inactive learner: Advance organizers in the secondary content classroom. *Learning Disability Quarterly, 10*(1), 53–67.

Lenz, B. K., & Bulgren, J. A. (1995). Promoting learning in the content areas. In P. A. Cegelka & W. H. Berdine (Eds.), *Effective instruction for students with learning problems* (pp. 385–417). Needham Heights, MA: Allyn & Bacon.

Lenz, B. K., Bulgren, J. A., Kissam, B., & Taymans, J. (2004). SMARTER planning for academic diversity. In B. K. Lenz & D. D. Deshler (Eds.), *Teaching content to all: Evidence-based inclusive practices in middle and secondary schools* (pp. 47–76). Boston: Pearson.

Lenz, B. K., Bulgren, J. A., Schumaker, J. B., Deshler, D. D., & Boudah, D. J. (1994). *The Unit Organizer Routine.* Lawrence, KS: Edge Enterprises.

Lenz, B. K. & Ehren, B. J. (1999). The strategic content literacy initiative: Focusing on reading in secondary schools. *Stratenotes, (8)*1, 1–3.

Lenz, B. K., Schumaker, J. B., Deshler, D. D., & Bulgren, J. A. (1998). *The Course Organizer Routine.* Lawrence, KS: Edge Enterprises.

Lovitt, T. C., & Horton, S. V. (1988). How to develop study guides. *Journal of Reading, Writing, and Learning Disabilities, 2,* 213–221.

Lovitt, T. C., Rudsit, J., Jenkins, J., Pious, C., & Benedetti, D. (1985). Two methods of adaptive science materials for learning disabled and regular seventh graders. *Learning Disability Quarterly, (8),* 275–285.

Mastropieri, M. A., & Fulk, B. J. M. (1990). Enhancing academic performance with mnemonic instruction. In T. E. Scruggs & B. Y. L. Wong (Eds.), *Intervention research in learning disabilities* (pp. 102–122). New York: Springer-Verlag.

Mastropieri, M. A., & Scruggs, T. E. (1989). Mnemonic social studies instruction: Classroom applications. *Remedial and Special Education, 10,* 40–46.

Mastropieri, M. A., Scruggs, T. E., Spencer, V., & Fontana, J. (2003). Promoting success in high school world history: Peer tutoring versus guided notes. *Learning Disabilities Research and Practice, 18,* 52–65.

Mayer, R. E. (1987). *Educational psychology: A cognitive approach.* Boston: Little, Brown.

Meheady, L., Sacca, M. K., & Harper, G. F. (1987). Classwide tutoring teams: The effects of peer-mediated instruction on the academic performance of secondary mainstreamed students. *Journal of Special Education, 21*(3), 107–121.

Meheady, L., Sacca, M. K., & Harper, G. F. (1988). Classwide Peer Tutoring with mildly handicapped high school students. *Exceptional Children, 55*(1), 52–59.

Merrill, M. D., & Tennyson, R. D. (1977). *Teaching concepts: An instructional design guide.* Englewood Cliffs, NJ: Educational Technology.

National Center for History in the Schools. (1996). *National standards for history: Basic edition.* Los Angeles: Author.

National Research Council (NRC). (1996). *National science education standards.* Washington, DC: National Academy Press.

National Research Council (NRC). (2000). *Inquiry and the national science education standards.* Washington, DC: National Academy Press.

No Child Left Behind Act of 2001. (2002). P. L. 107–110.

Scanlon, D., Deshler, D. D., & Schumaker, J. B. (1996). Can a strategy be taught and learned in secondary inclusive classrooms? *Learning Disabilities Research and Practice, 11*(1), 41–57.

Schumaker, J. B., Bulgren, J. A., Deshler, D. D., & Lenz, B. K. (1998). *The Content Enhancement Series: The Recall Enhancement Routine.* Lawrence: University of Kansas.

Schumaker, J. B., Deshler, D. D., & McKnight, P. C. (2001). Ensuring success in the secondary general education curriculum through the use of teaching routines. In M. A. Shinn, H. M. Walker, & G. Stoner (Eds.), *Interventions for academic and behavior problems II* (pp. 791–821). Bethesda, MD: National Association of School Psychologists.

Scruggs, T. E., & Mastropieri, M. A. (1989a). *Classroom applications of mnemonic instruction: Acquisition, maintenance, and generalization.* West Lafayette, IN: Purdue University, Department of Educational Studies.

Scruggs, T. E., & Mastropieri, M. A. (1989b). Mnemonic instruction of LD students: A field-based evaluation. *Learning Disability Quarterly, 12,* 119–125.

Scruggs, T. E., & Mastropieri, M. A. (1990). Mnemonic instruction for students with learning disabilities: What it is and what it does. *Learning Disability Quarterly, 13,* 271–280.

Scruggs, T. E., & Mastropieri, M. A. (1992). Classroom applications of mnemonic instruction: Acquisition, maintenance, and generalization. *Exceptional Children, 13,* 271–280.

Slavin, R. E. (1983). *Cooperative learning.* New York: Longman.

Slavin, R. E., Madden, N. A., & Leavey, M. (1984). Effects of cooperative learning and individualized instruction on mainstreamed students. *Exceptional Children, 50*(5), 434–443.

Swanson, H. L., & Ransby, M. (1994). The study of cognitive processes in learning disabled students. In S. Vaughn & C. Bos (Eds.), *Research issues in learning disabilities: Theory, methodology, assessment, and ethics* (pp. 246–275). New York: Springer-Verlag.

Thornton, S. J. (1991). Teacher as curricular-instructional gatekeeper in social studies. In J. P. Shaver (Ed.), *Handbook of research on social studies teaching and learning* (pp. 237–248). New York: Macmillan.

Vaughn, S., Schumm, J. S., & McIntosh, R. (1991, April). *Teacher adaptations: What students think.* Paper presented at the meeting of the American Educational Research Association, Chicago, IL.

Wiggins, G., & McTighe, J. (Eds.). (1998). *Understanding by design.* Alexandria, VA: Association for Supervision and Curriculum Development.

4

Teaching Adolescents to Be Strategic Learners

Jean B. Schumaker and Donald D. Deshler

One of the key elements of the program plan established for Jason was the specification of a set of key learning strategies that he would master so that he would be in a position to respond to the demanding high school curriculum. His plan specified that Jason would receive intensive learning strategy instruction to enhance his capacity to deal with the heavy language demands in middle school. For reading, Jason was taught strategies in paraphrasing, self-questioning, and predicting. In written expression, he was taught strategies for writing well-organized paragraphs and for taking notes in class. To ensure that the strategies he learned were relevant to and applied in the general education classes and out-of-school situations, special and general education teachers collaboratively planned and carefully monitored Jason's performance.

As students with disabilities, like Jason, move into adolescence, they are confronted with the rigorous demands inherent in the secondary school curriculum. Intervention procedures traditionally used with adolescents with high-incidence disabilities (that is, remedial instruction to overcome deficiencies in basic skills) often fall short in enabling these students to cope with the rigorous demands encountered in subject-matter classes. Educators face a significant challenge in selecting and delivering interventions that are sufficiently powerful to impact these students' performance. Since its inception in 1978, the University of Kansas Center for Research on Learning (KU-CRL) has had as a major goal the design and validation of interventions that educators can use to help adolescents with disabilities access and succeed in the general education curriculum. To this end, the center adopted a learning strategies instructional approach as one of the core elements of a larger intervention model called the *Strategic Instruction Model* (Deshler et al., 2001). As a result, several learning strategy interventions have been developed and validated over several years.

The major thrust of this instructional approach is to teach students "how to learn" by teaching them to use an array of task-specific learning strategies to respond to curriculum demands as well as to novel demands that they will likely encounter in the world of work. For the purposes of KU-CRL research, a learning strategy has been defined as "an individual's approach to a task. It includes how a person thinks and acts when planning, executing, and evaluating performance on a task and its outcomes" (Deshler & Schumaker, 1988). More comprehensive definitions have been proposed in the literature (e.g., Pressley & Hilden, 2004); however, this definition was chosen to guide KU-CRL research because of its direct relevance to classroom and world-of-work tasks. An example of a learning strategy is a set of steps that a student can use to study for a test. Another example is a set of steps that can be used to write a paragraph.

A major goal associated with teaching students with learning disabilities (LD) to use learning strategies such as these is to enable them to successfully analyze and solve novel problems and to respond to tasks in both academic and nonacademic settings. A key factor in realizing this goal, however, is the degree to which these students can be taught to generalize mastered learning strategies to other situations and settings over time. Researchers have found that, for this to occur, many students must be taught explicitly to generalize and transfer learning strategies to other settings and circumstances.

There are five major rationales for choosing a learning strategies instructional approach for adolescents with high-incidence disabilities. First, data convincingly show that at-risk adolescents, including those with disabilities, perform at levels that are markedly below their peers because they lack the necessary skills and strategies to successfully negotiate the demanding environment of a secondary school. According to the 2002 National Assessment of Educational Progress, for example, approximately one quarter of all adolescents tested read at or below the basic level. This means they probably have considerable difficulty reading a newspaper or even road signs (Hock & Deshler, 2003). As a result of this poor performance, only 56% of all students aged 14 to 21 with disabilities graduated with a standard diploma (U.S. Department of Education, 2002). Thus, at-risk students need instruction that will immediately help them gain access to and successfully cope with the demands of the secondary curriculum. Second, a large proportion of adolescents with disabilities do not invent productive strategies as they approach novel tasks (Warner, Schumaker, Alley, & Deshler, 1989), nor do they appear to approach tasks strategically (Deshler & Schumaker, 1986). Hence, they must be explicitly taught these important behaviors.

Third, the development and application of learning strategies appear to be related to age; older students have been found to be more proficient in the acquisition and use of cognitive and metacognitive behaviors than younger students (Armbruster, Echols, & Brown, 1984; Chi, 1981). Thus, teaching cognitive and metacognitive strategies seems to be developmentally appropriate. Fourth, adolescents with disabilities must be in a position to learn independently as they transition from school to postsecondary training or work. Rapid changes in the workplace require employees to be continual learners and to process information effectively (e.g., Bereiter & Scardamalia, 1993). Students who have learned how to learn in secondary school have a much better chance of being able to respond to these circumstances. Fifth, a learning strategies instructional approach requires students to accept major responsibility for their learning and progress in an academic setting. Such responsibility must be borne and commitments made by students if they are truly to become independent learners (Van Reusen, Deshler, & Schumaker, 1989). Although other intervention approaches tend to be based largely on teacher mediation, where teachers assume major responsibility for student progress, a learning strategies instructional approach is based on the premise that adolescents should have substantial control over their educational programs (Hock, Schumaker, & Deshler, 1999).

The purpose of this chapter is to describe how the KU-CRL staff has conceptualized and validated an array of learning strategy interventions for adolescents with disabilities. First, the *Learning Strategies Curriculum* will be discussed. This curriculum has emerged from a programmatic line of research conducted on strategic instruction. Second, instructional design principles that have served as underpinnings to each of the strategies in the curriculum will be described. Third, a detailed description of the instructional methodology found to be effective in helping students both master and generalize targeted strategies will be provided. The fourth section of the chapter will be devoted to describing research studies and findings related to different types of learning strategies. Finally, the results of an attempt to take learning strategies instruction to scale will be reported.

THE LEARNING STRATEGIES CURRICULUM

The Learning Strategies Curriculum operationalizes learning strategy instruction for students with disabilities at the junior high, senior high, and college levels (Deshler & Schumaker, 1988; Lenz et al., 1990). Each curriculum unit includes instructional procedures and materials that teachers

Figure 4.1   The Learning Strategies Curriculum

Acquisition Strand	Storage Strand	Expression Strand
Word Identification Strategy	FIRST-Letter Mnemonic Strategy	Sentence Writing Strategy
Visual Imagery Strategy	Paired-Associates Strategy	Paragraph Writing Strategy
Self-Questioning Strategy	Vocabulary Learning Strategy	Error Monitoring Strategy
Paraphrasing Strategy		InSPECT Strategy
Multipass Strategy		Theme Writing Strategy Assignment
		Completion Strategy
		Test-Taking Strategy

need to teach students to acquire and generalize a given learning strategy. The curriculum is organized into three major strands that correspond to three categories of demands presented by mainstream secondary and post-secondary curricula: acquisition, storage, and expression of information (see Figure 4.1). Through the curriculum, students can learn how to acquire information from written materials, store that information in some way (on paper or in their brains), and express that information on a test, in an assignment, or in a written paper. The curriculum has been designed to focus on these three broad demand areas so that teachers can have a complete picture of which intervention is required so that students can compensate for any effects of their learning disabilities. This focus is different from that of traditional remedial interventions, which emphasize understanding learner attributes as the primary basis for designing the instructional program (that is, if a student has difficulty reading, the instructional program focuses on remedial reading instruction). In contrast, this approach focuses on the skills and strategies that students need to succeed in required general education courses.

The first strand in the Learning Strategies Curriculum includes strategies that help students acquire information from written material. Five task-specific strategies have been developed within this strand. The *Word Identification Strategy* (Lenz & Hughes, 1990; Lenz, Schumaker, Deshler, & Beals, 1984) is used by students to decode multisyllabic words quickly. The *Visual Imagery Strategy* (Clark, Deshler, Schumaker, Alley, & Warner, 1984) is used by students to form mental pictures of events described in a reading passage. The *Self-Questioning Strategy* (Clark et al., 1984) is used to form questions about information that has not been provided by the author and to find answers to those questions later in the passage. The *Paraphrasing Strategy* (Schumaker, Denton, & Deshler, 1984) is used to paraphrase the main idea and important details of each paragraph after it is read. Finally, the *Multipass Strategy* (Schumaker, Deshler, Alley, Warner, & Denton, 1982) is used to attack textbook chapters by conducting three passes through the chapter to survey it, extract important information, and study that information.

The second strand in the Learning Strategies Curriculum includes strategies that enable students to identify, organize, and store important information. The *FIRST-Letter Mnemonic Strategy* (Nagel, Schumaker, & Deshler, 1986) and the *Paired-Associates Strategy* (Bulgren & Schumaker, 1996) provide students with several options for memorizing key information for tests. The *Vocabulary Learning Strategy* (Ellis, 1992) enables students to learn the meaning of new vocabulary words.

The final strand of the Learning Strategies Curriculum includes strategies for facilitating written expression and demonstration of competence. Seven strategies have been designed to enable students to cope with writing assignments at the secondary level. The *Sentence Writing Strategy* (Schumaker & Sheldon, 1985) provides students with a set of steps for creating a variety of sentence types, ranging from simple to compound-complex sentences. The *Paragraph Writing Strategy* (Schumaker & Lyerla, 1991) helps students organize and write several types of paragraphs. The *Error Monitoring Strategy* (Schumaker, Nolan, & Deshler, 1985) helps students detect and correct errors in written products. The *InSPECT Strategy* helps students to detect spelling errors through the use of a spellchecker. The *Theme Writing Strategy* (Schumaker, 2003) helps students organize and write short themes. The *Assignment Completion Strategy* (Hughes, Ruhl, Schumaker, & Deshler, 1995) helps students record and complete assignments on time. Finally, the *Test-Taking Strategy* (Hughes, Schumaker, Deshler, & Mercer, 1988) enables students to take classroom tests effectively.

Common Design Features in All Learning Strategies

The strategies included in the Learning Strategies Curriculum were designed to have common features (see Figure 4.2). First, each strategy contains a set of steps leading to a specific outcome, and the steps are sequenced in a manner that leads to successful task completion. Second, the strategy steps cue the learner to use specific cognitive and metacognitive strategies, to select and use appropriate procedures, skills, and rules, or to engage in observable actions. Third, the steps are short. They begin with a verb that is directly related to the cognitive or physical action the step is designed to cue, and they are organized in an easy-to-remember format. A mnemonic device has been designed for each strategy to facilitate students' memory of the steps. For example, the first-letter mnemonic device "ASK IT" is used to remember the steps of the Self-Questioning Strategy (see Figure 4.3). Finally, most of the learning strategies comprise "strategy systems" because steps often cue the use of several cognitive or metacognitive strategies for the same task (Ellis, Deshler, Lenz, Schumaker, & Clark, 1991).

The Instructional Methodology for Teaching Strategies

A specific instructional methodology has been designed for teaching learning strategies to students with disabilities (Ellis et al., 1991). This methodology

Figure 4.2   Strategy Design Features

The steps
Are sequenced
Lead to a specific outcome
Cue cognitive functions
Cue metacognitive functions
Are short
Begin with a verb
Are organized with a mnemonic device
Constitute strategy systems

Figure 4.3   Self-Questioning Strategy Steps

Step 1: **A**ttend to clues as you read

Step 2: **S**ay some questions

Step 3: **K**eep predictions in mind

Step 4: **I**dentify the answers

Step 5: **T**alk about the answers

has eight instructional stages (see Figure 4.4). The purpose of these stages is to ensure that students acquire the knowledge, motivation, and practice necessary to apply a strategy successfully in the general education setting in relation to tasks that are a regular part of requirements in that setting. In the *Pretest and Make Commitments Stage*, students are given a test to determine how they perform on a particular academic task. Then they are made aware of their strengths and weaknesses as learners and are asked to make a commitment to learn a new strategy to enable them to be better learners and performers. The teacher also makes a commitment to facilitate the student's learning. During the *Describe Stage*, the new strategy and where, when, how, and why the strategy should be used are described to the student. The strategic processes involved in the strategy and the mnemonic device that is used to remember the strategy's steps are presented. Finally, students are encouraged to set goals for learning the strategy. In the *Model Stage*, the teacher demonstrates the new strategy from start to finish while thinking aloud. Specifically, the cognitive behaviors of self-instruction, problem solving, and self-monitoring are demonstrated along with use of the strategy steps. Students become progressively more involved in subsequent demonstrations of the strategy. During this student-enlistment phase of the Model Stage of instruction, the teacher prompts involvement, checks the students' understanding of the strategy processes, corrects and expands on student responses, and engineers success.

Figure 4.4   Instructional Stages

Stage	Instructional Action
1	Pretest and Make Commitments
2	Describe
3	Model
4	Verbal Practice
5	Controlled Practice
6	Advanced Practice
7	Posttest and Make Commitments
8	Generalization
	Orientation
	Activation
	Adaptation
	Maintenance

Verbal Practice is the fourth instructional stage. This stage enhances students' ability to name and explain a strategy before they move to the fifth stage of instruction, the *Controlled Practice and Feedback Stage*. In this stage, students practice the new strategy to a specified performance criterion in controlled materials (that is, materials in which the complexity, length, and difficulty levels have been reduced). Initially, instruction is primarily teacher mediated through the use of guided practice activities. After students demonstrate some mastery with the strategy, the emphasis shifts to student-mediated learning through the use of independent practice assignments.

The *Advanced Practice Stage* commences once students have demonstrated mastery in the *Controlled Practice Stage*. Here, students practice using the strategy to mastery in materials and situations that closely approximate those encountered in required general education classes and other natural environments. Teachers guide students' use of the strategy in both guided and independent practice activities. Feedback provided during both the Controlled Practice and Advanced Practice stages is individualized, specific, and elaborated (Kline, Schumaker, & Deshler, 1991).

The seventh stage is *Posttest and Make Commitments*. During this stage, students are tested to determine whether they have mastered the strategy and are able to use it effectively. Once this is established, the student and teacher celebrate the student's success, and the student is asked to make a commitment to generalize the strategy or to use it in a variety of situations. The teacher also makes a commitment to help the student generalize the strategy.

In the eighth stage of the instructional sequence, the *Generalization Stage,* teachers focus their energies on engineering situations that will give students several opportunities to generalize the strategy across tasks, situations, and settings. Although this eighth stage explicitly targets generalization, instruction for generalization is emphasized throughout the other seven phases. For example, some generalization techniques (Ellis, Lenz, & Sabornie, 1987a, 1987b) are programmed into the first acquisition stage by enlisting student commitment to learn a particular strategy to be used in general education courses. Throughout the remaining stages, teachers continually incorporate different examples in their instruction as reminders about where the strategy can be used, and they program the student's actual application of the strategy to assignments received in general education classes whenever possible.

The Generalization Stage comprises four specific phases of generalization instruction. The first phase, *orientation*, makes students aware of the variety of contexts within which the learning strategy can be applied and the strategy's most helpful aspects, given varying course demands. During the second phase, *activation*, students are given ample opportunities to practice the strategy with different materials and in new settings. They also receive feedback on their general education class assignments to which they have applied the strategy. *Adaptation* is the third phase of generalization instruction. Here, teachers prompt students to identify how the strategy can be modified to better enable them to meet different setting demands. The final phase of the generalization process is *maintenance*. The purpose of this phase is to conduct periodic probes to determine whether the student is still using the strategy fluently in a variety of settings. These maintenance probes occur at intermittent intervals over a sustained period of time (over the academic year and across years).

Research on Strategy Instruction for Adolescents

During the 1980s and 1990s, a programmatic series of research studies was conducted to determine whether the eight-stage instructional methodology just described can be effectively used to teach learning strategies in the Learning Strategies Curriculum to adolescents with learning disabilities and to determine the effects of these students' use of the learning strategies. The studies share several common characteristics. First, two major research questions were addressed: (1) Can adolescents with learning disabilities be taught to use a given learning strategy? And (2) does their use of this strategy result in improved performance on academic tasks? Across the studies, the students' IQs ranged from 80 to 117; they were enrolled in Grades 7 through 12; and they were validated as meeting state guidelines for being classified as having learning disabilities. The studies took place in schools, and qualified teachers provided the instruction. Although a few of the studies took place after school or during summer school, the majority took place during regularly scheduled instructional time throughout the regular school year. In addition, the instructional stages described previously were adapted to the particular strategy being taught. To ensure standard application of the intervention, the procedures were documented in written form and followed in a step-by-step fashion during each lesson. In many of the studies, some form of a multiple-baseline design (Baer, Wolf, & Risley, 1968) or a multiple-probe design (Horner & Baer, 1978), a variation of the multiple-baseline design, was used to demonstrate experimental control. In other studies, a comparison-group design was used or combined with the multiple-baseline or multiple-probe design. Thus, in all of the studies reviewed here, a scientific experimental design that controlled for the effects of extraneous variables was used. In addition, a written document is available for each study, either in the literature or from the University of Kansas.

In many of the studies, two types of student performance measures were gathered: (1) a measure of the student's performance of the strategy, and (2) a measure of the effects of the student's use of the strategy. (In a few of the studies, only the student's performance of the strategy was measured.) This dual type of measurement distinguishes KU-CRL strategies research from much of the other strategies research in the learning disabilities field because researchers most often measure the indirect effects of strategy instruction (for instance, they use measures derived from a standardized reading test before and after reading strategy instruction, but they do not measure students' actual use of the reading strategy).

Measuring the effects of the use of a learning strategy in these studies typically involved measuring the students' performance on a task that closely approximates a task that students might face in mainstream classes. For example, when students were taught a textbook-attack strategy called Multipass (Schumaker, Deshler, Alley, Warner, & Denton, 1982), they applied the strategy to a textbook used in a mainstream content course in their school. When they were taught a strategy for organizing and memorizing facts, they were given a passage from a textbook chapter to study (Bulgren, Hock, Schumaker, & Deshler, 1995).

The final commonality across studies is that generalization across academic tasks was measured in every case. In some studies, generalization across settings was measured. That is, students were asked to apply the strategy they had learned to novel tasks that they had not previously encountered. Each time they applied the strategy, they applied it to a new task. Thus, for each study, a pool of similar tasks was developed, and each time a test probe was given, a new task was used. For example, when the research on the Test-Taking Strategy was conducted (Hughes & Schumaker, 1991), a pool of tests was designed. Each test had the same number and types of test items as other tests in the pool. The order of the types of items was varied across the tests, and items on each test were different from all other items on all other tests. All tests were similar in form to the kinds of tests that students encounter in secondary mainstream classrooms (Hughes, Salvia, & Bott, in press; Putnam, 1992). Each time a student received a probe test, a test the student had not previously encountered was randomly selected from the pool and then administered.

Research on Acquisition Strategy Instruction

Studies that have been conducted on acquisition strategy instruction following the paradigm and instructional methodology described previously focus on two main areas: reading decoding and reading comprehension. In both areas, researchers have worked to determine whether students with disabilities could learn to apply reading strategies to enable them to succeed on reading tasks involving materials written at their grade level. Because, on average, students with LD enter the seventh grade reading at a fourth-grade level and stay at that level throughout the remainder of their junior and senior high school careers if they do not receive the appropriate types of instruction (Warner, Schumaker, Alley, & Deshler, 1980), and because most high school textbooks are written at the 9th- to 17th-grade levels, enabling a student to close the gap in reading is an important goal.

Within the decoding area, Lenz and Hughes (1990) conducted a study in which 12 seventh, eighth, and ninth graders with LD learned the Word Identification Strategy (Lenz et al., 1984). At the beginning of the study, the students' reading achievement grade-level scores ranged from 3.5 to 7.0. A multiple-baseline across-students design was used to display the effects of the instruction on two measures: the number of errors students made when reading a passage aloud and the percentage of comprehension questions they answered correctly one day after reading each passage. Students read three types of 400-word passages: those written at their reading grade level, those written at their actual grade level, and passages taken from their actual science textbook (called "textbook passages").

Results showed that in the baseline condition, students made as many as 37 errors while reading grade-level passages. During strategy instruction, all students reached the mastery criterion of six or fewer errors while reading a 400-word ability-level passage within five practice attempts with the strategy and while reading a grade-level passage within nine practice trials. Mean comprehension scores improved from 83% to 88% for ability-level passages and from 39% to 58% for grade-level passages. Maintenance probes showed that the students maintained their use of the strategy at mastery levels for at least five weeks after the instruction was terminated on grade-level passages and textbook passages. Thus, this study showed that students could learn to use a decoding strategy and apply it to grade-level passages to reduce the number of errors they made and increase their comprehension, especially at their reading level. The authors suggested that comprehension instruction would be required in addition to decoding instruction to further improve comprehension levels.

Recently, Woodruff, Schumaker, and Deshler (2002) conducted another study on the Word Identification Strategy. Two matched groups of 62 ninth graders who had earned decoding scores two or more grades below their grade level on a standardized reading test were involved. Included in the experimental group were 11 students with LD. The experimental group received instruction in the Word Identification Strategy for four to eight weeks, depending on the time required for each student to reach mastery. The comparison group received traditional reading instruction. To obtain a decoding score, all students were tested at the beginning and end of the study using the Slosson Diagnostic Achievement Battery (Gnagey & Gnagey, 1994).

Results showed that students in the experimental group were decoding, on average, at a high-fourth-grade level when they entered high school. Seven months later, after experimental students had received instruction in the strategy, they were decoding, on average, at the high-eighth-grade level, a mean improvement of 3.4 grade levels. Every student made an improvement of at least 0.8 grade levels. The 11 students with LD made a mean improvement of 3.9 grade levels in decoding (range = 0.8–6.1). Their average decoding level was at the 4.9 grade level at the beginning of the study and at the 8.8 grade level at the end of the study.

Comparison students made little improvement. At the beginning of the study, they were decoding, on average, at the 6.1 grade level. Seven months later, they were decoding, on average, at the 6.3 grade level, for an average gain of 0.2 grade levels (range = 0.1–1.7 grade levels).

ANCOVA results indicated that there was a significant difference between the posttest scores of the experimental and comparison groups, $F(1, 121) = 31.078$, $p < .001$, $\eta^2 = .692$; this represents a large effect size. In addition, there was a significant difference between the posttest scores of students with LD in the experimental group and the posttest scores of comparison students who were matched with students with LD in the experimental group on the basis of pretest scores, $F(1, 19) = 29.673$, MSE = 43.93, $p < .001$, $\eta^2 = .610$; this represents a large effect size. However, the most significant finding was that, at the end of the study, all students in the experimental group were decoding, on average, at the ninth-grade level, their actual grade level. The students with LD were decoding, on average, at the high-eighth-grade level (8.8), very close to their actual grade level. Furthermore, the authors reported that similar results had been achieved by the school decoding program for eight years running.

With regard to reading comprehension strategies, Clark et al. (1984) conducted a study on students' acquisition of the Visual Imagery Strategy (Schumaker, Deshler, Zemitzch, & Warner, 1993) and the Self-Questioning Strategy (Schumaker, Deshler, Nolan, & Alley, 1994). Six students with LD in Grades 8 through 12 participated, and a multiple-probe across-strategies design was used for each student. Some students were taught the Visual Imagery Strategy first; others were taught the Self-Questioning Strategy first. However, all students received instruction in both strategies.

As in the Lenz and Hughes (1990) study, several measures were used. These included a measure of student use of each strategy while they were reading a passage, as well as a measure of reading comprehension after reading the passage. Two levels of 100- to 200-word passages were used to gather these measures: those written at the student's reading level and those written at the student's actual grade level. To gather the strategy-use measures, five dots were marked in the passage at relatively equally spaced intervals. The students were individually asked to read until they reached a dot and then to tell the researcher about the picture they had in their minds of the passage (visual imagery) or to tell the researcher about any questions they had asked themselves about the passage (self-questioning), depending on which strategy was being tested in a given session. The researcher scored each student response according to a written set of objective guidelines. For example, a question was scored as "appropriate" if it was relevant to the passage's content, if the answer did not include information that the student had already read, and if it did not repeat a previously asked question.

Results showed that all six students mastered both strategies with regard to applying them to ability-level materials. Five of the six students learned to apply both strategies to grade-level materials within four practice trials and did so in such a way as to improve their performance on the comprehension tests. In the baseline condition, the mean percentage of comprehension questions answered correctly on grade-level passages was 42%, even after the students were prompted to use visual images. After instruction in the Visual Imagery Strategy, the mean percentage of comprehension questions answered correctly on grade-level passages was 82% when students were prompted to use the strategy. Results for the Self-Questioning Strategy were similar. The mean percentage of comprehension questions answered correctly on grade-level passages was 46% in the baseline condition and 90% after instruction. Follow-up tests conducted after instruction was terminated showed some decrease in mean comprehension scores (down to 78% for Visual Imagery and 70% for Self-Questioning). Thus, these results show that after relatively small amounts of instructional time (five to seven hours per strategy), students with LD could learn to apply reading comprehension strategies to materials written at their grade level in such a way that their comprehension of those passages increased substantially.

These findings were replicated in another study that focused on a different reading comprehension strategy, the Paraphrasing Strategy (Schumaker et al., 1984). In that study (Schumaker & Deshler, 1992), six students with LD in Grades 10 through 12 were taught the strategy using the same instructional methodology applied in the other studies. A multiple-baseline across-students design was used to demonstrate experimental control. Again, students were instructed to stop at five points while they were reading each passage. At each point, they were asked to tell the researcher about what they had read. The student's response was scored as an accurate paraphrase according to a set of written guidelines. In addition, the students took a comprehension test on the passage's content the day after reading each passage. Again, students were tested using ability-level and grade-level passages before and after instruction.

Results showed that all students mastered applying the Paraphrasing Strategy. As the number of points they earned on paraphrases increased, the percentage of questions answered correctly on the comprehension test also increased. They required an average of four practice attempts to reach the mastery criterion (80% correct). In the baseline condition, the students earned a mean of 0% of the paraphrasing points available and answered a mean of 52% of the comprehension questions correctly on ability-level passages and a mean of 49.5% of the questions correctly on grade-level passages. After instruction, they earned a mean of 71% of the paraphrasing points available and answered a mean of 86% of the questions correctly on ability-level passages and a mean of 84% of the questions correctly on grade-level passages. The students were reading, on average, at the 5.9 grade level (range = 3.8–7.7) when they began the study. At the end of the study, they were performing the strategy and earning an average comprehension score of 84% on passages written, on average, at the 10.5 grade level.

In another study that focused on the instruction of two reading comprehension strategies, Beals (1983) taught the Self-Questioning Strategy and the Paraphrasing Strategy to a ninth-grade English class containing 23 students. A comparison class contained 25 students. Three students with disabilities, three high-achieving students, and three low-achieving students within each class served as targeted subjects for a multiple-probe across-strategies design. Thus, a comparison-group design was combined with a multiple-probe design so that individual student results could be highlighted, as well as group results. Students in the experimental class received instruction in the strategies through the use of the eight-stage instructional methodology described previously combined with cooperative-group structures. Students in the comparison class received traditional English class instruction. Measures included the same measures described for the Self-Questioning and Paraphrasing strategies, including a performance measure and a comprehension measure for each strategy.

Results showed that students with LD and low-achieving students in the two classes were somewhat comparable at the beginning of the study. For example, the targeted students with LD earned a mean self-questioning score of 8% in the experimental class and a mean score of 5% in the comparison class. Low-achieving students earned a mean self-questioning score of 7% in the experimental class and 10% in the comparison class. All students in the experimental class earned an average self-questioning score of 11%, and all students in the comparison class earned an average score of 9%. For paraphrasing, students with LD and low achievers earned an average score of 50% and 40% in the experimental class and 48% and 35% in the comparison class, respectively. All students earned an average paraphrasing score of 50% in the experimental class and 47% in the comparison class.

All targeted students in the experimental class mastered both strategies after instruction, as shown by the multiple-probe design. After instruction, the experimental students with LD earned an average self-questioning score of 100% and low-achieving students earned an average score of 80%. In contrast, comparison students with LD and low-achieving students earned average self-questioning scores of 30% and 18%, respectively. After instruction, all experimental students earned an average self-questioning score of 88%; all comparison students earned an average score of 20%. With regard to paraphrasing, experimental students with LD and low achievers earned mean scores of 80% and 90%, respectively. All experimental students earned a mean paraphrasing score of 90%. Comparison students with LD and low achievers earned mean scores of 60% and 50%, respectively. The mean score for all the comparison students was 40%.

Mean comprehension scores also increased for experimental students. For example, the mean comprehension score for experimental students with LD on grade-level materials increased from 24% to 70%; for experimental low achievers, it increased from 30% to 70%; for all experimental students, it increased from 50% to 70%. The only group to make gains in the comparison class was the low-achieving group; their mean comprehension score on grade-level materials increased from 48% to 60%.

Thus, this study showed that reading strategies could be taught in an inclusive general education high school class in such a way that students could make substantial gains in reading and comprehension skills. Nevertheless, these results were achieved when the eight-stage methodology was used and students had multiple opportunities to practice using each strategy. They also received help and feedback from peers in their cooperative groups. The cooperative-group structure was designed in such a way that students helped and encouraged each other to master each strategy (that is, points were awarded to individuals according to how well *all* members of the group performed). The teacher indicated, however, that scoring many practice attempts was a daunting task.

All of the studies on reading strategies instruction reviewed here used short written passages for the reading task that students were asked to complete. An additional study focused on a task that replicated a reading task that students encounter in subject-area courses in high school: reading whole textbook chapters (Schumaker, Deshler, Alley, Warner, & Denton, 1982). For this investigation, researchers taught a strategy called the Multipass Strategy to eight students enrolled in Grades 7 through 12. The strategy involves three passes through a textbook chapter. In the first pass, the *Survey Pass*, students survey the chapter to familiarize themselves with the chapter title, the relationship of the chapter to other chapters, chapter organization, the chapter's introduction and summary, and illustrations. Then they paraphrase that information silently to themselves. During the second pass, the *Size-Up Pass*, students gain information from the chapter. First, they review the questions at the end of the chapter. Next, they look for a textual cue such as a heading or a bold-faced word and ask themselves a question about that information. Then they skim for the answer to that question and paraphrase the answer to the question. They repeat this process for each textual cue throughout the chapter. At the end of the chapter, they paraphrase all of the information they can remember. During the third pass, the *sort-out pass*, they test themselves on chapter content using the questions at the end of the chapter. If the answers are not known, they skim the chapter for the answer and paraphrase it to themselves.

A multiple-probe across-strategies design was used to demonstrate control for each student. Students were administered tests that measured their performance of strategic behaviors during each pass through the chapter and their knowledge of chapter information at the end of each pass. For example, for the survey test, they were asked to learn as much information as they could within a specified period of time (one minute per page). They were observed during this time, and then they were asked to tell what they had learned. Students also took a test on chapter information after completing all three passes. Two types of textbook chapters were used for the tests: some written at a student's reading ability level, and those assigned in the student's actual subject-area courses and written at least at the student's grade level.

Results showed that all of the students mastered the use of the Multipass Strategy in ability-level chapters and then immediately generalized it to their grade-level textbook chapters without further practice. Mean pretest and posttest scores, respectively, for each of the passes with regard to knowledge gained in a grade-level chapter were 9% and 83% for the Survey Pass, 25% and 97% for the Sort-Out Pass, and 3% and 100% for the Self-Test Pass. On the 20-item written chapter test on a grade-level chapter, the mean pretest score was 40% (an F grade), and the mean posttest score was 91% (an A grade). The students' average reading ability was at the 6.0 grade level (range 4.3–7.3) when the study began, representing a significant gap between their reading-ability level and the grade-level materials to which they were able to productively apply the Multipass Strategy (the mean grade level of the materials was 10th grade, ranging from 7th through 12th grade).

The results of these studies on reading strategies, when taken as a whole, show that students with LD who exhibit significant reading deficits can master reading strategies and apply them to materials written at their grade level so that they can perform well on comprehension tasks. Only one student in the Visual Imagery/Self-Questioning study was unable to immediately generalize his use of reading strategies to grade-level materials. The gap between his reading-ability level and his grade level was five years. The researchers suggested that if a more scaffolded approach had been used—that is, if the student had been taught to use the strategy gradually on more and more difficult materials—he might have been able to navigate the more difficult task with grade-level materials, but this approach was not tested in the study. Nevertheless, this group of studies is significant because they show that given explicit strategy instruction, the gap that secondary students with reading disabilities experience between their reading-ability level and their grade level can be closed, and students can perform well on reading comprehension tasks. Such success is critical for secondary students who are taking required general education courses in which they must read textbooks and novels and pass state minimal competency tests in reading to graduate from high school.

Research on Storage Strategy Instruction

The second area of strategy instruction that has received attention from KU-CRL researchers and affiliates involves teaching students how to study for tests. Secondary students are required to study for and take tests in many subject-area courses. These tests often contain questions that require students to know as many as 60 to 80 information items (Schumaker & Deshler, 1984). They are required to know (1) meanings of vocabulary words, (2) pairs (such as a person's name and his or her accomplishment) or trios of informational items (such as a place, an event, and a date), and (3) lists of items (such as the names of the bones in the leg). Studies focused on the task of studying this kind of information have involved the teaching of some sort of mnemonic (memory) strategies to students so that they can use it in a generative way. That is, in each study, a particular set of mnemonic strategies was taught so that students could apply that set of strategies whenever they encountered similar kinds of information.

In a study focused on vocabulary learning, Wedel, Deshler, Schumaker, and Ellis (reported in Ellis, 1992) taught the *LINCS Vocabulary Strategy* to students in one sixth-grade social studies class. Students in a second class served as the comparison group. The LINCS Vocabulary Strategy comprises a set of mnemonic strategies including a keyword strategy, a visual imagery strategy, and a story strategy. Students use these strategies in combination, create study cards for themselves, and then test themselves on the information until they know it.

Study results showed that students with LD in the experimental class earned a mean score of 53% on vocabulary tests in their social studies class before using the strategy and a mean score of 77% after using the strategy. Students without LD in the experimental class earned a mean score of 84% on vocabulary tests before using the strategy and a mean score of 92% after using the strategy. Students in the comparison class earned mean scores of 86% and 85% on tests before and after the experimental class learned the strategy, respectively. None of the students in the comparison class had LD.

In another comparison study, Harris (in press) taught the LINCS Vocabulary Strategy to 87 eighth-grade students (including three students with LD) enrolled in five sections of an inclusive general education language arts course. Three classes served as Group A ($n = 54$), and two classes served as Group B ($n = 33$). The 20 vocabulary words to be learned were taken from two units of instruction (10 from each unit). A counterbalanced design was used. Students in Group A created mnemonic devices for the words in Unit 1; students in Group B wrote out dictionary definitions for those words. Then, students in Group B created mnemonic devices for the words in Unit 2; students in Group A wrote out dictionary definitions for those words. At the end of each unit, a vocabulary test was given in which students had to write the meaning of each word.

Results showed that the students who used the strategy earned significantly higher scores than the students who did not use the strategy for each unit. For example, their mean pretest score of the students who used the strategy on Unit 1 was 22%, and their mean posttest score was 67%. The mean pretest score of the dictionary group was 16%, and their mean posttest score was 36%. The mean pretest score of the students who used the strategy on Unit 2 was 17%, and their mean posttest score was 62%. The mean pretest score of the dictionary group was 15%, and their mean posttest score was 51%. The difference between the two types of instruction was found to be statistically significant.

To help high school students with LD learn pairs or trios of facts, Bulgren et al. (1995) taught them the Paired-Associates Strategy. This strategy initially involves the creation of one of four types of mnemonic devices: making mental images, relating information to prior knowledge, using keywords, and making a code. Then students create study cards and tests themselves on the information. Twelve students participated in the multiple-baseline across-students designs, with three students participating in each design.

Two types of tests were given for the repeated measures. In the first type of test (the controlled tests), students were given a list of 20 pairs or trios of facts and asked to learn them. Each type of mnemonic device that students had learned could be used to remember five of the pairs or trios in the list. Students were given 45 minutes to study the information. The next day, students were given a fill-in-the-blank test on the information. In the second type of test (called the content test), students were given a written passage, similar to a passage that they would encounter in a high school textbook, in which 20 pairs or trios of factual items had been embedded. Students were asked to study the information in the passage and make study cards on one day and then take a test over the information on the next day.

The authors reported that in the baseline condition, the 12 students earned an average score of 18% on the controlled tests and 22% on the content tests. Students learned the strategy quickly, meeting the mastery criterion for creating each type of mnemonic device within one or two trials. After instruction, the students' mean score on the controlled tests was 85% and on content tests 76%. With the exception of one score, all of the students' scores in the baseline represented failing performances. After instruction, 59 of the 66 test scores represented passing performances. Ten of the 12 students maintained their performance on follow-up tests. Two received additional instruction during the maintenance condition and then met their prior performance levels.

In a study focused on a third storage strategy, called the FIRST-Letter Mnemonic Strategy, Nagel (1982) taught students with LD how to remember lists of information. The FIRST-Letter Mnemonic Strategy involves the use of several first-letter devices, including (1) using the first letters of the items in the list to form a word, (2) inserting a letter among the first letters to form a word, (3) rearranging the letters to form a word, (4) creating a sentence using the first letters of the items in the list as the first letters of words in a sentence, and (5) using combinations of the first four devices. Nagel taught the students to try to create each of these types of devices in sequence for each list until one worked. Once they had created a device, they were to test themselves on the information.

A multiple-baseline across-students design was used with two students in each repetition of the design. Six students with LD in Grades 10 and 11 participated. Two types of tests were given to the students. For the first type of test, which was administered before and after instruction, students were given a piece of paper on which three lists were printed. These lists had been derived from textbooks written at the fifth-grade level, and the tests containing these lists will be referred to as *ability-level tests*. Each list had a heading and four items related to the heading written underneath the heading. Students were given time to study the lists and told that they would be tested on the information the next day. The next day, they took a test with three items on it. Each test question asked them to name the items in one of the lists they had studied (for instance, name the four types of spiders). For the second type of test, which was also administered before and after instruction, students were given a piece of paper with four lists that had been derived from textbooks for the courses in which the students were currently enrolled (these tests are referred to as *grade-level tests*). However, the students had not yet had instruction on the information in class. Again, each list had a heading and four items that were related to the heading. The students were given time to study the information, and on the next day, they were asked to take a test on the information.

Results showed that the students learned to use the strategy quickly, requiring just a few practice trials on each type of first-letter device. In the baseline condition, they earned a mean score of 53% on the ability-level tests and a mean score of 51% on the grade-level tests. After instruction, they earned a mean score of 95% on the ability-level tests and a mean score of 85% on the grade-level tests.

When considered as a group, the results of the studies conducted on the storage strategies are promising. They show that students with LD can learn to use mnemonic strategies to master a variety of items they are expected to learn for upcoming tests, and they can use them in a generative way when they face novel items they have not previously encountered. In addition, one of the studies (Bulgren et al., 1995) showed that students with LD could learn to find the items to be mastered within written passages and study them effectively. Furthermore, although they earned failing scores during baseline or pretest conditions, once they had learned a storage strategy, most students earned scores well above the passing range. Because none of the studies measured student performance on the number and variety of items required for typical secondary tests (many tests have 60 to 80 items, whereas the most items on any one test in the studies was 20 items), whether students with LD can learn to study that many items is not known.

Research on Expression Strategy Instruction

A number of research studies have been conducted to determine the effects of instruction in expression strategies on the academic performance of adolescents with disabilities. These studies are similar to the studies conducted on other reading strategies. However, measures vary across the studies. For example, in studies focused on writing strategies, measures relate to elements of writing such as sentence completeness, organization of paragraphs and themes, and spelling, punctuation, and capitalization errors. In studies focused on test taking, measures relate to successful test-taking behaviors. In studies focused on assignment completion, measures relate to skills involved in the successful completion of homework assignments. In other words, the goal of this group of studies was to create and validate interventions that would yield performance on written products (themes, tests, and assignments) that would be appropriate for required general education high school and college courses.

Kline et al. (1991) conducted a study on the Sentence Writing Strategy, the strategy typically taught first within the expression strand of the Learning Strategies Curriculum in which three groups of teachers and their students with LD participated. Twenty-four teachers (eight teachers per group) and 54 students (18 students per group) in Grades 4 through 12 were involved. After all the teachers had been instructed in how to teach the Sentence Writing Strategy in a daylong workshop and given all the materials needed to teach 10 students, one group of eight teachers received instruction on how to give elaborated feedback. Elaborated feedback involves meeting privately with a student after each practice attempt to make at least three positive statements about the student's performance, specify a category of error the student made, show examples of the error type, describe how to avoid the error in the future, model how to perform in the future, ensure that the student practices avoiding the error, and provide help and feedback until the student performs at least one example correctly.

Eight other teachers received instruction on how to give elaborated feedback and how to teach their students to accept that feedback using an "acceptance routine." Additionally, these teachers learned to prompt students to summarize the feedback and to write a goal statement related to the feedback. This goal was to be reviewed by the student immediately before the next practice trial. The third group of eight teachers was instructed to provide feedback as specified in the instructor's manual. This involved making three positive statements about the student's practice attempt, specifying a type of error the student made, reviewing the concept or rule associated with the error, and requiring the student to correct the error. The students of teachers in this third group are referred to as the *comparison students*.

Measures collected in the study included an observation measure of the teachers' implementation of the assigned feedback routine, an observation measure of student acceptance of the feedback, the number of student trials necessary for mastery within the instructional sequence for learning how to write simple sentences, and the number of errors made by the students on their learning sheets within six error categories.

Results showed, through the use of a multiple-baseline across-teachers design, that the teachers in the two elaborated feedback groups learned quickly and easily how to implement the elaborated feedback routine in conjunction with instruction in the Sentence Writing Strategy. Results also showed that their students learned the feedback acceptance routine easily. Student results showed that all students met the mastery criterion on all of the lesson sets (earned 90% or more of the points available). A 3×3 factorial design showed that significant differences were found in the average number of trials required to reach mastery across the three groups of students. The comparison students required a mean of 14.6 trials to reach mastery; students in the feedback group required a mean of 10.8 trials; students in the feedback plus acceptance group required a mean of 9.5 trials. Significant differences were found between the average number of trials to mastery required by the comparison students and the average number of trials to mastery required by the other two groups of students. No differences were found between the number of trials required by the two elaborated feedback groups.

Moreover, students in the two elaborated feedback groups, according to the $3 \times 3 \times 2$ repeated-measures factorial design, made substantially fewer errors on the second trial than on the first trial in all error categories across the lesson sets, whereas students in the comparison group did not. That is, students in the two elaborated feedback groups performed substantially better on the second trial within each lesson set. Thus, they met the mastery criterion on that trial. Students in the comparison group did not perform better on the second trial than on the first trial and required more practice trials to meet mastery. To summarize, this study showed that students with learning disabilities could learn to write simple sentences and that they could reach mastery within two trials on each lesson set, as long as teachers provided elaborated feedback to them after the first practice attempt.

Moran, Schumaker, and Vetter (1981) conducted two experiments focused on the instruction of the Paragraph Writing Strategy (Schumaker & Lyerla, 1991). In the first experiment, three adolescents with LD in the eighth and ninth grades were taught to use the Paragraph Writing Strategy to write enumerative, sequential, and compare-and-contrast paragraphs in sequence. In addition, they were taught to write a topic sentence, at least three detail sentences, and a clincher sentence in each type of paragraph. Students were first introduced to the strategy, and then one paragraph type was described and modeled before the students practiced writing that type of paragraph. Students were required to meet mastery on one paragraph type before proceeding to learn about another type. They earned points for each type of sentence appropriately written within each paragraph, and the percentage of points earned was calculated. Instruction was delivered in a one-hour time period each day. Results of the multiple-baseline across-paragraph-types design showed the instruction's effects on each student's paragraph organization. The average paragraph organization scores earned by the students were 59%, 50%, and 44% in the baseline condition and 95%, 90%, and 87% after instruction for enumerative, sequential, and compare-and-contrast paragraphs, respectively.

A follow-up experiment was conducted by Moran et al. (1981) because students had generalized their use of the strategy across paragraph types during the first experiment, which interfered with the usefulness of the experimental design. In the second experiment, five students with LD in the 7th through 10th grades participated. A multiple-baseline across-students design was combined with a multiple-baseline across-paragraph-types design to allow for possible generalization effects. The only other difference between the two experiments was that students in the second experiment had instruction in two-hour blocks each day because they were participating in summer school. In the baseline condition, the average paragraph writing scores earned by students were 49%, 49%, and 38%; after instruction they were 92%, 87%, and 91% for enumerative, sequential, and compare-and-contrast paragraphs, respectively. The multiple-baseline across-students design showed that improvements in paragraph writing occurred only in conjunction with instruction in the first paragraph type.

Moran et al.'s (1981) experiments show that instruction was equally effective in one- and two-hour time blocks and for a variety of students; students earned scores ranging from 19% to 71% on individual pretests. Interestingly, all students generalized their use of the strategy to at least one untrained paragraph type, and three of the students generalized their use of the strategy to both untrained paragraph types.

In another study focused on a strategy in the expression strand of the Learning Strategies Curriculum, Schumaker, Deshler, Alley, Warner, Clark, and Nolan (1982) taught the Error Monitoring Strategy to nine students with LD in Grades 8 through 12. This strategy enables students to edit four major categories of errors in their writing: capitalization, punctuation, appearance, and spelling errors. The strategy was described and modeled for students, and then the students memorized the strategy steps. Next, students practiced using the strategy on written passages in which 20 errors had been inserted (called teacher-generated passages). Students were expected to find and correct those errors, and their scores on each passage represented (1) the percentage of errors identified correctly and (2) the percentage of errors edited correctly. Once students had found and correctly edited 18 of the 20 errors in one passage, they practiced finding and correcting errors in passages that they had written themselves (student-generated passages). Students had to make fewer than one error in every 20 words (or fewer than 0.05 errors per word) in their final drafts of student-generated passages to reach mastery.

After students had learned the Error Monitoring Strategy, results of the multiple-baseline across-students design showed that they found and corrected substantially more errors than before instruction. In the baseline condition, each student corrected less than 25% of the errors in the teacher-generated passages. After instruction, all students corrected more than 90% of the errors, and they all met the mastery criterion within six practice attempts (mean score = 96%), with most students reaching mastery within three attempts. In the baseline condition, students made as many as one error in every two words in the final drafts of the student-generated passages. After instruction, some students made no errors; others made a few errors, such as one error in every 20 or 30 words. They all met the mastery criterion within one or two practice attempts. Thus, this study demonstrated that students with LD could learn to correct a variety of errors and could generatively use the strategy to detect and correct successive examples of different kinds of errors. It also showed that they could learn to detect and correct the errors in someone else's writing and in their own writing.

In another study focused on detecting and correcting writing errors, McNaughton, Hughes, and Ofiesh (1997) taught the InSPECT Strategy (McNaughton & Hughes, 1999) to three students with LD between 15 and 18 years old. This strategy enables students to detect and correct spelling errors through the use of a computerized spellchecker. McNaughton and Hughes evaluated the effects of the instruction using a multiple-baseline across-students design that included three phases: baseline, intervention, and maintenance. Maintenance of the strategy use was measured one, two, and four weeks after instruction was terminated. They measured strategy use and spelling errors.

The strategy was described and modeled for students, and students learned how to name the strategy steps in order until they met a 100% correct criterion. During the computerized controlled practice activities, students were asked to correct spelling errors in passages (designed by the researchers) that each contained 20 spelling errors representing both misspelled and incorrectly used words. Next, students practiced correcting spelling errors in their own writing. Finally, they participated in generalization training in which they committed to and discussed using the strategy in a variety of settings.

Before instruction, students used an average of 39% of the strategy steps. After instruction and during the maintenance condition, they used an average of 79% and 86% of the steps, respectively. Before instruction, an average of 7.6% of the words in their compositions contained spelling errors. They had corrected an average of only 41% of their spelling errors, even though they had a spellchecker at hand. After instruction (during the maintenance condition), an average of 3% of the words in their compositions contained spelling errors. They had corrected an average of 75% of their spelling errors, which is similar to the level of performance of peers who do not have spelling disabilities (McNaughton & Hughes, 1999). Thus, this study indicated that students who have disabilities in the area of spelling could learn a strategy for using a computerized spellchecker that helped them eliminate spelling errors in their writing and performed at a level comparable to peers who did not have such a disability.

In yet another writing strategy study, Hock (1998) taught the Theme Writing Strategy to 28 underprepared freshman scholarship athletes who had earned an average score of 17.7 on the American College Test (ACT, a college entrance test) and a grade point average (GPA) of 2.8 in high school. Two of the students in this group had learning disabilities, and one had attention deficit hyperactivity disorder. They were all enrolled in English 101, a required English course at a midwestern university, and were required to participate in academic tutoring for 6 to 10 hours per week because of their skill deficits. An additional group of 28 freshman scholarship athletes who had earned an average score of 23.2 on the ACT and a GPA of 3.3 in high school and who were also enrolled in English 101 participated in the comparison group. This comparison group had unlimited access to tutors for help with their coursework; however, they did not receive instruction in the strategy. The research question was whether a group of underprepared students who were taught the Theme Writing Strategy could perform as well in the English 101 course as a more prepared group of students who had not learned the strategy.

All of the students were required to write six themes for the English 101 course, including three in-class themes and three out-of-class themes. They had 90 minutes to write a 400- to 500-word theme in class without help. They had unlimited time to write the out-of-class themes. Student performance on the six themes made up the semester course grade.

Hock collected three measures. For the first, students were given a knowledge test in which they were asked an open-ended question about the steps they would take or the strategies they would use to write a theme. Students could earn up to 10 points on this oral knowledge test.

The semester grade earned by each student in the course was the second measure, and the semester GPA earned by each student for all college courses taken during the first freshman semester was the third measure.

The experimental students earned significantly lower scores on the theme writing knowledge pretest ($M = 1.6$) than the comparison students ($M = 2.7$). Nevertheless, at the end of the semester, they earned knowledge test scores that were significantly higher than the comparison students ($M = 3.5$). In the English 101 course, the experimental students earned an average grade of 2.5 (A = 4, B = 3, C = 2, D = 1, F = 0), and the comparison students earned an average grade of 2.6. The overall grade point average was 2.5 for the experimental group and 2.54 for the comparison group during their first semester in college. There were no significant differences between the groups' grades in the English 101 course or between their overall GPAs, even though students in the experimental group had entered college with poorer skills than the comparison students. All three students with disabilities in the experimental group earned C's in the English 101 course, and they earned overall GPAs of 2.50, 2.62, and 2.91 during their first semester of college.

Another expression strategy is the Test-Taking Strategy (Hughes et al., 1988). Two studies have been conducted on the effects of teaching this strategy to adolescents with disabilities. In the first study, Hughes and Schumaker (1991) taught six seventh- and eighth-grade students with LD how to apply the strategy while taking tests. To measure the students' test-taking skills, they constructed a pool of 10 equivalent tests, each containing five sections and a total of 29 items. Each item was specifically designed to measure whether a student was using a particular test-taking skill (for instance, whether the student crossed out obviously incorrect answers). A checklist was also designed to record student use of certain test-taking behaviors, as indicated by their responses on the test. For example, the following items appeared on the checklist: (1) Did the student underline words in a set of instructions that indicated how to respond? (2) Did the student underline words in the instructions that indicated where to respond? (3) Did the student follow the instructions correctly? Unit test scores were also collected from students' mainstream classes.

Results of the multiple-probe across-students design showed that students performed an average of 30% of the test-taking behaviors on the checklist before instruction began. After students had instruction in the strategy, they reached the mastery criterion (90% of the behaviors) in an average of two practice attempts. On the posttests, the students performed an average of 90% of the test-taking behaviors. They performed a mean of 85% of the test-taking behaviors during maintenance probes that lasted for 11 weeks after instruction was terminated. On their unit tests in mainstream courses, the students were earning an average score of 57% during baseline (an F grade). After instruction, they were earning an average score of 71% (a C grade) on unit tests.

Hughes, Deshler, Ruhl, and Schumaker (1993) repeated the same study with a group of six seventh- and eighth-grade students with emotional and behavioral disorders. The same Test-Taking Strategy was taught, and the same measures were used. Results of the multiple-probe across-students design showed that the students performed a mean of 32% of the test-taking behaviors in the baseline condition. On posttests, they performed a mean of 95% of the test-taking behaviors. During maintenance probes, they performed a mean of 88% of the test-taking behaviors. On unit tests in their general education courses, they earned a mean score of 57% in the baseline condition and 68% after instruction in the strategy.

Finally, Hughes, Ruhl, Schumaker, and Deshler (2002) conducted a study on the effects of teaching the Assignment Completion Strategy to students with LD who were enrolled in at least three general education courses in which homework was assigned. Nine students in the sixth through eighth grades participated. One repeated measure in the study was the percentage of assignment completion behaviors performed by the students on a series of simulated probe assignments. Another repeated measure was the percentage of assignment completion behaviors performed by the students on actual assignments given to them in their general education classes, determined from each student's recordings in his or her assignment notebook. Teachers in these general education classes supplied information about assignments given each week, as well as whether each assignment was turned in, whether it was turned in on time, and the student's quarterly grade.

Results of the multiple-probe across-students design showed that the students earned an average of 19% of the points available for assignment completion behaviors on simulated assignments during baseline. During instruction in the Assignment Completion Strategy, eight of the nine students earned an average of 81% of the points and met the mastery criterion of 90% of the points within three practice trials. During the maintenance condition, students earned an average of 90% of the points. One student improved from earning 11% of the points during baseline to 65% of the points during instruction. On actual assignments given in class, students earned an average of less than 1.7% of the points available for recording assignments and planning assignment completion per week. During the instructional and maintenance conditions, they earned an average of 28% and 60% of the points, respectively.

With regard to actual assignment completion, students turned in an average of 54% of their assignments in the baseline condition and an average of 58% of their assignments during instruction in the strategy. During the maintenance condition, they turned in 70% of their assignments. They earned a GPA of 1.7 in the targeted classes in the first school quarter before instruction in the strategy. During the fourth school quarter, after instruction in the strategy, they earned a GPA of 2.7 in those classes.

All of the studies reviewed thus far in the expression area focused on the instruction of only one expression strategy. Two studies focused on the instruction of more than one strategy. One such study focused on the effects of instruction of two writing strategies, and the other focused on instruction of four writing strategies.

In the first study, two writing strategies were taught in a 10th-grade English class containing 31 students (Beals, 1983). A comparison class contained 25 students. Three students with disabilities, three high-achieving students, and three low-achieving students within each class served as targeted subjects for the multiple-probe across-strategies design. Students in the experimental class received instruction in the Sentence Writing Strategy and then the Error Monitoring Strategy through the use of the eight-stage instructional methodology described previously combined with cooperative-group structures. Students in the comparison class received traditional writing instruction. Measures included the percentage of complete sentences, the percentage of complicated sentences (compound, complex, and compound-complex sentences), and an error score (the total number of errors divided by the total number of words written, subtracted from 100).

Results showed that students in the two classes were somewhat comparable at the beginning of the study. For example, targeted students with LD wrote an average of 45% complete sentences in the experimental class and an average of 35% complete sentences in the comparison class. Low-achieving students in the experimental class wrote an average of 35% complete sentences, and low-achieving students in the comparison class wrote an average of 50% complete sentences. All students in the experimental class wrote an average of 55% complete sentences, and all students in the comparison class wrote an average of 67% complete sentences.

All targeted students in the experimental class mastered both strategies after instruction, as shown by the multiple-probe design. After instruction, the experimental students with LD wrote an average of 90% complete sentences, and the low-achieving students wrote an average of 80% complete sentences. Comparison students with LD and low-achieving comparison students wrote an average of 40% complete sentences after traditional instruction. After instruction, all experimental students wrote an average of 95% complete sentences; all comparison students wrote an average of 55% complete sentences. Substantial gains were made by experimental students with LD on the other measures as well. Experimental high-achieving students did not make gains in sentence completeness and error monitoring. They did make substantial gains with regard to writing complicated sentences, as did the experimental low-achieving students. The comparison students made small gains on the error monitoring measure; otherwise, their performance was stable across the course of the study.

This study showed that writing strategies could be taught in an inclusive general education high school class in such a way that students made substantial gains in their writing skills. Nevertheless, caution is in order.

These results were achieved when the eight-stage methodology was used and when students had multiple opportunities to practice using the strategy. Peers within the cooperative groups provided help and feedback to those students who needed it, and the cooperative-group structure was tailored to ensure that all students mastered the strategy (that is, points were awarded to individual students according to how well *all* members of the group performed). Unfortunately, the experimental high-achieving students indicated they were not satisfied with the instruction because they did not like their role as teachers of other students. Moreover, the teacher also indicated that the scoring of multiple written practice attempts was very difficult.

Another study that focused on instruction of more than one strategy involved seven students with LD in Grades 10 through 12 who were taught two or more writing strategies: the Sentence Writing Strategy, the Paragraph Writing Strategy, the Error Monitoring Strategy, and the Theme Writing Strategy (Schmidt, 1983; Schmidt, Deshler, Schumaker, & Alley, 1988/89). For each student, a multiple-baseline across-strategies design was employed to show the effects of instruction in each strategy on products written in the special education class and in general education classes. For the Sentence Writing Strategy, measures were the percentage of complete sentences and the percentage of complicated sentences in a given written product. For the Paragraph Writing Strategy, the measure was the percentage of points earned on different kinds of required sentences in a paragraph. The measure associated with the Error Monitoring Strategy was the number of errors per word in a student's final draft. The measure associated with the Theme Writing Strategy was the percentage of points earned by the student on sentences contained in the student's theme. Students received instruction in the strategies in the sequence listed above.

Several written products were gathered in the special education classroom for each student before, during, and after instruction in each strategy. Throughout the study, written products were collected in the students' English and history classes without their knowledge to obtain measures of generalization across settings. In the following school year, at least one written product was gathered from a general education class to determine whether the students had maintained their use of the strategies. Other measures included students' scores on the Written Language Subtest of the Woodcock-Johnson Psychoeducational Battery and their scores on the school district's writing competency exam.

On all products written in the special education classroom, all students exceeded the mastery criteria related to each strategy. Three of the students received instruction in all four strategies. Because of the instructional time available or because some students had few errors in their writing, three students received instruction in three strategies, and one student received instruction in two strategies.

After students completed instruction in a given strategy, their written products were gathered from the general education teachers. Results were mixed. As a group, students generalized their use of the Sentence Writing Strategy, the Error Monitoring Strategy and the Theme Writing Strategy to some extent to products written in these classes (that is, their scores improved), but not at a level equivalent to mastery. The strategy teacher then used a variety of instructional procedures to promote generalization across classes. First, the teacher reviewed the strategy with the students and had them practice using the strategy. As a result, some students generalized their use of some strategies to general education classes. For example, four students met the criterion on their in-class writing samples for the percentage of complete sentences written. However, these performance levels were not maintained over time. Next, the teacher specifically told the students to generalize their use of a strategy to other classes, and they subsequently received individual feedback from the teacher on written products they produced in those classes. This condition produced higher mean scores than the review condition, and some students met the mastery criteria on several measures on products written in their general education classes. With two students who did not generalize at mastery levels, the teacher implemented a self-control condition. She guided students to set goals for themselves with regard to generalization and to deliver reinforcers to themselves when they met mastery. On behalf of one student, in a cooperative planning condition, the special education teacher taught the general education teacher how to prompt and cue the student to use the writing strategies. Both the self-control and cooperative planning conditions resulted in generalized use of the writing strategies in the general education classroom. By the end of the school year, six of the seven students had demonstrated that they could write as well in general education classes as they had in the special education class. One of the students was below the mastery criterion on only one measure, the percentage of complete sentences.

The students' GPAs and course enrollment changed over the course of the study. At the beginning of the study, the students' average GPA was 2.1 in English and social studies courses taught in the resource room by a special education teacher. After strategy instruction, their average GPA was 2.7 in English and social studies general education courses. Before the study, none of the students had earned GPAs of 3.0 or higher. After the study, four of the students did so. On the written language subtest of the Woodcock-Johnson Psychoeducational Battery, the students earned a mean grade-level score of 6.2 at the beginning of the study and 8.2 at the end of the study. (Statistically, this score was predicted to be 7.0 at the end of the study, given the students' previous growth on this measure.) Students who had learned the Theme Writing Strategy earned a mean overall score of 3.5 on the district's writing competency exam; the mean score for 11th graders at large in the district was 2.5. Students in the study who had not learned the Theme Writing Strategy earned a mean score of 2.4 on the district exam.

Thus, research conducted on expression strand strategies shows that students with disabilities can learn complex strategies that enable them to respond to the performance demands of secondary schools. They can learn to write themes that are favorably scored on writing competency exams and that allow them to enroll and succeed in general education classes in which themes are a required part of the curriculum. They can learn to take tests and complete assignments in such a way that their grades in secondary courses improve. Because strategies associated with these demands are complex, time needs to be devoted to teaching students to use and generalize them, usually across the course of a few semesters. Nevertheless, once this investment is made, students have the tools they need to use in combination to respond to many of the demands they face in secondary school and beyond.

A Scaling-Up Effort

One high school in Michigan is illustrative of the many schools across the nation that have adopted strategy instruction. The English staff of this school decided to implement instruction in two writing strategies (the Sentence Writing Strategy and the Paragraph Writing Strategy) in all English classes. The district's school board formalized the staff's decision in September of 2000 by adopting instruction in the Sentence Writing Strategy and the Paragraph Writing Strategy as part of the district's core curriculum.

The high school staff compared the results of their writing instruction to the results of instruction in other state high schools using the state competency test as their measure. Student participants learned the Sentence Writing Strategy and the Paragraph Writing Strategy in their 9th- and 10th-grade English classes. They were prompted by their general education teachers in subject-area courses (such as history or science) to generalize the writing strategies to these courses.

Results of the state writing competency exam taken in the 11th grade (class of 2001) showed that 94% of the students in the school who took the exam passed it. In addition, 9 of the 11 students with LD who took the exam also passed it. In contrast, a mean of only 74.5% of students in schools of comparable size and student populations passed. The average percentage of Michigan students who passed the state writing assessment in all schools was 85%. Thus, students who learned writing strategies outperformed students in other Michigan schools (S. Woodruff, personal communication, 2001).

SUMMARY

The research program described in this chapter represents a focused attempt to conceptualize, design, and validate a set of intervention procedures for adolescents with disabilities that enables them to succeed in the general education curriculum. The Learning Strategies Curriculum and the instructional methodology that have been the focus of this research have emerged in relation to the demands that these students are expected to meet as they access the general education curriculum.

Based on research presented in this chapter, the following conclusions can be drawn. First, the eight-stage instructional methodology that was designed to promote the acquisition and generalization of task-specific learning strategies has been shown to be a highly effective instructional system in terms of enabling students with disabilities to master different learning strategies. The studies involved in the line of research summarized here have involved more than 550 students. Of these, 197 students had disabilities. This means that the studies have demonstrated, with 197 replications of the phenomenon, that students with disabilities can, indeed, successfully master a task-specific strategy from the Learning Strategies Curriculum when the instructional methodology is implemented with fidelity. These replications, which involved a number of schools, teachers, students, and researchers, suggest that the design of the strategies and the accompanying instructional methodology are robust relative to their application in conjunction with a broad array of student and setting variables.

Second, this research program presents strong evidence that students with disabilities can generalize using a learning strategy across different types of instructional tasks. Furthermore, in most of the studies described here, students were able to use the strategy they had acquired to respond to tasks similar to those they typically encounter in subject-matter classes. Also, evidence from several studies suggests that students with disabilities can generalize their use of task-specific strategies across settings and situations. Most important, the evidence presented here showed that students who use the strategies in their general education classes can earn higher grades in those classes.

IMPLICATIONS FOR FUTURE RESEARCH

Although there are some data indicating that student outcomes on state assessment measures can be favorably impacted, additional work is required to determine how to best orchestrate a long-term instructional program spanning several years that will result in consistent and dramatic improvement on stringent outcome measures. A second area of investigation that is needed relates to the long-term effects of learning strategy instruction. Although a few research studies have addressed the issue of strategy maintenance, much remains to be learned about how to best ensure sustained use of a targeted strategy over a prolonged time period (for example, over several school years). In addition to studying how elements of the current instructional methodology need to be enhanced to ensure long-term strategy use, other elements related to the belief systems and intrinsic motivation of students to use the strategies need to be strategically incorporated into existing interventions to determine the effects on student outcomes.

Another important area for future investigation relates to the conditions under which learning strategies are taught to students with disabilities. The vast majority of studies reported here involved strategies instruction within the context of settings *other than* the general education classroom. Ways need to be found to enable subject-matter teachers to incorporate learning strategy instruction into the context of their ongoing course while subject-area content is being taught. This is a particularly vexing problem because of enormous pressures on subject-area teachers to teach large volumes of content to high levels of proficiency to prepare students to reach mastery on state assessments (Nolet & McLaughlin, 2000).

Finally, future research needs to address the cumulative effects of strategy instruction on the quality of life experienced by participating students. The bottom line for these students needs to include an increased probability of high school graduation, success in postsecondary education, and productive and meaningful employment. Research on the long-term effects of strategies programs that are coordinated across schools is only now becoming possible as whole school districts adopt the approach.

Central to addressing many of the foregoing areas for future research is the need to conceptualize what constitutes meaningful indexes of strategic performance that can be used for both formative and summative assessments. The design of various assessment devices and measurement systems for evaluating the degree to which students are becoming more strategic learners not only will facilitate research efforts to address these socially significant questions, but also will assist practitioners as they turn their attention to issues related to long-term and far-generalization effects.

IMPLICATIONS FOR IMPLEMENTATION IN SCHOOLS

Schools and school districts across the nation have implemented strategic instruction in a variety of service delivery settings. For example, some schools have implemented strategic instruction in their resource room programs for students with disabilities. Some schools have implemented short, intensive periods of instruction in the Word Identification Strategy with students who are reading two or more grades below their grade level. Some schools have implemented instruction in the reading comprehension strategies in a semester-long or yearlong course. Others have created summer school or afterschool programs in which students can learn the reading comprehension strategies. One state has mandated that a course in learning strategies be taught to students who meet certain criteria.

Some schools and districts have specified that certain strategies will be taught in certain core courses. For example, in one school, certain science teachers teach the Self-Questioning Strategy, social studies teachers teach strategies related to studying for and taking tests, and English teachers teach the writing strategies. Ninth graders learn the Sentence Writing Strategy, 10th graders learn the Paragraph Writing and Error Monitoring strategies, and 11th graders learn the Theme Writing Strategy.

All of these applications require the support of administrators. First, a plan needs to be created that specifies the structures within which strategic instruction will take place. That is, if strategic instruction is going to take place within a special course, the course needs to be designed. Second, personnel need to be assigned to that course or program. Third, the personnel need to receive instruction in how to teach strategies. Typically, teachers receive an overview presentation on strategic instruction and then at least three hours of instruction in each strategy that they are expected to teach. Fourth, teachers need time to plan, gather materials, set up the learning environment, and select students for the course or program. Selecting students might entail testing a pool of students who meet certain criteria. Once students are enrolled in strategic instruction, teachers need time to learn how to implement the instruction. Coaching, in the form of demonstrations, observations, and feedback, can be very helpful at this point.

Thus, administrators play a major role in ensuring that strategic instruction takes place in their schools. Structures and policies need to be created and put in place. Personnel need to be assigned and their roles specified. Professional development experiences need to be orchestrated. Materials need to be purchased. Student schedules need to be arranged. Coaching sessions need to be scheduled. Finally, programs need to be maintained with vigilance through frequent classroom visits and meetings with teachers regarding the outcomes of their instruction.

For more information on how to obtain assistance with professional development experiences for the interventions reviewed in this chapter, visit the University of Kansas Center for Research on Learning Web site at www.kucrl.org or contact the center's director of professional development at 785-864-4780.

REFERENCES

Armbruster, B. B., Echols, C. H., & Brown, A. L. (1982). The role of metacognition is reading to learn: A developmental perspective. *Volta Review, 84*(5), 45–56.

Baer, D. M., Wolf, M. M., & Risley, T. R. (1968). Some current dimensions of applied behavior analysis. *Journal of Applied Behavior Analysis, 1,* 91–97.

Beals, V. L. (1983). *The effects of large group instruction on the acquisition of specific learning strategies by learning disabled adolescents.* Unpublished doctoral dissertation, University of Kansas, Lawrence.

Bereiter, C., & Scardamalia, M. (1993). *Surpassing ourselves: An inquiry into the nature and implications of expertise.* Chicago: Open Court.

Bulgren, J. A., Hock, M. F., Schumaker, J. B., & Deshler, D. D. (1995). The effects of instruction in a Paired-Associates Strategy on the information mastery performance of students with learning disabilities. *Learning Disabilities Research and Practice, 10*(1), 22–37.

Bulgren, J. A., & Schumaker, J. B. (1996). *The Paired-Associates Strategy.* Lawrence: University of Kansas Center for Research on Learning.

Chi, M. T. H. (1981). Knowledge development and memory performance. In M. Friedman, J. P. Das, & N. O'Connor (Eds.), *Intelligence and learning* (pp. 221–230). New York: Plenum.

Clark, F. L., Deshler, D. D., Schumaker, J. B., Alley, G. R., & Warner, M. M. (1984). Visual imagery and self-questioning: Strategies to improve comprehension of written material. *Journal of Learning Disabilities, 17*(3), 145–149.

Deshler, D. D., & Schumaker, J. B. (1986). Learning strategies: An instructional alternative for low-achieving adolescents. *Exceptional Children, 52*(6), 583–590.

Deshler, D. D., & Schumaker, J. B. (1988). An instructional model for teaching students how to learn. In J. L. Graden, J. E. Zins, and M. J. Curtis (Eds.), *Alternative educational delivery systems: Enhancing instructional options for all students* (pp. 391–411). Washington, DC: National Association for School Psychologists.

Deshler, D. D., Schumaker, J. B., Lenz, B. K., Bulgren, J. A., Hock, M. F., Knight, J., & Ehren, B. J. (2001). Ensuring content-area learning by secondary students with learning disabilities. *Learning Disabilities Research and Practice, 16*(2), 96–108.

Ellis, E. S. (1992). *The LINCS Vocabulary Strategy.* Lawrence, KS: Edge Enterprises.

Ellis, E. S., Deshler, D. D., Lenz, B. K., Schumaker, J. B., & Clark, F. L. (1991). An instructional methodology for teaching learning strategies. *Focus on Exceptional Children, 23*(6), 1–24.

Ellis, E. S., Lenz, B. K., & Sabornie, E. J. (1987a). Generalization and adaptation of learning strategies to natural environments: Part 1. Critical agents. *Remedial and Special Education, 8*(1), 6–20.

Ellis, E. S., Lenz, B. K., & Sabornie, E. J. (1987b). Generalization and adaptation of learning strategies to natural environments: Part 2. Research into practice. *Remedial and Special Education, 8*(2), 6–23.

Gnagey, T., & Gnagey, P. (1994). *DST: Reading Diagnostic Screening Test* (3rd ed. rev., Forms A and B). East Aurora, NY: Slosson Educational Publications.

Harris, M. (in press). *The effects of a vocabulary teaching routine in general education classes.* Lawrence: University of Kansas Center for Research on Learning.

Hock, M. F. (1998). *The effectiveness of an instructional tutoring model and tutor training on the academic performance of underprepared college student-athletes.* Unpublished doctoral dissertation, University of Kansas, Lawrence.

Hock, M. F., & Deshler, D. D. (2003). Don't forget the adolescents. *Principal Leadership, 13*(4), 50–56.

Hock, M. F., Schumaker, J. B., & Deshler, D. D. (1999). Closing the gap to success in secondary schools: A model for cognitive apprenticeship. In D. D. Deshler,

J. B. Schumaker, K. R. Harris, & S. Graham (Eds.), *Teaching every adolescent every day* (pp. 1–51). Cambridge, MA: Brookline Books.

Horner, R. D., & Baer, D. M. (1978). Multiple-probe technique: A variation of the multiple baseline. *Journal of Applied Behavior Analysis, 11,* 189–196.

Hughes, C. A., Deshler, D. D., Ruhl, K. L., & Schumaker, J. B. (1993). Test-Taking Strategy instruction for adolescents with emotional and behavioral disorders. *Journal of Emotional and Behavioral Disorders, 1*(3), 188–189.

Hughes, C. A., Ruhl, K. L., Schumaker, J. B., & Deshler, D. D. (1995). *The Assignment Completion Strategy.* Lawrence, KS: Edge Enterprises.

Hughes, C. A., Ruhl, K. L., Schumaker, J. B., & Deshler, D. D. (2002). Effects of an Assignment Completion Strategy on the homework performance of students with learning disabilities in general education classes. *Learning Disabilities Research and Practice, 17*(1), 1–18.

Hughes, C. A., Salvia, J., & Bott, D. (1991). The nature and extent of test-wiseness cues in seventh and tenth grade classroom tests. *Diagnostique, 16,* 153–163.

Hughes, C. A., & Schumaker, J. B. (1991). Test-Taking Strategy instruction for adolescents with learning disabilities. *Exceptionality, 2,* 205–221.

Hughes, C. A., Schumaker, J. B., Deshler, D. D., & Mercer, C. (1988). *The Test-Taking Strategy.* Lawrence, KS: Edge Enterprises.

Kline, F. M., Schumaker, J. B., & Deshler, D. D. (1991). Development and validation of feedback routines for instructing students with learning disabilities. *Learning Disability Quarterly, 14*(3), 191–207.

Lenz, B. K., Clark, F. L., Deshler, D. D., Schumaker, J. B., Hazel, J. S., & Rademacher, J. A. (Eds.). (1990). *SIM training library: Implementing a strategic curriculum.* Lawrence: University of Kansas Institute for Research in Learning Disabilities.

Lenz, B. K., & Hughes, C. A. (1990). A Word Identification Strategy for adolescents with learning disabilities. *Journal of Learning Disabilities, 23*(3), 149–158, 163.

Lenz, B. K., Schumaker, J. B., Deshler, D. D., & Beals, V. L. (1984). *The Word Identification Strategy: Instructor's manual.* Lawrence: University of Kansas Institute for Research in Learning Disabilities.

McNaughton, D., & Hughes, C. A. (1999). *InSPECT: A starter strategy for proofreading.* Lawrence, KS: Edge Enterprises.

McNaughton, D., Hughes, C. A., & Ofiesh, N. (1997). Proofreading for students with learning disabilities: Integrating computer and strategy use. *Learning Disabilities Research and Practice, 12,* 16–28.

Moran, M. R., Schumaker, J. B., & Vetter, A. F. (1981). *Teaching a paragraph organization strategy to learning disabled adolescents* (Research Report No. 54). Lawrence: University of Kansas Institute for Research in Learning Disabilities.

Nagel, D. R. (1982). *The FIRST-Letter Mnemonic Strategy: A memorization technique for learning disabled high school students.* Unpublished master's thesis, University of Kansas, Lawrence.

Nagel, D. R., Schumaker, J. B., & Deshler, D. D. (1986). *The FIRST-Letter Mnemonic Strategy.* Lawrence, KS: Edge Enterprises.

Nolet, V. W., & McLaughlin, M. J. (2000). *Assessing the general curriculum: Including students with disabilities in standards-based reform.* Thousand Oaks, CA: Corwin.

Pressley, M., & Hilden, K. (2004). Cognitive strategies: Production deficiencies and successful strategies instruction everywhere. In D. Kuhn & R. Siegler (Eds.),

Handbook of child psychology: Vol. 2. Cognition, perception, and language. Hoboken, NJ: Wiley.

Putnam, M. L. (1992). The testing practices of mainstream secondary classroom teachers. *Remedial and Special Education, 13*(5), 11–21.

Schmidt, J. L. (1983). *The effects of four generalization conditions on learning disabled adolescents' written language performance in the regular classroom.* Unpublished doctoral dissertation, University of Kansas, Lawrence.

Schmidt, J. L., Deshler, D. D., Schumaker, J. B., & Alley, G. R. (1988/89). Effects of generalization instruction on the written language performance of adolescents with learning disabilities in the mainstream classroom. *Reading, Writing, and Learning Disabilities, 4*(4), 291–309.

Schumaker, J. B. (2003). *The Theme Writing Strategy.* Lawrence, KS: Edge Enterprises.

Schumaker, J. B., Denton, P. H., & Deshler, D. D. (1984). *The Paraphrasing Strategy: Instructor's manual.* Lawrence: University of Kansas Institute for Research in Learning Disabilities.

Schumaker, J. B., & Deshler, D. D. (1984). Setting demand variables: A major factor in program planning for the LD adolescent. *Topics in Language Disorders, 4*(2), 22–40.

Schumaker, J. B., & Deshler, D. D. (1992). Validation of learning strategy interventions for students with LD: Results of a programmatic research effort. In B. Y. L. Wong (Ed.), *Intervention research with students with learning disabilities* (pp. 22–46). New York: Springer-Verlag.

Schumaker, J. B., Deshler, D. D., Alley, G. R., Warner, M. M., Clark, F. L., & Nolan, S. (1982). Error Monitoring: A learning strategy for improving adolescent academic performance. In W. M. Cruickshank and J. W. Lerner (Eds.), *Best of ACLD* (Vol. 3, pp. 170–183). Syracuse, NY: Syracuse University Press.

Schumaker, J. B., Deshler, D. D., Alley, G. R., Warner, M. M., & Denton, P. H. (1982). Multipass: A learning strategy for improving reading comprehension. *Learning Disability Quarterly, 5*(3), 295–304.

Schumaker, J. B., Deshler, D. D., Nolan, S. M., & Alley, G. R. (1994). *The Self-Questioning Strategy: Instructor's manual.* Lawrence, KS: University of Kansas Center for Research on Learning.

Schumaker, J. B., Deshler, D. D., Zemitzch, A., & Warner, M. M. (1993). *The Visual Imagery Strategy.* Lawrence: University of Kansas Center for Research on Learning.

Schumaker, J. B., & Lyerla, K. D. (1991). *The Paragraph Writing Strategy: Instructor's manual.* Lawrence: University of Kansas Institute for Research in Learning Disabilities.

Schumaker, J. B., Nolan, S. M., & Deshler, D. D. (1985). *The Error Monitoring Strategy: Instructor's manual.* Lawrence: University of Kansas Institute for Research in Learning Disabilities.

Schumaker, J. B., & Sheldon, J. (1985). *The Sentence Writing Strategy: Instructor's manual.* Lawrence: University of Kansas Institute for Research in Learning Disabilities.

U.S. Department of Education. (2002). *Twenty-fourth annual report to Congress on the implementation of the Individuals with Disabilities Act.* Washington, DC: Author.

Van Reusen, A. K., Deshler, D. D., & Schumaker, J. B. (1989). Effects of a student participation strategy in facilitating the involvement of adolescents with learning disabilities in the individualized educational program planning process. *Learning Disabilities, 1*(2), 23–34.

Warner, M. M., Schumaker, J. B., Alley, G. R., & Deshler, D. D. (1980). Learning disabled adolescents: Are they different from other low-achievers? *Exceptional Education Quarterly, 1*(2), 27–36.

Warner, M. M., Schumaker, J. B., Alley, G. R., & Deshler, D. D. (1989). The role of executive control: An epidemiological study of school identified LD and low-achieving adolescents on a serial recall task. *Learning Disabilities Research, 4*(2), 107–118.

Woodruff, S., Schumaker, J. B., & Deshler, D. D. (2002). *The effects of an intensive reading intervention on the decoding skills of high school students with reading deficits* (Research Report No. 15). Lawrence: University of Kansas Center for Research on Learning.

5

Designing Instructional Materials to Promote Curriculum Access

Bonnie Grossen and Doug Carnine

One of the biggest challenges that Jason faced was being able to understand and cope with the instructional materials used in his classes, which he often found to be complex, abstract, and confusing. However, he began to experience some success in handling instructional materials when his teachers incorporated different elements from a framework of six principles of instructional design: namely, big ideas, judicious review, conspicuous strategies, background knowledge, modified scaffolding, and strategic integration. This framework was taught to all of Jason's teachers at a schoolwide inservice. The framework is based on findings from the National Center to Improve the Tools for Educators (NCITE), which conducted research to determine the design features of instructional materials that were most effective for struggling adolescent learners.

Many in education have embraced the concept that the design of an instructional tool (the content) is not critically important, that is, "A good teacher can make anything work." Several factors may have influenced this point of view. During the 1980s, for example, teachers had only "inconsiderate" tools available. The term "inconsiderate" was coined by

Armbruster (1984) to describe the serious barriers to comprehension that she found so prevalent in textbooks. Among these barriers were frequent inaccuracies, large numbers of unrelated facts, unclear explanations, and poor organization. Other research has identified additional inconsiderate features that have resulted in learning problems (Kantor, Anderson, & Armbruster, 1983; Lloyd, 1989; Newport, 1990; Osbourne, Jones, & Stein, 1985; Smith, Blakeslee, & Anderson, 1993).

When Berliner, Brophy, Good, Rosenshine, and others began studying effective teachers in the 1980s, they found that the differences lay in teaching behaviors, not in the tools that teachers used (Brophy & Good, 1986; Fisher et al., 1980; Rosenshine, 1983; Rosenshine & Stevens, 1986). Good teachers, given only inconsiderate tools, could control only their teaching behaviors. Thus, only variations in teaching behaviors emerged from that research as distinguishing effective from less effective teaching.

Moreover, a common assumption is that teachers respond better to student misconceptions if they react spontaneously rather than use a planned response from an instructional tool (Salomon & Perkins, 1989). Smith et al. (1993) compared two types of approaches to conceptual change, one that allowed the teacher to implement conceptual change strategies in the prescribed spontaneous fashion, and another that provided the teacher with curricular materials for producing conceptual change. The curricular material was designed to coordinate with the authors' analysis of "key issues on which students commonly hold misconceptions" (p. 118). Teachers using the curricular material achieved better learning outcomes than teachers who were given no print materials.

During much of the history of American education, instructional tools have probably had limited impact on overall school effectiveness. When schooling prepared mostly white, relatively affluent college-bound students, researchers may have been hard-pressed to demonstrate that one tool served teachers significantly better than another. Indeed, for affluent students with parents who had the skills to tutor their children and no discernible cognitive disability, one tool may have been as good as the next. Many such students seemed to get it, regardless of the instructional tools their teachers used.

A final factor relating to the use of well-designed instructional tools is that schools periodically shift from highly structured instruction directed by teachers to unstructured, child-centered instruction. Although child-centered education has become popular again, there are signs that the pendulum is swinging back toward more teacher-directed orientation based on skills and problem solving. Student-centered instruction develops from interests that students express, and therefore teaching tools, which are seen as directive, are considered inappropriate.

In reality, however, neither swing in educational approaches, from teacher-directed basics to student-centered problem solving, effectively addresses the reality of modern classrooms. An inherent danger in teacher-directed instruction is that learners become dependent on the teacher. That is, the learner appears to be successful, but only in the context of direct teacher support. An inherent danger in basics-oriented instruction is that learners receive inadequate opportunities to apply basic knowledge to higher-order thinking, including challenging, realistic problems.

Further, student-centered approaches to problem solving have never been documented as effective for low-performing students. Their effectiveness with higher-performing students also varies considerably (Catrambone & Holyoak, 1989; Hermann & Hincksman, 1978; Yates & Yates, 1990). At most, only 29% of subjects learned the targeted concept after instruction in several student-centered, computer-mediated interventions that were presented as successful (Brna, 1987, 1988; Finegold & Gorsky, 1988; Hewson & Hewson, 1983; Stavy & Berkovitz, 1980; White & Horwitz, 1988). Every student probably benefits from student-centered instruction *at some time,* but not all students benefit consistently.

Instructional tools can be designed to help synthesize these apparently disparate approaches by incorporating empirically validated characteristics that accommodate the natural learning progression. For example, a teacher can teach a strategy explicitly and provide substantial support to students as they practice the strategy. The teacher then gradually reduces support while giving students more discovery-oriented activities in which to apply the strategy. (This instructional feature will be referred to as *mediated scaffolding.*) Such an instructional approach circumvents the problem of student dependence on teachers by allowing students to acquire knowledge reliably and subsequently use that knowledge across a broad range of interests. Similarly, basics and higher-order thinking may be taught hand in hand (to the benefit of both).

REVIEW OF INSTRUCTIONAL DESIGN PRINCIPLES

Precise, highly useful instructional tools can serve teachers effectively in their quest to help all learners achieve their highest potential. At NCITE, researchers have synthesized findings on quality features in an instructional tool (Kameenui & Carnine, 1998) and identified six critical principles related to designing tools that can substantially influence the meeting of the effectiveness criterion (see Table 5.1).

Two research areas have converged to support these six principles as a critical focus for developing high-quality instructional tools. First, there is a large body of research describing specific causes of failure. Each cause implies a specific instructional design solution that can overcome a disability condition. Second, over the past 30 years, there has been an impressive base of empirical research on instructional design that supports these six specific design considerations. This database on instructional design includes technological media as well as other media formats.

Table 5.1   Six Principles of Instructional Design Related to Traditional
Instruction

Six Principles of Accommodation for Heterogeneous Groups	*Traditional Instruction*
Big ideas are concepts and principles that facilitate the most efficient and broad acquisition of knowledge across a range of examples. Big ideas encourage students to learn efficiently because "small" ideas can often be best understood in relationship to larger umbrella concepts.	A barrage of unrelated facts and details are presented. The links between concepts may be obscured.
Conspicuous strategies made up of specific steps can lead to solving complex problems.	Strategies are seldom taught.
Background knowledge improves the acquisition of new knowledge.	Important prerequisite learning is often not evaluated or taught.
Mediated scaffolding provides personal guidance, assistance, and support that gradually fades as students become more proficient and independent.	Little direction or provision for scaffolding the progression of learning toward greater independence is provided.
Judicious review requires students to draw on and apply previously learned knowledge over time.	Review is often minimal.
Strategic integration blends new knowledge with old knowledge to build bigger big ideas.	Spiraling of topics does not carefully integrate units.

In this second group, all studies that isolated variables of instructional design have been included in this review. However, it is not always possible to design studies to test the importance of a feature in isolation. Often the use of one design feature requires incorporating some aspect of another feature. Thus, combinations of features often must be compared in the research studies.

This chapter also describes recent studies that have evaluated the effectiveness of instructional tools that incorporated all six of the design features described in Table 5.1 to accommodate the needs of students with disabilities as they learned rigorous classroom content. Most of these studies were funded by the Education Department's Office of Special Education Programs to improve the quality of technology, media, and materials. The studies focused on adolescents, both at the middle and high school levels. Although the content of the instruction provided to middle school students may not, in all cases, be appropriate for high school students, the assumption is that the design of the instruction applies to both high school and middle school learning.

WHAT ARE THE CAUSES OF FAILURE?

To prevent failure, we must first understand what we mean by failure. Table 5.2 summarizes the characteristics of vulnerable learners and the implications relative to the design of instructional tools.

Background Research on the Six Principles of Instructional Design

A great deal of research has been conducted on the six principles of instructional design described previously. This section will provide additional information about each of the principles and their application to learning within high school contexts, as well as offer references that support each principle.

Big Ideas

Big ideas are the core concepts within a content area. By focusing instruction on big ideas, more mileage can be achieved with less instruction. For example, by focusing on the big idea of morphemic analysis for spelling, students can learn only 600 morphemes and three rules for connecting them (for instance, drop the *e* when you add a morpheme that begins with a vowel, such as *ing*), and be able to spell correctly 12,000 words. By focusing on the big idea of morphemic analysis for spelling, students can learn only 600 morphemes and three rules for connecting them, and be able to spell correctly 12,000 words.

Although these examples all focus on the application of big ideas to learning basic skills, big ideas may also be applied to learning higher-order concepts and processes. For example, Engelmann and Grossen (1995) used the big idea of a "ruling-out process" for constructing knowledge. This process is the essence of the scientific method. Figure 5.1 illustrates an early task in the instructional sequence: Students must figure out what is in the mystery box and write a paragraph describing their thinking process. The outline diagram provides a template for their paragraphs, and icons graphically represent the type of thinking involved. The first trapezoid prompts a summary statement or topic sentence. The boxes illustrate the stepwise nature of the ruling-out process used in constructing knowledge. The second trapezoid prompts a concluding sentence. To figure out the mystery object, students read the first clue, "The object is

Table 5.2   Characteristics of Vulnerable Learners and Instructional
Implications

Characteristic	*Instructional Implications*
Slow learning rate: Low achievers generally learn at a slower rate than other students. This is not necessarily the result of a within-child problem, but may be related to the fact that fewer opportunities to learn result in lower achievement and, as achievement increases, learning rate increases (Marston & Magnusson, 1985; O'Shea & Vacante, 1986).	**Big ideas:** Less should be taught for exposure; more emphasis on central understandings. **Explicit strategies:** More efficient than discovery-oriented instruction. Also, the time allocated to instruction should be used efficiently. First and most obvious, time should not be wasted, and active student engagement should be maximized.
Language deficits: Vulnerable learners perform below other students in a variety of language-related skills, including phonological, semantic, and syntactic tasks (Donahue, 1987; Dunlap & Strope, 1982; Levy & Schenck, 1981; Stanovich, 1988; Vellutino, 1987; Wagner & Torgensen, 1987).	**Explicit strategies:** Information should be explained in clear, concise language that is comprehensible to the learner, and the learner should receive feedback. **Background knowledge:** Student knowledge of language as a prerequisite to such explanations should be established (assessed and taught if necessary).
Memory deficits: Low achievers demonstrate deficiencies in remembering information covered in instruction (Bauer, 1987; Swanson, 1988; Torgeson & Kail, 1980; Torgeson, Murphy, & Ivey, 1979; Torgeson & Goldman, 1977; Wong, 1978, 1985).	**Big ideas and explicit strategies:** Memory is enhanced when information is meaningful and presented in a prearranged, structured manner (Bransford, Sherwood, Vye, & Rieser, 1986; Phillips, 1986; Swing & Peterson, 1988; Torgeson, Rashotte, Greenstein, & Portes, 1988). **Review:** Students should have ample cumulatively distributed opportunities to apply new meaningful information to retain it (Dempster, 1991; Mulligan, Lacey, & Guess, 1982; Pelligrino & Goldman, 1987; Resnick, 1989; Swing & Peterson, 1988; Trafton, 1984).
Automaticity: Because low achievers often lack automaticity with lower-level cognition, they are often preempted from acquisition of higher-level cognition (Ashcraft, 1985; Pelligrino & Goldman, 1987; Samuels, 1987).	**Review:** Automaticity is closely related to memory. Ample cumulatively distributed application opportunities contribute to automaticity as well as memory.

Characteristic	Instructional Implications
Attention: Various manifestations of attention difficulties (selective attention, meta-attention, metacognition) play a major role in the referral of students for special education services and the identification of students who are at risk for such referral (Bryan, Bay, Shelden, & Simon, 1990; Cooper & Farran, 1988).	**Integration:** Strategic knowledge should be made conditional, ensuring that students know when to apply it appropriately.
	Explicit strategies: The characteristics of new knowledge that promote transference (Gick & Holyoak, 1987) should be made explicit for students to mitigate inattention (Gersten, Woodward, & Darch, 1986).
Selective attention: See Hallahan & Reeve (1980), Koppitz (1971), Krupski (1985), Samuels & Miller (1985), and Snef (1971).	**Scaffolding:** Students need assistance in making the transition from the initial introduction of potentially confusing new strategies to self-regulated application, in the form of scaffolding, temporarily simplified instruction, and explicitness.
Meta-attention: See Loper, Hallahan, & Ianna (1982), Krupski (1985), and Miller (1985).	
Metacognition: See Deshler & Schumaker (1986), Englert, Raphael, Fear, & Anderson (1988), Palincsar & Brown (1984), Schumaker, Deshler, Alley, Warner, & Denton (1984), and Smiley, Oaken, Worthen, Campione, & Brown (1977).	**Review:** Repeated opportunities to apply new strategies result in better understanding (Wong, 1988).
	Background knowledge: Relating new, complex knowledge to prior knowledge can help simplify the new knowledge, thus making attention easier.
Attitudes and motivation: The relatively poor academic performance of low-achieving students correlates with poor attitudes toward school, a sense of failure, and inappropriate classroom behavior.	Although a cause-and-effect relationship between academic performance and attitudes has not been convincingly shown, an emphasis on all instructional factors that contribute to student success is presumed to have potential for improving students' attitudes and motivation.
Prior knowledge: Vulnerable learners frequently enter new instructional situations with a dearth of relevant background knowledge.	**Background knowledge:** Instruction should first determine whether students possess the relevant knowledge prerequisite to acquiring new knowledge and then provide such prerequisite knowledge when it is not present.

red," and then review the possibilities. Following the outline diagram, they write, "Clue A rules out the banana. That object is not red," and so on.

This thinking strategy has wide application. Figure 5.2 illustrates the application of the ruling-out process to shopping. Henry needs a jacket but

Figure 5.1   Mystery Box

Possibilities

banana
cherry
strawberry
apple
raspberry

Clues

A. The object is red.

B. The object is not taller than a silver dollar.

c. The object has a "stone" inside.

Outline diagram

The mystery object is
_____.

Clue A rules out _____.
That object is _____
_____.

The only remaining possibility is _____.

Grossen, Bonnie, *Reading and Writing Level E* (n.d.). Used with permission of McGraw-Hill.

has several requirements. In this scenario, there is a jacket that meets his requirements. In other scenarios, the students encounter situations in which no option meets all the requirements, so they must weigh the alternatives and choose the best option.

Students use the same ruling-out process for many other kinds of applications. For example, they use it to select the best plan for accomplishing a goal, such as learning how to ride a horse when a person lives in the city, has no money, and has no horse. The ruling-out process also represents the fundamental thinking behind setting up and interpreting the outcomes of scientific experiments. Figure 5.3 illustrates a problem requiring an experiment before a conclusion can be made. Not all of the possible explanations for an observation have been ruled out. The students describe a short experiment and how to interpret those data, depending on the results of the experiment. One of the remaining explanations for the observation will be ruled out in the experiment.

Figure 5.2 Henry's Shopping Problem

Henry's requirements

1. The jacket must cost less than $200.00.
2. The jacket must be washable.
3. The jacket must offer superior protection against the cold.
4. The jacket must weigh no more than 4 pounds.

Henry's requirements

Jacket	Stormbuster	Windblaster	Leader	King kold	Wilderness
Price	$179.00	$187.99	$156.00	$206.00	$187.00
Weight	4 lb.	3 lb. 2 oz.	2 lb. 8 oz.	3 lb. 7 oz.	4 lb. 3 oz.
Protection against cold	superior	superior	good	superior	superior
Cleaning	washable	dry clean only	washable	washable	washable

Outline diagram

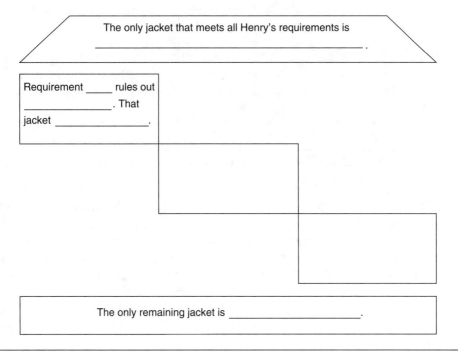

The only jacket that meets all Henry's requirements is _____ .

Requirement _____ rules out
_____ . That
jacket _____ .

The only remaining jacket is _____ .

Grossen, Bonnie, *Reading and Writing Level E* (n.d.). Used with permission of McGraw-Hill.

The outline diagrams shown in Figures 5.1 through 5.3 provide students with a clear model of the wording and thinking processes involved. After students have internalized the thinking patterns and can work successfully without prompts, these prompts are faded.

Figure 5.3   Sam's Experiment

Sam's test

Sam did an experiment with maple seeds. He planted 600 seeds at a depth of one-half inch below the surface of the dirt. He controlled the temperature of the soil so it was above 60 degrees Fahrenheit. Nearly all the seeds sprouted.

He planted another batch of seeds two inches deep. He put them in a place that had a temperature that was less than 60 degrees. Almost none of those seeds sprouted.

Sam's Conclusion

A temperature above 60 degrees causes the seeds to sprout.

Outline Diagram

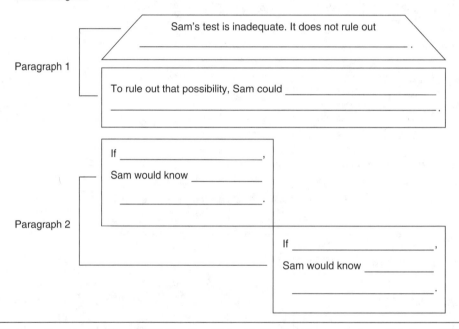

Grossen, Bonnie, *Reading and Writing Level E* (n.d.). Used with permission of McGraw-Hill.

Two research studies have focused on the application of big ideas within the curriculum. For example, Woodward (1994) compared the effects of an earth science curriculum designed around big ideas with those of a curriculum organized around traditional topics. Both curricula used the same media (videodisc) to present the lessons. The curricular material organized around a big idea (the causal principle of convection) produced significantly better learning than the material organized around traditional topics for both general education students and students with learning disabilities (LD).

Big ideas may also be used in writing instruction. Text structures are an example of a big idea for writing. Students who are required to use a particular type of text structure (such as an explanation) benefit from knowing the elements that are common to that type of structure (Armbruster, Anderson, & Ostertag, 1987). Once students have mastered the structure of an explanation, for example, they are prepared to write many explanations on widely varying topics with confidence. Therefore, a lot of mileage can be achieved with relatively little instruction on a handful of the most common structures. In one study, students learned two text structures in a single school year. Not only did they master the two targeted text structures (explanations and arguments), but also the knowledge they acquired made for a relatively quick and easy transfer to entirely new text structures (Hillocks, 1984).

Another source of converging evidence that supports the importance of big ideas is the body of research comparing the performance of experts and novices. In the 1970s, researchers hypothesized that the key difference between an expert and a novice is that the expert is better at general problem solving. This hypothesis turned out to be wrong, however. Extensive research during the 1980s found that experts differ from novices primarily in their knowledge base, which seems to be organized around big ideas. Specifically, researchers found the following:

- Experts have a large, hierarchically organized knowledge base; novices do not.
- Experts' knowledge is organized into big ideas (information patterns that are particularly useful in solving problems); novices' knowledge is more fragmented.
- Experts apply these solution patterns with greater automaticity in solving problems; novices spend more time analyzing and reflecting on the problem (Bruer, 1993; Weisberg, 1986; Woods, 1989).

Conspicuous Strategies

Big ideas relate to the content being taught, whereas the remaining instructional principles to be reviewed here, such as conspicuous strategies, are content independent; that is, they relate to *how* content (the big ideas) is presented to students. Before describing the principle behind conspicuous strategies, a clarification is in order. The notion of conspicuous instruction is based on empirical research that shows that explicit presentation methods are more effective than discovery or inductive methods in teaching both general content (Brophy & Good, 1986; Catrambone & Holyoak, 1989; Charles, 1980; Darch, Carnine, & Gersten, 1984; Fielding, Kameenui, & Gersten, 1983; Guzzetti, 1990; Guzzetti, Snyder, Glass, & Gamas, 1993; Hermann & Hincksman, 1978; Rosenshine & Stevens, 1986; Yates & Yates, 1990) and higher-level content, such as the scientific method or formal thinking (Ross, 1988; Rubin & Norman, 1992). However, the emphasis on conspicuous instruction is not an antidiscovery or anticonstructivist position. Research has shown, in fact, that explicit initial instruction actually facilitates students' ability to benefit from discovery-oriented instructional experiences. In other words, conspicuous strategy instruction does not preclude discovery-oriented activities; instead, it can be designed to facilitate them.

Some caution is also in order with regard to the use of the word "strategy." A strategy is defined here as a series of steps that one can follow to analyze content or solve problems. Not all strategies are created equal. "Narrow" strategies tend to result in rote learning instead of understanding. For instance, an algorithm in math, such as "invert and multiply" for dividing fractions, could be considered a strategy, but it is too narrow to be considered an effective strategy as the term is used here. A strategy may also be too broad, in that its use does not reliably lead to most students successfully solving problems. For example, the dictum "plan before you write" could be considered a strategy, but it lacks sufficient detail to be useful to the majority of students.

An effective strategy, then, is intermediate in generality—that is, it is just right, neither too narrow nor too broad. For example, a decoding strategy for beginning reading might include the following steps:

- Begin at the left end of the word.
- Say the sound for the first letter.
- Without stopping, say the sound for the next letter.
- When you've said all the sounds, say the word.

Students can use these steps in sequence to decode any word. With more difficult concepts or tasks, where the key features are more deeply embedded, explicit verbal information accompanying the experience can facilitate learning. A series of experimental studies has been especially informative in identifying the important features of effective instruction when it comes to applying strategies to difficult concepts. In the first study in the series, Gick and Holyoak (1980) taught college students the solution to a radiation problem (for example, how to treat a tumor with rays so that the surrounding tissue is not destroyed). Nearly all of the college subjects failed to apply the learned solution to a new example of an analogous radiation problem (a general directing an attack on a fort with roads leading to it so that only one soldier at a time can travel). Successfully solving the second radiation problem required subjects to abstract deep structural similarities between the problems (the key features identifying this problem type). This abstraction of similarities almost never occurs, according to Salomon and Perkins's (1989) review of transfer research.

In a subsequent study, Gick and Holyoak (1983) found that performance improved when they told the college students to use the first radiation problem to help them solve the second. Specifically, they asked the students to write summaries of how the problems resembled one another before solving the second problem. Salomon and Perkins (1989) believed this summary writing aided subjects in inducing the similarity between the problems and, without the mindfulness required to induce the abstraction (that is, the deep structural similarity), the abstraction would not have been understood.

Later studies have cast doubt on this analysis, however. In a series of five studies, Catrambone and Holyoak (1989) found that performance on radiation problems further improved as (1) the deep structural similarities between problems were presented more explicitly, and (2) more practice was provided. The instruction that presented the most instructional examples (three radiation problems) and made the similarities between the examples (that is, the abstraction) most explicit resulted in the greatest transfer to another radiation problem.

The instruction required students to memorize the ideal answers to six questions, one of which was the following verbal description of the deep structural similarity: "If a target is difficult to overcome because a large force cannot be aimed at it from one direction, then divide the force into parts and deliver it from many directions." Experimental conditions involving less explicit descriptions of the deep structural similarities (requiring students only to write answers to the six questions and receive corrective feedback) or fewer practice problems both resulted in less successful transfer (Catrambone & Holyoak, 1989). By providing practice and an explicit definition of the similarities between the problems, radiation problems were no longer novel problems for students; rather, they became a familiar problem pattern, a concept.

The instructional research by Gick and Holyoak (1980, 1983) and Catrambone and Holyoak (1989) suggests that making deeply embedded features explicit is key to better application and generalization. This finding is supported by research on nonexplicit methods of instruction. Overall, nonexplicit methods have not been shown to improve achievement. Howell, Sidorenko, and Jurica (1987) found that without a conspicuous strategy, students learned an inappropriate strategy for problem solving using the "rule of nines." However, when a strategy was made conspicuous and combined with drill and practice, students were able to unlearn the ineffective strategy and incorporate the new knowledge and skills.

Background Knowledge

Research across content areas supports the commonsense notion that the extent of students' background knowledge influences the extent to which they are able to acquire new knowledge. Students, especially students with disabilities, frequently enter new instructional situations with a dearth of relevant background knowledge. Desirable background knowledge may take the form of general knowledge of the world or more specific academic knowledge that relates to the new instruction. For example, students may have difficulty understanding a reading passage related to harvesting wheat if they have no general knowledge of farms and farming. Similarly, students may have a hard time understanding a new strategy if they need to have mastered some specific prerequisite academic or procedural knowledge that, in fact, they have not mastered.

In another example in the reading skills area, both phonemic awareness and understanding of alphabetic and sound relationships have been shown to be prerequisites for beginning decoding success (Torgesen, Wagner, & Rashotte, 1997). If students are to successfully sound out a word such as *stop,* they must know generally that the letters in the word correspond to sounds, and more specifically, the usual sounds for the particular letters in *stop.* In addition, they must be able to blend isolated phonemes into complete words. Research has shown that beginning decoding instruction is most effective when students have such background knowledge. That background knowledge itself is of limited value when it is not incorporated into explicit decoding instruction (Adams, 1990). This is true regardless of whether the nonreader is a child or an adult (Lyon, 1995).

Instructional materials can acknowledge the importance of background knowledge in two ways. First, students can be pretested for important background knowledge. Pretests may be used to determine placement within an instructional program or to alert teachers of the need to allocate time to background topics. Second, instructional programs may include important background knowledge in the scope of topics taught. Ideally, such background topics would be taught or reviewed shortly (a few days) before the introduction of new content that depends on those topics. If background topics are introduced earlier than that, students may forget some relevant aspects by the time the new content is introduced. If background topics are introduced in the same lesson as the new strategy, some students are likely to become overwhelmed by the quantity of new knowledge.

Mediated Scaffolding

In its most general sense, scaffolding refers to help, guidance, or assistance given to students as they acquire new knowledge. The benefits of scaffolding may be most apparent with respect to children learning new physical tasks. When observing parents at a playground, for example, numerous examples of scaffolding can be seen as young children learn a new activity, such as using a slide. Parents help the child climb the ladder, catch the child at the bottom, perhaps slide with the child a few times, or have the child initially slide only part of the way down the slide.

In textbooks, such as history texts, scaffolding can take the form of frequent questions interspersed throughout passages. Such questions help students to focus on the most critical aspects of a passage. The following examples are taken from a middle school history text:

An economic problem involves difficulty in getting and keeping items that people need or want.

- What is an economic problem?

At a basic level, people need three things: (a) food to eat, (b) shelter to keep them dry and out of the weather, and (c) clothing to keep them warm. People require these three basic items to live. For centuries, people have found ways to meet these basic needs.

- What three basic things must people have to live?

Crawford and Carnine (2000) documented the multiple positive effects for students with disabilities when these types of question prompts were used in a textbook. Other effective scaffolding methods include concept models (Mayer, 1989), speech feedback (Hebert & Murdock, 1994; Olson, Foltz, & Wise, 1986), coaching feedback (Jackson, Edwards, & Berger, 1993), immediate elaborated feedback (Collins & Carnine, 1988), prompts that require a deeper level of processing (Grossen & Carnine, 1990b), and attribution retraining (Okolo, 1992). Fading these scaffolds over time has a positive effect on the mastery and generalization of students with disabilities (Paine, Carnine, White, & Walters, 1982).

Judicious Review

Research has consistently shown that there are four characteristics of effective review. Review should be (1) adequate, (2) distributed, (3) cumulative, and (4) varied. In addition, it should be based on big ideas because the overall contribution of review to knowledge and understanding depends on the quality of what is being reviewed. That is, if small or marginal ideas are taught in the first place, the best that can be expected from implementation of effective review methods is the mastery of small ideas.

Each of these characteristics of a good review suggests something different about the way instructional materials can be designed to best facilitate learning. *Adequate review,* for example, is perhaps the most intuitive aspect of review. Some students need more review than others to achieve fluency and long-term retention. Instructional tools should address this variability in need among students (Dempster, 1991) by allowing students to have varying amounts of review depending on their needs.

Few aspects of instruction have been as well researched as *massed and distributed practice.* The consistent conclusion is that, initially, practice should be massed and then distributed (Dempster, 1991; Mulligan et al., 1982; Schmidt & Bjorke, 1992). An effective distribution review schedule involves an increasing ratio review. *Increasing ratio* refers to gradually greater periods of "nonreview" between review sessions. For example, when a new big idea is introduced, students might apply the new knowledge daily for a few days, then every other day, then every third day, then every fifth day, and thereafter only occasionally. Such a schedule stretches retention. Another advantage of an increasing ratio schedule of distributed practice is that students need only a small amount of practice during each review session. By distributing review, less total review is adequate than if most of the review were massed. Moreover, distributed review sessions provide a natural, built-in assessment from which teachers can determine whether more or less subsequent instruction is needed.

Cumulative Review

A review process that includes not only the most recently learned material, but also material from throughout the program, prevents the predictable confusion that many students experience within a content area when they encounter similar but different facts, concepts, principles, and strategies. For example, in mathematics, many students confuse the addition and multiplication of fractions. These types of problems appear to be similar, but they are conceptually quite different. Similarly, science students often confuse the concepts of mass, volume, and density, resulting in misconceptions such as "bigger objects float, and smaller objects sink." Beginning readers confuse the letters *b* and *d*. Beginning (and sometimes advanced) writers confuse *its* and *it's*.

Instruction can help prevent or correct such misconceptions by integrating them during initial instruction. This strategy has proved effective for preventing many misconceptions in science. Cumulative review is an effective follow-up to integration for preventing or correcting misconceptions (Howell et al., 1987; Schmidt & Bjorke, 1992). Assume, for instance, that students are learning how to multiply fractions. During initial instruction, a program might put what seems to be an unusual emphasis on the process of multiplication and the multiplication sign in anticipation of later instruction on adding fractions. Later, after multiplication of fractions has been introduced and mastered fairly well, instruction on integrating *both* multiplying and adding fractions is necessary. Then both skills can be cumulatively reviewed within the same review session.

Such mixing is crucial for understanding. Perhaps even more compelling, though, is that in the real world of mathematics, all of the mathematics knowledge a person possesses is mixed and cumulative. Thus, for knowledge to accumulate, review should be cumulative.

Finally, with regard to *varied review,* a major instructional goal is generalization or transference of learning. It is impossible to show students the entire range of possible applications of a set of knowledge when they are first acquiring that knowledge. Therefore, varied review combined with distributed, cumulative review is a major means of accomplishing transference. A criticism of much instruction is that it is contrived and decontextualized. Such criticism is frequently valid. One response is to attempt to make the initial instruction on new information as authentic as possible. Theoretically, that serves the goal of transference. However, new knowledge is often difficult to acquire when it is initially applied to a broad range of contexts. Therefore, the goal of transference may become inadvertently subverted.

Varied review offers a powerful alternative to achieving transference. At first, students can learn to apply a new strategy to decontextualized, possibly contrived tasks. For example, they can learn to evaluate which of two objects contains more mass using problems on worksheets with graphic displays of the two objects to be compared in each instance. Such contrived tasks serve to clearly communicate a deep but decontextualized understanding of mass and volume, which provides the foundation for subsequent, *varied* activities with actual substances in a naturalistic context. As related concepts are subsequently introduced, such as the effect of heat on density, review becomes increasingly varied and natural. Thus, the goal of transference to realistic contexts is uniformly achieved.

These different types of effective review apply differently to students of varying performance levels. For example, students with LD are likely to need more review than other students. That is, the amount of review that will prove to be adequate will probably be greater for students with LD than for their peers without disabilities. However, all students benefit equally from distributed review, cumulative review, and especially varied review, which is so crucial to understanding.

Comprehensive syntheses of the large volume of studies investigating the features of review that lead to mastery, retention, and generalization have concluded that these four features of review are critical (Dempster, 1991; Schmidt & Bjorke, 1992). Research using computer-assisted instruction has found that small sets are learned more quickly than large sets in the context of daily review (Johnson, Gersten, & Carnine, 1987). In other words, introducing a new item each day is better than presenting all of the items in a set and reviewing them constantly. Not only is learning faster, but also the tedium of review, often described as "drill and kill," is avoided. Thus, shorter sets combined with frequent practice create an alternative experience: "drill and thrill." The thrill of success (that is, the feeling that one knows the material as the review continues) is much better than the frustration of a large set that requires constant prompting.

Strategic Integration

Integrated curricula are currently popular. However, the term *integration* is somewhat ambiguous, and some ways of integrating knowledge are better than others. For example, there is tremendous potential benefit in compounding knowledge or blending knowledge that highlights important interrelationships. In this case, new, more complete knowledge structures result.

Additionally, potential confusion may be preempted or corrected through careful integration of knowledge. Indeed, the most important benefit of integration is to prevent or correct misconceptions. Misconceptions frequently manifest themselves as confusion over similar concepts, principles, or strategies. Such confusion is notorious in mathematics, as well as other content areas. For instance, one can predict with great assurance that some students will confuse adding fractions with multiplying fractions, given that these processes are rarely integrated in instructional materials.

Instructional materials designed for students with disabilities must anticipate and design against predictable confusion. Integration is the principal means of doing that. For example, Problem A is a straightforward proportion problem.

If an instructional program does not anticipate the confusion some students will encounter when they are faced with highly similar types of problems, those students would likely apply the same basic proportions mapping strategy that worked for Problem A to Problem B and get a wrong answer. To prevent such confusion, instructional materials should explicitly teach basic mapping strategies (for problems such as Problem A), then teach advanced mapping strategies (for problems such as Problem B), and explicitly integrate the basic and advanced strategies so that students learn *when* to apply each. Figure 5.4 illustrates such an advanced mapping strategy for solving complex proportion problems such as Problem B.

Problem A: A truck delivers cartons of juice to a store. Of those cartons, 2/7 of the juice is grape. The truck has 8,400 cartons of juice. How many cartons hold grape juice?

Mapping strategy for Problem A:

a. Map   *grape*
          total

b. Insert *grape* $\dfrac{2}{7} = \dfrac{}{8,400}$
           total

c. Solve   *grape* $\dfrac{2}{7} = \dfrac{2,400}{8,400}$ = 2,400 grape cartons
           total

Problem B appears to be similar to Problem A, but there is a crucial difference: There are *three* elements in Problem B (total juice, apple juice, grape juice) instead of just two, as in Problem A (total juice and grape juice).

Problem B: A truck delivers cartons of grape and apple juice to a store. Of those cartons, 2/7 of the juice is grape; the rest is apple juice. The truck will deliver 8,400 cartons of apple juice. How many cartons of grape juice will the truck deliver?

Figure 5.4   Advanced Mapping Strategy for Solving Complex Proportion
Problems

	Ratio	Juice Cartons
Step 1: Students map three units, not just two, and insert the relevant information.		
Grape	2	☐
Apple	☐	8400
Total	7	☐
Step 2: Students use their knowledge of missing addends to come up with the unknown value in the ration column.		
Grape	2	☐
Apple	5	8400
$7 - 2 = \boxed{5}$ Total	7	☐
Step 3: Students write and solve the proportion to determine the number of cartons of grape juice:		
Grape	2	3360
Apple	5	8400
$\dfrac{2}{5} = \dfrac{3360}{8400}$ Total	7	☐

This type of integration benefits all students because it is a major key
to achieving a depth of understanding within a content area. In addition,
to the extent that integration is a principal means for preventing or correcting

stubborn but predictable misconceptions, students with disabilities are especially likely to benefit. Indeed, research has shown that coordinating the various components of instruction so that concepts are clearly and unambiguously communicated and later combined has a positive effect on the learning of students with disabilities (Woodward, Carnine, & Collins, 1988). Research has also shown that perfecting strategic integration by reviewing student data to determine where misconceptions occur and adding strands of practice to prevent those misconceptions result in a significant improvement in the effectiveness of the instructional tool (Collins & Carnine, 1988).

STUDIES INVESTIGATING ALL SIX PRINCIPLES

Carnine's research team at the University of Oregon evaluated the effectiveness of instructional tools designed to incorporate all six principles. The findings of these studies related to closing the gap between the performance of students with disabilities and the performance of general education peers are summarized briefly. These studies involved middle and high school students and were conducted particularly in the area of higher-level thinking in various subject areas.

Grossen and Carnine (1990a) found that after receiving instruction in these skills with a program that integrated the six principles (referred to as a *six-principle program*), high school students with LD scored as high as high school students in an honors English class and higher than college students enrolled in a teacher-certification program on a variety of measures of argument construction and critiquing. In another study related to constructing arguments, high school students with disabilities scored significantly higher than college students enrolled in a teacher-certification program and scored at the same level as a group of college students enrolled in a logic class after receiving instruction on constructing arguments with a six-principle program (Collins & Carnine, 1988).

With regard to science, Woodward, Carnine, and Gersten (1988) used a six-principle program to teach health content to high school students with disabilities. The students with disabilities scored significantly higher on a test of problem solving to achieve better health than students without disabilities who had completed a traditional high school health class. Another group of researchers found that mainstreamed middle and high school students with disabilities who had used a six-principle science program scored higher than a class of general education students taught in a student-centered science program on a problem-solving test that required students to apply theoretical knowledge and predict results based on given information (Grossen, Carnine, & Lee, 1996).

Also in science, Muthukrishna, Carnine, Grossen, and Miller (1993) reported that mainstreamed middle school students with LD showed better conceptual understanding on a test of misconceptions in earth science after they had participated in a six-principle program than Harvard graduates interviewed in Schnep's 1987 film *A Private Universe.* Additionally, Woodward and Noell (1992) reported that mainstreamed middle school students with LD who had participated in a six-principle program scored significantly higher on a test of earth science problem solving than students without disabilities who had received traditional science instruction. Similarly, Niedelman (1992) found that most of a group of mainstreamed middle school students with LD who had received science instruction in a six-principle program scored higher on a test of problem solving involving earth science content than the mean score of the control students without disabilities who had received traditional instruction.

Finally, on an advanced placement chemistry test, high school students with disabilities and remedial students who had received instruction through a six-principle program scored higher on subscales covering chemical equilibrium than a group of high-performing students in an advanced placement chemistry class. Specifically, the students matched the performance of advanced placement students on subscales requiring the application of the concepts of chemical bonding, atomic structure, organic compounds, and energy of activation (Hofmeister, 1989).

With regard to mathematics instruction, on a test of problem solving requiring the use of ratios and proportions, mainstreamed high school students with disabilities who had received instruction on these concepts through a six-principle program scored as well as high school students without disabilities who had received traditional math instruction (Moore & Carnine, 1989). On a test requiring the application of fractions, decimals, and percentages, age-grouped, low-achieving middle school students who had learned about these concepts in a six-principle program scored significantly higher than high-achieving students in a constructivist math program (Grossen & Ewing, 1994).

In history, when students were given a history test that required them to analyze primary source documents, scores related to the use of principles and facts in writing earned by mainstreamed high school students with LD who had participated in a six-principle program did not differ significantly from those of control students without disabilities who had received traditional history instruction (Crawford & Carnine, 1996). Moreover, poor, urban middle school students and some students with limited English proficiency who had participated in a six-principle history program increased their history vocabulary proficiency at a rate five times that of suburban middle school students who had received traditional history instruction. Finally, with regard to behavior, studies of low achievers have consistently shown that their relatively poor academic performance correlates with poor attitudes toward school, a sense of failure, and inappropriate classroom behavior. Some researchers have found that improvements in academic performance as a result of participation in a six-principle program correspond to improvements in behavior (Burke, Hagan, & Grossen, 1998).

Implications for the Future

The design of instruction clearly plays a critical role in the effectiveness of instructional tools for students with disabilities. Research supporting the six design considerations described here derives not only from the large research base on instructional design, but also from descriptive studies of the causes of failure, a critical aspect for students with disabilities and those at risk. More recent studies evaluating the effectiveness of these design principles have indicated that design considerations should be a primary focus in selecting instructional tools if the success of students with disabilities is the educational goal.

For many students with disabilities, curricular materials within content-area high school courses can exacerbate difficulties, including problems with encoding, comprehending, remembering, or organizing material. Barriers within current secondary curriculum design include the presentation of a large number of unrelated facts that cover a breadth, but not depth, of information (Harniss, 1994). Further, the rapid pace at which teachers must cover material to achieve high school content-area objectives can further serve to undermine the success of students with disabilities (Mastropieri, Scruggs, & Graetz, 2003). Developers of instructional tools must be cognizant of the principles of effective instructional design to ensure that all students with disabilities are given every opportunity to benefit from their educational experience.

Educational Applications and Implications

With the passage of the No Child Left Behind Act, considerable attention has been given to the importance of teachers using scientifically based instruction. Although the number of instructional materials that have strong validation data behind them are limited, teachers can be confident in grounding their instruction in teaching practices, materials, and educational tools that embody some or all of the six principles of instructional design discussed in this chapter. Each of these principles is built on an extensive research foundation. Collectively, teachers and administrators can effectively leverage these principles as a framework in a variety of ways:

- to select new instructional materials or programs;
- to evaluate existing instructional materials relative to the soundness of the design principles that have been incorporated by developers or are recommended when the material is being used with students;
- to serve as the basis of an evaluation system for peer coaching and feedback; and
- to use as a framework for organizing staff development activities to ensure that the limited time available for teachers to acquire new skills is used effectively.

One of the most powerful mechanisms that teachers and administrators can employ for improving student outcomes is professional learning communities. These structures bring teachers together around professional issues and areas of interest that relate directly to the teaching process. The six design principles provide not only a framework to guide teacher thinking and analysis, but also a shared language around the core elements of the teaching process. As the academic diversity of classrooms continues to increase and the number of low-achieving students within those diverse classes grows, it will be critical for teachers to acquire the kinds of teaching skills that will enable at-risk students (including those with disabilities) to be successful in their classes. The track record of the principles described in this chapter provides a good starting point for any teaching initiative designed to improve student outcomes. Additional information on the six design principles can be found at the Web site of the National Center to Improve the Tools of Educators, http://idea.uoregon.edu/~ncite/.

REFERENCES

Adams, M. (1990). *Beginning to read: Thinking and learning about print.* Cambridge: MIT Press.

Armbruster, B. (1984). The problem of "inconsiderate text." In G. G. Duffy, L. R. Roehler, & J. Mason (Eds.), *Comprehension instruction* (pp. 202–217). New York: Longman.

Armbruster, B., Anderson, T. H., & Ostertag, J. (1987). Does text structure/ summarization instruction facilitate learning from expository text? *Reading Research Quarterly, 22,* 331–346.

Ashcraft, M. (1985). Is it farfetched that some of us remember our arithmetic facts? *Journal for Research in Mathematics Education, 16*(2), 99–105.

Bauer, R. H. (1987). Control processes as a way of understanding, diagnosing, and remediating learning disabilities. *Advances in Learning and Behavioral Disabilities, 2,* 41–81.

Bransford, J., Sherwood, R., Vye, N., & Rieser, J. (1986). Teaching, thinking and problem solving. *American Psychologist, 41*(10), 1078–1089.

Brna, P. (1987). Confronting dynamics misconceptions. *Instructional Science, 16*(4), 351–379.

Brna, P. (1988). Confronting misconceptions in the domain of simple electrical circuits. *Instructional Science, 17*(1), 29–55.

Brophy, J. J., & Good, T. (1986). Teacher behavior and student achievement. In M. C. Wittrock (Ed.), *AERA handbook of research on teaching* (3rd ed., pp. 328–375). New York: Macmillan.

Bruer, J. T. (1993). *Schools for thought: A science of learning in the classroom.* Cambridge: MIT Press.

Bryan, T., Bay, M., Shelden, C., & Simon, J. (1990). Teachers' and at-risk students' simulated recall of instruction. *Exceptionality, 1,* 167–179.

Burke, M., Hagan, S., & Grossen, B. (1998). What curricular designs and strategies accommodate diverse learners? *TEACHING Exceptional Children, 31*(1), 34–38.

Catrambone, R., & Holyoak, K. J. (1989). Overcoming contextual limitations on problem-solving transfer. *Journal of Experimental Psychology: Learning, Memory, and Cognition, 15*(6), 1147–1156.

Charles, R. I. (1980). Exemplification and characterization moves in the classroom teaching of geometry concepts. *Journal for Research in Mathematics Education, 11*(1), 10–21.

Collins, M., & Carnine, D. (1988). Evaluating the field test revision process by comparing two versions of a reasoning skills CAI program. *Journal of Learning Disabilities, 21,* 375–379.

Cooper, D. H., & Farran, D. C. (1988). Behavioral risk factors in kindergarten. *Early Childhood Quarterly, 3,* 1–19.

Crawford, D., & Carnine, D. (1996). *Promoting and assessing higher order thinking in history: Using performance assessment to evaluate effects of instruction* (Technical Rep. 101). Eugene: University of Oregon, National Center to Improve the Tools of Educators.

Crawford, D., & Carnine, D. (2000). Comparing the effects of textbooks in eighth-grade U.S. history: Does conceptual organization help? *Education and Treatment of Children, 23*(4), 387–422.

Darch, C., Carnine, D., & Gersten, R. (1984). Explicit instruction in mathematics problem solving. *Journal of Educational Research, 77,* 351–359.

Dempster, F. N. (1991). Synthesis of research on reviews and tests. *Educational Leadership, 48,* 71–76.

Deshler, D. D., & Schumaker, J. B. (1986). Learning strategies: An instructional alternative for low-achieving adolescents. *Exceptional Children, 52,* 583–590.

Donahue, M. (1987). Interactions between linguistic and pragmatic development in learning disabled children: Three views of the state of the union. In S. Rosenberg (Ed.), *Advances in applied psycholinguistics* (Vol. 1, pp. 126–179). Cambridge, UK: Cambridge University Press.

Dunlap, W. P., & Strope, G. J. (1982). Reading mathematics: Review of literature. *Focus on Learning Problems in Mathematics, 4,* 39–50.

Engelmann, S., & Grossen, B. (1995). *Reasoning and writing: Level E & F.* Columbus, OH: SRA/McGraw-Hill.

Englert, C. S., Raphael, T. E., Fear, K. L., & Anderson, L. M. (1988). Students' metacognitive knowledge about how to write informal texts. *Learning Disability Quarterly, 11,* 18–46.

Fielding, G. D., Kameenui, E., & Gersten, R. (1983). A comparison of an inquiry and a direct instruction approach to teaching legal concepts and applications to secondary school students. *Journal of Educational Research, 76*(5), 287–293.

Finegold, M. C., & Gorsky, P. (1988). Learning about force: Simulating the outcomes of pupils' misconceptions. *Instructional Science, 17,* 251–261.

Fisher, C. W., Berliner, D. C., Fibly, N. N., Marliave, R., Cahen, I. S., & Dishaw, M. M. (1980). Teaching behaviors, academic learning time, and student achievement: An overview. In C. Denham & A. Lieberman (Eds.), *Time to learn* (pp. 7–32). Washington, DC: National Institute of Education.

Gersten, R., Woodward, J., & Darch, C. (1986). Direct instruction: A research-based approach to curriculum design and teaching. *Exceptional Children, 53*(1), 17–31.

Gick, M. L., & Holyoak, K. (1980). Analogical problem solving. *Cognitive Psychology, 12,* 306–355.

Gick, M. L., & Holyoak, K. (1983). Schema induction and analogical transfer. *Cognitive Transfer, 15,* 1–38.

Gick, M. L., & Holyoak, K. (1987). The cognitive basis of knowledge transfer. In S. M. Cormier & J. D. Hagman (Eds.), *Transfer of learning: Contemporary research and applications* (pp. 9–46). Orlando, FL: Academic Press.

Grossen, B., & Carnine, D. (1990a). Diagramming a logic strategy: Effects on more difficult problem types and transfer. *Learning Disability Quarterly, 13*(4), 133–147.

Grossen, B., & Carnine, D. (1990b). Review of empirical evaluations of interventions for teaching logical and analogical reasoning. *Learning Disability Quarterly, 13*(3), 168–182.

Grossen, B., Carnine, D., & Lee, C. (1996). *The effects of considerate instruction and constructivist instruction on middle-school students' achievement and problem solving in earth science* (Technical Rep. 103). Eugene: University of Oregon, National Center to Improve the Tools of Educators.

Grossen, B., & Ewing, S. (1994). *Raising mathematics problem-solving performance: Do the NCTM teaching standards help?* (Technical Rep. 102). Eugene: University of Oregon, National Center to Improve the Tools of Educators.

Guzzetti, B. J. (1990). Effects of textual and instructional manipulations on concept acquisition. *Reading Psychology, 11,* 49–62.

Guzzetti, B., Snyder, T. E., Glass, G. V., & Gamas, W. S. (1993). Promoting conceptual change in science: A comparative meta-analysis of instructional interventions from reading education and science education. *Reading Research Quarterly, 28*(2), 116–159.

Hallahan, D. R., & Reeve, R. E. (1980). Selective attention and distractibility. In B. K. Keogh (Ed.), *Advances in special education* (Vol. 1, pp. 141–181). Greenwich, CT: JAI Press.

Harniss, M. K. (1994). Content organization and instructional design issues in the development of history texts. *Learning Disability Quarterly, 17*(3), 235–248.

Hebert, B., & Murdock, J. (1994). Comparing three computer-aided instruction output modes to teach vocabulary words to students with learning disabilities. *Learning Disabilities Research and Practice, 9*(3), 136–141.

Hermann, G. D., & Hincksman, N. (1978). Inductive versus deductive approaches in teaching a lesson in chemistry. *Journal of Research in Science Teaching, 15*(1), 37–42.

Hewson, M. G., & Hewson, P. W. (1983). Effect of instruction using students' prior knowledge and conceptual change strategies in science teaching. *Journal of Research in Science Teaching, 20*(8), 731–743.

Hillocks, G. (1984). What works in teaching composition: A meta-analysis of experimental treatment studies. *American Journal of Education, 93,* 133–170.

Hofmeister, A. (1989). Developing and validating science education videodiscs. *Journal of Research in Science Teaching, 26*(7), 665–677.

Howell, R., Sidorenko, E., & Jurica, J. (1987). The effects of computer use on the acquisition of multiplication facts by a student with learning disabilities. *Journal of Learning Disabilities, 20*(6), 336–341.

Jackson, D., Edwards, B., & Berger, C. (1993). The design of software tools for meaningful learning by experience: Flexibility and feedback. *Journal of Educational Computing Research, 9*(3), 413–443.

Johnson, G., Gersten, R., & Carnine, D. (1987). Effects of instructional design variables on vocabulary acquisition of LD students: A study of computer-assisted instruction. *Journal of Learning Disabilities, 20*(4), 206–213.

Kameenui, E. J., & Carnine, D. W. (1998). *Effective teaching strategies that accommodate diverse learners*. Des Moines, IA: Prentice Hall.

Kantor, R. N., Anderson, T. H., & Armbruster, B. B. (1983). How inconsiderate are children's textbooks? *Journal of Curriculum Studies, 15*, 6–72.

Koppitz, E. M. (1971). *Children with learning disabilities: A five-year follow-up study*. New York: Grune & Stratton.

Krupski, A. (1985). Variations in attention as a function of classroom task demands in learning handicapped and CA-matched nonhandicapped children. *Exceptional Children, 52*, 52–56.

Levy, W., & Schenck, S. (1981). The interactive effect of arithmetic and various reading formats upon the verbal problem solving performance of learning disabled children. *Focus on Learning Problems in Mathematics, 3*, 5–10.

Lloyd, C. V. (1989). *The relationship between scientific literacy and high school biology textbooks*. Paper presented at the annual meeting of the National Reading Conference, Austin, TX.

Loper, A. B., Hallahan, D. P., & Ianna, S. O. (1982). Meta-attention in learning disabled and normal children. *Learning Disability Quarterly, 5*, 29–36.

Lyon, G. R. (1995). Research initiatives in learning disabilities: Contributions from scientists supported by the National Institute of Child Health and Human Development. *Journal of Child Neurology, 10*, 120–126.

Marston, D., & Magnusson, D. (1985). Implementing curriculum-based measurement in special and regular education settings. *Exceptional Children, 52*, 266–276.

Mastropieri, M. A., Scruggs, T. E., & Graetz, J. E. (2003). Reading comprehension instruction for secondary students: Challenges for struggling students and teachers. *Learning Disability Quarterly, 26*, 103–116.

Mayer, R. E. (1989). Models for understanding. *Review of Educational Research, 59*(1), 43–64.

Miller, P. H. (1985). Metacognition and attention. In D. L. Forrest-Pressley, G. E. MacKinnon, & T. G. Waller (Eds.), *Metacognition, cognition and human performance* (Vol. 2, pp. 181–218). New York: Academic Press.

Moore, L. J., & Carnine, D. (1989). Evaluating curriculum design in the context of active teaching. *Remedial and Special Education, 10*(4), 28–37.

Mulligan, M., Lacey, L., & Guess, D. (1982). Effects of massed, distributed, and spaced trial sequencing on severely handicapped students' performance. *Journal of the Association for the Severely Handicapped, 7*, 48–61.

Muthukrishna, N., Carnine, D., Grossen, B., & Miller, S. (1993). Children's alternative frameworks: Should they be directly addressed in science instruction? *Journal of Research in Science Teaching, 30*(3), 233–248.

Newport, J. F. (1990). Elementary science texts: What's wrong with them? *Educational Digest, 59*, 68–69.

Niedelman, M. (1992). Problem solving and transfer. In D. Carnine & E. Kameenui (Eds.), *Higher order thinking: Designing curriculum for mainstreamed students* (pp. 137–156). Austin, TX: Pro-Ed.

Okolo, C. (1992). The effects of computer-based attribution retraining on the attributions, persistence, and mathematics computation of students with learning disabilities. *Journal of Learning Disabilities, 25*(5), 327–334.

Olson, R., Foltz, G., & Wise, B. (1986). Reading instruction and remediation with the aid of computer speech. *Behavior Research Methods, Instruments and Computers, 18*(2), 93–99.

Osbourne, J., Jones, B. F., & Stein, M. (1985). The case for improving textbooks. *Educational Leadership, 42,* 9–16.

O'Shea, L. J., & Vacante, G. (1986). A comparison over time of relative discrepancy of low achievers. *Exceptional Children, 53,* 253–259.

Paine, S. C., Carnine, D. W., White, W. T., & Walters, G. (1982). Effects of fading teacher presentation structure (covertization) on acquisition and maintenance of arithmetic problem-solving skills. *Education and Treatment of Children, 5*(2), 93–107.

Palincsar, A. S., & Brown, A. L. (1984). The reciprocal teaching of comprehension-fostering and comprehension-monitoring activities. *Cognition and Instruction, 1*(2), 117–175.

Pelligrino, J. W., & Goldman, S. R. (1987). Information processing and elementary mathematics. *Journal of Learning Disabilities, 20*(1), 23–32.

Philips, R. J. (1986). Computer graphics as a memory aid and a thinking aid. *Journal of Computer-Assisted Learning, 2*(1), 37–44.

Resnick, L. (1989). Developing mathematical knowledge. *American Psychologist, 44*(2), 162–169.

Rosenshine, B. V. (1983). Teaching functions in instructional programs. *Elementary School Journal, 83*(4), 335–351.

Rosenshine, B. V., & Stevens, R. (1986). Teaching functions. In M. C. Wittrock (Ed.), *AERA handbook of research on teaching* (3rd ed., pp. 376–391). New York: Macmillan.

Ross, J. A. (1988). Controlling variables: A meta-analysis of training studies. *Review of Educational Research, 58*(4), 405–437.

Rubin, R. L., & Norman, J. T. (1992). Systematic modeling versus the learning cycle: Comparative effects on integrated science process skill achievement. *Journal of Research in Science Teaching, 29*(7), 715–727.

Salomon, G., & Perkins, D. N. (1989). Rocky road to transfer: Rethinking mechanisms of a neglected phenomenon. *Educational Psychologist, 24*(2), 113–142.

Samuels, S. J. (1986). Why children fail to learn and what to do about it. *Exceptional Children, 53,* 7–16.

Samuels, S. J., & Miller, N. L. (1985). Failure to find attention differences between learning disabled and normal children on classroom and laboratory tasks. *Exceptional Children, 51,* 358–375.

Schmidt, R., & Bjorke, T. (1992). New conceptualizations of practice: Common principles in three paradigms suggest new concepts for training. *Psychological Science, 3*(4), 207–217.

Schumaker, J. B., Deshler, D. D., Alley, G. R., Warner, M. M., & Denton, P. H. (1982). Multipass: A learning strategy for improving reading comprehension. *Learning Disability Quarterly, 5*(3), 295–304.

Smiley, S. S., Oaken, D. D., Worthen, D., Campione, J. D., & Brown, A. L. (1977). Recall of thematically relevant material by adolescent good and poor readers as a function of written versus oral presentation. *Journal of Educational Psychology, 69*(4), 381–387.

Smith, E., Blakeslee, T., & Anderson, C. (1993). Teaching strategies associated with conceptual change learning in science. *Journal of Research in Science Teaching, 30*(2), 111–126.

Snef, G. M. (1971). An information-integration theory and its application to normal reading acquisition and reading disability. In N. D. Bryand & C. E. Kass

(Eds.), *Leadership training institute in learning disabilities: Final report* (Vol. 2, pp. 305–391). Tucson: University of Arizona.

Stanovich, K. E. (1988). Explaining the differences between the dyslexic and the garden-variety poor reader: The phonological-core-variable difference model. *Journal of Learning Disabilities, 21,* 590–604.

Stavy, R., & Berkovitz, B. (1980). Cognitive conflict as a basis for teaching quantitative aspects of the concept of temperature. *Science Education, 64*(5), 679–692.

Swanson, H. L. (1988). Memory subtypes in learning disabled readers. *Learning Disabilities Quarterly, 11,* 342–357.

Swing, S., & Peterson, P. (1988). Elaborative and integrative thought processes in mathematics learning. *Journal of Educational Psychology, 80*(1), 54–66.

Torgeson, J., & Goldman, T. (1977). Verbal rehearsal and short-term memory in reading-disabled children. *Child Development, 48,* 56–60.

Torgeson, J., & Kail, R. V. (1980). *Memory processes in exceptional children: Advances in special education* (Vol. 1). Greenwich, CT: JAI.

Torgeson, J., Murphy, H. A., & Ivey, C. (1979). The influence of an orienting task on the memory performance of children with reading problems. *Journal of Learning Disabilities, 12*(6), 396–401.

Torgeson, J., Rashotte, C. A., Greenstein, J., & Portes, T. (1988). Language comprehension in learning disabled children who perform poorly on memory span tests. *Journal of Educational Psychology, 80*(4), 480–487.

Torgesen, J., Wagner, R., & Rashotte, C. (1997). Prevention and remediation of severe reading disabilities: Keeping the end in mind. *Scientific Studies of Reading, 1*(3), 217–234.

Trafton, P. R. (1984). Toward more effective, efficient instruction in mathematics. *Elementary School Journal, 84*(5), 514–530.

Vellutino, F. R. (1987). Dyslexia. *Scientific American, 256*(3), 34–41.

Wagner, R., & Torgesen, J. (1987). The nature of phonological processing and its causal role in the acquisition of reading skills. *Psychological Bulletin, 101,* 192–212.

Weisberg, R. (1986). *Creativity: Genius and other myths.* New York: W. H. Freeman.

White, B., & Horwitz, P. (1988). Computer microworlds and conceptual change: A new approach to science education. In P. Ramsden (Ed.), *Improving learning: New perspectives* (pp. 69–80). London: Kogan Page.

Wong, B. Y. L. (1978). The effects of directive cures on the organization of memory and recall in good and poor readers. *Journal of Educational Research, 72*(1), 32–38.

Wong, B. Y. L. (1985). Metacognition and learning disabilities. In D. L. Forrest-Pressley, G. E. MacKinnon, & T. G. Waller (Eds.), *Metacognition, cognition and human performance* (Vol. 2, pp. 137–175). New York: Academic Press.

Wong, B. Y. L. (1988). An instructional model for intervention research in learning disabilities. *Learning Disabilities Research, 4*(1), 5–16.

Woods, D. R. (1989). PS corner: Novice versus expert research. *Journal of College Science Teaching, 18*(3), 193–195.

Woodward, J. (1994). Effects of curriculum discourse style on eighth graders' recall and problem solving in earth science. *Elementary School Journal, 94*(3), 299–314.

Woodward, J., Carnine, D., & Collins, M. (1988). Closing the performance gap: CAI and secondary education for the mildly handicapped. *Journal of Educational Computing Research, 4*(3), 265–286.

Woodward, J., Carnine, D., & Gersten, R. (1988). Teaching problem solving through computer simulation. *American Educational Research Journal, 25*(1), 72–86.

Woodward, J., & Noell, J. (1992). Science instruction at the secondary level: Implications for students with learning disabilities. In D. Carnine & E. Kameenui (Eds.), *Higher order thinking: Designing curriculum for mainstreamed students* (pp. 39–58). Austin, TX: Pro-Ed.

Yates, G. C., & Yates, S. (1990). Teacher effectiveness research: Towards describing user-friendly classroom instruction. *Educational Psychology, 10*(3), 225–238.

6

Using Technology to Access the General Education Curriculum

Betsy Davis, Jennifer Caros, and Doug Carnine

Without a doubt, one of the most pressing demands placed on any high school student is the expectation to learn a large number of new vocabulary words. Students who have rich vocabularies and a store of background knowledge have a better chance of succeeding in secondary schools than those who don't. Because of the struggles that Jason had in learning to read, he read much less frequently than his normal-achieving peers. Consequently, his grasp of vocabulary was significantly behind his counterparts. To address this problem, Jason's teachers utilized some of the vocabulary instructional programs that they found in a computer-based format. Jason was able to access these programs when he had time and could progress through them at his own pace. These programs also freed up some valuable instructional time for his teachers to work on areas of need with other students.

As in Jason's case, technology can play a critical role in addressing the educational needs of many high school students with disabilities. The key tenets of the Individuals with Disabilities Education Act (IDEA; 2004) place a financial responsibility on high schools to provide the technology necessary to improve a student's capabilities. Along with technology tools, schools must provide sufficient services to ensure that these tools are appropriately selected, implemented, and maintained. The magnitude of this responsibility is daunting in light of the high number of high school students who have been identified with high-incidence disabilities and, in particular, the large number with specific learning disabilities (U.S. Department of Education, 2002).

An important issue for the field of education research is how to move toward a workable but effective service-delivery system for these students in light of financial uncertainty at the state and federal levels. Certainly, researchers and consumers cannot control the financial aspects of school funding. However, they can focus on identifying and selecting the most effective uses of technology to ensure that high school students with high-incidence disabilities learn the skills needed to succeed in the general education curriculum. How can this goal be accomplished? First, there must be an agreed-upon conceptualization of technology; in other words, the parameters for the domain of technology relative to service delivery for students with high-incidence disabilities must be identified (Edyburn, 2000). Second, there must be a stronger focus on and demand for empirical research that will identify the most effective forms of technology to serve the needs of these students.

CONCEPTUALIZATION OF TECHNOLOGY

An early impetus for developing federal laws for the education of all children was to include populations of students who had been relegated to special schools (such as schools for the deaf) or who had received inappropriate or no services from public schools. More severe forms of low-incidence disability hindered the educational pursuits of a large number of these children. For these children, "assistance" had a clear purpose: to provide necessary, medically related accommodations so that the deficit associated with their disability did not limit their capacity to benefit fully from public education.

Over time, although technological advances have proliferated, there has been a simultaneous identification of more disability categories, including disabilities with less explicit physical manifestations (such as learning disabilities). As a result, questions have begun to arise regarding the conceptualization of technology and service delivery for these students.

The current view of the purpose of technological assistance for students with disabilities is to compensate for or circumvent a disability to provide an alternative mode of performing a skill or accomplishing a task (Lewis, 1998). An assistive technological tool replaces an ability that is either missing or impaired, thereby providing the needed support to accomplish a goal (Quenneville, 2001). For students with high-incidence disabilities, this view presents an important question relative to the best way to meet their needs. That is, if technology for mild disabilities is seen as circumventing a missing ability and any associated skill deficits, the focus shifts from finding tools that alternatively and successfully teach skills for success to circumventing the skill entirely and moving toward success only in the presence of the technological tool.

Though the focus on circumventing a missing ability may be appropriate for students with certain forms of low-incidence physical disability, a question arises as to whether this is the most appropriate and beneficial framework for viewing technology relative to students with high-incidence disabilities. Indeed, if the missing skills are necessary for success after the student exits high school, a focus on circumvention may not benefit the student in the future, when assistance is no longer mandated. Therefore, the technological search for this student population should shift to alternative methods of teaching skills so that future success does not depend on technology, but on the skill the individual possesses.

Edyburn (2000) presented a conceptualization that can expand our view of technological services to accommodate the diversity of disabilities that are currently represented in the educational system. Drawing from Blackhurst (1997), four forms of technology were specified: (1) teaching technology with a pedagogical focus on the effective instruction of students with disabilities; (2) medical technology for addressing physical and medically related disabilities; (3) instructional technology for software and hardware that will improve teaching and thereby student learning; and (4) assistive technology that enhances students' functional performance, enabling them to complete tasks more effectively than would be possible otherwise.

This separation of forms of technology depicts the range of assistance that is possible for students with high-incidence disabilities while suggesting important questions about the purpose of the technology. The breakdown distinguishes instructional goals (such as teaching a student to add independently) from functional outcomes (for example, the student can calculate the correct answer to an addition problem with a calculator). It shifts the focus from directly teaching skills to enhancing performance, with the associated technology shifting from instructional to assistive (Edyburn, 2000). The delineation helps to focus attention on critical issues surrounding the selection of beneficial technology services for high school students with high-incidence disabilities. In essence, a critical issue is determining whether the goal of using technology is to teach a skill that is necessary for future success outside the school environment (that is, instructional) or to compensate for a skill deficit in one area to enhance performance in another (that is, assistive). Educators, technology developers, and researchers must begin discussing the purpose of technology assistance for high school students with high-incidence disabilities within the framework of how that purpose affects students' future functioning and success within the larger society.

Need for Empirical Focus

In addition to reconceptualizing the view of technology to best meet the needs of students with high-incidence disabilities, understanding the effectiveness of current technologies for these students is an important step in informing potential consumers. Carnine (1999) has suggested that to become a more mature profession, education should use scientific methods to determine the efficacy of any educational implementation. Without empirical evidence of efficacy, student success becomes one of hope rather than certainty. This is particularly critical for high school students with disabilities who have limited time remaining in the educational environment. Edyburn (2000) has argued that to fully understand the importance of technology, researchers must document student-performance evidence on specific tasks under both technology-aided and unaided conditions to gauge the effects of the technology. In short, focusing on academic performance as the critical outcome for technology users is essential (Hauser & Malouf, 1996) if educators are to ensure appropriate accountability and address IDEA mandates (Edyburn, 2000).

Focus and Process of the Review

Within the framework just presented, this chapter will examine the state of empirical research on the use of technology in schools to improve the learning of high school students with high-incidence disabilities. The form of technology discussed in this review reflects what is typically thought of as technology: software and hardware. However, the educational goal associated with a given technology determines whether the medium remains within what Edyburn (2000) would classify as instructional technology or moves to the assistive-technology realm. For example, if a computerized system is used to circumvent a deficit that remains after the technology is removed, the computerized system is classified as an *assistive device*. On the other hand, if the computerized system supports skill development in a deficit area so that the student can perform the skill after the technology is removed, the system is a form of *instructional technology*.

The process used to identify relevant articles involved searching two major databases, ERIC and PsychLit, for general content terms reflecting (1) technology (computers, media, hypermedia, multimedia, personal digital assistants, instructional technology, technology of learning, and instructional materials); (2) high school students (secondary and high school students); and (3) disability (learning, behavioral, and emotional disabilities and disorders). Studies containing middle school students were included only if they were captured under the "secondary" label and the topic under study was generalizable across grades, or if the middle school focus tapped high-level skills that would be considered applicable to students with disabilities entering high school. Articles from 1984 to the present were considered. As a further limiting criterion, selected articles had to be journal articles or other peer-reviewed research reports that are available to the public.

Sixty-six abstracts emerged from the PsychLit search and 187 from the ERIC search. These abstracts were reviewed and further limited to the requirement that the studies be data driven, with either intraindividual (pretest–posttest) or interindividual (groups of students) comparisons of student academic performance outcomes. The search and review processes resulted in 32 articles related to technology, of which one was a review article and two were meta-analyses. Because of restrictions of time and space, the review is not completely exhaustive, and the authors regret any published omissions.

EVIDENCE FOR TECHNOLOGY USE IN HIGH SCHOOLS

This section will focus on published studies that have examined how technology has been incorporated into the educational environment, the intent of these technological tools, and how they have fared relative to effectiveness. The empirical studies were conducted in the content areas of language arts (reading, vocabulary, and writing), mathematics, and social studies. Some of the studies used specific technological hardware; however, they were actually testing the impact of specific instructional design principles that fall within Edyburn's (2000) concept of teaching technology (see Chapter 5 in this volume).

The review is organized by content area, with different types of technologies applied to and tested in each area presented. The organization is not intended to reflect a static, definitive structural arrangement. Many technology terms used in the literature are often used interchangeably (such as multimedia, hypermedia, and hypertext); as a result, the creation of meaningful grouping categories by technology form is difficult. Further, sorting studies by content area was often a difficult task. For example, certain articles related to content-area reading comprehension were included in the reading content domain, whereas other sets of articles were relegated to their own content domain heading (such as social studies) even though comprehension was the desired outcome. The decision to group studies under a specific content domain was based on the number of similar studies in the content area and the focused nature of the line of research.

Research on Writing

Quenneville (2001) noted that for students with learning disabilities (LD), computers and related software can provide communicative benefit by improving the quality and quantity of writing. Furthermore, the advancement of spelling and grammar supports may enable writers to succeed by decreasing their focus on writing mechanics, thereby freeing up resources for planning time and content generation. The following sections review the empirical evidence available to evaluate support for these expectations.

Word Processing

Only two studies meeting the search criteria were identified relative to word processing and writing performance at the secondary level. In the first, Vacc (1987) examined differences between letters that were written by hand and those composed on a computer. Subjects were four mildly mentally handicapped eighth-grade students. Within a single-subject, repeated-measures design, each student completed 24 letters: 12 handwritten and 12 using a word processor. Results indicated that students who used the computer spent more time writing and revising their letters and produced noticeably longer letters than when they composed by hand. Evaluations of quality, however, did not differ between the two production methods. Given the small sample and the fact that all subjects were male, few generalizations can be made. The author contends that the results suggest the computer is an effective tool in writing instruction with mildly mentally handicapped students. Nevertheless, whether increased time spent writing, more revisions, and greater length in the absence of improvements in quality, constitute significant benefits remains unclear.

The second study was a meta-analysis of research findings involving the use of word processing in writing instruction (Bangert-Drowns, 1993). To be included in the meta-analysis, each study had to compare two groups of students receiving identical writing instruction, allow only one group to use word processing, and report quantitative treatment outcomes. The authors located 32 articles, but not all studies included sufficient information to permit the calculation of effect sizes. Only two of the studies included high school samples; both were unpublished dissertations.

Results across studies indicated an average effect size of 0.27 standard deviations ($SE = 0.011$), a small but significant effect. The authors concluded that, overall, word processing improved the quality of writing, especially for weaker writers. Word processing allowed students to write longer documents, but it did not result in more positive attitudes toward writing. The meta-analysis was conducted 10 years ago with no published data at that time on high school students with high-incidence disabilities. Empirical evidence is still virtually nonexistent that word processing, in isolation, produces any meaningful benefits for the writing performance of high school students with disabilities.

Thus, in spite of the *apparent* assistive benefits of word processing over handwriting (that is, features that remove the need for recopying and erasures, as well as those that can transform writing into a collaborative endeavor), the *actual* benefits for improving the writing performance of high school students with disabilities are unknown.

Spelling and Grammar Supports

In a society that emphasizes written communication, those who cannot successfully navigate the written word are at a definite disadvantage. The correctly spelled word is a critical feature of comprehensible writing—a deficit that, unfortunately, is demonstrated by many students with disabilities (Bailet, 1990; Bailet & Lyon, 1985). If the writing of students with disabilities is to benefit from computerized spelling supports, the efficacy of computerized spell-checkers needs to be examined.

The only study found relative to the computerized spell-check function was an examination by Montgomery, Karlan, and Coutinho (2001), in which 199 writing samples produced by 111 students with disabilities were submitted to different spell-check programs to analyze misspellings. Writing samples drawn from various content domains were submitted to nine spell-check programs. Misspellings were classified according to the level of phonetic mismatch to the target word and the proportion of correct two-letter sequences. The goal was to determine the accuracy with which the spell-check functions generated the target word for misspellings. The authors noted that although spell-checkers can identify the misspelling of words with 100% accuracy, they do not always provide the target word in the suggested list of replacements, and, if they do, the correct word is not always the first suggested change. It is possible that students with LD who have spelling deficits may not be able to recognize that the spell-check function has not provided the correct spelling of the desired word in its list of suggested changes. Also, for students with attention deficits, if the target word is not the first suggested replacement, they may not be able to focus their attention on the list long enough to sort through multiple suggestions or may impulsively select the first incorrect suggestion (Montgomery et al., 2001).

Generally, the results indicated that spell-checkers were ineffective at producing target words first in the replacement list for misspellings generated by students with LD. Of the spelling errors submitted, only 53% resulted in the identification of the target words at any position within the suggestion lists, and, of those identified, only 22% were placed in the first position. Further, spell-checkers were more efficient at providing the target word when misspellings were closer in phonetic match to the target word and when they contained a higher percentage of correct letter sequences. Unfortunately, the sample of middle school students with disabilities was spelling at such a low level that the spellchecker did not identify the correct word as the first word in the displayed list. The authors made several suggestions for changing the spell-check function to enhance its effectiveness for students with disabilities. Although this study was based on students in the third through eighth grades, it was included in the current review because the results reflected the efficacy of a technological tool that is not necessarily age dependent. Earlier examinations of spell-check efficacy have been conducted (e.g., Dalton, Winbury, & Morocco, 1990; MacArthur, Graham, Haynes, & DeLaPaz, 1996), but the most recent validation study was selected for review because of the rapid pace of technological advance and the potential for improvements in the word-suggestion dictionaries and algorithms across time.

With regard to computerized grammar supports, no studies were found for high school students with disabilities relative to grammar and style checkers. However, authors have suggested that these technologies may have limited value. For example, MacArthur (1996) noted that these types of support can identify relatively minor grammatical and stylistic problems, but often they misinterpret more serious grammatical and mechanical errors. The author further reported on an internal study conducted on one program that had been specifically designed to meet the needs of students with LD (MacArthur, 1994). Here, the checker was used to proofread 10 writing samples written by LD students and the same papers with the errors corrected. The checker did not flag the majority of grammatical errors in the uncorrected writing versions, and it incorrectly flagged many errors in the corrected version. Thus, at this time, there appears to be no empirical support for grammar tools as assistive devices to improve the writing performance of high school students with high-incidence disabilities.

Word-prediction software is another spelling and grammar support system that may have potential for helping students communicate more clearly through written language (Hasselbring & Glaser, 2000). As the writer types, these programs display words that have the highest probability of being correct within a sentence and writing passage based on the initial letters typed, prior frequency of use, most recent use, and grammatical correctness (Quenneville, 2001). Because these programs supply words as the writer composes, they may influence writing during the composition process rather than during revision (MacArthur, 1996). To date, no empirical studies have examined the efficacy of this software in improving the writing process and outcomes of students with high-incidence disabilities. However, given the cautions associated with spell-checkers relative to the difficulties that students with disabilities have with knowing when a correct word has been suggested, word-prediction software is likely to suffer from the same issues.

Multimedia

For students with limited literacy skills or prior knowledge deficits in content areas, the use of visual and other media as writing assists may have particular benefit (Daiute, 1992). According to the National Center to Improve Practice in Special Education (NCIP; 2004), integrating text, graphics, video, music, and sound effects offers students with disabilities alternative ways to access and represent information. It also capitalizes on strengths that allow for fuller participation in the learning process. Unfortunately, there is no empirical support for this expectation relative to improving the writing performance of high school students with disabilities.

Although using the multimedia capabilities of computers may motivate students with disabilities to communicate complex ideas (Behrmann & Jerome, 2002), caution is warranted relative to assuring the level of learning that is taking place. For example, if multimedia projects are group assigned within diverse classrooms, and students with disabilities are paired with nondisabled peers, teachers must make certain that students with disabilities are meaningfully participating in the group activity, not merely being assigned nonessential production tasks. Further, although multimedia publishing is becoming a commonplace activity, written communication is still a prerequisite for general success. Thus, multimedia projects should not constitute the majority of writing experiences for students with disabilities. Multimedia technology should be viewed as an assistive device that allows high school students with disabilities to present information in content-area courses, but emphasis should also be placed on instructional technology that addresses written-expression skill deficits for generalizable future success.

Speech Synthesis

Speech-synthesis technology translates text written by students into an audio format, thereby allowing students to hear what they have written and monitor the adequacy of their writing. Unfortunately, no empirical evidence suggests that this type of technology can improve the writing performance of high school students with disabilities. MacArthur (1996) noted that in academic settings that depend on meaningful communication, a requisite in high school courses, speech synthesis may provide a link between the ideas that students want to express and the skills they possess to write about those ideas. However, in a review of text-to-speech research, the Center for Applied Special Technology (Ruzic & O'Connell, 2002) identified only one article reporting on the impact of speech synthesis on writing, and that study was conducted on elementary students (Borgh & Dickson, 1992). Although speech synthesis resulted in more formative text revisions for the young children in that study, no differences were found in the length or quality of writing between word processing with and without speech synthesis. Thus, although there may be an impetus to try speech synthesis within content-area courses to allow high school students with disabilities to express their ideas, there is little evidence to support this decision. Thus, the focus should remain on addressing the underlying written-expression deficits.

Outlining and Semantic Webbing

Students with LD often experience problems with organizing and retaining information, focusing and sustaining attention, and integrating prior knowledge with new information (Hunter, 2004; Reyes, Gallego, Duran, & Scanlon, 1989; Saski, Swicegood, & Carter, 1983). Most successful writers take time to plan their activities, gather information, and formulate a plan to adequately organize and address their chosen topic. Therefore, technology that is designed to assist students with LD to gather information, as well as to plan and organize that information, could prove beneficial to their writing performance. Computer software such as *Inspiration* (2003, 2004), which allows students to gather information from multiple sources, develop concept maps of the relationships between ideas, and formulate flexible outlines, has been developed to serve this purpose. The assistive benefit of this type of program for improving the writing of students with disabilities has been suggested in the literature (e.g., Castellani & Jeffs, 2001); however, no empirical evidence exists to support this contention.

Research on Reading Comprehension and Vocabulary

A major distinction between secondary and elementary academic environments is the increased need in high school to understand extensive content-area text and vocabulary that represent a wide diversity of topics and ideas. In other words, secondary students must have adequate skills to encode, comprehend, remember, organize, and link together a great deal of information. For many students, "inconsiderate" content-area textbooks (Armbruster, 1984), which lack organization and contain only surface coverage of a breadth of content, and the rapid pace at which teachers must present related information (Mastropieri, Scruggs, & Graetz, 2003) increase the challenge and frustration posed by content-area reading requirements. For students with disabilities in particular, many of whom read far below grade level and have difficulty assimilating information, the challenge can seem insurmountable. Thus, identifying the most efficacious forms of technology to address the reading challenges faced by these students is of great importance. The following sections synthesize the empirical literature on this topic.

Computer Display of Text and Comprehension

Keene and Davey (1987) assessed the effects of computer-presented text on the reading behaviors of high school students with LD. Fifty-one students were randomly assigned to one of two groups: those who read expository passages from a computer monitor, and those who read from a comparably formatted printed page. Before reading the passages, students were told to try to use six reading strategies to aid their comprehension.

Results indicated that the computer-displayed text format did not have a significant effect on reading comprehension, on most of the strategic behaviors, or time on task compared with the traditional printed text. However, using computer-presented text did appear to increase the students' positive attitude toward the reading task. If processing, integrating, and remembering information is difficult for students with LD and contributes to reading and language difficulties (Hunter, 2004; Scruggs & Mastropieri, 1990), one would expect that facing expository reading passages in any format would result in reading difficulty. Thus, the findings from this early study on the simple display of text on the computer screen are not surprising.

Based on the importance of breaking down sentences into smaller groups of meaningfully related words for enhancing the retention and comprehension of students with LD, Casteel (1988) investigated the effects of two methods of chunking information on reading performance. Thirty 10th- and 11th-grade students with LD were assigned to one of three groups: (1) a training group that received chunked passages displayed on a computer screen using computer-assisted instruction, (2) a group for whom the chunked passages were administered in a traditional paper-based mode, and (3) a control group who used computer-assisted instruction with nonchunked passages. Pretest–posttest gains revealed that, although the computer-assisted, chunked-passage group made larger gains, the mean posttest reading scores did not differ significantly between the two chunked-passage groups; both chunked-passage groups outperformed the nonchunked group. Thus, the technological medium was not the critical factor in influencing student performance; rather, the manner in which the information was presented to students made the difference.

Recognizing that computers can not only display textbook material but also enhance text through hypermedia, MacArthur and Haynes (1995) designed a study to investigate the impact of enhancement on content-area comprehension. The researchers created two versions of reading passages from a 10th-grade basic biology textbook using the *Student Assistant for Learning Text*, a software system for developing hypermedia textbook material. The basic computerized text version contained all of the elements found in the original textbook, including headings, boldface print, questions, and graphics. The enhanced computer version comprised these same features, in addition to links between questions and text, highlighted main ideas, speech synthesis, an online glossary, and teacher-supplied summaries or restatements of important ideas. Ten students with LD in Grades 9 and 10 read one text passage using the basic version and another passage using the enhanced version. Results indicated that the use of the enhanced hypermedia program significantly influenced student comprehension, as measured by paper-and-pencil tests of key terms and main ideas. The enhanced version resulted in 56% correct answers, whereas the basic version resulted in 45% correct, a moderate effect size.

Thus, at this time, there seems to be no major benefit of reading material from a computer screen compared with reading from a textbook. However, hypermedia-enhanced text, as constructed by MacArthur and Haynes (1995), does show promise for improving the reading comprehension of students with disabilities in content-area classes and indicates a line of research that should be pursued.

Computerized Reading Assessment

In a programmatic line of research, Horton, Lovitt, and colleagues at the University of Washington recognized the instructional difficulties inherent in content-area classrooms with learners of diverse reading abilities. Given that textbooks serve as one of the main information sources in secondary schools, even in diverse classrooms, and that texts can be overwhelming to students, particularly students with disabilities, the researchers saw a great need for matching the reading skills of students within a classroom to differential levels of textbook instruction.

The first strand of their research focused on modifying textbook information and developing methods for matching students to their level of independent content comprehension within their assigned textbook using paper-and-pencil modality (e.g., Horton & Lovitt, 1989). In this earlier work, three classroom instructional groups were formed, based on content-area reading inventories: students whose level of content comprehension reflected a need for (1) teacher-directed (0%–47% correct), (2) peer-dyadic (53%–73% correct), or (3) independent (80%–100%) instruction. Several studies indicated that multilevel instructional treatments relative to these groupings significantly benefited lower-performing students (e.g., Horton, Lovitt, & Christensen, 1991a, 1991b).

The second strand of research focused on changing the paper-and-pencil procedures into a computerized format. Relevant to the domain of content-area reading and paralleling their focus on matching students to their level of reading independence within the curriculum, Horton and Lovitt (1994) assessed the extent to which a computerized format for reading assessment and diagnostic procedures resulted in the same instructional groups that were formed through paper-and-pencil assessment. The assumption was that when dealing with diverse classrooms of learners, teachers must be able to match instructional levels to differing reading levels to structure the classroom for the most efficient and effective instructional delivery. If a computerized method of prescribing instructional levels of textbook comprehension is viable, the computer could increase task efficiency because assessments could be conducted in the group setting of the computer lab.

Within this framework, 7th-grade middle school students and 10th-grade high school students (remedial, $n = 16$; LD, $n = 13$; typically achieving, $n = 120$) completed reading inventories under two conditions:

computerized and paper-and-pencil administration. In the paper-and-pencil condition, teachers followed a protocol that directed students to read a 1,000-word passage from their textbook for 10 minutes, complete a 15-item study guide using the textbook to find the answers, study the completed guide for five minutes, and take a 15-item multiple-choice test. In the computerized group, the teacher directed students to perform the same set of tasks, except that these tasks were computerized. All students were assessed using both formats of the reading inventory, with the assessment format randomly distributed across eight assessment points. The middle school reading passages came from social studies and science textbooks; the high school passages came solely from social studies textbooks. Dependent measures were scores on eight multiple-choice tests administered across passages. Results indicated close alignment between the diagnostic information gained from the two methods at the individual level of analysis for all students. Specifically, 72% of the students were placed in the same instructional level by both methods, with the remaining students being placed within one instructional level of each other by the methods. Further, the majority of mismatched cases between methods were based on correct score differences of two or fewer points.

Although the choice of design for the study (that is, the equivalent time samples design; Campbell & Stanley, 1963) limited the generalizability of the computerized assessment results outside the context of alternating administration with the paper-and-pencil version, these results have practical value for teachers who are attempting to deal with diverse learners within the classroom environment. Thus, efficient methods for pre-assessing students' reading level in content-area textbooks and designing instructional groups relative to that level can not only make the delivery of instruction more efficient and effective for all students but can also allow teachers to focus on the more important goal of achieving content objectives.

Audio Text and Comprehension

Much attention has focused on alternative methods of effectively conveying content-area information to students with disabilities, particularly audio recordings that preserve the format of the original text but present information in an alternative modality (Baskin & Harris, 1995). Two studies were identified in which this technology was used by high school students with disabilities. The initial study by Torgesen, Dahlem, and Greenstein (1987) reported the results of three separate experiments that examined the effect of audio-text recordings on the comprehension of textbook information for adolescents with LD.

In the first experiment, the effect of supplemental verbatim recordings on comprehension was tested under conditions in which the need for special study strategies was minimized, short passages were used, and comprehension was tested immediately. Student participants were 16 adolescents with LD in Grades 9 through 12, selected from a pool of 92 students. The 16 students were selected to represent all possible combinations of average and low IQ and average and low reading skills within the initial pool. Reading passages were taken from textbooks used in American history, civics, or health classes. The design of the study incorporated three conditions that alternated on successive treatment days for all subjects: read only, listen only, and read-listen (reading and listening to text simultaneously). Subjects were counterbalanced according to which condition they had received first and moved successively through the conditions. All subjects experienced each condition six times. Ten students without LD served as a comparison group and performed under the read-only condition, reading the same passages that were given to the students with LD.

Results indicated that the effect of supplemental auditory text on comprehension was immediate and consistent over time. The control students (students without LD) earned a mean comprehension score of 65% correct, considerably higher than that of the students with LD in the read-only condition ($M = 38\%$), but not significantly different from the students with LD in the read-listen condition ($M = 55\%$). Further, a significant relationship was found between the initial reading level and the amount of learning achieved by students with LD in the read-listen condition. The eight students with LD with the poorest initial reading scores showed an average improvement of 23% in the read-listen condition compared with students with LD with higher initial reading scores, who improved by 11%. Thus, within this study, supplemental auditory information may have compensated for deficiencies in basic reading skills.

The second experiment reported by Torgesen et al. (1987) sought to test the effectiveness of verbatim recordings under more realistic conditions than those found in the first experiment. Thus, students read or read and listened to passages for 10 minutes a day, three days a week and were tested once a week to reflect a weekly exam format within the academic environment. Subjects in this study were 16 students, selected in the same manner as the subjects for Experiment 1.

Results did not support the benefit of the read-listen condition for students with LD. That is, the average test performance of students with LD on the weekly quizzes did not differ when the students experienced the read-only or read-listen conditions. Thus, the availability of supplemental audio recordings did not appear to increase learning of the chapter content when the tests were taken over a weeklong period. Furthermore, there was no relation between the initial reading level and the amount of learning within the read-listen condition, as was found in the first experiment. Consequently, under the weekly time frame, the supplemental audio recording did not appear to compensate for basic reading deficits.

The findings in Experiment 2 led to a third experiment (Torgesen et al., 1987), which followed the same format and used the same subjects as

Experiment 2 but attempted to strengthen the impact of the read-listen intervention. In the third examination, the amount of time was increased from six to eight weeks and supplemental study worksheets were added. The worksheets consisted of 15 questions that were formed to test understanding of the passage's main ideas. Worksheets were designed to require little preparation but lend assistance to students. Students in both the read-only and read-listen conditions received the worksheets. Text passages were highlighted to indicate when the student was to stop reading and answer a worksheet item. Under these conditions, the average comprehension quiz score in the read-only condition was 39.7%, whereas the average score in the read-listen condition was 51.4%. Combining the results from Experiments 2 and 3, the authors concluded that verbatim auditory text materials are a useful tool for students with LD in learning content information from textbooks, but only when study aids are included as part of the reading experience. However, one might note that none of the auditory text conditions across the three studies assisted the students with LD in earning mean scores above the passing level (60% correct).

More recently, in response to findings from prior research and to address the technical difficulties of traditional books on tape, Boyle and colleagues examined the effects of CD-ROM audio text paired with a structured study strategy intervention on content acquisition (Boyle et al., 2003). Subjects were 95 students from eight self-contained special education history classes in six comprehensive northeast high schools. The researchers compared three conditions: CD audio text alone, audio paired with strategy instruction, and a control condition consisting of traditional instruction. To be included in the study, students had to have an individualized education program (IEP) designation of needing specialized accommodations in secondary history content. The strategy instruction received by the audio-strategy group involved a procedure to assist students in attending with and taking notes on important information in the reading. The authors included strategy instruction within their design in recognition of the importance of providing students with disabilities strategies for notetaking, as well as organizing and integrating new information (Deshler et al., 2001). Six weeks were allotted for the intervention.

Results indicated that following the intervention, both audio groups scored significantly higher than the control group on cumulative knowledge acquisition scores. The audio-only and the audio-strategy conditions evidenced improvements of 38% and 39% in correct responding, respectively, compared with a 22% improvement in the control condition. The authors noted that audio textbooks can be effective tools for increasing the acquisition of high-level academic content over time for students with disabilities. The lack of significance of the strategy addition to audio text was surprising, but, as the researchers and teachers noted, the students involved had deficits in notetaking skills. The strategy involved a time-consuming process requiring students to select the appropriate information to be synthesized within the 20 minutes allotted for reading and notetaking. Further, the six-week intervention may have been too short for students to fully incorporate the strategy skills into their repertoires. Despite these difficulties, many students did begin to display appropriate notetaking skills, such as identifying important information and outlining reading passages.

Given the small number of studies that have been conducted on audio text, additional research is needed to substantiate the benefit of this technological form for students with disabilities. Further, whether incorporating supplemental study material with audio recordings results in increased acquisition of content-area knowledge is unclear. Future research should focus on identifying the most user-friendly, efficient, and effective study guide and strategy elements to supplement audio text.

Outlining and Semantic Webbing and Comprehension

The only published study that was identified for outlining programs did not focus specifically on high school students with disabilities, but on the lowest-performing third of two ninth-grade global studies classes (Anderson-Inman, Redekopp, & Adams, 1992). The authors sought to investigate the effects of computer-based outlining programs as study tools in an effort to identify conditions under which they are effective in enhancing knowledge acquisition and comprehension in content-area texts.

Seven low-performing students in two classes participated; one class was academically stronger (Class 2) than the other class (Class 1). The same teacher taught both classes and provided the same focus of instruction. Over the course of the study, nine sessions took place for each class covering nine chapters or shorter reading selections. The weaker class (Class 1) began the outlining procedure after the first preoutlining session (Sessions 2–9); the stronger class began outlining at Session 6 (Sessions 6–9). Implementation of the outlining procedure was staggered across classes to evaluate the effects of electronic studying compared with other study strategies the students were already using. In essence, for four sessions (Sessions 2–5), Class 1 performed the outlining routine, whereas Class 2 was still in the preoutlining phase using the SQ3R strategy (Robinson, 1961) taught in class.

Outcomes were assessed using text-embedded mastery tests administered across the course of the nine study sessions. Pretest–posttest comparisons indicated that some students performed better across time when they used the computer-based outlining as a study strategy, whereas others remained stable or decreased in performance. The mean increase in the percentage correct between the preoutlining and outlining sessions was 14% for Class 1 students, who had eight outlining sessions, and 7% for Class 2 students, who had only four sessions. Although no statistical comparisons were possible, the increased exposure to the outlining routine for Class 1 may have led to the greater performance increase. The researchers staggered implementation across the classes to view performance during Sessions 2 through 5 while Class 1 was outlining and Class 2 was not. However, they did not make any statistical comparisons. Raw numbers in the report indicate that for Sessions 2 through 5, the outlining group in Class 1 had an average of 69% correct answers. During the same time, the preoutlining staggered group in Class 2 had an average score of 54% correct. Interestingly, the authors specified that a 15% or greater gain across time represented a significantly meaningful increase in knowledge acquisition for each student. However, they did not apply this criterion to the mean-level differences between classes during Sessions 2 through 5. If they had, the results would have indicated that, on average, the outlining function had a beneficial impact on content acquisition. More recently, researchers have moved toward using *Inspiration* (2003) software (e.g., Anderson-Inman, Knox-Quinn, & Horney, 1996). However, no published report of empirical work examining the impact of this new outlining program on the academic performance of high school students with disabilities could be found.

Computers and Vocabulary Enhancement

Two studies were identified in which computerized programs were used to enhance the content-area vocabulary of high school students with disabilities. Johnson, Gersten, and Carnine (1987) examined two computer-assisted instructional (CAI) approaches to teaching vocabulary to 25 high school students with LD in Grades 9 through 12. Subjects were randomly assigned to one of the two CAI programs after being matched on pretest scores. The distinguishing instructional characteristics between the two programs were the amount of information presented to the students at one time and the procedures used to provide cumulative review.

The instructional characteristics of the Small Teaching Set approach (Carnine, Rankin, & Granzin, 1984) included (1) individualized lessons based only on words the student did not know; (2) practice sets consisting of no more than seven words at any time; (3) a specified mastery criterion that had to be met on two consecutive lessons before the word was considered learned; and (4) cumulative review on words after 10 words were learned. The instructional characteristics of the Large Teaching Set approach (Davidson & Eckert, 1983) included (1) presentation of words in sets of 25; (2) word sets presented in the same order until mastery was reached; and (3) multiple options for displaying the word, including word-and-definition display, multiple-choice questions, sentence-completion items, or an arcade matching game. This program contained no cumulative review. Both programs provided feedback to subjects on the accuracy of their responses and the number of words correct.

Results indicated that significantly more students reached mastery more quickly when they were taught with the Small Teaching Set program than the Large Teaching Set program. The mean number of sessions to mastery of 50 words was 7.6 for the Small Teaching Set approach and 9.1 for the Large Teaching Set approach. However, students learned vocabulary knowledge (approximately 85% correct) and retained this knowledge two weeks later (approximately 82%) equally well across both instructional conditions. Thus, students learned the material more efficiently when it was presented in smaller chunks with cumulative review, but they did not necessarily gain and retain more vocabulary knowledge with this approach. Given the limited amount of time that high school students with disabilities have remaining in school and the vast amount of content-area knowledge imparted during this time, teaching efficiency is an important criterion for evaluating any instructional program. Furthermore, although the study design did not test the effect of the implementation of computer technology on improving students' vocabulary acquisition, one might argue that using this technology could provide benefits to these students. Through this technological format, vocabulary acquisition in content areas could be accomplished proactively outside the classroom before introducing vocabulary within the context of content-area instruction.

The previous study examined vocabulary acquisition related to adjectives and verbs. Horton, Lovitt, and Givens (1988) followed up with two studies focusing on content-specific vocabulary that incorporated aspects of instructional design identified by Johnson et al. (1987). In the first study, a pretest design was used in which 35 difficult geography vocabulary terms were identified and 28 terms were incorporated into a self-paced, computerized vocabulary program. Students completed as many seven-word sets as possible within a 30-minute period, with corrective feedback and cumulative review provided during each session. Overall, three 30-minute computer sessions were conducted in the computer lab on consecutive school days. Pretest and posttest knowledge of all 35 terms was tested, with 28 instructed items serving as experimental items and the remaining 7 nonprogrammed terms serving as control items.

One class of high school students who were enrolled in a remedial ninth-grade world geography class participated in the study, including seven remedial students and six students with LD. Results indicated a significant gain in knowledge on the 28 instructed items for all students, but no gain in control-item knowledge. On average, remedial students and those with LD improved their accuracy on the 28 instructed vocabulary terms across the three computerized sessions. Specifically, the mean score of students with disabilities increased from 26% at pretest to 68% at posttest. The mean score of remedial students increased from 30% at pretest to 80% at posttest. Further, remedial students made their largest improvements after the first session, with smaller increments upward with each successive session. In contrast, students with disabilities made equal levels of smaller gains across the first two sessions, with a small increment after the final session. One caution is warranted relative to drawing conclusions from this study. Nonprogrammed words served as the control comparison against which improved vocabulary acquisition of programmed words was viewed. Therefore, separating out the relative contribution to improvement of the computerized vocabulary program from simple repeated exposure to the programmed words is not possible.

The second study conducted by Horton, Lovitt, and Givens (1988) involved two general education ninth-grade health classes. The classes contained students of varying ability levels, including below-average performers, but no students with disabilities. Within a pretest–posttest control-group design, one class served as the control group; the other was selected to receive computerized vocabulary intervention. The procedures used for the experimental condition were identical to those used in the first study, with the exception that students received two computer lab intervention sessions instead of three. The teacher in the classroom where students routinely received instruction tested the control students.

On average, the results indicated that students in the experimental group answered 75% of the items correctly on the second posttest, an increase of 9.3 points from the pretest, whereas their control-group counterparts answered only 38% of the items correctly at posttest, an increase of 2 points. For the eight experimental students who had not reached the criterion set for mastery (80%) by the end of the second session, a third session was conducted. Seven of these eight students improved their scores after this session, with four earning a score of 80% correct or higher.

Results across the two Horton et al. studies suggest that computer-assisted instruction in content-area vocabulary was successful for all students, whether they were classified as LD, remedial, or general education. Identifying methods for teaching content-specific vocabulary that meet the needs of all students and conducting this instruction outside content-area instruction may help to free up teacher time within the classroom to achieve content objectives.

Vocabulary and Audio Presentation of Words

In an early study focusing on efficiency, Freeman and McLaughlin (1984) sought to use a low form of technology to assist resource-room teachers in helping students develop sight-word reading skills. The authors focused on teaching survival-oriented sight-word vocabulary in different content areas using vocabulary sheets that were constructed from district curricula. With tape recordings as a model for correctly pronounced words, response and error rates in sight-word reading were assessed using a multiple-baseline across-subjects design. In the baseline condition, no modeling of correct pronunciation was given. Results indicated an increase in correct oral response rates of isolated words and a sharp decrease in each student's oral error rates when the tape recorder was used to provide models, compared with baseline rates. As reported by the authors, using the tape recorder rather than the teacher for modeling increased the teacher's time for other kinds of instruction, and therefore it was considered a highly efficient intervention.

Within the area of synthesized speech feedback, one study was identified that met the criteria for this review. Farmer, Klein, and Bryson (1992) examined the efficacy of a computer program that provided whole-word synthesized speech feedback to adolescents with severe reading disabilities. The study's goal was to determine whether speech feedback for difficult words would lead to improved word recognition and possibly improved comprehension by enhancing students' reading experience and encouraging them to spend more time practicing reading. Fourteen students with reading disabilities from a special school for students with LD volunteered to take part in the study. The average age of the subjects was 15 years, 8 months.

Students were presented with 36 stories stored on three disks in order of reading level. Half the stories within each level were programmed so that when one of the words was clicked (called "tagged" words) with the mouse, the speech synthesizer would pronounce it. For the other half, the words were not pronounced. After a student had read each story, a set of four short multiple-choice questions was presented to test comprehension. In addition, students were tested for word recognition approximately once a week. The recognition test consisted of tagged words in the stories, intermixed with a number of words from the stories that were preselected as likely to be difficult to decode ("untagged" words). The time required to read the words in each test and the percentage of words read correctly were recorded for each student.

The results showed no between-group differences in the mean percentage of comprehension questions answered correctly or the mean reading time when the speech synthesizer was turned on versus off. Further, having the speech synthesizer turned on had no significant impact on word-recognition ability, with the mean percentage correct of tagged words being virtually identical to the untagged words (46 vs. 43). Also, there was no significant difference between the time taken to correctly read tagged words and the time taken to read untagged words. Ultimately, there was no evidence that using a computer-assisted reading program with synthesized vocabulary feedback benefited adolescents with severe reading disabilities by improving their specific word-recognition skills.

The authors noted reasons the lack of substantial findings may have occurred, the most salient being the short amount of time spent practicing. The study's design allowed for one hour of practice per week for seven weeks, and each student spent less than the allowable time on the computer. The average amount of time spent over the course of the study by students was two hours. The authors suggested that, because of a habit of skimming over words they could not easily read, students may not have taken the time to use the system to its full advantage. They recommended the presence of an instructor during early sessions to monitor and encourage use of the system to maximize its potential. Given that this study took place in a special school for students with severe problems, results are not immediately generalizable to the public school environment and to students who experience lesser but significant reading problems.

Mathematics

Computer Instruction

The influx of computers into educational settings during the early 1980s was seen as holding great promise for improving the learning of special education students. Relative to mathematics, several forms of math-focused software were in existence, including drill-and-practice and tutorial-type programs. With computer games beginning to flood the mass market and gaining popularity, math-related instructional software programs incorporating the action and competitive nature of these games were also developed in hopes of increasing students' motivation, and thereby their learning (Chaffin, Maxwell, & Thompson, 1982).

Research on these types of programs focused mainly on young children. However, Howell, Sidorenko, and Jurica (1987) used a single-subject design with a 16-year-old sophomore male whose math functioning was at the fifth-grade level to begin to determine the effectiveness of math software. The student had specific difficulties in reproducing and recalling multiplication facts. Researchers compared two conditions: computerized practice alone and in combination with teacher intervention. Two studies were conducted. The first used an ABAB design involving drill-and-practice software (Galaxy Math, 1984); the other used a multiple-baseline withdrawal design involving tutorial-based software (MemorEase; Mind Nautilus Software, 1985) under varying conditions of teacher intervention.

Findings indicated that both drill-and-practice and tutorial software had an initial but transitory effect on the number of errors and the amount of time required to successfully complete multiplication problems. Results also indicated that without a specific teacher intervention designed to foster problem-solving strategies, any gains made during the computer interactions may not hold over time. Because only a single subject was involved, results of this early work were limited with regard to their generalizability to the larger population of high school students having trouble in mathematics. Further, the authors did not provide enough detail on the teacher intervention to fully specify aspects that could serve in a heuristic manner to spur future larger-scale studies. However, the authors did stress the importance of the interaction between computer technology and teacher support and guidance.

Testing the possibility that incorporating game-like features into computerized math instruction may interfere with math performance rather than enhance it, Bahr and Rieth (1989) compared the effects of a drill-and-practice approach with an instructional-game approach on the acquisition of multiplication skills related to decimal numbers. Both approaches to teaching math were taken from the *Math Blaster* software package (Eckert & Davidson, 1983). Within a multiple-baseline across-students design, both approaches were manipulated across time with 50 students with LD who were being taught within either self-contained or resource-room math classes. The baseline condition was established during their regular math instruction. Over the course of nine weeks, students used each approach for three weeks at a time, 10 minutes per session, three days per week. The baseline phase lasted two to four weeks for each class. During all three phases, teachers were asked to administer a 70-item paper-and-pencil decimal multiplication quiz three times per week.

Results indicated that, although neither software program had a detrimental effect on learning, neither contributed significantly to learning. The computer software programs were not integrated into the instruction conducted in the general education classroom. Rather, 10 minutes a day were set aside for using the programs, with no teacher involvement. Thus, the lack of interaction between computer technology and teacher support and guidance may have contributed to the weakened technology results in this study.

Most mathematics computer software programs offer some sort of feedback after student responses. Typically, for math problems, feedback takes a neutral form, indicating the correctness or incorrectness of an answer with either a "good job" or "try again" statement. Okolo (1992) performed an important study on the type of feedback that students receive when performing tasks. Specifically, she examined the impact of attribution feedback to students when it was embedded in a computer-assisted mathematics-instruction program. Underlying this investigation were the notions that a lack of motivation interferes with the academic performance of students with LD, that a lack of academic success and motivation for these students may be the result of a certain attribution style (that is, attributing successes to luck and failures to lack of ability), and that attributions can be retrained. Okolo chose to embed attribution retraining into a computer-assisted program because these types of programs can analyze students' performance on an ongoing basis and provide individualized feedback, thereby providing an established format to give adaptive attributional feedback to students. Measured outcomes included change in attributions of the cause of math success and failure, persistence, and mathematics-computation performance.

The CAI program selected was the public-domain math program *Drill* (Davis, n.d.), which contains four sets of multiplication problems of increasing difficulty displayed in 25-problem sets at 5 problems per screen. Students were instructed to start with the easiest set and were allowed a 20-second-per-problem time limit. After reaching the mastery criterion (80%) three times within the time limit, students could progress to the next difficulty level. The study was conducted across eight 30-minute sessions. Twenty-nine students with LD who were one to two years below grade level in mathematics (average age 13.3 years) were randomly assigned to one of two conditions. The attribution-retraining condition provided not only accuracy feedback but also attribution statements reflecting ability-success when meeting successive within-session goals (for example, "You really know these") and effort feedback when successfully completing the session ("You're really trying hard"). For failure, effort-failure feedback was given (for example, "You can get it if you keep trying") as students progressed through each successive within-session goal. The control condition involved neutral accuracy feedback throughout the program.

A trend was noted in both conditions for increasing effort-success and lack of effort-failure attributions. Persistence, as measured by the average number of sessions completed, differed significantly between groups. The retraining students completed an average of 15 levels, and the control students completed an average of 11.6 sessions. With regard to skill attainment, students in both conditions performed similarly at pretest, but the attribution-retraining students performed significantly better than the control students at posttest, the magnitude of difference reflecting a moderate effect size. Although Okolo (1992) did not manipulate technology, but rather supplemental attribution training, the study brings to light the importance of considering the characteristics of individual learners and how they may interact with technology. Quite clearly, receipt of constructive, self-attributional statements as feedback positively influenced math performance. In the absence of positive attribution feedback in math software programs, students with disabilities who possess a negative attribution style may not benefit as much from these technologies as would be possible otherwise. Although the current study was conducted with seventh- and eighth-grade students, it was included in this review because of the generalizable nature of attribution style and its relation to performance across developmental periods.

Laser and Videodisc Instruction

Five studies were identified as using laser and videodisc technology as an instructional tool to teach math skills (four studies) and problem-solving skills (one study). These studies differed from the majority of the reviewed technological studies, which focused on assistive devices, in that they examined instructional technology and focused on improved teaching and learning rather than improvements in functional performance. The studies paid close attention to teaching technology (pedagogy) and important issues related to principles of effective instructional design (see Chapter 5 in this volume).

In the first study, Kelly, Carnine, Gersten, and Grossen (1986) examined the teaching of basic fractions concepts to remedial and mildly handicapped high school students. Students learned fractions concepts through either a traditional basal program or a videodisc program. The videodisc condition provided a wide range of examples for new concepts and included multiple discrimination practice opportunities. The basal condition, on the other hand, followed a traditional, less-structured approach to teaching math concepts, with less emphasis on multiple examples and discrimination practice.

Results indicated that students in the basal treatment condition made four times as many errors as students in the videodisc treatment. Further, the performance of students taught with the videodisc on a criterion-referenced posttest was high (the mean score was 95%). Furthermore, these positive effects were maintained on a measure given several weeks later. Rates of academic engagement were also significantly higher for the videodisc students. Results demonstrated the promise of videodisc delivery (hardware) of math instruction combined with structured instruction incorporating elements of effective instructional design (teaching technology).

A long-standing question in the educational technology literature centers on whether the medium (technology hardware) contributes to learning or whether it is the message the medium imparts, in terms of structured instruction (pedagogy), that is the critical factor in learning (e.g., Clark, 1994; Hasselbring & Glaser, 2000; Kozma, 1994; Okolo, Bahr, & Rieth, 1993). In addressing the question of medium versus message, Hasselbring and colleagues (1988) manipulated both elements across three groups: (1) computerized instruction, (2) analogous instruction presented through a teacher, and (3) a basal curriculum presented through a teacher. The focus of the mathematics instruction was the teaching of fractions concepts using the same program that was used in the Kelly et al. (1986) study described previously.

Results indicated no difference in student performance between those who had received computerized instruction and those who had received analogous instruction through a teacher. However, both groups outperformed students who had been instructed in the less-structured basal curriculum. Thus, computerized instruction in this instance appeared to be equivalent to live instruction when the content and structure of the instruction were controlled, thus supporting the importance of message over medium.

Moore and Carnine (1989) conducted a study that centered on instruction in the area of ratio word problems. High school students with LD and remedial high school students were assigned to one of two conditions. The experimental students received a highly structured videodisc mathematics program, whereas the comparison students were taught with an enhanced basal curriculum using active teaching procedures. The content of the basal curriculum was derived from four general math and pre-algebra textbooks. This procedure was followed to ensure that the comparison group had an equivalent amount of practice with ratio problems. The basal strategies were not altered. Instead, the strategies and examples used in the composite curriculum were derived from those most commonly found throughout the four basal series.

Results showed significant between-group differences on a posttest containing representative problems from basal texts, standardized achievement tests, and the two curricula used in the study. The authors noted that the results provided evidence that a highly structured presentation of information through videodisc technology can make a substantial difference in a specific content area for remedial students and students with LD. Once again, although it did not test the effects of the technological medium, the study provided evidence of the importance of pedagogy in designing software.

Woodward and Gersten (1992) examined factors contributing to successful implementation and use of the fractions-related mathematics videodisc program examined in the previous studies. Focusing on high school students with high-incidence disabilities, the authors collected pretest and posttest student-performance data on a criterion-referenced test that covered all major curriculum topics to determine the program's impact on student performance. Subjects were 57 students from seven classrooms in secondary resource-room programs for students with high-incidence disabilities. Students were tested before and 30 days after instruction. Results indicated that the mean pretest performance of students was quite low ($M = 29.4$; $SD = 9.38$). The mean posttest score was considerably higher ($M = 79$; $SD = 10.08$). Almost two-thirds of the students (64%) reached or exceeded a criterion performance of 80%. Observational data further indicated that, on average, students were engaged in academic activities at a reasonable rate (on-task rate = 87%, $SD = 4.4$). Data on independent work were also collected, showing that the average student score was 82% ($SD = 7.37$).

Results of this study demonstrated the potential benefit of a structured, videodisc-based mathematics program for high school students with high-incidence disabilities. Unfortunately, within the pretest–posttest design, there was no external control against which to compare the relative performance gains of the students.

In a study that did contain a randomized control condition, Bottge and Hasselbring (1993) compared two groups of ninth-grade adolescents ($n = 36$) with learning difficulties in mathematics. They tested students' ability to generate solutions to a contextualized problem after being taught problem-solving skills under two conditions: standard specific instruction in word problems and instruction involving a contextualized problem on videodisc. The fractions videodisc program described in the previous studies was used to strengthen the fractions-computation skills of students before they were randomly assigned to an experimental condition. Instruction in each condition lasted five days. Students in the contextualized condition first viewed a video problem about buying a small pet and building a home for it. This video problem served as an instructional anchor for facilitating students' ability to solve a real-world problem. The course of instruction was centered on solving the contextualized problem and progressed through several phases: review, guided practice, feedback and corrective suggestions, independent practice, and formative review. Students in the standard-word-problem condition were guided through a series of word problems and given independent worksheets that contained one or more practice problems after every lesson. Pretest and posttest measures on both a contextualized problem and a word problem were administered. Also, two transfer tasks were administered one day and three weeks after the posttest.

Results indicated that both student groups improved their performance on solving word problems. However, students in the contextualized-problem group did significantly better on the contextualized problem at posttest and were able to retain and generalize their performance on the two transfer tasks.

Once again, the results of this study highlighted the importance of software instructional design in improving the math performance of high school students with LD. As the authors noted, the study also indicated that placing the students' problem-solving instruction within an anchored contextualized environment rather than a decontextualized environment improved their ability to solve complex, meaningful mathematics problems and to transfer these skills to other real-world tasks. However, significant differences were marginal between the two groups on both the word-problem transfer task administered one day after the posttest and the contextualized-problem task administered three weeks after the posttest. Given that initial performance differences existed between these groups, the initial differences may account for any transfer effects found.

In recognition of high content standards and the need to improve the intellectual quality of students' learning experiences in mathematics, as well as the lack of research on how to accomplish this goal, Bottge, Heinrichs, Chan, and Serlin (2001) conducted a study to determine whether low-achieving remedial math students could learn to solve problems intended for general education use. The researchers assigned four classes, a total of 75 eighth-grade students, to either an enhanced anchored instruction (EAI) condition or a traditional problem instruction (TPI) condition. One class assigned to the EAI condition was a remedial math class. The other three were pre-algebra classes containing 11 special education students whose math achievement did not warrant placement in the remedial class. One pre-algebra class was assigned to the EAI condition because of scheduling logistics; the other two classes were placed in the TPI condition.

The EAI intervention used a video-based anchor called *Kim's Komet* from a series of episodes, *The New Adventures of Jasper Woodbury* (Learning Technology Center at Vanderbilt University, 1996). *Kim's Komet* helps students develop an understanding of algebraic concepts such as non-linear functions, independent and dependent variables, rate of change, and measurement error. To solve problems, students must make predictions of rate, time, and distance using information from tables and graphs. The videodisc format allows students to search locations in the video where information for solving the problems is located. The solution to the problem is not evident, and students must test hypotheses before arriving at a solution. The authors note that the EAI intervention is aligned with standards put forth by the National Council of Teachers of Mathematics (NCTM; 2000).

In the TPI condition, a variety of standard word problems involving distance, rate and time, graphing, and prediction were used to teach students how to solve traditional text-based problems. These problems were selected from basal math texts. As a supplement to this instruction, the teacher also incorporated a two-week project that required students to plan a trip that involved reading maps and charts, calculating travel times based on average speed, computing miles per gallon, tracking trip costs, and monitoring travel budgets. Teacher-led discussions focused on how to solve the word problems, and teachers taught students how to calculate, graph, and make predictions. Instruction lasted for 12 class periods of 90 minutes each. Before and after instruction, all students were assessed on computation using the arithmetic subtest of the WRAT-III, on problem solving using a researcher-developed test, and on maintenance using two measures that had been developed to assess student performance on problems similar to the ones solved during the intervention.

Results indicated that, for problem solving only, remedial students who had received the enhanced instruction did not differ significantly in performance from students in the pre-algebra class who had received either enhanced or traditional instruction, with gains of 8.25, 9.04, and 10.61 for enhanced remedial, enhanced pre-algebra, and traditional pre-algebra students, respectively. Based on these results, the authors concluded that remedial students using the technology-based EAI matched the problem-solving performance of the pre-algebra students. The major limitation of this conclusion is that the researchers' planned comparison sought to confirm rather than disconfirm the null hypothesis of no difference between groups. Such an approach significantly weakens the ability to adequately test the hypothesis. Furthermore, the remedial students did not show gains on measures of computation or maintenance. Thus, there is limited evidence that enhanced instruction of this sort is beneficial for secondary remedial students. Furthermore, no conclusions could be drawn for students with disabilities in this study because their data were presented in combination with all pre-algebra students.

Computers and Test Accommodations

In the last math study identified, Calhoon, Fuchs, and Hamlett (2000) compared the effects of computer-based test accommodations, non-computer-based test accommodations, and no test accommodations on the math performance assessment scores for secondary students with LD. The impetus for this study was that a lack of reading skills can result in significant crossover effects on the overall academic life of students with LD. This fact, paired with current trends in accountability and a focus on problem-solving performance assessments that rely heavily on ability to read and apply multiple skills and strategies, can result in great disadvantage for students with LD. Therefore, there is a need to determine the impact of testing accommodations, as allowed by federal legislation, on the performance of these students. Over four weeks, 81 secondary (9th–12th grade) students with LD were tested on four parallel mathematics performance assessments, each under a different condition: (1) standard administration, (2) teacher-read, (3) computer-read, and (4) computer-read with video. Conditions were counterbalanced, as were performance assessments. After each performance assessment, students filled out questionnaires assessing their perceptions of the benefits of the testing condition.

Results indicated that providing a reader, either human or computer, increased students' scores on mathematics assessments, with no significant differences between the conditions. Furthermore, there were no condition effects on the students' perceptions of the test conditions or their perceptions of earning higher scores. However, the data did show that 65% of students preferred to some degree the anonymity provided by the computer when it came to rereading. These results are important because the goal of any mathematics assessment is to measure math skills, not reading skills; thus, separating out the entities is critical. Furthermore, the study supported the idea that students or schools can select the most amenable approach to providing a reader without significant impact on outcome. Further validation of these results is warranted.

Social Studies

Computers and Hypertext Study Guides

Five studies were identified that focused on social studies and the use of technology. Four of the studies examined the use of hypertext to provide a study guide structure to increase knowledge acquisition of high school social studies content. Hypertext differs from the format of traditional CAI programs in that it allows the user to navigate nonlinearly through multiple layers of linked information. In CAI, all that is there is what is on the screen. With hypertext, the first screen is only the first layer of information. It is linked to infinite layers of underlying information, accessible by a click of the mouse. For instructional purposes, hypertext can provide in-depth information about any surface topic of interest.

An early study that used computer graphic capabilities will be presented for background purposes before other, more recent studies are discussed. This study was one of the first to use microcomputer graphics to teach geography to high school students with LD and remedial high school students in the general education setting. Horton, Lovitt, and Slocum (1988) compared two methods for teaching geographic locations. In one condition, students used an atlas and wrote their findings on a work map. In the other condition, students completed a computerized map tutorial that was part of a generic computer program called the *Instructional System for Graphics Facts* (Slocum, 1986). The computerized program contained several aspects associated with effective instructional design, including individualized pacing, sequenced instructions, frequent responding, corrective feedback, and cumulative review.

Twenty-seven students—12 students with LD and 15 remedial students—enrolled in two remedial world geography classes participated in the study. Both classes completed a pretest measure that contained 28 Asian cities that were virtually unknown to all the students. The 28 cities were then randomly divided into two groups of 14. The two sets of 14 cities were taught using one of the two methods (atlas vs. computer). The order of the treatments and cities was counterbalanced across the two classrooms. The posttest for each condition consisted of questions on the 14 cities covered by the instruction in that condition.

Results indicated that the computerized map tutorial had a significantly greater impact on students' geographic-location knowledge than the atlas condition. This effect was equal for students with LD and for remedial students. At pretest, the average score across the two classes was fewer than one item correct. At posttest in the computer condition, both students with LD and remedial students in the two classes earned an average score of 13 correct (92%). At posttest, in the atlas condition, the students with LD and remedial students earned an average score of three correct (22%). These findings indicate that the computerized map tutorial was effective at teaching geographic city locations to students with LD and remedial students, at least during immediate posttesting. Whether students can retain the knowledge across a longer period is unknown.

Horton, Lovitt, Givens, and Nelson (1989) investigated the effectiveness of a computerized study guide for 13 students with LD and 18 remedial education students enrolled in a ninth-grade general education world geography class. Student performance was assessed using a text comprehension test. Results indicated that the computerized study guide produced significantly higher performance than notetaking condition for both types of student categories. Unfortunately, in this study both the technological medium and the content were varied, rendering impossible any conclusions about the impact of the hypertext technology facet. Thus, whether the hypertext study guide contributed to the difference in student performance or whether a study guide presented in any form would have resulted in similar performance gains is not known.

Higgins and Boone (1990) examined the impact of using hypertext computerized study guides on social studies learning, specifically the acquisition of information regarding state history. Two studies were conducted to investigate the extent to which study guides could serve as both a substitute and an enhancement for teacher-led instruction. In the first study, subjects included a diverse set of 40 ninth-grade learners (10 students with LD, 15 remedial students, and 15 general education students) enrolled in Washington State history classes. The intervention consisted of a 10-day instructional unit in these classes. Students were randomly assigned to three intervention conditions that were designed to present the instructional material to students: (1) computerized study guide alone, (2) teacher-presented material alone, and (3) combined computerized and teacher-presented material.

Electronic study guides were designed to contain highly interactive instructional activities and incorporate elements of good screen design. The screen was made up of text (with word or graphic enhancement), text plus a multiple-choice question (with word or graphic enhancement), or a graphic (with word enhancement). Questions were placed in text on the same screen where the answer was located. Accuracy feedback was given for each item response. The teacher-led instructional material contained the same information as the computer-assisted study guides and consisted of teacher lecture, a reading passage, and a worksheet with questions. Pretest, posttest, and retention assessments consisted of the same 50-item multiple-choice test drawn from daily class quizzes, with the posttest occurring one day after the completion of the instructional unit and retention testing two weeks after the posttest.

Curiously, the authors chose to analyze pretest, posttest, retention, and daily quiz scores separately, thereby eliminating the ability to view any improvement across time resulting from the intervention. Posttest values, without a consideration of pretest differences between groups, are meaningless. Further, given the presentation of numerous individual pieces of data, no cohesive conclusions could be drawn. Thus, the basis for the authors' conclusion that the study guides were effective is unclear.

In a second study, Higgins and Boone (1990) used the same study guides as a follow-up to teacher-presented instruction in a small-group ABA design. The goal was to determine whether computerized study guides could be used to bring the performance of low-achieving students up to the passing level. Five students who had the lowest unit test scores at the end of Study 1 participated. Two students had learning disabilities, and three were remedial students. Three weeks after the completion of Study 1, students participated in an instructional unit covering 10 hypertext study guide lessons presented in a separate computer lab. The retention test from Study 1 served as the pretest measure, and the unit test served as the posttest immediately after instruction and as the retention measure administered two weeks after the end of the unit. The authors conducted no statistical tests on these data, but they discussed individual trends in general. With no comparison or control in this study, the gains reported for low-performing students could be attributed to the additional review activities rather than the study guide format. Thus, as in Study 1, no strong statement can be made regarding the actual impact of the hypertext study guides.

Horton, Boone, and Lovitt (1990) investigated the effectiveness of a computer-based study guide using hypertext software to increase textbook comprehension among four students with LD in a remedial high school social studies class. Two students were situated at individual workstations in the classroom, and two were in a computer lab. The hypertext software was self-paced as students worked through the study guide. Students had the option of choosing from four levels of guidance: (1) given the question to answer; (2) given additional assistance by fading the portion of text that did not contain answers (reducing extraneous information); (3) given additional typographical cues by boldfacing lines of text around the answers; and (4) providing the correct answer for the question. A 45-item unit test covering the information presented over the course of three days (30 items), in addition to 15 items that were related but not directly covered, served as the pretest, posttest, and retention test, which was given 30 days after the posttest. Students' average performance on the lesson tests was higher for the computer-presented items than the test-only items, 97% versus 67%, respectively. Furthermore, the subjects retained more information from the computer-presented items compared with the test-only items (77% and 63%, respectively). Finally, larger pretest–posttest gains were found for the computer-presented items (45% to 83%) than for the test-only items (52% to 67%).

The manner in which the authors established a control comparison in this study leads to caution in interpreting the results. The authors viewed the 15 items appearing on the pretest, posttest, and retention tests that were not presented in the computer program as a comparative base in the absence of a control group. However, by doing so, they confounded the comparisons relative to the mechanism posited to improve student learning and retention. The "control" items were those that the students did not have prior exposure to; this was not the case for the study guide items. Under these circumstances, comparing scores on the two sets of items is analogous to testing the mechanistic explanation of exposure to items rather than the structure and process of the hypertext study guides. Thus, caution is warranted relative to attributing any comparative gains to a hypertext study guide effect.

Higgins, Boone, and Lovitt (1996) examined the use of pop-up text windows within study guides to support or extend information in a high school social studies text. Twenty-five ninth-grade students in a social studies class participated in the study: 13 students with LD and 12 remedial students. Students were randomly assigned to one of three educational methods: (1) lecture, (2) lecture/hypermedia study guide, or

(3) hypermedia study guide alone. In the lecture condition, students listened to and took notes from a lecture given by the teacher, read an assigned passage from the textbook, and filled out a worksheet containing eight multiple-choice questions from the passage. Students assigned to the lecture/hypermedia study guide condition listened to and took notes from a lecture given by the teacher and went through the hypermedia study guide. Finally, students in the hypermedia study guide condition worked with the hypermedia study guide for the entire 30 minutes of the instructional period. A 50-item multiple-choice quiz on the material served as a comprehension measure administered before and after intervention, as well as two weeks after the conclusion of the instructional unit.

Results indicated no significant differences in performance on both the daily quiz and the retention test scores among the groups. When test items were reviewed, answers to factual questions, which were displayed either through a hypermedia note window or in the body of the text, were answered correctly more often than inferential questions. Though the study had the strengths of random assignment and manipulation of treatment conditions, the small sample leads to reduced confidence in the data presented. The authors acknowledged the power issues when discussing nonsignificant results, but the generalizability of their significant findings should also be viewed with caution.

In spite of the weaknesses found within the electronic study guide literature relative to methodological issues that preclude strong conclusions about effectiveness, the researchers are to be commended for their attempts to intervene with students with disabilities in the real-life setting of the general education curriculum. However, future research that addresses the existing weaknesses is needed before strong support can be garnered for using hypertext study guides.

General Application Across Content Areas

Hypermedia

Three articles were identified that reviewed hypermedia across content domains. In one study, Edyburn (1991) sought to identify and understand student characteristics that are likely to interfere with successful search and retrieval from electronic databases. The study was based on the increasing importance of being able to retrieve information from electronic databases and the lack of research on this skill focusing on students with mild disabilities. Students with learning difficulties are likely to be less successful than their nondisabled peers at this task because of their documented difficulties in processing and retrieving information (e.g., MacMillan, Keogh, & Jones, 1986).

Fifteen middle school students with LD and 15 students without disabilities were randomly assigned to one of three treatment-order conditions representing ways that information is retrieved from databases (print, command, and menu). The print condition involved retrieval tasks centered on printed encyclopedias. The command condition involved retrieving information from an electronic database by entering command codes along with the search term and other limiting parameters. Access within this condition was linear, such that information at the end of the article could be accessed only by viewing everything before it. Finally, in the menu condition, students had to retrieve information from electronic data sets by menu-driven commands. This required fewer direct commands from the student than the command condition and allowed access to text in specified sections of documents, thus eliminating the need to view the entire article.

Subjects were asked to conduct four retrieval tasks under each treatment condition. The tasks were broken down by the characteristic of "simple" (searches that required only one word to retrieve the answer to the question) or "complex" (searches that required more than one article and higher-order thinking skills). Tasks were also broken down by whether the questions were assigned by the experimenter, reflecting common classroom uses of the encyclopedia, or self-generated by the student, reflecting a common use of encyclopedias for self-directed learning. A maximum of five minutes was allowed to complete each search.

Data on students' performance included an indicator of search success or failure, as well as the search aspects of keywords used, error messages, help accessed, print volume selected, and time required for the search. Results indicated that, regardless of the retrieval method, students with learning difficulties were significantly less successful in retrieving information than their nonhandicapped peers. However, the author was surprised at the apparent lack of success for students with and without disabilities, with an overall retrieval success rate of 16% and 43%, respectively. Results further indicated that for both groups of students, there were no significant differences in success relative to whether print or electronic encyclopedias were used for fact retrieval. The combined results across student groups raise important questions about the process of allowing walk-up access to electronic encyclopedias in school media centers. Students in both groups were considerably more successful when information retrieval involved simple rather than complex tasks and assigned rather than self-generated tasks. These findings suggest a need to identify effective aspects of interventions for preparing students to better function as independent, self-directed learners.

Two studies conducted within the same year attempted to summarize findings across all hypermedia studies. Dillon and Gabbard (1998) presented a review of hypermedia research in education and found that, across grade levels and subject areas, the benefits of hypermedia were limited to learning tasks that relied on repeated manipulation and information searching. According to the review, methodological and analytical shortcomings limited the generalizability of all findings. Furthermore, of the studies reviewed by Dillon and Gabbard, only two were identified as examining the impact of hypermedia on high school students with disabilities.

Liao (1998), taking a more empirical approach to summarizing the hypermedia research, performed a meta-analysis that compared the effects of hypermedia and traditional instruction on students' achievement. Using three different search sources, 35 articles were located. Of these, 69% of the study-weighted effect sizes were positive, favoring hypermedia. The overall grand mean effect size was 0.48, representing the low range for a moderate effect size. Of the 35 articles, only four (11%) were conducted with students in Grades 7 through 12; the average effect size for these studies was 0.091, representing a very small effect. Thus, although Liao concluded that the results of the studies provided classroom teachers with accumulated research-based evidence of positive outcomes relative to technology use in instruction, this conclusion does not appear to apply to teachers at the high school level, particularly for students with disabilities, a variable that was not examined in Liao's analysis.

Conclusions for Assistive and Instructional Technology

The current search across the last 20 years resulted in 32 research articles that contained academic performance data, comparisons that are relevant to secondary students with high-incidence disabilities, and technology in the form of hardware or software that served either an assistive or instructional purpose. Identified studies were described in sections of this review reflecting technological form and content area. This organization highlights an overall lack of content-related studies over the last 20 years, Additionally, where studies exist, the focus and purpose of the research relative to technological form is sometimes diffuse and substantiated with only one or two studies or no studies at all—simply a hunch. Thus, one of the biggest gaps in the special education literature is the lack of empirical research examining the impact of technological tools on high school student performance. Furthermore, many of the existing studies suffer from methodological problems, including small sample sizes and confounded designs that weaken any conclusions drawn. These findings support Edyburn's (2000) conclusion that education must begin to acknowledge and respond to the need to appropriately document technology's effectiveness on student performance to ensure accountability.

In addition to the lack of research studies designed to isolate the impact of technology so that an empirical base to support its use can be built, this research field has been influenced by the tremendously rapid rate of technological advance. Given the rapid pace at which technology development moves relative to the educational field, by the time educational studies have been conducted and data analyzed and published, the technology used may be obsolete. As a result, educators may find themselves in a position where newer areas of technology have no current empirical base while others areas of technology, where empirical studies exist, seem antiquated (Edyburn, 2000). The overwhelming feeling that may come with developing a strong empirical base for educational technology, however, should not dissuade people from continuing to move toward examining theory relative to the best uses of technology for successfully educating all students.

With regard to the state of technology research and what is known about the content domain of writing, few studies have focused on the assistive devices of word processing, spell-checkers, and grammar supports, as well as speech synthesis and semantic webbing relative to high school students with high-incidence disabilities. Furthermore, the conclusions drawn from these studies were not promising. More studies must be focused on the population of high school students with high-incidence disabilities, with an eye toward appropriately designed studies. Second, educators must be cognizant that simply providing computers and associated writing supports does not automatically result in improvement in students' writing. Rather, as MacArthur (1996) has suggested, effective instructional methods must be developed to make use of the power provided by these tools to enhance the writing of students with disabilities. Particularly relevant for high school students with learning problems, in addition to supplying the assistive computer supports necessary for functional improvement in writing, educators must continue to focus on the deficit skill responsible for the supportive need (such as a spelling deficit) and not turn away from instructional technology to remediate the deficit. Thus, the compensation should be viewed as a support to move students forward in other content area domains, whereas remediation takes place to remove the need for the assistive support.

No empirical research was found involving multimedia and writing for high school students with high-incidence disabilities. However, MacArthur (1996) cautioned in advance that adding graphics and sounds to compositions may not result in the desired benefits. Educators must be aware that the introduction of these enhancements may reduce focus on the actual text being written. Text may become relatively less important in transferring meaning and, because creating graphics and sounds requires time and attention, may detract attention from the written text. Support for this contention has been demonstrated in younger students when they were presented with a graphics option for producing a story. They spent more time manipulating graphic devices than writing the story (Bahr, Nelson, & Van Meter, 1996). Clearly, for high school students with disabilities, more research in this area is needed. Being able to communicate through the written word is a critical skill for future success after public education. Good writing instruction must be a focus, along with multimedia enhancement.

Technological devices for increasing content-area vocabulary acquisition have had mixed results. Early, low-tech assistive devices for vocabulary presentation showed promising results, but only with regard to the acquisition of isolated sight words (Freeman & McLaughlin, 1984). Incorporating more advanced speech-synthesis technology to prompt for vocabulary embedded in content-area text did not result in improvements (Farmer et al., 1992). Thus, at this time, there is little evidence for using assistive devices to build the vocabulary of high school students with learning difficulties. Instructional technology for this purpose, however, does show promise. The two CAI studies (Horton, Lovitt, & Givens, 1988; Johnson et al., 1987) focused on elements of effective instructional design and demonstrated significantly improved and efficient acquisition of content-related vocabulary.

For enhancing content-area reading comprehension, advances in assistive technology have shown promise. Early studies on the impact of computer-screen display and audio presentation of content-area text did not result in significant reading comprehension improvements for high school students with LD (Keene & Davey, 1987; Torgesen et al., 1987). However, technological advances using hypertext links in text (MacArthur & Haynes, 1995) and CD-ROM audio technology (Boyle et al., 2003) led to stronger positive results. Although research is limited in this area, these types of assistive supports must continue to be considered for use by schools. Therefore, research must continue to identify the most effective use of these technologies and the conditions under which their effectiveness can be maximized.

Using assistive devices to compensate for the reading deficits of high school students cannot suffice in the absence of attention to these deficits. Some students enter high school reading below the fifth-grade level (Archer, Gleason, & Vachon, 2003). Thus, although technology may be available to provide reading support to these students to benefit from content-area coursework, instruction must simultaneously focus on ensuring sufficient skill learning so that students have a chance of success outside the school environment.

Technology to address reading issues, when it is focused on the area of assessment, can be of great benefit to high schools in educating diverse learners. Reading deficits can limit the benefits of content-area instruction for many students and, through crossover effects, undermine their performance on assessments of content-area knowledge—a particularly salient issue for high school students facing high-stakes tests. Horton and Lovitt (1994) demonstrated that computers can provide flexibility and increased administration options for conducting reading assessments, such that learning environments can be designed to maximize the effectiveness of content-area instructional time. Calhoon and colleagues (2000) also demonstrated that computers can serve the function of a human reader when administering content-area assessments in which reading is not the major focus. Furthermore, students preferred the anonymity of this option. These research lines warrant continued investigation.

Several studies in the current review involved improving comprehension in social studies classes. Most of these studies were conducted by investigators who followed a line of research for developing hypertext study guides. Although the studies suffered from methodological flaws and produced equivocal evidence supporting the use of guides to increase student performance, the instructional aspects of providing more opportunities for student review and more structure through guided prompts are sound. Therefore, research in this area should continue with an eye toward designing studies that can lead to the further evolution of study guides to maximize their efficacy.

No research was identified that examined assistive technology and its support to students with high-incidence disabilities in mathematics. Although these forms of technology (such as calculators) are currently being implemented in schools, the question of purpose must be raised. If students leave high school with limited foundational math skills such that simple computations in the real world without technological support are compromised, the perceived benefits of assistive technology should not override a focus on instructional technology to remediate the students' skill deficits.

The majority of studies in mathematics focused on instructional technology, with the principles of effective instructional design incorporated into the software (e.g., Bottge & Hasselbring, 1993; Hasselbring et al., 1988; Moore & Carnine, 1989). In several instances, the study goals were not to test the impact of technological hardware. Rather, they were to test principles of effective instructional technology tools that served to support effective teaching goals, not to supplant them. The general conclusion from these instructional technology studies indicates the importance of instructional design in creating educational software to increase the math functioning of high school students with LD. In their review of the literature, Okolo and colleagues (1993) agreed that instructional design and the curriculum in which computer-based instruction is embedded are essential for producing learning effects. For students with high-incidence disabilities, if the goal is learning, simply plugging technology into a classroom does not bring certainty that the technology will have an effect on learning (Hasselbring & Glaser, 2000).

IMPLICATIONS FOR FUTURE RESEARCH

In testing the effectiveness of assistive technology, Edyburn (2000) noted that two conditions, technologically aided and unaided conditions, must be compared to gauge the success of technology. The same conditions are important when testing instructional technology, but the assumptions differ. With tests of assistive technology, the instructional methods should be controlled across conditions to assess the impact on functioning by adding the technology device. For tests of instructional technology effectiveness, on the other hand, because instruction and learning are the variables of interest, the instructional methods may differ across conditions. Regardless of the technology focus, however, all studies should manipulate the technology and observe its influence on student outcomes. Focusing on performance and learning as the critical outcome is essential (Hauser & Malouf, 1996) if appropriate accountability is to be assured and relevant IDEA mandates are to be addressed (Edyburn, 2000).

In the current review, there is good news in the fact that a relatively large number of studies compared groups that used or did not use the technology program to be tested. Unfortunately, some studies lacked the control necessary across comparative groups to isolate extraneous variables that may also have contributed to observed increases in functioning (for example, practice effects were not controlled), thus weakening the conclusions drawn about technological effectiveness. Still other studies contained sample sizes too small to place firm confidence in their findings.

To build a stronger evidentiary base for education technology, research should move in the direction of a study design and process like that called for by the National Institutes of Health. Within that agency, two different types of studies are used to test treatments: efficacy and effectiveness. Efficacy studies test an intervention under well-controlled experimental conditions with randomly selected subject samples for whom the intervention is purported to be effective. Effectiveness studies test an intervention under looser conditions in the natural environment. Generally, to establish the validity of an intervention, several well-designed studies from independent researchers must demonstrate improvement over a control condition and provide specified protocols for intervention that include the purpose of the intervention, the factors necessary for successful implementation, and the population(s) for whom the intervention is intended.

A large amount of educational technology research is conducted within the school environment, which inherently imposes design issues that weaken the internal validity of the findings. Thus, researchers must conduct several effectiveness trials, each building on the others to strengthen the internal validity of the examination before any conclusions can be drawn. Independent researchers should also take part in a series of multiple trials to reduce the possibility of experimenter bias. Furthermore, trials for each technology device and, if used for multiple purposes, for each purpose, should be carried out. As this review has illustrated, the field is far from having established a strong, validated evidentiary base, particularly in the areas of writing and science at the high school level.

Even in content areas where focused studies have been conducted, few studies have elicited impressive evidence on maintenance of intervention gains. This is a critical variable when testing instructional technology, where the goal is learning rather than circumventing a deficit skill. If knowledge is learned well, carrying this knowledge forward should be a given. Also, for certain purposes of assistive technology, such as supports for content-area comprehension, maintenance of gains may be just as critical as acquisition, especially if the information learned in one instructional unit is needed for success in future units. Researchers should be clear not only about the purpose of the technology they are testing, but also the place of technology outcomes within the larger educational picture for students with disabilities.

Finally, in addition to measuring the maintenance of gains from technology, researchers should also consider measuring the transfer of knowledge. Many researchers develop outcome measures that are specifically geared to the design of their technological implementation. These measures often involve items drawn directly from the content and structural presentation of the technology and usually involve an instructional unit or brief textbook passage. Nevertheless, there also should be interest in drawing conclusions that are more generalizable. If items of this type are used and generalizable performance or learning is desired, researchers must include a transfer measure that assesses knowledge gain or performance enhancement on items that are less dependent on the implementation format.

In sum, to achieve the goal of successful and effective implementation of technology for students with disabilities, funding opportunities must be available to researchers to engage in collaborative, sustainable, and financially feasible research efforts. Collaboration is necessary to fulfill the need for independent investigations. Further, sustainability of funding over a sufficient length of time is necessary to conduct studies that not only allow for the adequate examination of maintenance and transfer of knowledge gains, but also the achievement of successful implementation. Implementation of a technological intervention within a school requires time; acceptance of and fidelity to that implementation takes even longer. If researchers are forced by time and funding constraints to implement and test technological interventions in a less than rigorous manner and forgo attention to maintenance and transfer of improvements to the larger educational picture, educators will remain in the arena of unknowns relative to the successful education of high school students with disabilities.

Future Technology Development

Pace of Development

In addition to the difficulty of establishing studies to isolate the impact of technology so that an empirical base can be built, it was noted earlier that the field of educational technology research is influenced by the rapid rate of technological advance. Paired with the fact that companies can promote and sell technology with little or no effectiveness evidence, such quick advancement makes research on technology out of date before it can be completed and findings published (Achacoso, 2003).

If researchers keep on a course toward building a strong evidentiary base, the rapid advancement of technology should not pose an impossible barrier to research. Technical enhancements of technology, in terms of processing speed, power, and memory, can occur without seriously influencing prior conclusions of effectiveness. That is, the theoretical base of the "old" technology can be carried forward to the "new" technology if the efficiency of implementation is the advancing variable. The purpose of and theory behind the technological device remains the same. Other advancements, however, such as those resulting in new technologies or substantive changes to existing technology, may be more susceptible to rapid advancement. In the instance of new technologies, new empirical bases must be formed. However, in the latter example, assuming an existing evidence base, an empirical test could be conducted and, if supportive, placed in context with the existing evidence to support the use of the substantive change.

Purpose of Development

Developers of technology should play an integral part in the conceptual discussion of technology purpose, requiring them to substantiate the use of their technology for that educational purpose and identify the intended population(s) of students for whom the technology was developed. For-profit companies that develop and market educational technology to schools and parents should be able to provide initial efficacy evidence to support the claims they make about their product. Further, private developers should actively recruit independent researchers to examine the effectiveness of their products so that consumers can have confidence in the outcomes.

In designing technology to assist or instruct students with disabilities, all developers should base their products on the existing literature. Although the literature is not fully developed as a strong evidentiary base, there is evidence to suggest that instructional technology, which has improved learning as its purpose, should incorporate elements of effective instructional design into its software. Developers of assistive technology, as evidenced by this review, can also incorporate elements of effective design to improve product outcomes. For example, design elements can be seen in developing study guides to improve comprehension in content-area courses. The use of hypertext, with links to additional information and explanation, can be seen as an attempt to incorporate aspects of scaffolding (such as providing further explanation of a concept) and background knowledge (such as providing definitions of words contained in text). Some researchers combine their technology implementation with strategy instruction, thereby attempting to provide conspicuous strategies for the student. These design characteristics are promising signs.

Further efforts should be made to incorporate design aspects into assistive technology, particularly when implementing technology to assist students in improving their content-area comprehension given reading deficits. The goal associated with this technology is not to instruct in reading, but to improve comprehension of content-area material. By including aspects of instructional design, assistive technology could serve to improve maintenance gains in comprehension and aid students as they move through subsequent coursework.

Future Practice

The great technology debate in education centers on whether technology itself can improve learning or whether it simply serves as a medium through which the instructional message is relayed to students, with the message being the important variable related to success (Achacoso, 2003). Despite ongoing debate among theorists and researchers, and although the research base addressing this debate for high school students with high-incidence disabilities is relatively small, enough knowledge has been accumulated to provide some reasonable guidance to schools.

First, high school personnel should identify the specific reading, writing, and math skill deficits of students with high-incidence disabilities. This knowledge will help determine the best use of technology to ensure that these students leave high school not only as functionally literate citizens, but also as individuals with more rigorous content-area knowledge that will further enhance their lives.

Second, school personnel should become familiar with the conceptual underpinnings of technology so as to understand the uses of existing technology, both assistive and instructional, that will best serve the needs of their students with high-incidence disabilities. In this regard, the focus should be on assistive technology that helps students with high-incidence disabilities participate successfully in content-area courses and on instructional technology that addresses the skill deficits. The hope is that by addressing skill deficits efficiently and effectively, some forms of assistive technology will no longer be needed. As a result, students with high-incidence disabilities will become more independent in their learning in content-area coursework, and thus more independent in their future lives.

Third, school personnel should be aware of evidence supporting existing assistive and instructional technologies to address the needs of students with high-incidence disabilities and call for more research to assist them in doing what is best for their students. Evidence shows that technology that incorporates the principles of effective instructional design can promote successful learning in this population, and developers of assistive technologies are becoming more cognizant of the need to incorporate these elements. Although evidence is sparse for high school students with high-incidence disabilities, positive signs have emerged to indicate that research is moving in the right direction. Higgins, Boone, and Williams (2000), for example, provided a framework for educators to begin evaluating for themselves the appropriateness of educational software for students with disabilities. Within their evaluation criteria, a noticeable segment focuses on aspects related to effective instructional design.

Fourth, technology can offer access to information more efficiently than traditional instructional methods, allowing students to spend less time searching for information and more time using information for higher-level tasks. Technology can also provide simulations that can place knowledge into context for students, making learning more meaningful. However, the evidence for technology use, particularly advanced technologies such as multimedia, is still minimal in terms of whether it can actually improve the performance of high school students with disabilities. In fact, the more complex the technology, the more difficulties these students may encounter relative to utilization, sustained performance, and comprehension. Thus, judicious design and implementation must be undertaken to increase the probability that the intended assistive help will occur.

Fifth, schools are short on personnel to support the implementation and maintenance of technology within the school environment (Edyburn, 2000). Therefore, schools should join in the call for more training programs for technology specialists and funding for full-time positions. These individuals could then serve as gatekeepers of current technological knowledge, identify the best implementations of these technologies for the identified needs of students with high-incidence disabilities, and ensure the appropriateness of technology's use relative to its purpose.

Finally, school personnel should remember that, as the main consumers, they have the power to determine whether they will accept the existing evidence of validity relative to technology effectiveness. Thus, they need to ask themselves whether they are content with one or two studies with less than rigorous evidence. If the answer is no, they alone have the strongest right to call for more thorough research on effectiveness and information on how to best implement effective technology in their educational environment.

REFERENCES

Achacoso, M. (2003). *Evaluating technology and instruction: Literature review and recommendations* (Division of Instructional Innovation and Assessment, Final Report for 2002–2003). Austin: University of Texas.

Anderson-Inman, L., Knox-Quinn, C., & Horney, M. A. (1996). Computer-based study strategies for students with learning disabilities: Individual differences associated with adoption level. *Journal of Learning Disabilities, 29*(5), 461–484.

Anderson-Inman, L., Redekopp, R., & Adams, V. (1992). Electronic studying: Using computer-based outlining programs as study tools. *Reading and Writing Quarterly, 8*(4), 337–358.

Archer, A. L., Gleason, M. M., & Vachon, V. L. (2003). Decoding and fluency: Foundation skills for struggling older readers. *Learning Disability Quarterly, 26*(2), 89–101.

Armbruster, B. (1984). The problem of "inconsiderate text." In G. G. Duffy, L. R. Roehler, & J. Mason (Eds.), *Comprehension instruction* (pp. 202–217). New York: Longman.

Bahr, C. M., Nelson, N. W., & Van Meter, A. M. (1996). The effects of text-based and graphics-based software tools on planning and organizing of stories. *Journal of Learning Disabilities, 29*(4), 355–370.

Bahr, C. M., & Rieth, H. J. (1989). The effects of instructional computer games and drill and practice software on learning disabled students' mathematics achievement. *Computers in the Schools, 6*(3/4), 87–101.

Bailet, L. L. (1990). Spelling rule usage among students with learning disabilities and normally achieving students. *Journal of Learning Disabilities, 23*(2), 121–128.

Bailet, L. L., & Lyon, G. R. (1985). Deficient linguistic rule application in a learning disabled speller: A case study. *Journal of Learning Disabilities, 18*(3), 162–165.

Bangert-Drowns, R. L. (1993). The word processor as an instructional tool: A meta-analysis of word processing in writing instruction. *Review of Educational Research, 63*(1), 69–93.

Baskin, B. H., & Harris, K. (1995). Heard any good books lately? The case for audio books in the secondary classroom. *Journal of Reading, 38*(5), 372–376.

Behrmann, M., & Jerome, M. K. (2002). Assistive technology for students with mild disabilities: Update 2002 (Report No. EDO-EC-02-01). Arlington, VA: ERIC Clearinghouse on Disabilities and Gifted Education. (ERIC Document Reproduction Service No. EDD00036).

Blackhurst, A. E. (1997). Perspectives on technology in special education. *TEACHING Exceptional Children, 29*(5), 41–48.

Borgh, K., & Dickson, W. P. (1992). The effects on children's writing of adding speech synthesis to a word processor. *Journal of Research in Computing in Education, 24*(4), 533–544.

Bottge, B. A., & Hasselbring, T. S. (1993). A comparison of two approaches for teaching complex authentic mathematics problems to adolescents in remedial math classes. *Exceptional Children, 59*(6), 556–566.

Bottge, B. A., Heinrichs, M., Chan, S., & Serlin, R. C. (2001). Anchoring adolescents' understanding of math concepts in rich problem-solving environments. *Remedial and Special Education, 22*(5), 299–314.

Boyle, E. A., Rosenberg, M. S., Connelly, V. J., Washburn, S. G., Brinckerhoff, L. C., & Banerjee, M. (2003). Effects of audio texts on the acquisition of secondary-level content by students with disabilities. *Learning Disability Quarterly, 26*(3), 203–214.

Calhoon, M. B., Fuchs, L. S., & Hamlett, C. L. (2000). Effects of computer-based test accommodations on mathematics performance assessments for secondary students with learning disabilities. *Learning Disability Quarterly, 23*(4), 271–282.

Campbell, D. T., & Stanley, J. C. (1963). Experimental and quasi-experimental designs for research. Boston: Houghton Mifflin.

Carnine, D. W. (1999). Campaigns for moving research into practice. *Remedial and Special Education, 20*(1), 2–6.

Carnine, D., Rankin, G., & Granzin, A. (1984). Learning Vocabulary [computer software]. Eugene: University of Oregon.

Casteel, C. A. (1988). Effects of chunked reading among learning disabled students: An experimental comparison of computer and traditional chunked passage. *Journal of Educational Technology Systems, 17*(2), 32–37.

Castellani, J., & Jeffs, T. (2001). Emerging reading and writing strategies using technology. *TEACHING Exceptional Children, 33*(5), 60–67.

Chaffin, J., Maxwell, B., & Thompson, B. (1982). ARC-ED curriculum: The application of video game formats to educational software. *Exceptional Children, 49*(2), 173–178.

Clark, R. E. (1994). Media will never influence learning. *Educational Technology Research and Development, 42*(2), 21–29.

Daiute, C. (1992). Multimedia composing: Extending the resources of kindergarten to writers across the grades. *Language Arts, 69*(4), 250–260.

Dalton, B., Winbury, N. E., & Morocco, C. C. (1990). "If you could just push a button": Two fourth grade boys with learning disabilities learn to use a computer spelling checker. *Journal of Special Education Technology, 10*(4), 177–191.

Davidson, J. G., & Eckert, R. K. (1983). Word Attack! [computer software]. Rancho Palos Verdes, CA: Davidson & Associates.

Davis, S. H. (n.d.). Drill [computer software]. Washington, DC: Gallaudet University Precollege Programs, Software Shopper.

Deshler, D. D., Schumaker, J. B., Lenz, B. K., Bulgren, J. A., Hock, M. F., Knight, J., & Ehren, B. J. (2001). Ensuring content-area learning by secondary students with learning disabilities. *Learning Disabilities Research and Practice, 16*(2), 96–108.

Dillon, A., & Gabbard, R. (1998). Hypermedia as an educational technology: A review of the quantitative research literature on learner comprehension, control and style. *Journal of Educational Research, 68*(3), 322–349.

Eckert, R., & Davidson, J. (1983). Math Blaster [computer software]. Rancho Palos Verdes, CA: Davidson & Associates.

Edyburn, D. L. (1991). Fact retrieval by students with and without learning handicaps using print and electronic encyclopedias. *Journal of Special Education Technology, 11*(2), 75–90.

Edyburn, D. L. (2000). Assistive technology and students with mild disabilities. *Focus on Exceptional Children, 32*(9), 1–24.

Farmer, M. E., Klein, R., & Bryson, S. E. (1992). Computer-assisted reading: Effects of whole-word feedback on fluency and comprehension in readers with severe disabilities. *Remedial and Special Education, 13*(2), 50–60.

Freeman, T. J., & McLaughlin, T. F. (1984). Effects of a taped-word treatment procedure on learning disabled students' sight-word oral reading. *Learning Disability Quarterly, 7*(1), 49–54.

Galaxy Math [computer program]. (1984). New York: Random House.

Hasselbring, T., & Glaser, C. W. (2000). Use of computer technology to help students with special needs. *Children and Computer Technology, 10*(2), 102–110.

Hasselbring, T., Sherwood, R., Bransford, J., Fleener, K., Griffith, D., & Goin, L. (1988). An evaluation of a level-one instructional videodisc program. *Journal of Educational Technology Systems, 16*(2), 151–169.

Hauser, J., & Malouf, D. B. (1996). A federal perspective on special education technology. *Journal of Learning Disabilities, 29*(5), 504–511.

Higgins, K., & Boone, R. (1990). Hypertext computer study guides and the social studies achievement of students with learning disabilities, remedial students, and regular education students. *Journal of Learning Disabilities, 23*(9), 529–540.

Higgins, K., Boone, R., & Lovitt, T. C. (1996). Hypertext support for remedial students and students with learning disabilities. *Journal of Learning Disabilities, 29*(4), 402–414.

Higgins, K., Boone, R., & Williams, D. L. (2000). Evaluating educational software for special education. *Intervention in School and Clinic, 36*(2), 109–115.

Horton, S. V., Boone, R., & Lovitt, T. (1990). Teaching social studies to learning disabled high school students: Effects of a hypertext study guide. *British Journal of Educational Technology, 21*(2), 118–131.

Horton, S. V., & Lovitt, T. C. (1989). Using study guides with three classifications of secondary students. *Journal of Special Education, 22*(4), 447–462.

Horton, S. V., & Lovitt, T. C. (1994). A comparison of two methods of administering group reading inventories to diverse learners. *Remedial and Special Education, 15*(6), 378–390.

Horton, S. V., Lovitt, T. C., & Christensen, C. (1991a). Matching three classifications of secondary students to differential levels of study guides. *Journal of Learning Disabilities, 24*(9), 518–529.

Horton, S. V., Lovitt, T. C., & Christensen, C. (1991b). Notetaking from textbooks: Effects of a columnar format for three categories of secondary students. *Exceptionality, 2*(1), 19–40.

Horton, S. V., Lovitt, T. C., & Givens, A. (1988). A computer-based vocabulary program for three categories of student. *British Journal of Educational Technology, 19*(2), 131–143.

Horton, S. V., Lovitt, T. C., Givens, A., & Nelson, R. (1989). Teaching social studies to high school students with academic handicaps in a mainstreamed setting: Effects of a computerized study guide. *Journal of Learning Disabilities, 22*(2), 102–107.

Horton, S. V., Lovitt, T. C., & Slocum, T. (1988). Teaching geography to high school students with academic deficits: Effects of a computerized map tutorial. *Learning Disability Quarterly, 11*(4), 371–379.

Howell, R., Sidorenko, E., & Jurica, J. (1987). The effects of computer use on the acquisition of multiplication facts by a student with learning disabilities. *Journal of Learning Disabilities, 20*(6), 336–341.

Hunter, Z. (2004). *Learning disabilities and the Haverford community.* Retrieved from Haverford College, Office of Disabilities Services Web site: www.haverford .edu/ods/ld/intro.html

Individuals with Disabilities Education Act (IDEA), 20 U.S.C. § 1400 *et seq* (2004). Retrieved from the U.S. Department of Education, Office of Special Education and Rehabilitative Services Web site: www.ed.gov/policy/speced/guid/ idea/idea2004.html

Inspiration Software. (2003). Inspiration (Version 7.5) [computer software]. Portland, OR: Author.

Inspiration Software. (2004). Inspiration for Palm OS [computer software]. Portland, OR: Author.

Johnson, G., Gersten, R., & Carnine, D. (1987). Effects of instructional design variables on vocabulary acquisition of LD students: A study of computer-assisted instruction. *Journal of Learning Disabilities, 20*(4), 206–213.

Keene, S., & Davey, B. (1987). Effects of computer-presented text on LD adolescents reading behaviors. *Learning Disability Quarterly, 10*(4), 283–290.

Kelly, B., Carnine, D. W., Gersten, R., & Grossen, B. (1986). The effectiveness of videodisc instruction in teaching fractions to learning handicapped and remedial high school students. *Journal of Special Education Technology, 8*(2), 5–17.

Kozma, R. B. (1994). Will media influence learning? Reframing the debate. *Educational Technology Research and Development, 42*(2), 7–19.

Learning Technology Center at Vanderbilt University. (1996). The new adventures of Jasper Woodbury [videodisc]. Mahwah, NJ: Lawrence Erlbaum.

Lewis, L. B. (1998). Assistive technology and learning disabilities: Today's realities and tomorrow's promises. *Journal of Learning Disabilities, 31*(1), 16–26.

Liao, C. Y. K. (1998). Effects of hypermedia versus traditional instruction on students' achievement: A meta-analysis. *Journal of Research on Computing in Education, 30*(4), 341–359.

MacArthur, C. A. (1994). Review of grammar checker designed for students with learning disabilities [data file]. Newark: University of Delaware.

MacArthur, C. A. (1996). Using technology to enhance the writing processes of students with learning disabilities. *Journal of Learning Disabilities, 29*(4), 344–347.

MacArthur, C. A., Graham, S., Haynes, J. B., & DeLaPaz, S. (1996). Spell checkers and students with learning disabilities: Performance comparisons and impact on spelling. *Journal of Special Education, 30*(1), 35–37.

MacArthur, C. A., & Haynes, J. B. (1995). Student assistant for learning from text (SALT): A hypermedia reading aid. *Journal of Learning Disabilities, 28*(3), 150–159.

MacMillan, D. L., Keogh, B. K., & Jones, R. L. (1986). Special education research on mildly handicapped learners. In M. C. Wittrock (Ed.), *Handbook of research on teaching* (3rd ed., pp. 686–724). New York: Macmillan.

Mastropieri, M. A., Scruggs, T. E., & Graetz, J. E. (2003). Reading comprehension instruction for secondary students: Challenges for struggling students and teachers. *Learning Disability Quarterly, 26*(2), 103–116.

Mind Nautilus Software. (1985). MemorEase [computer software]. Pleasanton, CA: Author.

Montgomery, D. J., Karlan, G. R., & Coutinho, M. (2001). The effectiveness of word processor spell check programs to produce target words for misspellings generated by students with learning disabilities. *JSET eJournal, 16*(2), 1–15.

Moore, L. J., & Carnine, D. (1989). Evaluating curriculum design in the context of active teaching. *Remedial and Special Education, 10*(4), 28–37.

National Center to Improve Practice in Special Education (NCIP). (2004). *Multimedia and more: Help for students with learning disabilities.* Newton, MA: Education Development Center. Retrieved from http://www2.edc.wor/NICP/library/mm/toc.htm

National Council of Teachers of Mathematics. (2000). *Principles and standards for school mathematics.* Reston, VA: Author.

Okolo, C. (1992). The effects of computer-based attribution retraining on the attributions, persistence, and mathematics computation of students with learning disabilities. *Journal of Learning Disabilities, 25*(5), 327–334.

Okolo, C. M., Bahr, C. M., & Rieth, H. J. (1993). A retrospective view of computer-based instruction. *Journal of Special Education Technology, 12*(1), 1–27.

Quenneville, J. (2001). Tech tools for students with learning disabilities: Infusion into inclusive classrooms. *Preventing School Failure, 45*(4), 167–170.

Reyes, E., Gallego, M., Duran, G., & Scanlon, D. (1989). Integration of internal concepts and external factors: Extending the knowledge of learning disabled adolescents. *Journal of Early Adolescence, 9*(1/2), 112–124.

Robinson, F. P. (1961). *Effective study.* New York: Harper & Row.

Ruzic, R., & O'Connell, K. (2002). Technology tools. Wakefield, MA: Center for Applied Special Technology. Retrieved from www.cast/org/ncac/index.cfmi=1668

Saski, J., Swicegood, P., & Carter, J. (1983). Notetaking formats for learning disabled adolescents. *Learning Disability Quarterly, 6*(3), 265–272.

Scruggs, T. E., & Mastropieri, M. A. (1990). Mnemonic instruction for students with learning disabilities: What is it and what it does. *Learning Disability Quarterly, 13*(4), 271–280.

Slocum, T. (1986). *Instructional design and computer delivered instruction.* Unpublished master's thesis, University of Washington.

Torgesen, J. K., Dahlem, W. E., & Greenstein, J. (1987). Using verbatim text recording to enhance reading comprehension in learning disabled adolescents. *Learning Disabilities Focus, 3*(1), 30–38.

U.S. Department of Education. (2002). *Twenty-fourth annual report to Congress on the implementation of the Individuals with Disabilities Education Act.* Washington, DC: Author. Retrieved from www.ed.gov/about/reports/annual/osep/2002/index.html

Vacc, N. N. (1987). Word processor versus handwriting: A comparative study of writing samples produced by mildly mentally handicapped students. *Exceptional Children, 54*(2), 156–165.

Woodward, J., & Gersten, R. (1992). Innovative technology for secondary students with learning disabilities. *Exceptional Children, 58*(5), 407–421.

7

Strategies for Enhancing Self-Determination, Social Success, and Transition to Adulthood

Laurie E. Powers, Donald D. Deshler,
Bonnie Jones, and Marlene Simon

About four months before Jason was to transition to high school, a meeting was scheduled to review his individualized education program (IEP) and to put in place a long-term plan encompassing his high school years, as well as his postschool plans. Prior to the IEP meeting, Jason's special education teacher had taught him the Self-Advocacy Strategy to ensure that he could take an active and meaningful role in the planning process and in determining his future. As a team, Jason, his parents, and key educators in his school put in place a set of goals and long-range plans that took into account things that Jason wanted to learn and accomplish, his learning strengths and weaknesses, and the types of resources to leverage on behalf of Jason within school as well as the community. A vitally important part of Jason's high school experience was the attention given to building transition plans that would assist him in setting meaningful goals for his life after high school, expose him to a broad array of career alternatives, and provide him some very meaningful experiences with employers in his community to enable him to gain on-site experiences to assist him in decision making. In all of these planning sessions, both Jason and his parents were centrally involved and had a major say in final decisions. Additionally, Jason was taught social skills to enable him to more effectively engage in cooperative group activities, resist peer pressure, and perform well in interactions with others. As Jason mastered these strategies and skills, his confidence grew, as did his capacity to respond to the demands he encountered meeting nonacademic requirements.

The goal of secondary education is to ensure that young people successfully complete high school and leave prepared to participate in adult life, including employment, postsecondary education, and independent living. During the last two decades, intensive effort has been devoted to expanding opportunities for adolescents with disabilities to assume typical adult roles. As a result, expectations have shifted dramatically for the achievement and participation levels of young people with disabilities. Furthermore, significant progress has been made in identifying approaches that promote students' academic, social, and transition success.

This chapter begins by reviewing the current postschool outcomes of secondary students with disabilities with respect to school completion, employment, and postsecondary education. The second part of the chapter focuses on effective secondary education practices that foster self-determination, social success, and transition preparation.

HIGH SCHOOL COMPLETION RATES

The importance of high school completion for students' future success abounds in the literature. Students who do not complete high school are more likely to be unemployed, less likely to be employed full-time, and make up a disproportionate percentage of the prison population (Wagner et al., 1991). High school completion rates for all students in the United States rose considerably during the early 1980s and have been relatively stable since then. In 1992, the rate was 87% for youths age 19 to 20 (U.S. Department of Education, 1998). Despite progress, however, in 2000, some 3.8 million young adults were not enrolled in a high school program and had not completed high school. These youths accounted for nearly 11% of the 16- to 24-year-olds in the country.

The challenge of improving graduation rates is exacerbated by the fact that many states require students with disabilities to meet the same graduation requirements as other students to receive a standard diploma. However, 31 states offer differentiated diplomas for students with disabilities; nine states award a standard diploma to students with disabilities who complete their IEPs; and others award modified diplomas or certificates of completion to students who do not meet the requirements for a standard diploma. Considering the broad array of graduation requirements that are currently employed, caution must be exercised in comparing graduation statistics from one state to another.

During the 1999–2000 academic year, 56% of all students ages 14–21 with disabilities graduated with a standard diploma, an increase from 53% in 1995–96 (U.S. Department of Education, 2002). Of these students, those with mental retardation had the lowest graduation rate (39.5%), and students with visual impairment had the highest (73.4%). Students with deaf-blindness (48.5%), autism (47.5%), multiple disabilities (39.5%), and emotional disabilities (40.1%) had lower graduation rates than all students with disabilities. Graduation rates varied by state, with statewide reading and math achievement and per-pupil expenditures in education accounting for much of the variance.

Variables such as household and community income, ethnicity, percentage of education revenues from state sources, teacher salaries, and life in an urban area are significant factors in predicting graduation rates, as well as the receipt of a diploma or certificate of completion. For example, data collected on race and ethnicity indicate that African American students are the least likely to graduate with a standard diploma, whereas European American students are most likely to graduate with a standard diploma (U.S. Department of Education, 2002).

A report from the U.S. Department of Education (2002) noted some encouraging trends in drop-out rates for students with disabilities from the mid-1990s to the turn of the century. Namely, the drop-out rate for students with disabilities decreased from 34.1% to 29.4%. Students with speech and language, learning, orthopedic, hearing, and emotional disabilities demonstrated the greatest improvement in drop-out rates. Students with emotional disabilities were the only disability group that had a drop-out rate above that for all students with disabilities (51.4%). As with the population as a whole, however, the drop-out rates for students of color exceeded those for students from European American backgrounds (Wagner, Cameto, & Newman, 2003).

EMPLOYMENT

Individuals with disabilities continue to be employed at disappointingly low levels, despite numerous employment initiatives undertaken in the last two decades. It is estimated that one-third of working-age persons with disabilities are in the labor force (that is, those employed or seeking employment), while only 28% are actually employed (U.S. Census Bureau, 1997). About 69% of young adults with disabilities are unemployed three to five years after high school, with African American and Hispanic youth significantly less likely than European American youth to find competitive employment (Blackorby & Wagner, 1996).

On a slightly more positive note, recent findings from the second National Longitudinal Transition Study (NLTS2) suggest that increasing numbers of youths with disabilities are holding paid jobs, with an overall one-year employment rate of 60% and two-thirds earning more than the minimum wage. However, youths with disabilities also demonstrated declines in the average number of hours worked per week, as well as rates of continuous employment. Only youths with mental retardation did not experience a significant increase in earning more than the minimum wage. In comparison to other ethnic groups, only European American youths had a significant increase in pay. Finally, in terms of gender, the gap in employment appears to be narrowing; however, males are still more likely than females to meet or exceed the minimum wage.

The median annual income for employed individuals with disabilities is about $16,000 (less than $14,000 for those with severe disabilities), compared with almost $22,000 for employees who do not experience disabilities (U.S. Census Bureau, 1997). Most individuals with disabilities are employed in low-status occupations that offer low pay, few opportunities for advancement, and limited benefits (White, 1992). African American and Hispanic youths with disabilities earn significantly less than their European American peers (Blackorby & Wagner, 1996).

To date, most employment initiatives have focused on areas such as job training, work experience, and job placement (Gajar, Goodman, & McAfee, 1993), and, traditionally, professionals have attempted to find short-term employment solutions for individuals with disabilities. Increasing attention is now being directed toward assisting individuals to build careers and long-term employment capacity. Bolstering student self-determination has become paramount in planning and carrying out educational and transition goals, given the expanded academic and transition opportunities available to youths with disabilities (Grayson, 1998).

POSTSECONDARY EDUCATION

Access to employment opportunities has become increasingly dependent on postsecondary education and training (Berryman & Bailey, 1992). The U.S. Department of Education's *Strategic Plan, 1998–2002,* describes postsecondary education as "America's traditional gateway to the professions, more challenging jobs, and higher wages" (p. 1). Thus, it is clear that postsecondary schooling enhances an individual's chances of achieving high status, wealth, and job stability (Gingerich, 1996; Tinto, 1987).

The number of individuals with disabilities attending postsecondary education programs has substantially increased in the past two decades. For example, it is estimated that more than 9% of college freshmen and more than 10% of all college students experience a disability, up from 3% in 1978 (Gajar, 1998). However, despite these advances, a lower percentage of people with disabilities attend postsecondary programs, compared with individuals without disabilities. Thus, youths with disabilities transition to postsecondary education at only about one-quarter the rate of youth without disabilities & one-third the rate of economically disadvantaged youth (Blackorby & Wagner, 1996; Fairweather & Shaver, 1991). Further, young people with disabilities have the highest level of representation in vocational schools. In community colleges, they are represented at about half the rate of youths without disabilities. By comparison, young people with disabilities make up about 6% of freshmen at four-year colleges and universities, a modest decrease from prior years (Henderson, 2001). The NLTS2 findings suggest that two-year colleges were considered a much more likely option in 2001, compared with 1987, for youths in all disability categories, for males and females, and for European American and African American youth (Wagner et al., 2003).

The rate of postsecondary participation among people with disabilities varies by factors such as socioeconomic status, gender, and ethnicity, as well as postsecondary setting and type of disability. As is the case with individuals who do not experience a disability, socioeconomic level is consistently associated with postsecondary enrollment. Thus, parents' level of education and family income are related to enrollment (Fairweather & Shaver, 1991; Plisko, 1984). Although the gender gap appears to be closing (Blackorby & Wagner, 1996), female students with disabilities continue to be underrepresented (Henderson, 1995). Ethnicity and culture also affect postsecondary attendance. For example, African Americans, Hispanics, and Native Americans lag Caucasians and Asian Americans in postsecondary attendance rates for individuals both with and without disabilities (Blackorby & Wagner, 1996; Western Interstate Commission for Higher Education & The College Board, 1991).

Much of the increase in postsecondary enrollment by individuals with disabilities reflects major growth in participation by one specific group, that is, students with learning disabilities. Enrollment of students with learning disabilities increased from 15% of all students reporting disabilities in 1988 to 40% in 2001 (Henderson, 2001). From an institutional perspective, the distribution of students with disabilities attending college has shifted dramatically, with those who experience learning disabilities replacing students with visual impairment as the largest group with disabilities on campus (Henderson, 2001). However, based on a comparative analysis of postsecondary attendance rates among specific disability categories, individuals with learning, emotional, and developmental disabilities are still much less likely to attend college than individuals with sensory, health, or orthopedic disabilities (Blackorby & Wagner, 1996).

In summary, evidence suggests that, as a whole, students with disabilities have demonstrated improvement in their rates of school completion, employment, and postsecondary participation. However, their success remains well below that of peers without disabilities, and critical barriers must be addressed if youths with disabilities are to successfully assume valued roles as full citizens in our society.

INTERVENTIONS FOR IMPROVING NONACADEMIC OUTCOMES

Previous chapters of this book have focused primarily on interventions designed to enhance academic outcomes for students with disabilities. The interventions and programs described in this chapter address nonacademic domains. Inasmuch as success in life involves much more than how well an individual performs in school, it is important to consider the myriad factors that are central to success and happiness in postsecondary life. They include goal setting, independent decision making, and appropriate social interactions. First, self-determination will be examined. It is central to any intervention designed to produce significant outcomes for adolescents with disabilities. Subsequent sections will deal with specific intervention strategies, programs, and principles that have been found to enhance social and transition performance of adolescents with disabilities.

ENHANCING SELF-DETERMINATION

One of the most important themes to emerge in secondary education during the past decade is self-determination. Halloran described self-determination as the "ultimate goal of education . . . . [The acquisition of self-determination] should not be assumed to be a natural occurrence but rather the result of purposeful strategies, properly implemented, to achieve the desired outcome of independence . . . . Actualizing this emphasis would require a major change in the current approach to educating, parenting, or planning for children and youth with disabilities" (1993, p. 214).

The growing emphasis on self-determination is, in part, a response to limited progress achieved in secondary and transition outcomes for students with disabilities using traditional professionally driven models. The emphasis also reflects a recognition that attention must be directed to building the capacities of youth to act as key agents in their own educational decision making, planning, and instruction. The focus on self-determination in special education may be viewed as part of the larger school-reform movement aimed at promoting decision making, self-sufficiency, and competence among all students (Apple & Beane, 1995).

The Education Department's Office of Special Education and Rehabilitative Services began a self-determination initiative in January 1989, when a national conference of individuals with disabilities, as well as educators, parents, and state and local administrators, was convened to recommend activities that could be sponsored at the federal level to promote self-determination (Ward, 1999). Following the conference, a discretionary funding program was launched through the Secondary Education and Transitional Services for Youth with Disabilities Program to support 26 demonstration projects of self-determination models during fiscal years 1990 through 1993.

The focus of these projects was to identify and teach the skills necessary for self-determination, as well as to identify systemwide activities that would help students have more input into decisions that would affect their lives (Ward & Kohler, 1996). The initial demonstration program was followed by research initiatives that developed methods for assessing self-determination and identified factors that promoted student involvement in transition planning. Prompted by the activities and outcomes of these projects, the value of self-determination has been widely embraced, and practices have been adopted and replicated by state systems and outreach projects. Further, key professional associations, such as the Division on Career Development and Transition of the Council for Exceptional Children, have formally endorsed the development and delivery of educational programs based on self-determination (Field, Martin, Miller, Ward, & Wehmeyer, 1998b).

Defining Self-Determination

Several overlapping definitions of self-determination have been put forth in education, beginning with one by Ward, who defined self-determination as referring to "both the attitudes which lead people to define goals for themselves and to their ability to take the initiative to achieve these goals" (1988, p. 2). Further, he saw self-actualization, assertiveness, creativity, pride, and self-advocacy as a set of characteristics necessary for self-determination. Accordingly, people must be (1) self-actualizing to achieve their full potential; (2) assertive to act self-confidently and express their needs clearly and directly (Weiner, 1986); (3) creative to expand beyond stereotyped roles and expectations; (4) proud to recognize their abilities and contributions to society; and (5) self-advocating to ensure access to services and benefits needed to achieve their full potential.

Field and Hoffman later defined self-determination as "one's ability to define and achieve goals based on a foundation of knowing and valuing oneself" (1994, p. 159). Addressing the cognitive, affective, and behavioral components that promote self-determination leads to five major directives: (1) know yourself, (2) value yourself, (3) plan, (4) act, and (5) experience outcomes and learn.

In another attempt to define self-determination, Wehmeyer saw it as "acting as the primary causal agent in one's life and making choices and decisions regarding one's quality of life free from undue external influence or interference" (1996, p. 22). According to Wehmeyer, individuals are self-determined if their actions reflect four essential characteristics: (1) the person acts autonomously, (2) behaviors are self-regulated, (3) the person initiates and responds to events in a psychologically empowered manner, and (4) the person acts in a self-realizing manner.

Finally, Powers and her colleagues defined self-determination as "self-directed action to achieve personally valued goals" (Powers et al., 1996, p. 292). From this perspective, self-determination is bolstered through (1) information and skills that foster a person's capacities for decision making and self-direction, such as strategies for planning, achieving goals, developing partnerships with others, and self-management; (2) access to opportunities to express self-determination, such as participation in a full range of educational opportunities or having control over supports and resources; and (3) facilitative support from family, friends, professionals, and mentors.

Inherent in each of these definitions is a contextual perspective that suggests that self-determination is promoted through interaction between a person and environmental factors. Therefore, students with disabilities must develop the capacities necessary to promote more positive outcomes in their lives (Mithaug, 1991; Wehmeyer, 1992; Wehmeyer & Ward, 1995). Concurrently, our education system must be structured to support students in directing their lives, exercising responsibility over their actions, and accessing a wide range of experiences and opportunities.

Self-determination also must be understood and supported within the context of culture. For example, outcomes that are commonly associated with the expression of self-determination in mainstream culture—such as individuality, control over one's environment, and a focus on the future—may directly oppose the values of students from cultural backgrounds that emphasize interconnectedness, harmony with nature, and the importance of past and present time. Student goals for achieving independence are often identified and fostered within the context of family norms and relationships. A student from a European American family may focus on living independently from family, whereas a student from a Hispanic background may desire to remain at home following graduation and assume increasing responsibility for contributing to family resources or caring for other family members.

Likewise, a European American youth may steadfastly desire to make independent decisions, whereas an Asian student may defer decision making to others or perceive that making a decision is not necessary because he or she is guided by cultural traditions and norms. Thus, although self-determination is relevant for virtually all students, the outcomes that youths value for their lives and the processes they use to define and work toward their goals are often culturally embedded and must be respected in that context.

What Research Says About Improving Outcomes Through Self-Determination

Although self-determination is a relatively new concept in special education, a considerable body of knowledge exists regarding its effect on secondary and transition outcomes. For example, Wehmeyer and Schwartz (1997) found that one year after graduation, students with learning or cognitive disabilities who had high levels of self-determination were more likely to be employed and earn higher wages than peers who had low levels of self-determination.

Other studies have shown the positive effect of making decisions, expressing preferences, and setting goals on educational and behavioral outcomes (e.g., Dunlop et al., 1994; Kennedy & Haring, 1993; Newton, Ard, & Horner, 1993; Schunk, 1985). For example, Schunk (1985) demonstrated that students with learning disabilities who participated in selecting their mathematics goals showed greater improvement in math than students who did not select their goals. Similarly, Dunlop et al. (1994) found that the opportunity to choose from a menu of academic tasks was associated with increased task engagement and decreased disruptive behavior for students with emotional and behavioral disabilities.

Research also points out the positive association between self-directed learning and motivation and performance. Malone and Mastropieri (1992) found that middle school students with learning disabilities performed better on reading comprehension tasks when they self-monitored their performance. Self-instruction training has also been shown to improve the academic and vocational performance of students with disabilities (Graham & Harris, 1989; Hughes & Peterson, 1989).

Keys to Increasing Self-Determination

Most research on promoting self-determination underscores the importance of systematic instruction in self-determination skills, support from family and other key people in a student's life, educator expectations, and school characteristics. For example, German, Huber Marshall, and Martin (1997) demonstrated that students with cognitive disabilities increased their achievement of daily goals when they participated in a goal-setting curriculum. Powers and colleagues (Powers, Turner, Ellison, et al., 2001) studied secondary students with orthopedic disabilities plus mental retardation, other health impairment, or learning disabilities. The students participated in TAKE CHARGE, a program that included coaching in skills such as goal setting, problem solving, negotiation, emotional self-regulation, parent support, and mentoring. Findings showed that these students experienced higher levels of psychosocial adjustment, goal accomplishment, and empowerment than a randomized comparison group of students who did not participate in the program.

Wehmeyer and colleagues developed a model of teaching, the Self-Determined Learning Model of Instruction (Mithaug, Wehmeyer, Agran, Martin, & Palmer, 1998; Wehmeyer, Palmer, Agran, Mithaug, & Martin, 2000), based on component elements of self-determination, the process of self-regulated problem solving, and research on student-directed learning. Implementation of this model consisted of a three-phase instructional process in which students solved problems by posing and answering a series of questions per phase that the students had learned. Each instructional phase included a list of educational supports that teachers could use to enable students to self-direct learning (see Figure 7.1). Based on a field test of the model with 21 teachers responsible for instructing 40 students with mental retardation, learning disabilities, or emotional or behavioral disorders, Wehmeyer et al. (2000) found that the model was effective in enabling students to attain educationally valued goals.

Finally, other research has suggested that parent involvement and support; collaborative planning among educators; school autonomy and flexibility; and participatory governance by students, parents, educators, and administrators have helped to empower students, parents, and educators (Golarz & Golarz, 1995).

Promising Self-Determination Practices

Several good summaries of exemplary and promising self-determination practices are available (e.g., Field, Martin, Miller, Ward, & Wehmeyer, 1998a, 1998b; Ward & Kohler, 1996). The practices reviewed in the following section are supported by research findings and have been incorporated into models developed to promote self-determination and student involvement.

Figure 7.1   Self-Determined Learning Model of Instruction

Phase I: Set a Goal

What do I want to learn?
What do I know about it now?
What must change for me to learn what I don't know?
What can I do to make this happen?

Phase II: Take Action

What can I do to learn what I don't know?
What could keep me from taking action?
What can I do to remove these barriers?
When will I take action?

Phase III: Adjust the Goal or Plan

What actions have I taken?
What barriers have been removed?
What has changed about what I don't know?
Do I know what I want to know?

Used with permission by Michael Wehmeyer.

- *Student decision making.* At an individual level, self-determination is promoted by enabling students to (1) make key decisions, such as choosing their courses, extracurricular activities, and career goals; (2) participate in the entire general education curriculum; and (3) be active in their educational and transition planning. At a systems level, self-determination is promoted by enabling students to participate in leadership activities (such as peer mediation or community service programs), as well as to make decisions related to curriculum content, scheduling, governance, and extracurricular activities.

- *Providing important information to students.* To make informed decisions and successfully participate in individual or leadership opportunities, students must have information about (1) their strengths, challenges, and needs; (2) the options available; and (3) the requirements or process for becoming involved. For example, to choose a course schedule, students must know what is being offered, how different course options address their academic and career goals, and how to sign up for courses. Such information must be provided in straightforward language and in a format that students can understand.

- *Instruction in self-determination skills.* There is general agreement that building students' self-determination requires specific instruction in self-determination skills such as planning, goal setting, problem solving, self-advocacy, self-regulation, and participation in educational or transition-planning meetings. Self-determination instruction should be available to all secondary students, with and without disabilities. Several effective self-determination and student-involvement curricula have been developed and field-tested (e.g., Curtis, 1998; Field & Hoffman, 1996; Fullerton, 1994; Halpern et al., 1997; Powers, Ellison, Matuszewski, Wilson, & Turner, 1995; Powers, Ellison, Matuszewski, Turner, & Wilson, 1997; Martin & Huber Marshall, 1995; Wehmeyer & Kelchner, 1997). Instruction in these curricula can be infused in existing courses or offered as an elective or required course.

Although the content, format, and strategies of various curricula vary to some extent, most emphasize achievement skills such as planning, goal setting, and problem solving. Some also focus on interpersonal skills such as assertiveness, self-advocacy, managing assistance provided by others, and listening skills. Several curricula focus specifically on preparing students to participate in their educational and transition-planning meetings. On a more personal level, some curricula address such issues as self-talk, coping, self-management, and self-esteem, and include activities to draw on and activate a person's creative potential.

Generally, curriculum formats consist of individual, small-group, and class activities delivered in school- and community-based settings. Some curricula are more easily delivered in small classes or cooperative learning groups (e.g., Fullerton, 1994; Powers, Sowers, & Stevens, 1995; Wehmeyer & Kelchner, 1997), whereas others are designed for delivery to larger classes (e.g., Field & Hoffman, 1996; Halpern et al., 1997; Martin & Huber Marshall, 1995). Although instruction is provided, the role of educators who work with students is more like that of a coach, facilitator, or consultant than a traditional instructor or teacher.

• *Experiential learning.* Experiential learning is a cornerstone of promoting self-determination, and therefore a key part of virtually every model. For example, in identifying their goals, students may actively seek out information (for example, go to the guidance office to get the course schedule or take an interest assessment). Depending on the goal that students identify, they may engage in a range of activities, such as studying for exams, visiting employment or postsecondary sites, filling out applications, or joining clubs. In most cases, students' goals inherently involve experiential learning—they participate directly in activities that are designed to let them learn by doing. Because self-determination skills are generic and intended to be learned and applied across settings, it is important to structure experiences that provide multiple opportunities for students to practice their newly learned skills in different environments.

• *Involvement in education and transition planning.* Clearly, the ability and opportunity to plan for one's future are central to self-determination. Such involvement occurs throughout secondary school and includes participating in ongoing planning, working toward goals, and using experiences gained in the process to restructure plans, as well as participating in specific planning activities such as IEP and transition-planning meetings. Students may participate in specific curricular activities through which they do future planning, identify goals, select strategies for achieving their goals, and then take action toward their goals through in-school or community-based activities. Students may also conduct self-evaluation and evaluation by significant others to identify their skills and challenges, then participate in curricular activities that will help them direct their educational planning.

Generally, to be truly involved in planning meetings, students need to be invited, assisted to prepare, welcomed, listened to, and supported as they try to participate. Research suggests that many students do not participate because they do not feel welcomed, acknowledged, or respected (Powers, Turner, Matuszewski, Wilson, & Loesch, 1999). In support of their involvement, most students benefit from specific coaching in participation skills. Also, it is typically best if they begin by participating in one or two parts of their meeting—for example, helping to identify whom to invite, welcoming everyone, and describing goals—and then increase their level of involvement as they become more experienced and comfortable.

• *Involvement in assessment.* Students need to be active participants in deciding that assessment is needed, what should be assessed, the most appropriate assessment methods, and how results will be used (Field et al., 1998b). Specifically, students may help decide what questions need to be answered, participate in gathering data (such as conducting interviews), approve the involvement of other participants, assemble portfolio information, and use assessment information to define their needs and goals. Throughout the assessment process, student input should be solicited and respected. Typically, involving students in assessment activities will increase their investment in acting on the results.

• *Mentoring opportunities.* Mentoring is a popular approach for promoting living skills, academic success, self-confidence, and motivation. Many schools introduce students to older peer or adult mentors who have achieved success in a particular area that is perceived to be important for students (for example, employers, college students, recovering substance abusers). Interaction with successful role models with disabilities enhances the disability-related knowledge and self-confidence of adolescents with disabilities, as well as parents' perceptions of the knowledge and capabilities of their children with disabilities (Powers et al., 1995). Mentoring and modeling activities can be used to deliver instruction (for example, share life experiences through panel discussions or assist with role play and videotaped practice of skills) and to support students in working toward their goals (for example, provide encouragement, accompany the student on a community activity, follow up on progress, and assist with problem solving).

There are many ways to involve students with mentors, including individual activities, classroom- or community-based workshops, and group outings of students and mentors. Mentoring programs may be organized by schools or existing community organizations, such as the YMCA, Boys and Girls Clubs, and independent living centers. Systematic recruitment, training, and ongoing support of mentors is critical to the success of mentoring programs.

• *Family involvement.* Research suggests that positive parent expectations and support are key to promoting self-determination of adolescents with disabilities (Powers et al., 1999; Sands, Bassett, Lehmann, & Spencer, 1998). Families typically require information and support to work optimally in partnership with school staff to bolster self-determination in their sons and daughters. In many cases, students are not actively involved in self-determination and transition planning unless their families are also involved.

In contrast to giving prescriptive support to parents (for example, "Susan is working on a goal and I'd appreciate it if you could do . . ."), self-determination is often fostered by other actions. These include

(1) providing parents with information about their children's activities and opportunities; (2) validating parents' strengths, efforts, and accomplishments; (3) assisting parents in identifying strategies that they believe are appropriate for encouraging the self-determination of their children; (4) supporting parent involvement in educational planning by keeping the cost of their involvement as low as possible; and (5) encouraging students and families to communicate with one another. Many parents also appreciate opportunities for contact with other parents of students with disabilities.

• *Enhancing educators' capacities to support self-determination.* Like students and parents, educators can encourage self-determination to the extent that they have the necessary information, skills, opportunities, and support to build their capacities. Promotion of self-determination requires a basic shift in how educators work with students and the way school environments are structured. Beginning at the preservice level, educators must have opportunities to develop their capacities for self-determination, as well as become acquainted with specific practices to support student self-determination. Likewise, school environments must be structured to enable students to access a full range of educational and extracurricular opportunities; communicate clear expectations for student self-direction and responsibility; facilitate parent involvement and collaborative planning with educators; and permit participatory governance by students, parents, educators, and administrators.

In summary, the self-determination movement in education has taught us several important lessons. The first lesson is that it is imperative for youths with disabilities to receive school instruction to develop their capacities to express self-determination and have multiple opportunities to practice these skills (Ward & Kohler, 1996). The second lesson is that self-determination can be expressed by students with diverse disabilities, including those with severe cognitive disabilities. For example, using a switch or gesture to indicate a choice of food may be as important an expression of self-determination as conducting one's own transition-planning meeting. What is important is that each student is supported to express self-determination at his or her optimal level.

The third lesson is that self-determination instruction and opportunities must begin when children are very young to reverse the cycle of dependency, learned helplessness, control by others, and feelings of inability that too often characterize individuals with disabilities. The fourth lesson is that expression of self-determination is fostered by having real opportunities to make decisions and direct one's life, not by a "readiness" approach that requires students to demonstrate a specified level of competence before they can participate in self-direction activities. The final and perhaps most important lesson is that promoting self-determination requires a shift in thinking among educators and others from an attitude of control to an attitude of empowerment and trust. In short, we must believe in the capacities of youths to be change agents in their lives and in our own capacities to support them.

ENHANCING SOCIAL SUCCESS

One of the most important factors contributing to adolescents' achievement in school, in the world of work, and in their personal lives is their ability to engage in a variety of social behaviors to successfully communicate with, relate to, and work with peers, teachers, employers, and other adults (Van Reusen, 1999). Students with good social skills know how and when to modify and redirect their interactions and behavior as situations change. These students regulate their behavior through the effective use of social skills. The degree to which students demonstrate appropriate social behaviors and skills in specific situations represents their social competence (Hazel & Schumaker, 1988). Regrettably, many adolescents with disabilities evidence significant difficulties in social competence. These difficulties have frequently been underscored in the research literature.

Deshler, Schumaker, Alley, Warner, and Clark (1981) found that adolescents with learning disabilities participated less actively than peers in activities that were formally arranged. For example, these students were involved in few extracurricular activities in high school; by comparison, their typically achieving peers spent as much as three times as many hours per week on such activities. On the other hand, students with disabilities participated as much as or more than their typically achieving peers in informal peer interactions (such as hanging around the neighborhood or having friends over to their house). The reason for these differences was unclear. One possibility is that, although individuals with learning disabilities interacted with peers on an informal basis as frequently as adolescents without disabilities, the quality of their interactions lacked whatever was necessary for them to be socially acceptable. This disconnected them from the nonacademic flow and fabric of the school experience.

In another study, Schumaker, Hazel, Sherman, and Sheldon (1982) found adolescents with disabilities to be less socially skilled than peers without disabilities. Thus, in eight role-play situations, students with learning disabilities earned significantly fewer points on observation checklists than peers because of markedly fewer appropriate responses. This same study found that the social performance of adolescents with learning disabilities was similar to the performance of students who had been referred to juvenile probation authorities as a result of social problems they had created in the community. Indeed, their scores were not significantly different in seven of the eight situations. These findings underscore the potential difficulties that youths with learning disabilities may face if their social performance largely mirrors that of youths who are considered by society to be at risk socially.

Some individuals with disabilities demonstrate even more severe difficulties than students in the studies just described. That is, current data paint a dismal picture of how adolescents who are severely emotionally disturbed respond to the rigors of high school. Highly antisocial and destructive behavior often characterizes the actions of many of these students. They can be potentially dangerous to themselves and others in a school environment.

Social competence plays a vital role in overall school and postschool success, and a lack of social skills can have negative effects for adolescents who are trying to gain acceptance and approval. Therefore, careful attention must be given to structuring school environments to promote the acquisition and demonstration of positive social behaviors, as well as to provide specific opportunities for instruction in social skills. The highly diverse needs presented by adolescents with disabilities underscore the importance of developing service options that are sufficiently comprehensive and flexible to meet these needs. At the same time, services should meet the myriad challenges presented by students without disabilities who also lack the necessary social skills to be successful in school and life and contribute positively to the overall school climate and culture.

Increased attention has been devoted to strategies for addressing the social and emotional needs of adolescents with disabilities. They need help developing social competencies to cope with the demands of high school, as well as the rigors of successfully competing in the world of work. The following sections describe some recent advances in defining strategies for promoting social success of adolescents with disabilities. First, the issue of *what* structures and instructional programs are available to educators will be discussed. Second, the issue of *how* students should be taught various social strategies will be addressed.

Programming Options: What to Teach

Ideally, programming for adolescents should be conceptualized along a continuum, given that most adolescents have the necessary social skills to perform satisfactorily if they are placed in a reasonable environment. Hence, it is important to conceptualize instruction in social skills within an environment that is conducive to appropriate performance. The first step in carefully considering the nature of the overall school environment is to set parameters within which specific instruction in social skills can be provided to adolescents who need individualized, specially designed instruction.

There are no simple answers to eliminating or reducing antisocial behavior among adolescents. However, a consistent message has emerged in the literature in recent years. Namely, to make significant and sustained gains, it is necessary to have in place a well-orchestrated, comprehensive program that involves all staff in the school setting. Such programs are both extensive and intensive (Nelson, Crabtree, Marchand-Martella, & Martella, 1998; Turnbull & Ruef, 1997; Walker et al., 1996). The programs described here are illustrative of the array of services and instruction that should be available to adolescents with disabilities.

Effective Behavioral Support

Significant work has been done in recent years under the broad rubric of positive behavior supports (e.g., Horner, Sugai, & Horner, 2000; Sprick, Garrison, & Howard, 1998). One of the largest centers funded by the Office of Special Education Programs, the Center on Positive Behavioral Interventions and Supports, is designed to deal solely with the challenges that teachers and parents face in teaching students proper behavioral repertoires. The work of Sugai and Horner (1994) will be highlighted as an exemplar of these intervention systems.

Schools are generally viewed as networks of four interactive systems that collectively enable students to learn and teachers to teach. The *school-wide* system is designed to accommodate most students by establishing rules and expectations by and teaching desired academic and social behaviors to the student body. This system is geared toward all students and is designed to establish the norms and prevailing culture of the school. The *specific setting* system details policies and rules that are in place in common areas in a building (such as hallways, cafeteria, auditorium) where all students spend time. The procedures and guidelines to be followed in these areas tend to be less rigid or structured than in the classroom. *Classroom* systems, in turn, are developed by teachers to facilitate the instructional and learning mission of the class. These procedures are designed to enhance classroom productivity and student outcomes. An example of a classroom management plan is CHAMPS, designed by Sprick et al. (1998; see Figure 7.2). General schoolwide rules (for example, show respect to others) are shaped to meet specific classroom requirements (such as encouraging those who are shy to speak and give them good eye contact when they do). Finally, *individual student* systems provide specific procedures for responding to students whose needs are not met within the broader school context and programs.

Walker et al. summarized this comprehensive design of services as follows: "Collectively, these four systems provide a comprehensive matrix in which behavioral supports, services, and interventions can be established that accommodate the behavioral challenges and needs of students who display the most antisocial and destruction forms of behavior" (1996, p. 198).

Related to Sugai and Horner's comprehensive model for implementing interventions across a setting, Walker et al. (1996) conceptualized

Figure 7.2   CHAMPs: An Example of a Classroom Management System

Conversation:	Can students talk to each other during this activity or transition?
Help:	How can students get questions answered during this activity or transition? How do they get your attention?
Activity:	What is the task or objective of this activity or transition? What is the expected end product?
Movement:	Can students move about during this activity or transition? For example, are they allowed to get up to sharpen a pencil?
Participation:	What does appropriate student behavior for this activity or transition look and sound like? How do students show that they are fully participating?

Used with permission from Pacific Northwest Publishing.

services in terms of the types of students to be served. Specifically, they suggested that various interventions were needed to address the broad diversity of student characteristics.

For *typical students,* primary prevention or universal interventions are required. These include schoolwide discipline plans, instruction in strategies for conflict resolution and anger management, and effective teaching and schooling procedures. For *students at risk for antisocial behavior patterns,* secondary prevention or individualized, one-on-one interventions are required. These include the identification of at-risk clusters of students and families; direct instruction in moral reasoning, anger management, and self-control; family support and parent management training; and consultant-based one-on-one interventions.

Finally, for *students who show chronic, persistent behavior patterns,* tertiary prevention or wraparound, comprehensive interventions are required. These include the connection of youths and caregivers to community-based social service agencies; the development of individually tailored, wraparound interventions; coordination with social service agencies, law enforcement, courts, and correction officers; drug or alcohol counseling; and alternative placements such as day-treatment centers, specialized schools, and residential environments.

Instruction in Specific Social Skills

Studies conducted with adolescents with high-incidence disabilities by staff at the University of Kansas Center for Research on Learning showed encouraging evidence that students with disabilities can learn social skills strategies to mastery at a rate and level comparable to that of typically achieving peers (Schumaker et al., 1982; Schumaker, Hazel, & Pederson, 1988; Whang, Fawcett, & Mathews, 1981). These studies also showed that adolescents generalized their newly learned social behaviors to naturally occurring situations. These intervention studies focused on social skill "packages" involving complex systems or sequences of social skills, including both verbal and nonverbal behaviors that individuals can apply to particular categories of social tasks. Examples included recruiting help, giving positive feedback, accepting negative feedback, joining group discussions, resisting peer pressure, and negotiating. Each strategy comprised a set of generic steps—for example, face the person, make eye contact, use a serious voice tone, have a serious facial expression, and keep a straight body posture. Each strategy also comprised a corresponding set of behaviors that might be used within a specific situation. For example, in recruiting help or assistance students might say the person's name, ask if the person has time to help them, explain the task they are working on, explain the problem, ask for advice, listen carefully, ask questions if they do not understand, do the task while the person watches, ask for feedback, and thank the person.

It is important to note that strategic social performance must be viewed as more than performing steps associated with a given strategy. It also involves such factors as (1) accurately perceiving the present social situation, (2) motivating oneself to interact, (3) selecting the best social-skills strategy to use, (4) translating generic steps of the strategy into appropriate words and actions to fit the situation, (5) performing those steps fluently and in appropriate combinations according to current social mores, (6) accurately perceiving the other person's verbal and nonverbal cues, and (7) monitoring and adjusting parts of the performance to react appropriately to the other person's responses.

In short, to be a competent social performer, an individual must know and understand the reasons why each step is important, the benefits of using the steps, and the social rules associated with using the steps (Schumaker, 1992).

Self-Advocacy and Problem-Solving Training

One of the most highly valued goals for most adolescents is to become independent and sufficiently empowered so that their needs are met and they feel a sense of happiness (Snyder, 1994). To the extent that adolescents with disabilities can be taught to effectively advocate for themselves and solve problems, they also can feel a sense of efficacy and accomplishment. Van Reusen, Bos, Schumaker, and Deshler defined self-advocacy as "an individual's ability to effectively communicate, convey, negotiate, or assert his or her own interests, desires, needs, and rights. It involved making informed decisions and taking responsibility for those decisions" (1994, p. 4).

The Self-Advocacy Strategy (Van Reusen et al., 1994) taught adolescents how to identify and prioritize their needs, set and monitor their learning and developmental goals, and work toward the attainment of those goals. Using the strategy, students were systematically taught a set of social behaviors that are important in self-advocacy situations (see Figure 7.3). They were also taught behaviors to use when advocating for something they want (for example, clearly state your goals, identify and state your strengths and weaknesses when appropriate). Adolescents who were taught these behaviors were more effective in taking responsibility for their decisions and actions. Furthermore, socially and academically competent adolescents who were taught self-advocacy skills understood that, regardless of the learning situation, *they* ultimately controlled what, how, how well, and why it was important to learn. These students recognized that they must assertively but calmly state their needs, wants, and desires. Likewise, they determined and pursued supports they needed to attain their goals and assumed responsibility for obtaining them.

Crank, Deshler, and Schumaker (1995) found that adolescents are often preoccupied with social concerns: "Why have I not been asked out for Friday night?" "Why does my math teacher always seem to pick on me?" "Why does Charles always tease me in PE class?" When these concerns become the central focus of students' lives, academic progress can be adversely affected, the degree of social isolation can increase, and demonstration of antisocial behaviors can increase in response to feelings of rejection. In response to these concerns, Crank and his colleagues developed a procedure called *surface counseling*.

The surface counseling procedure was developed for professionals who are not formally trained as psychologists or counselors to help adolescents with disabilities deal constructively with much of the turmoil and stresses that are typically associated with adolescents. The procedure was not designed to address deep-seated difficulties caused by traumatic events—such as abuse or observing violence—or major psychological difficulties. In brief, the surface counseling procedure was designed to teach students how to independently size up a problem they are facing (such as

Figure 7.3   The "Share" Behaviors for Use During Self-Advocacy

---

Sit up straight.

Have a pleasant tone of voice.

Activate your thinking.

- Tell yourself to pay attention.
- Tell yourself to participate.
- Tell yourself to compare ideas.

Relax.

- Don't look uptight.
- Tell yourself to stay calm.

Engage in eye communication.

---

being picked on by a teacher), specify alternatives for addressing the problem, compare alternatives and make a choice, role-play the selected option, and finally, carry out the chosen course of action. Data showed that adolescents with high-incidence disabilities could be taught this problem-solving strategy and could apply it effectively to solve social problems they encountered. Figure 7.4 summarizes the problem-solving steps used in the surface counseling program.

How to Assess and Teach Social Skills

In cases in which certain students do not respond to schoolwide, specific setting, or classroom interventions (defined by Sugai & Horner, 1994) that other students respond to, it is important to understand why the system did not work for these students. One of the most effective tools developed in recent years in this regard is the *functional assessment* (e.g., Dadson & Horner, 1993; Fitzsimmons, 1998; Kamps et al., 1995). The functional assessment attempts to discover the purposes, goals, or functions of behavior by answering the following questions: (1) What is the problem? (2) Why does the problem exist? (3) What should be done to address the problem? (4) Did the interventions work, and what should be done next? (Tilly et al., 1998). In essence, the purpose of the functional assessment is to (1) understand what maintains problem behaviors; (2) predict the occurrence and nonoccurrence of problem behaviors; (3) gain information that can be used to prevent problem behaviors; and (4) gather information to be used to respond to problem behaviors when they do occur (Horner & Carr, 1997).

Research has shown that students learn targeted social-skill strategies best through two means: (1) explicit instruction and (2) multiple opportunities to practice the social skill in an array of naturally occurring situations. Schumaker (1992) described an example of an explicit instructional methodology comprising five stages. In the first stage, each student's

Figure 7.4   Surface Counseling Problem-Solving Steps

Step 1: Specify the problem.

Step 2: Plan solutions.

Step 3: Summarize solutions.

Step 4: Specify the consequences of solutions.

Step 5: Rate solutions and select the "best."

Step 6: Rehearse and role-play the solution steps.

Step 7: Set a time to discuss the outcome.

Step 8: Enact the solution.

Step 9: Review the outcome.

current performance in social situations was assessed and analyzed. In the second, descriptive stage, students were made aware of the name and general definition of the social-skill strategy, the steps of the strategy, the circumstances in which using the strategy would be appropriate, examples of situations in which the strategy would be appropriate, the benefits of using the strategy, and the rules associated with using the strategy. In the third stage, the strategy was modeled for students.

In the fourth stage, the students rehearsed naming the steps in the proper sequence at a criterion of 100% correct. This step was implemented to ensure that each student would be able to self-instruct about what to do each time the strategy was applied in a new social situation. In the fifth stage, students practiced performing the strategy in role-playing situations. After each practice attempt, students received positive and corrective feedback from the teacher or other students until mastery was reached. During the final instructional stage, students were provided with ample opportunities to practice using the newly learned social strategy in novel situations so that generalization and maintenance was ensured. It is important that students be required to use the new strategy in as many settings and with as many different individuals as possible so that they can become accustomed to the subtle nuances that exist in the social world.

ENHANCING TRANSITIONS

To adequately prepare students for adult life, schools must not only help to ensure that students complete high school, but also promote their transition from secondary education to employment and postsecondary education. For the past 20 years, significant attention has been devoted to enhancing the transition success of students with disabilities. Since 1984, the Office of Special Education Programs has funded more than 400 transition-related model programs. The transition context has changed dramatically over the years. Expectations that students would transition to sheltered employment, low-wage jobs, and never go to college or other postsecondary training yielded to expectations that young adults would work, live, and attend college alongside their peers without disabilities. At the same time, general education has shifted toward an increasing focus on outcome-based learning and preparing all young people for careers in the global marketplace.

Despite these advancements, transition outcomes for many young adults with disabilities remain bleak. About 69% of young adults with disabilities are unemployed three to five years after high school, and only 29% of employed young adults with disabilities earn wages above the poverty level (Blackorby & Wagner, 1996). Historically, most employment initiatives have focused on areas such as job training, work experience, and job placement (Gajar et al., 1993). There has been an emphasis on finding short-term employment solutions, not on assisting individuals with disabilities to build careers and long-term employment capacity.

In a global economy that requires a technically skilled workforce, access to employment opportunities has become increasingly dependent on postsecondary education and training (Berryman & Bailey, 1992). The number of individuals with disabilities attending postsecondary education programs has increased substantially in the past two decades. However, it is estimated that youths with disabilities transition to postsecondary education at only about one-quarter the rate of youth without disabilities and one-third the rate of economically disadvantaged youth (Blackorby & Wagner, 1996; Fairweather & Shaver, 1991). Postsecondary students with disabilities are much more likely to withdraw from school without graduating than their nondisabled counterparts (Sitlington & Frank, 1990). Most students attend vocational schools (Fairweather & Shaver, 1991; Henderson, 1995). In community colleges, they are represented at about half the rate of youth without disabilities, whereas at four-year colleges and universities, young people with disabilities attend at about one-quarter the rate of their counterparts without disabilities.

Although progress has been made in recent years in providing students with disabilities with transition support, comprehensive transition-planning services are not provided to a high proportion of youths. For example, a survey of adolescents with disabilities in Minnesota found that, of almost 1,500 youths surveyed, only 50% had even heard of transition planning (Wright, 1996). Case studies (e.g., Lichtenstein, 1993; Lichtenstein & Michaelides, 1993) suggested that, following high school, many young adults with disabilities find themselves confused about the future, socially isolated, and unable to get jobs and live independently. Transition outcomes are particularly poor for ethnic minority students (Blackorby & Wagner, 1996).

Thus, transition expectations and opportunities for students with disabilities are at unprecedented heights; however, their level of transition preparation and outcomes remains disappointing. Our most critical challenge is to help students successfully obtain employment and postsecondary education that will promote the acquisition of increasingly high-status, high-wage careers. There is general agreement that (1) transition goals should be identified based on students' abilities, needs, interests, and preferences; (2) educational instruction and experiences should prepare students for postschool goals; and (3) a variety of individuals, including the student, should work together to assist the student in achieving those goals (Kohler, 1998a).

Exemplary and Promising Transition Practices

Although numerous models and practices have been identified to enhance student transition, a limited amount of research has documented the effect of these practices on transition outcomes. Existing syntheses of research and model demonstration findings suggest some practices that appear to enhance transition outcomes for students with disabilities (Kohler, 1998b; Kohler & Chapman, 1999; Kohler & Troesken, 1999). They include (1) strategies to promote transition preparation and planning, (2) comprehensive and coordinated services to facilitate transition into employment and postsecondary environments, and (3) supports to ensure success in employment and postsecondary settings. The most prominent effective and promising approaches are described in the following sections.

Transition Planning and Preparation With Longitudinal Focus

The Individuals with Disabilities Education Act of 2004 requires that transition planning be undertaken for all youths with disabilities. Specifically, the regulations mandate that transition planning be conducted for students ages 16 and older, that students be invited to their transition-planning meetings, and that decisions be based on students' interests and preferences. Longitudinal, incremental transition preparation is critical to assist students in identifying and successfully working toward their career goals. Therefore, transition and school-to-work programs are placing increased emphasis on beginning transition exploration and planning activities in the late elementary and middle school grades (Morgan & Hecht, 1990).

Culturally Competent Transition Support

The gap between ethnic and cultural minority and nonminority youths with disabilities on measures of successful transition outcomes suggests that "minority status may present further obstacles to successful transition beyond those that youth experience because of disability alone" (Blackorby & Wagner, 1996, p. 410). Culturally and ethnically diverse youth may face a number of barriers, such as language diversity, lack of system accommodation to diverse cultural norms, increased risk of poverty, lack of recognition of the role of family and community in transition preparation, and frank racism and prejudice (Brookins, 1993; Geenen, Powers, & Lopez-Vasquez, 1999; Geenen, Powers, Lopez-Vasquez, & Bersani, 2003; Gortmaker, Walker, Weitzman, & Sobol, 1990; Groce & Zola, 1993). In addition, culturally and ethnically diverse youth may not have equal access to transition services. For example, evidence suggests that European American individuals are more likely to use vocational rehabilitation services, experience greater placement rates, and receive higher wages than culturally and ethnically diverse individuals (National Council on Disability, 1993).

Traditionally, transition services have not focused on issues related to cultural diversity (Meier-Kronick, 1993). This is particularly critical considering that one defines "successful adulthood" by culture-specific values and expectations. For example, achieving independence is often viewed as a fundamental transition goal for youth with disabilities. However, focusing on this goal may be antithetical to a youth's cultural background unless it is undertaken within a context of interdependent family relationships (Harkness, Super, & Keefer, 1992).

Numerous authors have argued for increasing attention to multicultural issues in transition (Chesapeake Institute, 1994; Franklin, 1992; Harry, 1992). Examples of strategies that can promote the success of culturally and ethnically diverse youth include (1) hiring culturally and ethnically diverse transition staff, (2) providing training to enhance staff's cultural and linguistic competence, (3) reaching out to youth with similar backgrounds who are not linked to transition resources, (4) collaborating with community organizations and networks that provide natural connections for youth and their families, and (5) actively supporting parental involvement.

Supporting parental involvement may be particularly important because an active partnership between parents and school can promote cultural understanding and responsiveness in transition planning. Parents can be a valuable resource in helping educators understand, identify, and support transition outcomes that are valued within a family's culture. When educators engage in truly collaborative relationships with parents, schools can more effectively meet the needs of ethnically and culturally diverse students (Keith et al., 1998). As stated by Cummins, "When educators involve minority parents as partners in their children's education, parents appear to develop a sense of efficacy that communicates itself to children, with positive academic consequences" (1986, p. 26).

Student-Centered Transition Planning

As detailed in the section on self-determination, there is general support and validation for involving students in their educational and career planning. For example, Schunk (1985) demonstrated that students with learning disabilities who participated in selecting their mathematics goals showed greater improvement in math than students who did not have the opportunity to select their goals. Similarly, Halpern, Yovanoff, Doren, and Benz (1995) found that student participation in transition planning was associated with postsecondary success. Van Reusen et al. (1994) conducted a multiple-baseline study of the effect of a strategy in which students participated in educational planning. They found that adolescents with learning disabilities who were exposed to self-advocacy procedures demonstrated increases in their relevant positive verbal contributions during educational planning meetings.

In another investigation, Sands et al. (1998) studied factors that predict student involvement in transition planning. They found that critical factors included (1) participation in general education classes; (2) the opportunity to plan, work toward goals, and evaluate progress; (3) self-regulation and social skills; (4) teacher and family support for student involvement; and (5) a democratic versus patriarchal family climate.

Powers, Turner, Matuszewski, et al. (2001) investigated the effect of a model called TAKE CHARGE for the Future to promote student involvement in transition planning. The intervention included coaching youth with learning, emotional, cognitive, and orthopedic disabilities to apply student-directed planning skills to achieve transition goals; peer-based mentoring and parent support; and inservice education for school transition staff. Students in the intervention group demonstrated significant increases in their involvement in transition-planning activities, empowerment, transition awareness, and level of participation in transition-planning meetings compared with youth in the wait-list comparison group.

Collaborative planning by students, parents, school staff, and representatives from agencies and community organizations also appears to be associated with positive transition outcomes (Gugerty, 1994). Additional promising planning practices include assessing student interests, skills, and achievement; offering support services, such as academic or vocational counseling and coaching; and providing students with information and instruction on how to request services and accommodations. For example, many youths want to work or attend postsecondary education, but they worry about the loss of disability benefit payments and health insurance. Students and their families can receive information about work incentives that may enable them to retain their benefits while employed (Schulzinger, 1998).

Successful Participation of Students With Disabilities in General Education

Education reform is gradually moving toward a unified system of quality education for all students (Nisbet, 1996). Central to positive transition outcomes for students with disabilities is successful participation in general education (Halpern et al., 1995; Miller, Snider, & Rzonca, 1990). For example, Miller et al. (1990) found that participation in high school extracurricular activities and academic success in math and reading were associated with participation in postsecondary education by students with disabilities. Likewise, participation in general vocational education courses and vocational experiences, such as apprenticeships, job shadowing, and career planning, were important for facilitating student exposure, selection, and movement into valued careers.

Successful Participation of Students With Disabilities in Postsecondary Education

The U.S. Department of Education's *Strategic Plan, 1998–2002,* described postsecondary education as "America's traditional gateway to the professions, more challenging jobs, and higher wages" (p. 16). There is general agreement that postsecondary schooling enhances an individual's chances of achieving high status, wealth, and job stability (Tinto, 1987). For example, Rumberger and Daymont (1984) found that participation in postsecondary vocational training was more strongly related to long-term employability than completion of secondary vocational programs. Increasing participation of students with disabilities in four-year colleges and universities is particularly important because they are most significantly underrepresented in these settings. In addition, four-year and graduate degrees are associated with increased status, wages, and career advancement (Gingerich, 1996; Greenbaum, Graham, & Scales, 1994).

Individualized support plays a critical role in the success of postsecondary students with disabilities. When appropriate services are provided, students with disabilities succeed at levels that are commensurate with their abilities and with their peers without disabilities (Dalke, 1993; Gajar, Murphy, & Hunt, 1982). Conversely, failure to provide appropriate supports is associated with reduced grade point averages and early withdrawal from school (Dalke, 1993).

Important postsecondary educational supports include programs to prepare for college entry, tutoring, assistive technology, adaptive equipment, accommodations and compensatory techniques, advocacy, counseling, peer support, career planning, job-seeking skills, internships, and career placement with follow-up (HEATH Resource Center, 1993; Huer, 1990; U.S. Department of Education, 1998). Postsecondary institutions that support the participation of students with disabilities generally have a strong institutionwide administrative commitment to student success. They offer an array of flexible support services for students, and they provide faculty with training and consultation to enhance their capacities to accommodate students.

Vocational Education, Work Experience, and Job Placement

Many students benefit from instruction in career awareness, work-related skills, vocational exploration, and work experience. Research suggests that training in work-related skills such as job-seeking and work behavior improves employment success. For example, Posthill and Roffman (1991) found that employers rated highly the work behaviors of students who had completed training in work-behavior skills. Similarly, Benz, Yovanoff, and Doren (1997) found that student participation in career-awareness training and vocational exploration was associated with productive engagement, and participation in two or more work experiences during high school was related to competitive employment.

Traditionally, career development and vocational education have not been emphasized for students with severe disabilities. Instead, these students were placed in jobs with the lowest skill requirements, typically in food service, janitorial, and cleaning occupations without considering factors such as student interests, job status, and advancement opportunities (Hagner & Dileo, 1993; Mank, 1994). There is now an increasing focus on assisting students with severe disabilities to select and work in meaningful careers. Innovative practices have been identified to facilitate career planning and placement of students with severe disabilities. For example, Sowers, McAllister, and Cotton (1996) developed strategies for employment consultants to assist students and their families in exploring the student's interests, talents, and career goals; conduct a job search; and support coworkers to train the student on the job. Practices included person-centered planning directed as much as possible by the student; assisting students and their families to identify, use, and expand personal connections to find jobs; and involving students in activities to seek and keep jobs (such as choosing which jobs to apply for, making a résumé, interviewing with employers, consulting with coworkers who will provide support, and problem-solving solutions to on-the-job problems). It is essential that students find and successfully maintain meaningful jobs or postsecondary education before their eligibility for school services ends at age 21.

Life Skills

Research underscores the importance of life skills instruction and student-centered education and career planning. Instruction in social skills, self-advocacy, independent living skills, and self-determination are associated with enhanced employment or independent living (Benz et al., 1997; Posthill & Roffman, 1991; Wehmeyer & Schwartz, 1997). For example, Benz et al. (1997) found that high social skills were predictive of employment. Wehmeyer and Schwartz (1997) noted that, one year following high school, students with high levels of self-determination were more likely to be employed than those with low levels of self-determination.

In a narrow study, Geenen, Powers, and Sells (2003) found that students with special health needs, as well as their parents, wanted to learn health management strategies and how to access needed supports. However, they often did not receive this information from their health care providers, and there was little opportunity for coordination among health providers and school staff. The benefits of life skills education are clear. To be most effective, skills must be taught as one component of a coordinated set of activities for all students. As Kohler pointed out, "We must be careful to truly expand the options. In the past, by focusing on the 'needs' of individuals with disabilities, we limited their opportunities by herding them into functional life skills curricula" (1998a, p. 189).

Partnerships With Business, Labor, and Community Resources

Partnerships among schools, businesses, labor unions, community service organizations, and government agencies appear to be key to effective transition and school-to-work programs. Interagency agreements, coordinating bodies, established methods of communication, and clearly articulated roles facilitate involvement of community organizations (Kohler & Chapman, 1999).

Promising models involve employers and community organizations in program planning and classroom-based vocational education. Furthermore, the mentoring of students and teachers by employers, representatives of community organizations, and successful adults with disabilities serves as an important link between school and work. Moreover, partnerships with employers and unions facilitate the identification of additional apprenticeships, work experiences, and jobs, particularly in areas that are traditionally underrepresented in special education (such as trades, technology, banking, professions, and administrative occupations). Finally, direct and ongoing relationships between schools and employers promote the establishment of successful coworker supports for students in the workplace (Nisbet & Hagner, 1998).

Structures and Policies That Support Successful Transition

Successful school–community partnerships are enhanced by organizational structures that support integrating special education transition and school-to-work programs (Peters, Templeman, & Brostrom, 1987). Programs must collaborate in program planning, working with employers and community organizations, and developing and implementing transition plans for students with and without disabilities. Establishing policies that reflect shared values across programs is essential. Such values may include (1) a commitment to inclusive education, outcome-based instruction, cultural competence, program evaluation, and teamwork; (2) ongoing staff training and technical assistance; (3) program goals related to economic trends and other workforce development activities; and (4) a long-term approach to transition preparation.

Family Involvement

There is general agreement that family involvement greatly enhances student transition planning and outcomes (Halpern, 1998; Halpern et al., 1995; Morningstar, Turnbull, & Turnbull, 1995; Posthill & Roffman, 1991; Powers et al., 1999). For example, Halpern et al. (1995) found that family involvement was a significant predictor of postsecondary success. Powers et al. (1999) found that students considered the support they received from their parents to be critical for their transition preparation.

Nevertheless, research suggests that, although families appear to be critical in helping children learn transition skills and make resource connections, their efforts are not often well understood by school staff or coordinated with school-based transition activities. This issue is particularly serious for minority parents, whose efforts in supporting their transitioning children may not be recognized or acknowledged (Geenen, Powers, Lopez-Vasquez, & Bersani, 2003). School staff must proactively reach out to involve families in transition planning and to work with them to help students achieve transition goals.

Next Steps in Improving the Success of Transition

A number of effective and promising practices promote the transition success of students with disabilities. However, empirical evidence for many of these practices is difficult to ascertain because studies are frequently field-tested as a package; thus, their effect is not specifically evaluated with respect to employment and postsecondary outcomes. There is a critical need to more rigorously evaluate the impact of specific transition practices on employment and postsecondary outcomes. In addition, existing transition-promotion practices must be described at a level of detail that permits their replication.

The focus on transition preparation for students with disabilities has substantively shifted in recent years. The shift has been from a specialized, professionally directed approach that is centered on the interaction of special education staff, vocational providers, and students to an inclusive, student-centered approach that is supported through collaborative partnerships among students, special education and general education staff, families, employers, and community organizations. This shift necessitates clarifying and restructuring the roles and relationships of all transition partners: students, special education and general education teachers, families, administrators, community rehabilitation providers, guidance counselors, and transition specialists (Kohler, 1998b).

From this perspective, the primary responsibility of special education and general education teachers is to become specific subject and skill instructors within their areas of expertise (for example, vocational education, compensatory reading, math). That is, transition specialists would focus on coordinating transition services, such as identifying job opportunities; working with adult service providers, students, families, and educators; and building employer networks. Guidance counselors would provide career and postsecondary information; assist students in assessing their skills and interests and selecting courses that support their education and career goals; and facilitate transition planning. Vocational rehabilitation counselors would work with educators, students, and families to identify assistive technology, accommodations, and other supports that facilitate student goal achievement.

Furthermore, administrators would become responsible for restructuring educational policies, programs, and schools to incorporate transition planning and services for all students, including the allocation of sufficient staff and resources to achieve targeted outcomes. Their activities are informed by and accomplished in partnership with educators, students, and families. Families would be invited to become active in program and policy development and evaluation, provide input related to student abilities and support needs, and provide support to the student consistent with their capacities and values (Kohler, 1998a). Finally, students would assume a primary role in planning and preparing for their adult lives. This means participating in planning activities, working toward transition goals, evaluating their progress, and revising their goals accordingly. Students might also be involved in program and policy planning, development and evaluation, and staff training.

Successfully bringing about this shift in staff roles and relationships requires significant policy and programmatic enhancement, as well as new approaches to professional development. Increased emphasis must be placed on teaching school and community staff effective practices to promote transition planning and preparation, as well as to collaborate successfully with one another, students, families, and employers. Accomplishing these objectives requires support to develop a school transition culture that promotes positive postsecondary outcomes for all students.

EDUCATIONAL APPLICATIONS AND IMPLICATIONS

The pressures of the No Child Left Behind Act for schools to ensure the academic success of all students, including those with disabilities, runs the risk that nonacademic aspects of a student's programs will be shortchanged or neglected altogether. Although the academic needs of students with disabilities are significant, they cannot be pursued at the exclusion of other areas that are critical to long-term success, such as social skills, transition skills, and self-determination competencies. One of the greatest challenges facing teachers of adolescents is to find the time to teach many of the skills and strategies described in this chapter. Many teachers have been successful when they have looked for ways to integrate this instruction within other aspects of a student's life within school. For example, it is common for subject-matter teachers to use cooperative groups as a means of having students meet certain academic objectives. This is a natural opportunity to teach an entire class social-interaction skills and then to set an expectation that these behaviors be used during all cooperative group activities. The probability of students learning and using these behaviors with fidelity will increase to the degree that the classroom teacher explicitly models the desired behaviors, sets clear expectations for the ongoing use of the targeted behavior, and carefully monitors and gives feedback to students on an ongoing basis.

Although some social skills can be taught in the course of other instructional activities, it is sometimes necessary for teachers to have opportunities to explicitly model, teach, and have students practice new social, self-determination, or other nonacademic behaviors in smaller groups, away from the ongoing academic activities of the mainstream class. Smaller, controlled conditions are often more conducive to role playing, practice, and feedback. Ultimately, however, it is imperative that students be afforded opportunities to practice these newly learned behaviors in natural settings.

AFTERWORD

Clearly, the probability of students with disabilities making it through 12 grades of school and successfully graduating from high school with a good sense of direction for their lives and for what they will do following high school is very low unless there is a very well planned, coordinated plan of action in place to guide the student's educational experience. This plan must carefully engage the students so that they feel a strong sense of ownership in what is happening. It also must deliberately engage parents, community agencies, and teachers across settings and years. Jason achieved success on June 6 because a majority of the factors that are critical to achievement were in place in a highly coordinated fashion. Anything less would have, in all likelihood, resulted in Jason's absence from the graduation ceremony—as well as a life of underachievement, discouragement, and failure, both in school and beyond.

REFERENCES

Apple, M. W., & Beane, J. A. (1995). *Democratic schools.* Alexandria, VA: Association for Supervision and Curriculum Development.

Benz, M. R., Yovanoff, P., & Doren, B. (1997). School-to-work components that predict postschool success for students with and without disabilities. *Exceptional Children, 63*(2), 151–165.

Berryman, S. E., & Bailey, T. R. (1992). *The double helix of education and the economy.* New York: Columbia University, Teachers College, Institute on Education and the Economy.

Blackorby, J., & Wagner, M. (1996). Longitudinal postschool outcomes of youth with disabilities: Findings from the National Longitudinal Transition Study. *Exceptional Children, 62*(5), 399–413.

Brookins, G. K. (1993). Culture, ethnicity, and bicultural competence: Implications for children with chronic illness and disability. *Pediatrics, 91*(5), 1056–1062.

Chesapeake Institute. (1994). *National agenda for achieving better results for children and youth with serious emotional disturbance* (Report for the U.S. Department of Education, Office of Special Education and Rehabilitative Services). Washington, DC: Author.

Crank, J. N., Deshler, D. D., & Schumaker, J. B (1995). *Surface-counseling.* Lawrence, KS: Edge Enterprises.

Cummins, J. (1986). Empowering minority students: A framework for intervention. *Harvard Educational Review, 56,* 18–36.

Curtis, E. (1998). It's my life: Preference-based planning for self-directed goals. In M. L. Wehmeyer & D. J. Sands (Eds.), *Making it happen: Student involvement in education planning, decision making and instruction* (pp. 241–261). Baltimore: Paul H. Brookes.

Dadson, S., & Horner, R. (1993). Manipulating setting events to decrease problem behaviors. *TEACHING Exceptional Children, 25*(3), 53–55.

Dalke, C. (1993). Making a successful transition from high school to college: A model program. In S. A. Vogel & P. B. Adelman (Eds.), *Success for college students with learning disabilities* (pp. 57–80). New York: Springer-Verlag.

Deshler, D. D., Schumaker, J. B., Alley, G. R., Warner, M. M., & Clark, F. L. (1981). Social interaction deficits in learning disabled adolescents—Another myth? In W. M. Cruickshank & A. A. Silver (Eds.), *Bridges to tomorrow: Vol. 2. The best of ACLD* (pp. 57–65). Syracuse, NY: Syracuse University Press.

Dunlap, G., DePerczel, M., Clarke, S., Wilson, D., Wright, S., White, R., & Gomez, A. (1994). Choice making to promote adaptive behavior for students with emotional and behavioral challenges. *Journal of Applied Behavior Analysis, 27*, 505–518.

Fairweather, J. S., & Shaver, D. M. (1991). Making the transition to postsecondary education and training. *Exceptional Children, 57*(3), 264–270.

Field, S., & Hoffman, A. (1994). Development of a model for self-determination. *Career Development for Exceptional Individuals, 17*(2), 159–169.

Field, S., & Hoffman, A. (1996). *Steps to self-determination.* Austin, TX: Pro-Ed.

Field, S., Martin, J., Miller, R., Ward, M., & Wehmeyer, M. (1998). *A practical guide for teaching self-determination.* Reston, VA: Council for Exceptional Children.

Field, S., Martin, J., Miller, R., Ward, M., & Wehmeyer, M. (1998). Self-determination for persons with disabilities: A position statement of the Division on Career Development and Transition. *Career Development of Exceptional Individuals, 21*(2), 113–128.

Fitzsimmons, M. (1988). *Functional behavioral assessment and behavior intervention plans.* Reston, VA: ERIC Clearinghouse on Disabilities and Gifted Education. (ERIC/OSEP Digest E571)

Franklin, M. E. (1992). Culturally sensitive instructional practices for African-American learners with disabilities. *Exceptional Children, 59*(2), 115–122.

Fullerton, A. (1994). *Putting feet on my dreams: A program in self-determination.* Portland, OR: Portland State University.

Gajar, A. H. (1998). Postsecondary education. In F. R. Rusch & J. G. Chadsey (Eds.), *Beyond high school: Transition from school to work* (pp. 383–405). Belmont, CA: Wadsworth.

Gajar, A. H., Goodman, L., & McAfee, J. (1993). *Secondary schools and beyond: Transition of individuals with mild disabilities.* New York: Charles E. Merrill.

Gajar, A. H., Murphy, J., & Hunt, F. M. (1982). A university program for learning disabled students. *Reading Improvement, 19*, 282–288.

Geenen, S., Powers, L. E., & Lopez-Vasquez, A. (1999). Parents as partners: Understanding and promoting the multi-cultural aspects of parent involvement in transition planning. *Exceptional Children, 67*(2), 265–282.

Geenen, S., Powers, L. E., Lopez-Vasquez, A., & Bersani, H. (2003). Understanding and supporting the transition of minority youth. *Career Development for Exceptional Individuals, 26*, 27–46.

Geenen, S., Powers, L. E., & Sells, W. (2003). Understanding the role of health care providers during the transition of adolescents with health conditions and disabilities. *Journal of Adolescent Health, 32*, 225–233.

German, S. L., Huber Marshall, L., & Martin, J. E. (1997). *Goal attainment through using the Take Action curriculum.* Colorado Springs: University of Colorado, Center for Self-Determination.

Gingerich, J. (1996). *Vast spaces and stone walls: Overcoming barriers to postsecondary education for rural students with disabilities.* Presentation to the American Council on Rural Special Education Conference, Portland, OR.

Golarz, R. J., & Golarz, M. J. (1995). *The power of participation: Improving schools in a democratic society.* Champaign, IL: Research Press.

Gortmaker, S. L., Walker, D. K., Weitzman, M., & Sobol, A. M. (1990). Chronic conditions, socioeconomic risks, and behavioral problems in children and adolescents. *Pediatrics, 85*(3), 267–276.

Graham, S., & Harris, K. R. (1989). Components analysis of cognitive strategy instruction: Effects on learning disabled students compositions and self-efficacy. *Journal of Educational Psychology, 81*(3), 353–361.

Grayson, T. E. (1998). Dropout prevention and special services. In F. R. Rusch & J. G. Chadsey (Eds.), *Beyond high school: Transition from school to work* (pp. 77–98). Boston: Wadsworth.

Greenbaum, B., Graham, S., & Scales, W. (1996). Adults with learning disabilities: Occupational and social status after college. *Journal of Learning Disabilities, 29*(2), 167–173.

Groce, N. E., & Zola, I. K. (1993). Multiculturalism, chronic illness, and disability. *Pediatrics, 91*(5), 1048–1055.

Gugerty, J. (1994). Characteristics of services provided by two-year colleges that serve students with learning or cognitive disabilities in highly effective ways. *Issues in Special Education and Rehabilitation, 9*(1), 79–87.

Hagner, D., & Dileo, D. (1993). *Workplace culture, supported employment and people with disabilities.* Cambridge, MA: Brookline.

Halloran, W. D. (1993). Transition services requirement: Issues, implications, challenge. In R. C. Eaves & P. J. McLaughlin (Eds.), *Recent advances in special education and rehabilitation* (pp. 210–224). Boston: Andover Medical Publishers.

Halpern, A. S. (1998). Next S.T.E.P.: Student transition and educational planning. In M. L. Wehmeyer & D. J. Sands (Eds.), *Making it happen: Student involvement in education planning, decision making and instruction* (pp. 167–185). Baltimore: Paul H. Brookes.

Halpern, A. S., Herr, C., Wolf, N., Doren, B., Johnson, M., & Lawson, J. (1997). *The next S.T.E.P. (Student Transition and Educational Planning) curriculum.* Austin, TX: Pro-Ed.

Halpern, A. S., Yovanoff, P., Doren, B., & Benz, M. R. (1995). Predicting participation in postsecondary education for school leavers with disabilities. *Exceptional Children, 62*(2), 151–164.

Harkness, S., Super, C., & Keefer, C. (1992). Culture and ethnicity. In M. Levine, W. Carey, & S. Crocker (Eds.), *Developmental-behavioral pediatrics* (pp. 103–108). Philadelphia: W. B. Sauders.

Harry, B. (1992). *Cultural diversity, families, and the special education system: Communication and empowerment.* New York: Teachers College Press.

Hazel, J. S., & Schumaker, J. B. (1988). Social skills and learning disabilities: Current issues and recommendations for future research. In J. F. Kavanagh & T. J. Truss, Jr. (Eds.), *Learning disabilities: Proceedings of the national conference.* Parkton, MD: National Press.

HEATH Resource Center, Association on Higher Education and Disability, and Educational Testing Service. (1993). *Study spreads the word about successful practices for students with disabilities.* Washington, DC: Author.

Henderson, C. (1995). The American freshman: National norms. *College freshmen with disabilities: A statistical profile.* Washington, DC: U.S. Department of Education, American Council of Education, HEATH Resource Center.

Henderson, C. (2001). *2001 College freshmen with disabilities: A biennial statistical profile.* Washington, DC: U.S. Department of Education, American Council of Education, HEATH Resource Center.

Horner, R. H., & Carr, E. G. (1997). Behavioral support for students with severe disabilities: Functional assessment and comprehensive intervention. *Journal of Special Education, 31,* 84–104.

Horner, R. H., Sugai, G., & Horner, H. F. (2000). A school wide approach to student discipline. *School Administrator, 57*(2), 4–7.

Huer, M. B. (1990). Special facilities and services for university student with mobility impairment: A demographic study (U.S.A.). *Assistive Technology, 2*(4), 125–130.

Hughes, C. A., & Peterson, D. L. (1989). Utilizing a self-instructional training package to increase on-task behavior and work performance. *Education and Training in Mental Retardation, 24,* 114–120.

Individuals with Disabilities Education Act, Amendments of 1997, Pub. L. No. 105-17, 20 U.S.C. § 1400 *et seq.*

Kamps, D. M., Ellis, C., Mancina, C., Wyble, J., Greene, L., & Harvey, D. (1995). Case studies using functional analysis for young children with behavior risks. *Education and Treatment of Children, 18,* 243–260.

Keith, T., Keith, P., Quirk, K., Sperduto, J., Santillo, S., & Killings, S. (1998). Longitudinal effects of parent involvement on high school grades: Similarities and differences across gender and ethnic groups. *Journal of School Psychology, 36*(3), 335–363.

Kennedy, C., & Haring, T. (1993). Teaching choice making during social interactions to students with profound multiple disabilities. *Journal of Applied Behavior Analysis, 26,* 63–76.

Kohler, P. D. (1998a). Implementing a transition perspective of education: A comprehensive approach to planning and delivering secondary education and transition services. In F. R. Rusch & J. Chadsey (Eds.), *High school and beyond: Transition from school to work* (pp. 179–205). Belmont, CA: Wadsworth.

Kohler, P. D. (1998b). *Transition from school to work: Promising practices and programs.* Champaign: University of Illinois at Urbana-Champaign, Transition Research Institute.

Kohler, P. D., & Chapman, S. (1999, March). *Literature review on school-to-work transition.* Retrieved from http://www.ed.uiuc.edu/sped/tri/stwpurpose.html

Kohler, P. D., & Troesken, B. J. (1999). *Improving student outcomes: Promising practices and programs.* Champaign: University of Illinois at Urbana-Champaign, Transition Research Institute.

Lichtenstein, S. (1993). Transition from school to adulthood: Case studies of adults with learning disabilities who dropped out of school. *Exceptional Children, 59*(4), 336–347.

Lichtenstein, S., & Michaelides, N. (1993). Transition from school to young adulthood: Four case studies of young adults labeled mentally retarded. *Career Development for Exceptional Individuals, 16*(2), 183–196.

Malone, L. D., & Mastropieri, M. A. (1992). Reading comprehension instruction: Summarization and self-monitoring training for students with learning disabilities. *Exceptional Children, 58,* 270–279.

Mank, D. (1994). The underachievement of supported employment: A call for reinvestment. *Journal of Disability Policy Studies, 5*(2), 1–24.

Martin, J. E., & Huber Marshall, L. H. (1995). Choicemaker: A comprehensive self-determination transition program. *Intervention in School and Clinic, 30*(3), 147–156.

Meier-Kronick, N. (1993). Culture-specific variables that may affect employment outcomes for Mexican-American youth with disabilities. In T. Dais, N. Meier-Kronick, P. Luft, & F. R. Rusch (Eds.), *Selected readings in transition: Cultural differences, chronic illness and job matching* (pp. 22–40). Champaign: University of Illinois at Urbana-Champaign, Transition Research Institute.

Miller, R. J., Snider, B., & Rzonca, C. (1990). Variables related to the decision of young adults with learning disabilities to participate in postsecondary education. *Journal of Learning Disabilities, 23*(6), 349–354.

Mithaug, D. E. (1991). *Self-determined kids.* Lexington, MA: Lexington Books.

Mithaug, D., Wehmeyer, M. L., Agran, M., Martin, J., & Palmer, S. (1998). The self-determined learning model of instruction: Engaging students to solve their learning problems. In M. L. Wehmeyer & D. J. Sands (Eds.), *Making it happen: Student involvement in educational planning, decision-making and instruction* (pp. 299–328). Baltimore: Paul H. Brookes.

Morgan, D., & Hecht, J. (1990). *Report on the methodology for the West End Special education transition program evaluation.* Riverside: California Educational Research Cooperative. (ERIC Document Reproduction Service No. ED327021)

Morningstar, M. E., Turnbull, A. P., & Turnbull, H. R. (1995). What do students with disabilities tell us about the importance of family involvement in the transition from school to adult life? *Exceptional Children, 62*(3), 249–260.

National Council on Disability. (1993). *Meeting the unique needs of minorities with disabilities: A report to the president and the Congress.* Washington, DC: Author.

Nelson, J. R., Crabtree, M., Marchand-Martella, N., & Martella, R. (1998). Teaching behavior in the whole school. *TEACHING Exceptional Children, 30*(4), 4–9.

Newton, J., Ard, W., & Horner, R. (1993). Validating predicted activity preferences of individuals with severe disabilities. *Journal of Applied Behavior Analysis, 26,* 239–245.

Nisbet, J. A. (1996). The interrelationship of education and self-esteem. In L. E. Powers, G. H. S. Singer, & J. Sowers (Eds.), *On the road to autonomy: Promoting self-competence for children and youth with disabilities* (pp. 155–170). Baltimore: Paul H. Brookes.

Nisbet, J. A., & Hagner, D. (1998). Natural supports in the workplace: A reexamination of supported employment. *Journal of the Association for Persons With Severe Handicaps, 13*(4), 260–267.

Peters, J. M., Templeman, T. P., & Brostrom, G. (1987). The school and community partnership: Planning for students with severe handicaps. *Exceptional Children, 53*(6), 531–536.

Plisko, V. (1984). *The condition of education.* Washington, DC: National Center for Education Statistics.

Posthill, S. M., & Roffman, A. J. (1991). The impact of a transitional training program for young adults with learning disabilities. *Journal of Learning Disabilities, 24*(10), 619–629.

Powers, L. E., Ellison, R., Matuszewski, J., Turner, A., & Wilson, R. (2005). *TAKE CHARGE for the Future*. Portland, OR: Portland State University Regional Research Institute.

Powers, L. E., Ellison, R., Matuszewski, J., Wilson, R., & Turner, A. (2005). *TAKE CHARGE*. Portland, OR: Portland State University Regional Research Institute.

Powers, L. E., Sowers, J., & Stevens, T. (1995). An exploratory, randomized study of the impact of mentoring on the self-efficacy and community-based knowledge of adolescents with severe physical challenges. *Journal of Rehabilitation, 61*(1), 33–41.

Powers, L. E., Sowers, J., Turner, A., Nesbitt, M., Knowles, E., & Ellison, R. (1996). Take charge: A model for promoting self-determination among adolescents with challenges. In L. E. Powers, G. H. S. Singer, & J. Sowers (Eds.), *On the road to autonomy: Promoting self-competence for children and youth with disabilities* (pp. 291–322). Baltimore: Paul H. Brookes.

Powers, L. E., Turner, A., Ellison, R., Matuszewski, J., Wilson, R., Phillips, A., & Rein, C. (2001). A controlled field-test of TAKE CHARGE: A multi-component intervention to promote adolescent self-determination. *Journal of Rehabilitation, 67*(4), 14–20.

Powers, L. E., Turner, A., Matuszewski, J., Wilson, R., Ellison, R., Westwood, D., & Phillips, A. (2001). *TAKE CHARGE* for the Future: A controlled field-test of a model to promote student involvement in transition planning. *Career Development for Exceptional Individuals, 24*(1), 89–104.

Powers, L. E., Turner, A., Matuszewski, J., Wilson, R., & Loesch, C. (1999). A qualitative analysis of student involvement in transition planning. *Journal of Vocational Education, 21*(3), 18–26.

Rumberger, R. W., & Daymont, T. N. (1984). The economic value of academic and vocational training acquired in high school. In M. E. Borus (Ed.), *Youth and the labor market: Analyses from the National Longitudinal Survey* (pp. 157–191). Kalamazoo, MI: W. E. Upjohn Institute for Employment Research.

Sands, D. J., Bassett, D. S., Lehmann, J., & Spencer, K. C. (1998). Factors contributing to and implications for student involvement in transition-related planning, decision making, and instruction. In M. L. Wehmeyer & D. J. Sands (Eds.), *Making it happen: Student involvement in education planning, decision making and instruction* (pp. 25–44). Baltimore: Paul H. Brookes.

Schulzinger, R. (1998, September). *Key issues for youth with disabilities and chronic health conditions*. Gainesville, FL: Institute for Child Health Policy.

Schumaker, J. B. (1992). Social performance of individuals with learning disabilities: Through the looking glass of KU-IRLD research. *School Psychology Review, 21*(3), 387–399.

Schumaker, J. B., Hazel, J. S., & Pederson, C. S. (1988). *Social skills for daily living: A curriculum*. Circle Pines, MN: American Guidance Service.

Schumaker, J. B., Hazel, J. S., Sherman, J. A., & Sheldon, J. (1982). Social skills performance of learning disabled, non-learning disabled, and delinquent adolescents. *Learning Disability Quarterly, 5,* 388–397.

Schunk, D. H. (1985). Participation in goal setting: Effects of self-efficacy and skills of learning-disabled children. *Journal of Special Education, 19,* 307–317.

Sitlington, P. L., & Frank, A. R. (1990). Are adolescents with learning disabilities successfully crossing the bridge into adult life? *Learning Disability Quarterly, 13*(2), 97–111.

Snyder, C. R. (1994). *The psychology of hope: You can get there from here.* New York: Free Press.

Sowers, J., McAllister, R., & Cotton, P. (1996). Strategies to enhance the control of the employment process by individuals with severe disabilities. In L. E. Powers, G. H. S. Singer, & J. Sowers (Eds.), *On the road to autonomy: Promoting self-competence for children and youth with disabilities* (pp. 325–346). Baltimore: Paul H. Brookes.

Sprick, R. S., Garrison, M., & Howard, L. M. (1998). *CHAMPS: A positive and proactive approach to classroom discipline.* Longmont, CO: Sopris West.

Sugai, G., & Horner, R. (1994). Including students with severe behavior problems in general education settings: Assumptions, challenges, and solutions. In J. Marr, G. Sugai, & G. Tindal (Eds.), *The Oregon conference monograph 6* (pp. 102–120). Eugene: University of Oregon.

Tilly, W. D., Kovaleski, J., Dunlap, G., Knoster, T. P., Bambara, L., & Kincaid, D. (1998). *Functional behavioral assessment: Policy development in light of emerging research and practice.* Washington, DC: National Association of State Directors of Special Education.

Tinto, V. (1987). *Leaving college: Rethinking the causes and cures of student attrition.* Chicago: University of Chicago Press.

Turnbull, A. P., & Ruef, M. (1997). Family perspectives on inclusive lifestyle issues for individuals with problem behavior. *Exceptional Children, 63*(2) 211–227.

U.S. Census Bureau. (1997). Survey of income and program participation. Tables B2–B5. Retrieved from www.census.gov

U.S. Department of Education. (1997). *1998–2002 strategic plan.* Retrieved May 21, 2005, from www.ed.gov/pubs/StratPln/index.html

U.S. Department of Education. (1998). *Twentieth annual report to Congress on the implementation of the Individuals with Disabilities Education Act.* Washington, DC: Author.

U.S. Department of Education. (2002). *Twenty-fourth annual report to Congress on the implementation of the Individuals with Disabilities Act.* Washington, DC: Author.

Van Reusen, A. K. (1999). Developing social competence in diverse secondary schools and classrooms. In D. D. Deshler, J. B. Schumaker, K. R. Harris, & S. Graham (Eds.), *Teaching every adolescent every day: Learning in diverse middle and high school classrooms.* Cambridge, MA: Brookline.

Van Reusen, A. K., Bos, C., Schumaker, J. B., & Deshler, D. D. (1994). *The Self-Advocacy Strategy: Instructor's manual.* Lawrence, KS: Edge Enterprises.

Wagner, M. (1991). *Dropouts with disabilities: What do we know? What can we do?* Menlo Park, CA: SRI International.

Wagner, M., Cameto, R., & Newman, L. (2003). *Youth with disabilities: A changing population; A report of findings from the National Longitudinal Transition Study (NLTS) and the National Longitudinal Transition Study–2 (NLTS).* Menlo Park, CA: SRI International.

Walker, H. M., Horner, R. H., Sugai, G., Bullis, M., Sprague, J. R., Bricker, D., & Kaufman, M. J. (1996). Integrated approaches to preventing antisocial behavior patterns among school-age children and youth. *Journal of Emotional and Behavioral Disorders, 4*(4), 194–209.

Ward, M. J. (1988). The many facets of self-determination. *National Information Center for Children and Youth with Handicaps: Transition Summary, 5*, 2–3.

Ward, M. J. (1996). Coming of age in the age of self-determination: A historical and personal perspective. In D. J. Sands & M. L. Wehmeyer (Eds.), *Self-determination across the life span: Independence and choice for people with disabilities* (pp. 3–16). Baltimore: Paul H. Brooks.

Ward, M. J. (1999). Self-determination for people with developmental disabilities and autism: Two self-advocates' perspectives. *Focus on Autism and Other Developmental Disabilities, 14*(3), 133–139.

Ward, M. J., & Kohler, P. D. (1996). Teaching self-determination: Content and process. In L. E. Powers, G. H. S. Singer, & J. Sowers (Eds.), *On the road to autonomy: Promoting self-competence for children and youth with disabilities* (pp. 275–290). Baltimore: Paul H. Brookes.

Wehmeyer, M. L. (1992). Self-determination: Critical skills for outcome-oriented transition services. *Journal for Vocational Special Needs Education, 15*(1), 3–7.

Wehmeyer, M. L. (1996). Self-determination as an educational outcome: Why is it important to children, youth, and adults with disabilities? In D. J. Sands & M. L. Wehmeyer (Eds.), *Self-determination across the life span: Independence and choice for people with disabilities* (pp. 17–36). Baltimore: Paul H. Brooks.

Wehmeyer, M. L., & Kelchner, K. (1997). *Whose future is it anyway? A student-directed transition-planning program.* Arlington, TX: The Arc of the United States National Headquarters.

Wehmeyer, M. L., Palmer, S., Agran, M., Mithaug, D., & Martin, J. (2000). Promoting causal agency: The self-determined learning model of instruction. *Exceptional Children, 66*, 439–453.

Wehmeyer, M. L., & Schwartz, M. (1997). Self-determination and positive adult outcomes: A follow-up study of youth with mental retardation or learning disabilities. *Exceptional Children, 63*, 245–255.

Wehmeyer, M. L., & Ward, M. J. (1995). Student involvement in transition planning: Fulfilling the intent of IDEA. *Journal of Vocational Special Needs Education, 17*, 108–111.

Weiner, F. (1986). *No apologies: A guide to living with a disability, written by the real authorities–people with disabilities, their families and friends.* New York: St. Martin's.

Western Interstate Commission for Higher Education & The College Board. (1991). *The road to college: Educational progress by race and ethnicity.* Boulder, CO: Author.

Whang, P. L., Fawcett, S. B., & Mathews, R. M. (1981). Teaching job-related social skills to learning disabled adolescents. *Analysis and Intervention in Developmental Disabilities, 4*, 29–38.

White, W. J. (1992). The postschool adjustment of persons with learning disabilities: Current status and future projections. *Journal of Learning Disabilities, 25*, 448–456.

Wright, B. (1996). Teens say job training their top need. *Point of Departure, 2*(2), 3–5.

Index

**CORWIN
PRESS**

The Corwin Press logo—a raven striding across an open book—represents the union of courage and learning. Corwin Press is committed to improving education for all learners by publishing books and other professional development resources for those serving the field of PreK–12 education. By providing practical, hands-on materials, Corwin Press continues to carry out the promise of its motto: **"Helping Educators Do Their Work Better."**